# ZANUCK

### THE RISE AND FALL OF
### HOLLYWOOD'S LAST TYCOON

**Books by Leonard Mosley**

*Nonfiction*

Zanuck: The Rise and Fall of Hollywood's Last Tycoon   1984
Marshall: Hero for Our Times   1982
The Druid   1981
Blood Relations: The Rise and Fall of the du Ponts of
    Delaware   1980
Dulles: A Biography of Eleanor, Allen, and John Foster Dulles
    and Their Family Network   1978
Lindbergh: A Biography   1976
The Reich Marshall: A Biography of Hermann Goering   1974
Power Play: Oil in the Middle East   1973
Backs to the Wall: London in World War II   1971
On Borrowed Time: How World War II Began   1969
Hirohito: Emperor of Japan   1966
The Battle of Britain   1965
Haile Selassie: The Conquering Lion   1964
Faces from the Fire: Biography of Sir Archibald
    McIndoe   1962
The Glorious Fault: The Life of Lord Curzon   1962
The Last Days of the British Raj   1961
The Cat and the Mice: A German Spy in Cairo   1960
Duel for Kilimanjaro   1959
Castlerosse: The Life of a Bon Vivant   1956
Gideon Goes to War: A Biography of Orde Wingate   1948
Report from Germany, 1945   1945
Downstream, 1939   1939
So Far So Good: A Fragment of Autobiography   1934

*Fiction*

The Seductive Mirror   1952
Each Had a Song   1951
War Lord   1950
No More Remains   1938
So I Killed Her   1937

# ZA

## THE RISE AND FALL OF

# NUCK

## HOLLYWOOD'S LAST TYCOON

### *by* LEONARD MOSLEY

**McGraw-Hill Book Company**

New York  St. Louis  San Francisco  Bogotá  Guatemala
Hamburg  Lisbon  Madrid  Mexico  Montreal  Panama
Paris  San Juan  São Paulo  Tokyo  Toronto

Excerpts and photograph from *Don't Say Yes Until I Finish Talking*
by Mel Gussow. Copyright © 1971 by Mel Gussow. Reprinted by
permission of Doubleday & Company, Inc.

Reprinted by arrangement with Little, Brown and Company

First McGraw-Hill Paperback Edition, 1985

1 2 3 4 5 6 7 8 9 D O C D O C 8 7 6 5

ISBN 0-07-043465-4

**Library of Congress Cataloging in Publication Data**

Mosley, Leonard, 1912–
   Zanuck: the rise and fall of Hollywood's last
tycoon.

   Reprint. Originally published: Boston: Little,
Brown, c1984. 1st ed.
   Filmography: p.
   Includes index.
   1. Zanuck, Darryl Francis, 1902–    . 2. Moving-
picture producers and directors — United States — Biography.
I. Title.
PN1998.A3Z4243   1985        791.43′0232′0924 [B]      85-154
ISBN 0-07-043465-4 (pbk.)

To D.

# INTRODUCTION

WAY BACK in the 1930s, when it seemed that every hungry young man in America was trekking to California, I limped into Hollywood in a Model A Ford and got a job in the movies. This is no place to explain how it was that an eighteen-year-old Englishman found himself on the West Coast of the United States in such a dire moment of global depression, nor of the complicated means I had used to get there. Let it simply be said that Carl Laemmle, Jr., whose father owned Universal Pictures, liked to play tennis at six o'clock every morning, and it inflated the large ego in his small body if he won. I did not mind rising early and was just poor enough a player to lose to Junior narrowly but with clockwork regularity.

In Hollywood in those days, what better qualifications could you ask for in a screenwriter? I was hired by Universal and was given a collaborator named Irving Allen (later well-known as a movie producer) who, since he was also an expert film editor, scooped up the discards from the cutting room floors and spliced them together. From these highly disparate droppings, I knitted together plots for some of Universal's program of "B" pictures. That was one reason why avid film fans who caught these curiosities when they were slipped unannounced into obscure movie houses were sometimes puzzled when John Boles, seen to be singing with a big band in one scene, turned out to be Slim Summerville riding a bicycle with ZaSu Pitts in the next.

The main point of this reminiscence is that it was shortly after I went to work for Universal Pictures that I was introduced to Darryl Zanuck for the first time, and it was hardly a meeting of the minds. I was being paid $35 a week for my work at the studio, which was not only more than I was probably worth but also enough, in those happy days, for a young man to run a car, rent an apartment, and eat strawberry waffles every night for supper. But then I acquired a girlfriend and needed extra money to pay for the escalopes de veau and French wines to which she was partial, and for this purpose I secured assignments to write articles about film stars for a highly popular fan magazine called *Photoplay*. The magazine paid well and I found it enjoyable work since I have always been an enthusiastic film fan myself. I was soon moving in head-spinning circles. I became on first-name terms with such inhabitants of Olympus as Jimmy Stewart, Clark Gable, Constance Bennett, Myrna Loy, Betty Grable and a wonderfully friendly star named Carole Lombard, who liked to shock my middle-class English susceptibilities by saying, whenever I politely addressed her as "Miss Lombard": "Honey, don't be so piss-pious. Call me Carole." Clark Gable, who was her constant companion, boomed with laughter.

"I always call her You Old Cow," he said.

One of the stars who was playing hard to get for the fan magazines at that time was the girl known in the tabloids as "The Blonde Bombshell." In other words, Jean Harlow. I was mad about her. I was not only anxious to interview her for *Photoplay* but thought the opportunity to meet her would be the fulfillment of a dream. It should be emphasized, perhaps, that I was a very uncynical young Englishman in those days, and apt to judge people on their looks. Nothing annoyed me more than to overhear the vulgar sexual remarks everyone made about Miss Harlow, who was, in my fantasy, as shiningly pure as her silvery hair, cherishing to her admirable bosom an innocence belied by her sexy reputation.

Imagine my joy, therefore, when a friend at M-G-M studios arranged to get me on the set where Miss Harlow was currently making a film called *Red Dust* with Clark Gable. I watched her doing what subsequently became a famous scene in the movie, taking an open-air shower. Being the 1930s, it was very discreet except for the odd glimpse of an arm, a leg and a shoulder, but delightful to watch. Afterwards, in a silk dressing gown, she came back to her canvas chair on the edge of the set and began to chat with Gable and members of the crew while the next set-up was finished. My friend and I were just about to move in for introductions when I noticed a man approaching the little group.

He was small, slight, slim, dressed in riding breeches and boots, and he carried a crop under his arm. His lightly tanned face was sharp and, I thought, ferretlike, his eyes gleaming, his thin mustache glinting gold in the studio lights. Stealthily, as I watched, he crept up to the back of Miss Harlow's canvas chair, and suddenly he bent down. Reaching out a hand under the canvas seat, *he goosed her!* She leaped to her feet like a startled fawn, twisted around, saw who it was, laughed out loud, and sat down again. Once more the man leaned down, and he goosed her again — but *this time he goosed her with his riding crop!* I was outraged. But amazed, too, because Miss Harlow didn't even leap up this time, only squirmed lower in her chair and giggled softly. A few moments later, I was taken over and introduced. Miss Harlow responded with a friendly welcome, then turned in her chair and indicated the grinning man in the breeches and boots. "And do you know this filthy son of a bitch?" she asked. "This is Darryl Zanuck."

He came around, took her in his arms, and began immediately pouring out a stream of affectionate obscenities at her to which, to my dismay, she replied in kind. Neither of them was even aware, of course, that they were shattering my illusions.

I grew older and wiser — and, I suppose, more cynical — during the next two years in Hollywood, and among the things I learned was that there was much more to Darryl Francis Zanuck than a predilection for prodding beautiful film stars when and where they were least expecting it (though I learned more about that too). Despite the fact that we never met again during that period of our lives, I became enough of a cineaste to appreciate his skill and vision as a filmmaker and of the part he was playing in the renaissance of Hollywood, which needed a revival then, God knows.

I had two brief encounters with him in 1942/3 under very different circumstances. Back from watching the successful campaign against the German General Erwin Rommel, at El Alamein in the Egyptian desert, I flew to Algiers to see General Dwight D. Eisenhower, then commanding the Allied forces in North Africa. At that moment Darryl Zanuck was attached to Ike's command as a colonel in the U.S. Signal Corps, and I was a war correspondent. He was in North Africa to shoot an action film about the war, and Commander John Ford, USN, was supposed to be collaborating with him but professed to find him "a difficult and cocky little bastard." Eisenhower, when introducing him at a press conference, jocularly remarked:

"Colonel Zanuck will probably make this campaign look as entertaining as one of his Hollywood films. I only hope to God he never forgets which side he's on, and makes sure we get a happy ending!"

Later, I ran into him again during a tricky moment of the war in Tunisia, after he had had a narrow escape from death under German bombardment. He was glowing with the excitement of it all and obviously thriving on danger.

In the postwar years, it seemed as if I was always encountering Zanuck. I became the film critic of a major London newspaper and was in Hollywood at least twice every year to look over the studios and their productions, and that always included a visit to 20th Century–Fox, where he was in charge. It seemed to me that Zanuck was still the pushiest producer in America, but that his choice of movie subjects was improving along with his skills and percipience. His movies had grown bolder, more controversial, tackling subjects never seen on the screen in American films before. When I talked to him, he admitted he was deliberately challenging the rules laid down by the industry's self-censorship organization, the Breen Office, but he complained of the fact that its bans and prohibitions and general timidity were still impeding any real breakthrough in ideas.

We would also meet every year at the Cannes Film Festival in the South of France, where he would express his envy at the freedom French and Italian film producers possessed, and he would bitterly inveigh against the way in which the Breen Office constantly "debollicked," as he termed it, any attempt he made to deal with controversy and new thinking. It was a period when his wife, Virginia, traveled with him, and the rapport between them, and the easy manner in which she talked about their relationship, gave no hint that their marriage would soon be ripped apart. But to anyone who spoke to him at any length, it was obvious that, even in those days, he was highly dissatisfied with Hollywood, and already longing for what he believed was the "freedom" of movie-making in Europe. So it was not much of a surprise when he announced in 1956 that he was leaving America and would henceforth be making his movies overseas.

It was hard not to become fascinated with Zanuck both as a filmmaker and a man, and each new meeting I had with him provoked new speculation about him. For instance, how could one who was so courageous in his pursuit of bold new film subjects, who was so eager to break the old cinematic taboos, be so hairy-chested and old-fashioned in his personal life? Why could his films seem so fresh and even belligerently provocative up there on the screen, when he was so much of a conformist off it? I do not mean by conformist that he was "respectable." Just the opposite. But why did he have to be so macho, especially towards women? Why was he always flexing his muscles and treating women like sex machines, always so determinedly putting them down in both senses of the phrase?

What had women done to him that he must always behave towards them like a professional Texan and set out to demonstrate at once that they were his inferiors? Did he have some deep dark Freudian secret tucked away there in the recesses of his subconscious?

It was after I had asked these questions several times that I realized I had better start searching for the answers.

I have gone to many and varied sources in search of material for this book. Not unnaturally, I gathered much useful information during my years as a film critic, and it was rare that a conversation with any producer, director, writer, or player who ever happened to work with Zanuck (and most of them had) did not produce some new sidelight on him both as a human being and a conceiver of films. In this regard, my talks with directors like Joseph L. Mankiewicz, Anatole Litvak, Orson Welles, Henry Hathaway and Henry King (whom I saw in Hollywood just before his death in 1982) elicited some fascinating data. Sam Spiegel and, while they were alive, Sam Goldwyn and Jack Warner, always had stories about him and his activities. I found in my notes much interesting information about Zanuck provided by stars like Bette Davis, Lauren Bacall, Ava Gardner, Elizabeth Taylor, Richard Burton, James Mason, James Stewart, Cary Grant, Loretta Young, and Jennifer Jones, to mention those Hollywood stars who are still around, if not as active.

One of those with whom my conversations proved to be particularly fruitful was that beautiful former star Linda Christian. I have known Miss Christian ever since I met her, a plump teenager, in the censor's office in Haifa during World War II, when it was still part of the British mandated territory of Palestine. Her father was a Dutch official of the Iraq Petroleum Company, whose pipeline terminated in Haifa, and her mother was a charming and attractive Mexican. They had both given Miss Christian a gift for languages and she worked in the local censor's office checking outgoing communications in English, Dutch, German, French, and Spanish. She went off to Hollywood to become a star and subsequently married Tyrone Power, who became one of Zanuck's biggest male box-office attractions. One summer in the 1950s, after Power's sudden death, Linda Christian and I came to the South of France together to work on a project, and the late Prince Aly Khan lent us his villa, the Château de l'Horizon, at Juan-les-Pins, while we worked together. Among the many visitors who came to see us there were Otto Preminger, Jean Seberg, Deborah Kerr, Elga Andersen, Françoise Sagan (all of whom had had some association with Zanuck), and, finally, Zanuck himself.

He was a in confidential, almost confessional, mood, and he talked a great deal of the last production he had done with Tyrone Power, the movie version of Hemingway's *Sun Also Rises*, when Linda Christian had been on the set in both Spain and Mexico. It was during the making of this film that Miss Christian watched her husband failing (he died shortly afterwards) and Zanuck beginning his stormy affair with the French night-club singer Juliette Greco, who was also in the film, and their mutual memories made absorbing listening.

Among other distinguished Hollywood figures whose reminiscences of Zanuck were extremely helpful to me, I would like to express my thanks to four well-known producers, Frank McCarthy, Milton Sperling, Pandro Berman, and Elmo Williams, all of whom were closely associated with Zanuck during crucial periods of his life. They talked to me freely and were generous in their stories and memories of their collaborations and, on occasion, clashes.

My old friend, Trevor Howard, had some salty reminiscences of what it was like to be acting in a Zanuck film when we talked together in the South of France. Another close friend, Ken Annakin, who directed the major portions of Zanuck's most cherished film, *The Longest Day*, and went on to make his enjoyable aerial entertainment, *Those Magnificent Men in Their Flying Machines*, had frequent conversations with me at his home and at my house at Malibu; he was joined on several occasions by another of my neighbors, Jack Davies, who wrote the script of *Flying Machines*, and first introduced me to Zanuck's patient wife, Virginia, when we both lived in the South of France; and by another distinguished director, Guy Green, and his wife, Jo.

Finally, for facts about Darryl Zanuck's character, actions, motivations, and behavior as a family man as well as a movie tycoon, facts which, I may say, I would have been able to obtain nowhere else, I must offer my heartfelt thanks to his son, Richard D. Zanuck, without whose help there would have been a great gap in this book. I have watched Richard Zanuck's movie career over the years and seen him grow in stature as a filmmaker so that today he matches his father's brilliant achievements, and adds to them the balance of a much more worldly-wise and solid human being.

Richard Zanuck gave up much of his time to talk to me about every facet of his father's activities, both personal and professional, and did so while seeing into the cinemas his latest film. We talked at length and he was never less than honest and forthcoming, as readers will discover in these pages, even about the most distressing moments of his relationship with his parents. He also allowed me free use of the scrapbooks he has been keeping on his father ever since he began making films. In Hollywood, which is not a community too full of mature characters, I found him firm as a rock and always willing to advise and help. It should be emphasized, however, that he is in no way responsible for the opinions expressed in this book about either his father's actions or motivations. Like all other views here expressed, they are the sole responsibility of the author.

In the course of this book, readers will find a detailed list of all the sources I have used. I have of course consulted many of the vast library of books about Hollywood. For my purpose, by far the most invaluable has been the study of Darryl Zanuck, published while he was still alive, in 1971, by Mel Gussow, *Don't Say Yes Until I've Finished Talking*. It includes the transcripts of many conversations with Zanuck himself, and I have quoted some of the most illuminating of them.

I have also relied heavily on that fascinating undertaking, the Oral Histories of the Motion Picture Industry in America, which was originally sponsored by the Film Department of the University of California at Los Angeles and then passed on to the American Film Institute and the Louis B. Mayer Foundation. The oral histories set out the memories of many of Hollywood's veteran writers, producers, directors, cameramen, art directors, cartoonists, and publicists, and it is a unique collection, indispensable to anyone seeking information about the early days of the movie industry in America. I hope the quotations I have used will give younger readers some idea of what Hollywood was like in the days when it was the movie capital of the world.

One other person I must single out for particular thanks in doing so much to shape this book and keep it to what is, I hope, its hard-driving narrative line is my editor at Little, Brown, William Phillips, who was full of advice, patient yet persistent, from rough draft to final manuscript.

For photographs and help with facts and figures there are many people and institutions I must thank, including the Motion Picture Academy of Arts and Sciences in Beverly Hills and the British Film Institute in London.

And once more, my love and thanks to my dearest collaborator, for her unfailing vigilance and encouragement.

# ZANUCK

THE RISE AND FALL OF
HOLLYWOOD'S LAST TYCOON

# THE PRODIGAL FATHER

ATURDAY, January 12, 1974, was one of those days when Palm Springs comes into its own. From all over the nation, reports of bitter winter weather were coming in, and even the Florida Keys were having storms. But here in the California desert a warm, gentle breeze was barely stirring the palm trees and the last touches of morning mist were melting away as the sun climbed higher. Etched against the brilliant sky, the purple mountains surrounding the desert colony were, for once, as clear and sharp as a film shot in old-time Technicolor.

The press had been summoned to the Raquet Club in Palm Springs for midday, and so had some of the most famous, powerful, and influential names in Hollywood. To make sure that the guests of honor would want for nothing before their departure for the party, the staff of the villa had been up early and on the qui vive. But no one had risen as early as Darryl Zanuck. At first light, sweaty from a restless night, his son, Richard, had come out of the bathroom of the guest-house annex and looked out of the window. And there, in the pool, was his father laboriously swimming up and down, length after length. There was a stir of drapes in the bedroom of the main house, across the pool, and it became obvious that Virginia Zanuck was watching too.

She had waited eighteen years for this day, and Richard couldn't help wondering what she must be thinking at this moment. Many years ago someone had compared her husband's body to "a bantam cock, a whippet, a jaguar," and added that it was "very stringy but also very strong."

Sadly, it gave no impression of strength now, and seemed, on the contrary, puny and frail; the general impression of vulnerability was exacerbated by the way in which the elder Zanuck was puffing and blowing

3

so stertorously, like a sick seal in distress, as he struggled up and down the pool with such dogged, almost despairing, determination.

Not for the first time, Richard Zanuck wondered why his father persisted in trying so hard. Why did he not accept the fact that he was seventy-one years old and his powers were waning? Why could he not recognize that although he still had demons inside him prodding his urges, his appetites, and his lusts, the passage of the years had sapped the ability of his flesh to respond to them? Why was he so unwilling to swallow the fact, unpalatable though it might be, that time was working against him?

Watching those thin arms angrily flailing the water, Richard Zanuck found himself fervently wishing — surely not the first son to do so — that his father would resign himself to old age, and do it gracefully. Especially on this day, his wedding anniversary.

The celebration at the Raquet Club to which close friends of the family and members of the media had been summoned was, in fact, the fiftieth anniversary of Darryl Zanuck's wedding to his wife, the former Virginia Fox, and it was their only son, Richard, who had sent out the invitations. Under normal circumstances, he might have expected little attention to be given by press and TV to such an occasion, especially on a weekend. A year earlier, in 1973, Zanuck had been ousted, after a particularly nasty boardroom coup, from his position as chairman of the board of the 20th Century–Fox Film Corporation, and so the man who had founded and made famous what had once been Hollywood's most prestigious movie production company was toppled from his throne and fobbed off with the derisorily meaningless courtesy title of chairman emeritus. Since no one is less newsworthy in Hollywood than a fallen film chief, why should anyone travel all the way from Los Angeles to report his anniversary celebrations? Richard Zanuck knew why and so did his mother, Virginia. They were well aware that there were too many savory elements connected with the occasion for the press, particularly the Hollywood columnists, to miss.

There was, for instance, the piquant marital situation between Darryl and Virginia on this fiftieth anniversary of their wedding. It was indeed true that Virginia had been waiting eighteen years for this day, but that was because Virginia and Darryl had been separated for eighteen years, and this would be the first time they had been together in public since Zanuck had walked out on his wife. Now they were suddenly back together again, and no one knew exactly how or why.

Nor was Virginia the only member of the family whose relations with Darryl could hardly be described as normal. There was the case of his younger daughter, Susan. Back in 1956, when she was twenty-two years old, she had had a blazing row with her father in which wild accusations had been flung around concerning her relations with Zanuck's then-mistress, and for several years afterwards she had hardly spoken to him. His second daughter, Darrylin, who had most adored and admired her father, had never succeeded in getting really close to him. As for Zanuck's son, Richard, he had perhaps been treated most unfeelingly of them all. Confident of his father's love and trust, he had worked long and hard to match his achievements in the movie world, only to be thrown out of his job in a sudden spasm of paternal jealousy and envy. DEAR DICK: YOU'RE SACKED. LOVE, DAD was the way the newspapers had headlined the story. It had been a brutal act of public humiliation — the execution of a son by his own father, in fact — which had so appalled those who knew them both that they were convinced Richard would never forgive his father nor bear to be in his presence again.

Yet here they all were, wife, daughters, son, and their errant husband-father, all back together again on this lovely desert morning, ready to play happy-family for the guests and the press who would soon be arriving to greet and salute them.

The Zanuck house in Palm Springs was called Ric-Su-Dar and had once been a showplace of the colony, much more renowned among the cognoscenti than the desert palaces of Frank Sinatra, Bob Hope, Gerry Ford, and the Annenbergs. It had originally been built and owned by one of the famous names of old-time Hollywood, Joseph Schenck, who, with his brother, Nicholas, had been in movies since the days of the nickelodeon. But like most of the early studio bosses, Joe Schenck had cheated on his taxes, and when the IRS decided to make an example of Hollywood, it was he who volunteered to be the sacrificial lamb. All the other cheats, including Louis B. Mayer, Sam Goldwyn, William Fox, and the brothers Cohn, had sworn at the time that they would be eternally in his debt and would never forget his bigheartedness in taking blame and public punishment on behalf of all of them. But of course they did. Schenck was heavily fined and sent to jail. When he came back to Hollywood his powerful friends were suddenly too busy to see him, and things were never the same again for him.

To help him pay off his debts, Darryl Zanuck had bought the Palm

Springs house from him after he went to jail, and Virginia, who loved inventing names, called it Ric-Su-Dar after her children, Richard, Susan, and Darrylin. It was a luxurious property surrounded by a wall and an electric fence, with a pool, a tennis court, a large guest house, a main house, and, after Darryl had finished rebuilding, a croquet lawn. Here, every weekend, publishers, politicians, writers, wartime generals, and all the most prominent Hollywood stars and directors met to fight needle-matches that sometimes went on all night under floodlights. There was a visitors' book in which the guests wrote some choice comments about those games. Playwright Moss Hart and his wife, Kitty Carlisle, for instance, left behind a long screed which included this verse:

> This is a roundelay, this is a song
>   Of lunches late and dinners long
> Of bitter croquet and games at the table
>   Of hitting the ball when you're hardly able
> To see your partner, much less the wicket,
>   Of hiding from Darryl way up in some
>   thicket.
> Of starting at noon and playing all night
>   Of knowing your strategy never is right.

But there were those with personalities powerful enough to keep out of these games and just sit and watch, like Aly Khan and Olivia de Havilland. Among them, Henry Luce of *Time* magazine and his wife, Clare, who were frequent visitors, wrote in the book:

> Some speak of Arizona and some of Waikiki
>   Of Nassau and Bermuda, and places where they ski,
> But of all the sun-kissed heavens
>   There's none that can compare
> With the zestful, restful, guestful
>   Home of Zanucks, mere and pere.

And then, suddenly, in 1956, it was all over. The marriage, always considered the most solid in Hollywood, was abruptly wrecked by a monumental crisis. Zanuck walked out and departed for Europe, swearing he would never come near Virginia or Hollywood ever again. It was ages, in fact, before he even visited California, and Virginia did not see him for eighteen years.

But she could follow his exploits in the newspapers. There were always stories or pictures of him, and he was to be seen in all manner of places — Paris, mostly, Monte Carlo, Cannes, St. Moritz, Mexico City, Rome, Africa, Greece — always with a cigar in his mouth, sunshades masking his eyes, and a beautiful girlfriend on his arm. She could hardly help noticing the girlfriends seemed to get younger year by year.

Ric-Su-Dar was taken over by a caretaker. The great dining room in the guest building, once the scene of some memorable parties, was denuded of the trophies around the walls. Sometimes Virginia came on a visit to see the house was kept in order, and then she would wander through the rooms, weeping silently, whispering that "this place used to be alive with happy voices and laughter." Sometimes she would stay late and go to the croquet lawn, kept mown but unused, and flick on the floodlights, turn on the hi-fi system, and stand there like a frozen wraith, and the sight of her in the baleful glow, combined with the dull thud of the music, would make the neighbors murmur that the place was haunted. As, in a way, it was.

And then, in 1973, after the debacle in the boardroom, all sorts of rumors were heard in Hollywood about Darryl Zanuck. Some said he had been stricken with a heart attack and had been abandoned by his latest girlfriend. Others whispered that he had been seen sitting in a wheelchair beside a Riviera swimming pool, the girlfriend still very much with him — so close to him, in fact, that she had been sighted sunbathing naked only a hand's reach away.

Whether that was true or not, a year later Darryl Zanuck was definitely back at Ric-Su-Dar, reunited with Virginia. How had he got there? No one seemed to know, except that an ambulance plane had brought him in from the East.

The story in Palm Springs was that his beautiful young girlfriend, a charming and attractive Frenchwoman, had followed him alone from New York and pleaded to be allowed to see him, but had been denied entry to Ric-Su-Dar. All she wanted was to talk to him herself, she explained in her French-accented English, to make sure her darling Darryl was happy, contented, and that everything went well with him. She was crisply told that he did not wish to be disturbed, but that everything went very well with him indeed. *"Vraiement bien,"* Virginia assured the girl. It was just that he was very tired. *"Très, très fatigué,"* she said.

But not too tired for his anniversary party.

To that, of course, his girlfriend was not invited. Richard Zanuck had made sure that it was a very exclusive occasion. By midday everybody had managed to reach the Raquet Club and there was a quietly discreet crowd of friends, relatives, and press crowding around the bar. None of the columnists present were saying what they were going to ask the happy couple when they appeared, but you could almost hear the questions hovering in the air.

There was a sudden stir and then the Zanucks, husband, wife, daughters, and son, advanced from the clubhouse. The cameramen put down their drinks and surged forward. Everyone was looking at Darryl Zanuck. He seemed thin, worn, much older than the last time most people present had seen him, but his face was sunburned and his appearance was immaculate. Always a snappy dresser, today he was in uniform, in the ceremonial uniform of a colonel of the U.S. Signal Corps: gleaming white silk, with a bow tie, medals up and flashing on his chest, a red silk cummerbund around his waist to conceal his paunch. On his shoulder straps it was obvious from the way they sparkled in the sun that his colonel's wings were made of solid gold.

Virginia Zanuck looked older too, and a nerve was jumping at her temple. But there was a glow coming from her — of happiness? contentment? triumph? — that made her seem positively radiant. She was in a white, floor-length gown, a necklace of diamonds and emeralds at her throat. Her arm was through her husband's and she was clinging on hard, the expression on her face serene as she smiled up at her husband. Everyone had forgotten how tiny she really was, and those present were mostly too young to remember that as a Mack Sennett Bathing Beauty she had once been the smallest of the belles. Now, still smiling, she held up a hand and almost immediately silenced the chatter of the crowd. "Welcome to our anniversary party and thank you for coming," she said. "Today is a particularly happy one for us because, as you know, it is our fiftieth wedding anniversary. I am overjoyed that my husband and I are spending it together. I can assure you we will never be separated again."

Then, before anyone could speak, the place was suddenly full of waiters bearing trays of glasses filled with bubbling champagne. Richard, with a glass in his hand, stepped forward.

"Ladies and gentlemen," he shouted above the hubbub, "I would like you all to drink a toast to my father and mother." He turned to them. "To you both! It is wonderful to see you together. Happy anniversary!"

A waiter was at his side and took his glass. He enveloped them in his arms, kissing them both, first his mother on both cheeks, then his father on cheek and forehead. Then came the turn of his sisters.

As the cameramen moved in, Virginia turned and touched her husband's cheek affectionately, and he reached out for her hand and took it. There were tears in the eyes of both of them. Richard's eyes were swimming. Susan and Darrylin were weeping openly, and so were many of the guests. It was quite a sentimental moment.

It was at this moment that a small phalanx of attendants moved between the Zanucks and their guests, and began shepherding the group back towards the clubhouse. The guests, pressmen among them, watched in bemused and stunned silence and were then distracted by the arrival of more waiters with more trays of champagne and bearing bottles of Dom Perignon. By the time they had finished with all the refills, the Zanucks were gone.

"My God," a columnist was heard to remark, "is that *all?* No one asked a single question!"

Perhaps it was just as well. They were not likely to have received satisfactory answers. Not on that occasion, anyway.

# ONE

# WAHOO

I
N LATER LIFE, whenever Darryl Zanuck spoke about his parents
(which was not too often) he always referred to his father with a
kind of rueful contempt.

"Like most American boys," he once said, "I didn't just love my
father. I wanted to admire and look up to him too. And that was difficult,
because my father was a failure, and, as I came to realize later, not
particularly ashamed of it either. For instance, anyone who puts down
his occupation as a hotel night clerk is acknowledging that he has no
ambition for a start. And that's how my father described himself — as a
night clerk. It's like admitting you're a mouse," he added, contemptuously, "and only dare to come out after dark and snuffle around for
cheese."

He might have added that his father, Frank Zanuck, was usually snuf-
fling around for other things besides cheese, mostly booze and card games,
and when he found both of them it was with almost invariably disastrous
results.

Frank Zanuck was a farm boy from Iowa who hated the wide open
spaces of the Middle West and dreamed of one day settling down in
California. In the years before the turn of this century, he was gradually
working his way west by easy stages. To begin with, he started out as a
salesman, peddling underwear and dress fashions for a Des Moines mail-
order house. But he found he lacked the persistence and the patience to
make a decent living, and changed his occupation to itinerant hotel employee, preferring whenever possible a night job behind the reception
desk of one of those small hotels where the more successful drummers
stayed. Despite his own failure at the trade, he liked drummers and found
their company congenial. At the end of their day's rounds and after their

evening meal, they had a tendency to forgather for drinks and cards, and Frank Zanuck could think of no more pleasant way to spend the night hours. He liked the free-and-easy company, the banter, the kidding, the jokes, and he particularly liked the poker games. With a drink in one hand, cards in the other, and a pile of money on the table, there was nothing mouselike about Frank Zanuck. Gambling fed his fantasy that one night he would scoop up a fortune off the table, and he boldly upped the ante in every game, convinced that he could outsmart his raucously merry and relaxed opponents. Unfortunately, Frank was a poor player and the drummers knew it, and they took him every time.

In 1892, Frank Zanuck was working as a night clerk in the quaintly named Le Grande Hotel, the only hostelry in the small city of Wahoo, some thirty-five miles west of Omaha, Nebraska. He had been there for some months and was unable to move on to the next town because his nightly gambling games had severely depleted his financial resources. During one of these noisy and enjoyable parties — for Frank was a good loser — he emerged from the smoke-filled room in which it was being held and wandered down a corridor of the hotel in search of some receptive soul who might give him a drink, his money and his liquor having run out. He found a door open, a bedside lamp discreetly lit, and whiskey and glasses on the dressing table. He awoke next morning to find himself lying in a strange bed beside a young woman with long ash-blond hair, who seemed quite undismayed by his presence and happily folded him in her arms. He recognized her at once. Her name was Louise Torpin and she was his boss's daughter.

Everyone in Wahoo knew Louise, not just because of her striking ash-colored hair but because she painted her nails a vivid green, and no one had ever seen that color nails in that part of the world before. In the circumstances, there was little else Frank could do but marry her. Louise's father, Henry Torpin, who owned Le Grande Hotel, had soon learned what had happened between his night clerk and his daughter, and he would not have been satisfied with less. He arranged the wedding ceremony himself and then saw off his daughter and new son-in-law for a short honeymoon in Omaha. When they returned, Frank found he had been promoted to assistant manager, but he continued to work the night shift, and ceased to be itinerant for the next few years. If Louise, however, expected marriage to cure him of his propensity for midnight tippling and nocturnal gambling, she was soon disillusioned. His frequent all-night absences from her bed and his inebriated condition when he eventually did fall into it soon had Louise complaining bitterly. For a time,

the birth of a son, in 1893, eased the strain. A second son was born on
September 5, 1902, and was christened Darryl Francis Zanuck. His presence did something to relieve the pain for both parents when, three
months later, the first child was killed by a kick from a horse.

As he began to grow, Darryl realized that there was strife between his
father and mother, constant rows over Frank's drinking and gambling
losses. This distressed him deeply and drove him into his mother's arms,
especially when she wept in distress after a particularly violent quarrel.
And then, when he was about four or five years old, Louise seemed to
become resigned to her husband's weaknesses. She even seemed to encourage Frank to "get out of here and have a game with your friends"
when he fidgeted restlessly around the family apartment in the hotel. So
far as Darryl was concerned, this hardly improved anything, since Louise
began neglecting him too and often put him out of the apartment and
told him to "go play with your friends" or go visit his grandfather, Henry
Torpin, who had a land office farther down Broadway, in Wahoo. Instead,
Darryl would often follow in his father's wake along the hotel corridors
and hang around the door of the room where the card game was taking
place, trying to will Frank Zanuck into getting out of the game quickly
and returning to his mother. It was in this way Darryl discovered that
the salesmen with whom his father gambled were not only taking his
money but were stealing his wife as well. They waited until Frank was
deeply involved in a game and plentifully tanked up with liquor, and then
one or another of them, with much winking and laughter, would deal
himself out of the game and creep along to the family apartment.

Young Darryl discovered to his surprise that his mother was ready and
waiting for the visitor. Soon he found himself peeking at the shocking
spectacle of his mother wrestling on the couch with the stranger, and
behaving in a manner that made him feel ill. He had never seen her
acting like this, even with his father, and he hated the man who was
responsible for it. At first he presumed his mother was being attacked
and his instinct was to rush in and kill the loathsome individual who was
so brutally assaulting her. He was stopped from doing so only by the
puzzling realization that, from her expression and her cries, she actually
seemed to be enjoying what was being done to her, and he was appalled.
One day, when Louise took her son with her on a visit to Grandpa Torpin,
she was asked about a bruise on her cheek and said it was the result of
a fall on the stairs. But Darryl blurted out the truth — that it was "one
of those drummers" who had hit her "because she bit him so hard on the

ear." He was told to leave the room, and while he waited outside he could hear Grandpa Torpin raging at his daughter, who was weeping bitterly when she eventually rejoined him.

Shortly afterwards Louise left Wahoo for a stay with relatives in Arizona. It was announced that she was suffering from incipient tuberculosis and had gone to the desert to recover from a bad cough and weakness in the chest. Since Frank was not trusted to look after his son, Darryl was taken in by Grandpa and Grandma Torpin at their home in Oakdale. He was allowed to take the coach into Wahoo once a week to see his father, who promised on each visit that Louise would soon be back and they would resume life together again. They never did, for Louise never came back. Instead, Grandpa Torpin informed his grandson one day that his mother now had a new husband and had gone to live in Glendale, California. She had asked that her son be returned to her as soon as possible. In a separate note to Darryl she gushed that she was divinely happy and couldn't wait to be reunited with him. He would soon be meeting someone "who will be a *real* father to you."

When the bewildered boy took the coach into Wahoo and went into Le Grande Hotel to seek his father's views on these strange developments, he discovered that Frank Zanuck was no longer around. Grandpa Torpin had sacked him the moment news of his daughter's remarriage reached him, and Frank had quietly departed, without informing his son, on his resumed search for new night desks and new nocturnal poker games. He was rumored to have found a berth in a hotel in Fremont, and Grandpa Torpin subsequently informed his grandson he was unlikely to see his father ever again. He did, though. On the night that Darryl departed to rejoin his mother in California, Frank turned up at the railroad depot to bid him goodbye, and there were tears in his eyes as he embraced his son for what he believed would be the last time.

Young Darryl was less discomposed. In the weeks since his mother's departure, he had begun to miss her badly and had long since forgiven her for her behavior with "those drummers" back at the hotel. If anything, he blamed his father, his drinking, his gambling, his neglect of his mother, for her behavior. He had heard his grandfather and grandmother talking about Frank's "weakness" and come to share their opinion that it was all his fault that the marriage had broken up. He couldn't wait to be reunited with his mother again, whom he thought of as the most beautiful woman in the world, and he was eager to meet his new "father," with whom, apparently, she was now so divinely happy.

*    *

It proved to be a disillusioning reunion. Louise was a bad picker of men, and in choosing her second husband she had done worse than in her choice of the first. Joseph Norton, like Frank Zanuck, turned out to be addicted to alcohol if not to gambling, but whereas liquor had made Frank bold and reckless, drink turned Joseph into a violent and vicious individual. He was the son of a California preacher and he had inherited his father's fierce passion for old-time religion, roaring through life with a bottle in one hand and a Bible in the other. Within a few days of his arrival in Glendale, Darryl watched, terrified, as his mother cringed in fear before her new husband. He would burst into their room, reeling drunk, screaming of hellfire and the wrath of a vengeful God, holding his Bible aloft, his frenzied, flashing eyes looking for trouble. Words like "whore" and "slut" and "harridan" came out of his mouth like ectoplasm as he verbally opened fire upon his wife. One word of reproach from Louise and he substituted fists and feet for his torrents of abuse, tearing at her hair, flinging her across the bed, kicking her violently as she cowered beneath him. When her son rushed in to protect his beloved mother, he found himself seized and thrown across the room amid a crash of breaking furniture and crockery.

Joseph Norton made it plain from the start that he hated and resented his stepson, and he went out of his way to hurt and humiliate him.

"I hated him back," Darryl said later. "He had a disregard for me. He would slap my mother down and I'd jump into the middle of it and he'd hit me . . ." He added: "I remember lying in my cot. My mother in her bed. Waiting for him to come home. I would be shivering almost . . . as I heard footsteps coming up to the door. Reeling drunk! Falling down! And with the Bible, always with the Bible. A big black Bible under his arm."

Sometimes the fights got so noisy that the neighbors would burst into the apartment and order his stepfather to calm down and his mother to stop screaming. The boy was astonished that the neighbors failed to take his side or his mother's, even when they could see that it was Louise who was bruised, bleeding and racked with sobs. He was too young to suspect that his mother might like being roughly handled by her men, and that perhaps the neighbors knew more about that than he did. He shivered in his cot and dreamed of the day when he would be big and strong enough to carry her out of danger, and it did not occur to him to wonder why it was that, in the middle of all this marital mayhem, Joseph would suddenly substitute embraces for blows, slobbering kisses for imprecations, and his mother's cries of pain and outrage would change to groans of passion. All he felt was hate against the one who was hurting the mother he loved so much.

"If I had had a gun," he said later, "I would have killed him a couple of times."

Sometimes, when his stepfather was out, he would plead with Louise to leave him.

"Let's run away and go back to Grandpa," he would urge her.

She would turn her pale blue eyes upon him and look at him with sheer astonishment, then tell him not to be silly, and assure him that "your stepfather is a good man, really. You'll grow to love him too. Things will get better, really they will. Just be nice to him." But even she, after a time, began to realize the extent of her son's loathing for his stepfather, and of her husband's resentment of her son, and she took steps to do something about it. Darryl was aware that a crisis had been reached when, during a particularly noisy quarrel, his stepfather suddenly seized him by the shoulders, lifted his puny body high in the air, and shook him violently.

"This is the viper in your bosom!" he cried. "Tear him out, tear him out!"

He then flung the sobbing boy violently to the ground, and Darryl lay there, terrified, waiting for his mother to rescue and comfort him. But she did not come. Finally, when he dared to look up, it was to discover that the two adults were in the throes of their usual slobbering reconciliation, tearing at each other with grunts and sobs and declarations of undying affection. He crawled away to a corner of the room and lay there, crying quietly to himself and listening to the thrashing on the bed next door. For the rest of the night, he could hear them whispering urgently to each other, and he made out his stepfather's voice angrily insisting:

"Tell him! Tell him in the morning! You have to choose between me and him!"

Next morning Louise informed her son that all arrangements had been made, and he was being sent away to military school. She had already enrolled him in the Page Military Academy in Los Angeles. He was eight years old. Even at that age, he realized there was no use arguing, that he could no longer rely on his mother.

"She just didn't want me around," he said.

In some ways it was a relief to get away from all that raw, tearing emotion. At least he didn't have to go on watching his mother "make a goddam spectacle of herself," as he put it later. "Being with a lot of boys, in a way, was a refuge."

But he was not the kind of child who made friends easily, and he was lonely. With the resilience of childhood, he began to forget the humiliations he had watched her suffer, and longed to be with his mother again. He counted the days to the summer holidays and waited for her to come for him. She failed to turn up. He was curtly informed by his class commander that special arrangements had been made and he would be spending the summer at the academy.

That was when he began running away from school.

"I would just wander, look in windows," he said later. "I ran away out of just pure boredom."

It was on one of these escapades that his real father, Frank Zanuck, found him wandering the streets of downtown Los Angeles. Frank had made his way to California at last and was working in a city hotel — as a night clerk, of course. It was a moment when his son felt miserable, neglected and forsaken, and he poured it all out to his father, sobbing bitterly as he recounted the unhappy tale of his mother's perfidy, his stepfather's brutality, his dislike of his school. Frank, who loved his son, listened sympathetically and finally persuaded the boy to return to the academy, promising that in return he would come and visit him regularly. This he did, twice a week. They almost invariably ended up at a movie house, and for both of them it was the highlight of their outing, almost certainly because, for an hour or two, they were transported into a world of make-believe where all problems, particularly the emotional ones, were always solved at the final fadeout. Years later, Darryl Zanuck could still name most of the films he saw with his father: Clara Kimball Young in *My Official Wife* and *Happy-Go-Lucky*, Helen Gardner as Becky Sharp in *Vanity Fair*, Marguerite Snow in *Lucile*, and Norma Talmadge in *A Tale of Two Cities*. It is interesting that he could remember the female stars of these films but never the male actors who played opposite them, and this was probably because he made a mental transference of himself into the male roles. Those were the days when the heroines of Hollywood films were weak and vulnerable and virtuous only because they were saved from moral ruin in the end by the protection of strong men. He persuaded his father to take him to see Clara Kimball Young no less than five times in *My Official Wife*, and fell in love with her. He said later she reminded him of his mother, and maybe that was because she usually played roles in films where she was being sexually tempted; but, unlike his mother, was saved from a fate worse than death by a love of a dominating male. He must have sighed each time he met his father for their outings and wished that he could be such a man, and he confessed later that so long as Frank Zanuck was in Los Angeles he toyed with the idea of trying to arrange a reconciliation between his father and his mother.

But then Frank Zanuck let him down again. One day he failed to turn up for the biweekly meeting, and when Darryl hurried around to the hotel to find out what had happened, it was to discover that Frank had been sacked (for playing poker during working hours) and had already gone on his way. He had left no forwarding address behind, and his son never saw or heard from him again.

He did not go back to the academy that night, or the next night either. Instead, he wandered around Los Angeles, looking into the lobbies of small and shabby hotels in the hope that he might see or hear of his father there. In vain. After about a week of this, tired, dirty, and hungry, he was picked up by the police and delivered to his mother, to whom the academy had already indicated that they did not want him back. He flung himself into Louise's arms and was comforted until the moment his stepfather burst in and, drunk as usual, began to abuse him. Once more there was a fearful row, but once more his mother failed to take his part, and it was both of the grown-ups who upbraided him for being a worthless, ungrateful, and, worst of all, unwanted boy. Louise made it plain that he was unwelcome, and got busy at once sending telegrams. Two days later she took him down to the depot, perfunctorily embraced him, and shipped him back to the care of Grandpa and Grandma Torpin in Nebraska.

The last he saw of his mother was through the open window of the railroad coach. She was not even looking in his direction, but had turned to his stepfather, who had been hanging back while the goodbyes were said, and was now holding his hand and smiling up at him. Already it was obvious that she had forgotten about her son.

The year was 1915 and Darryl Francis Zanuck was twelve and a half years old. That was the moment, it seems most likely, that he not only fell out of love with his mother, but decided that he would never trust a woman again.

## T W O

# BOYHOOD HERO

W HEN YOUR father has let you down and your mother has turned her back on you, to whom do you look for affection, solace, and guidance? It was fortunate for young Darryl Zanuck that his grandfather took him over when he did. At least for a year or two he lavished love and attention upon the boy and did his best to guide his transition from childhood to manhood. And, according to his lights, he did a good job.

Henry Torpin was what, in those days, was admiringly referred to, even by women, as "a man's man," and he was the antithesis in every way of his son-in-law, Frank — which is probably why he had despised him. Frank Zanuck was not only short in stature but he was "small" in other ways too. He looked and dressed like a clerk, in neat, dark suits, a pince-nez perched on his nose, and he had a way of looking at anyone who accosted him as if he were beneath notice. He had never mounted a horse or handled a gun in his life. His shirts were white, his collars starched, and his boots highly polished, and Grandpa Torpin condemned him as a sissy the moment he discovered he doused himself with eau de cologne after bathing. (Actually, Frank used it in an attempt to mask the smell of liquor on his breath, but Torpin didn't know that.) In contrast, Grandpa Torpin was six feet tall and broad and handsome into the bargain, with fair hair and clear blue eyes. When he strode the wooden sidewalk of Oakdale township in his leather jerkin, open shirt, breeches, and riding boots, he looked as if he had just ridden in from a hunting trip through the forest, and it was more than likely that that was just what he had done. He was very much an outdoorsman, a fine rider, a first-class shot, a great survivor. The first time he took Darryl into the woods, he stripped to the waist to chop logs for the fire and revealed a bronzed back ridged with scars. They were the marks left by Indian arrows, he told his awed grandson, and they were a legacy of the days when he had worked for Union Pacific and had survived a raiding party of Apaches who had attacked a band of railroad workers. He taught the boy to catch trout with his hands, decoy ducks and imitate game birds, track moose, trap and skin jackrabbits and coons, and survive in the bitter snows of a wilderness winter.

Grandpa Torpin liked nothing better than to talk about his pioneer days on the plains or tell romantic tales of his ancestors in England, whence the Torpin family had immigrated, and in his grandson he had an avid listener. He had once been a judge in Laramie, Wyoming, and spoke of leading vigilante posses through the forests in pursuit of cattle thieves and murderers, and he made the boy's eyes pop with wonder and horror as he described railhead trials and hanging parties.

But the character who came alive most vividly for Darryl was one of the Torpin ancestors, and therefore one of his forebears too. He was the legendary English highwayman, Dick Turpin. (The family had changed their name from Turpin to Torpin when they arrived in America.) Dick Turpin was a character for Darryl to relish. He had been the scapegrace son of the family back in the days when the Turpins lived in the Yorkshire dales, in the North of England. After quarreling with his father and being disinherited, he left home astride his sturdy horse, a mare named Black Bess, and took to the highways, where he robbed the rich and gave to the poor. Soon he was famous and notorious throughout the land, wearing his mask and brandishing his pistol as he rode up and down the Great North Road, holding up the Royal Mail and stripping the passengers of their money and jewels. Grandpa Torpin stressed that Turpin killed only when his life was threatened (mostly by the notorious Bow Street Runners), and that he had always treated old folks with great courtesy and young women with a gallantry that won their hearts. Young Darryl's eyes gleamed as he listened, and in later life, Dick Turpin was the only member of his family — his grandpa excepted, of course — of whom he ever talked with any pride. In fact, years afterwards, when he first visited England, he set out from London to drive along the Great North Road, where his highwayman forebear had operated, and he did his best to track down the ancestral home of the Turpins/Torpins in the neighborhood. The house where they had lived was called Bolton Abbey, but for some reason, he never found it, and finally decided it had fallen into ruin and disappeared.* He also wanted to make a film about Dick Turpin's adventures, but discovered that a British film company had already got in before him.

Everything there was to know about wood lore and survival in the wilderness Grandpa Torpin passed on to his grandson, and though he failed to make him grow to his own stature (Darryl was never more than five feet six inches tall), he challenged him into becoming wiry and strong, a good swimmer, an expert trapper, and a first-class horseman. But if his grandfather was highly skilled with animals, he was not much good at human relations, especially with women. The great sorrow of his life was the fact that his wife had failed to give him a son. He blamed Mrs. Torpin — a long-suffering woman who cooked, scrubbed, and waited hand and foot on her husband without complaint — for bearing him a girl instead, especially since the girl had turned out to be the weak and willful Louise. But what could you expect? Women would always let you down unless you kept a constant eye on them. That was why Louise had turned out so badly, he said, firmly. It was all the fault of Darryl's father, Frank. He had never been firm enough with the girl.

"Your daddy should have whaled the tar out of her," he told Darryl. "If he'd done that, shown her who was boss, he'd never have had any trouble with her. He was a goldarned fool about women, that daddy of yours."

He warned his grandson not to be taken in by these newfangled ideas that were being spread around about votes for women and equal rights. Females were not made for such things, and never would be.

"They're weak and they get tempted, and then you have trouble," he said. "The fact is, they can't grasp masculine logic nor keep consecutive thoughts in their heads. You've got to tell them what's right for them, give them a set of rules to follow, and then see that they don't deviate. That's the only way to treat them. Never let them get the upper hand — that's the only thing to remember. There's no sadder sight in all the world than a henpecked husband, and there's nothing more dangerous than an emancipated woman."

Once, on a trip to Omaha, they watched a pretty woman step down from a train at the depot and show what, for those days, was an inordinate

---

*In fact, Bolton Abbey is still standing in the Yorkshire dales not far from the Great North Road where Dick Turpin pillaged the Royal Mail. The Abbey was one of the homes of a member of the Mosley family, and it would be intriguing if Darryl Zanuck and the author turned out to be blood relations.

amount of leg. She smiled at them, saucily and confidently, until she caught the expression of disapproval on Grandpa Torpin's face. He stared after her angrily.

"Sometimes," he then remarked, with gloomy conviction, "I think them Ayrabs have the right idea. They make *their* young women wear veils."

But he did not explain to his grandson what veils had to do with a furtive glimpse of a female calf.

In fact, so far as girls were concerned, Darryl was at an age when he was both repelled and attracted to them. It would not have been surprising had the whole idea of sex been repugnant to him. He had seen too much, too closely, of his mother's encounters with hotel salesmen and her drunken second husband not to be nauseated at the whole idea of it, and at the way she had behaved when it was happening to her. He was tempted to run a mile when a girl at school smiled at him or made advances. Yet he was thirteen years old and thought about girls and sex most of his waking and sleeping hours. He later confessed of this period of his life in Oakdale that he was always dreaming of girls. Night after night he would see himself as a dashing Dick Turpin, riding the roads with his finger on the trigger of his pistol, brandishing it in the face of terrified young women, then dropping to his knees in homage to them. The dream always ended in the same way. One particularly young and beautiful girl would lean towards him in supplication, her bare breasts heaving and palpitating before him, and then he would awake, wet with sweat, excited, relieved — yet also guilty and ashamed.

Years after leaving Oakdale, he revealed that when he was thirteen years old and still in the ninth grade at school, he had his first sexual experience with a girl. She was one of his fellow pupils, and she enticed him into the fields, then dropped her panties and lifted up her skirt.

"This older girl practically raped me," he said, afterwards.

He was particularly shocked when he discovered the girl was actually the local minister's daughter. How could he have been so daring? And what about her? How could she be so shameless, with her family background? But then he made a discovery from his classmates. He wasn't the only one. Despite her religious background, the girl was one of those easy ones, and "half the other guys in school had had her."

Somehow that made him feel better. Grandpa Torpin must be right after all, and that was the way girls were made: weak, easily tempted, not to be trusted. Just like his mother.

*       *

It was 1916, and even in Nebraska they were beginning to smell war in the air. Involvement in World War in Europe was looming. In Omaha, the army was in process of beefing up its forces, and recruiting offices had been opened and color sergeants strutted the sidewalks, urging young men to join up. To stimulate interest, and because they were short of their own, the army had imported recruiting posters from Europe, and Darryl Zanuck remembers being fired up by the famous one from Britain of General Kitchener staring out, his finger jabbing at the passersby, with the legend underneath: YOUR COUNTRY NEEDS YOU! But what inflamed him even more was a French poster showing a fierce German soldier cutting off the breast of a half-naked Belgian woman, while she piteously cries: SAUVEZ-MOI, JE VOUS EN PRIE! [Save me, please!] He could hardly wait to get in there and avenge her.

He was just going on fifteen years of age, and it was an unhappy and restive period of his life, a moment when he was more than ever impatient with being still treated as a child and eager to be accepted as a man. Whenever he saw the recruiting sergeant's uniform, he became convinced that only when he himself could walk around in Uncle Sam's khaki would folks begin treating him as a grown-up. So on one trip to Omaha, he sneaked into the recruiting office and volunteered his services. When asked his age, he told the recruiter he would be "seventeen on my birthday," carefully not specifying which birthday he meant. With carefully concealed skepticism, the recruiter took his measurements and his weight, and then announced Darryl had failed because he was half an inch below the minimum height and four pounds short in weight. He was told to come back on his next birthday.

He went back to Oakdale and began a regimen of stretching exercises and a diet of butter, eggs, and red meat, and just before his fifteenth birthday he was back, having reached the requisite height requirement and lacking only a pound to make the minimum weight of 110 pounds. He did not, of course, mention that he was still two years short of the minimum age. As he told Mel Gussow, many years later, he arrived half an hour early for his test and filled up with water from the cooler to put on the extra pound in weight he needed to make the grade. But the first thing the recruiter noticed were the braces on his teeth, and told him tersely that they certainly would not let him into the army wearing those. The boy asked for a buttonhook and ripped them off.

Then, his mouth oozing blood, his bladder bursting with water, and naked, he moved into line for the inspection. Immediately he was conscious of the fact that he had an erection, the result of the pressure of all the water he had drunk. The doctor looked down at him, astonished. "Is it always like that?" he asked. "Yes, sir," mumbled the boy through his bleeding teeth. "You're very lucky," the doctor said.

And passed him for service with the U.S. Army.

Later that day, when he rejoined his grandfather, he told him what he had done, and begged him not to tell the army how old he really was, nor allow his mother to prevent him from joining up. In fact, Grandpa Torpin was both proud and impressed with what his grandson had done, and promised he would do nothing to impede him. He told the boy to leave Louise to him.

"I'll take care of your mother," he said.

"He had a helluva time with her," Darryl Zanuck said later. "She was going to write to the authorities, but he told her I might be liable for arrest."

He later recalled that on his first night in the army three of his mates in the Omaha barracks took him to a downtown brothel.

"They invited me," he said. "I was afraid to say no. I wanted to be accepted as one of the boys."

But this time he was not so lucky, and "when it came to my turn, I couldn't make it."

The prostitute shrugged her shoulders as she looked down at him.

"Don't worry, kid," she said, "it happens to half of them."

Not to Zanuck, it didn't — not now that he was in the U.S. Army, and a man. He was back next night, and this time he performed as any girl had a right to expect, even when you were paying her for it.


The boot camp to which the fifteen-year-old rookie was posted turned out to be Deming, New Mexico, and he bustled into the barracks with all the eagerness of a cockerel looking for a fight. The camp was close enough to Mexican rebel territory for him to demand, as soon as he got there:

"When do we go after Pancho Villa?"*

His new comrades greeted him with hoots of raucous laughter, and quickly made it clear that Mexico would not be the scene of their first engagement. The U.S. Army under General "Black Jack" Pershing had already been in and out of Mexico in pursuit of the rebel leader, but it was unlikely that any of the recruits at Deming would be given the chance

*Who was on the rampage along the border at that time.

to follow him. The global military situation was changing so fast (it was 1917) that it was now the war in Europe that was concentrating Washington's attention, and not long afterwards, while Darryl Zanuck was still learning how to use a bayonet and slogging round the barracks square, Congress had declared war on Germany and America was involved in World War I.

He spent another six months in New Mexico before being shipped to Fort Dix, New Jersey, as part of the 34th U.S. National Guard Division, and two months later he was on his way to France, by way of England, aboard the troopship *Baltic*. He still couldn't wait to get into battle, but was beginning to understand why his comrades got so irked by the routine of army life — mainly as a result of a spell of potato-peeling and other kitchen duties. On the other hand, his first sight of the actualities of war chastened him. The division disembarked at Brest after crossing the English Channel by night, and the first French citizen to greet him was a ragged kid who sold him a bottle of "real champagne," which, as he quickly learned, "tasted like warm piss" and turned him off champagne for a lifetime. He marched with his unit to the railhead in the blazing sun, weighted down by full kit, and, while waiting for transport, queasily watched a hospital train pull in, full of American casualties from the fighting in Belgium.

He was stunned by the sight of "three hundred guys, with arms gone, holes in their chests. They were staring at us — my first real shock. This was a war where they were killing people. Jesus Christ!"

All through the summer of 1918, the 34th Division trained in Belgium for the eventual thrust that would take them, their officers assured them, right into Germany and eventually on to Berlin. But as the weeks of drilling passed by and nothing happened, morale began to droop. Soon five percent of the men had been arrested and locked in the stockade for going AWOL and visiting the local brothels, which were out of bounds. He managed to escape arrest because he was one of the few visitors to the bordellos who failed to contract gonorrhea.

"You got six months in the stockade for getting a dose of clap," he said later. "I was lucky. Either I took better precautions or mine was the only girl in the house who didn't have it."

In fact, he had other things on his mind besides whorehouses, because the drill sergeant had discovered he was a tough little fighter with his fists, and tried him out in the ring. Soon he was traveling around the rear lines fighting in area championships. He fought as a flyweight and was fast on his feet, skillful and aggressive, and he won every bout. Finally, he was picked to represent the U.S. Army in his category and won all but the last of his engagements, and that was only because, he said later, "this Limey referee hated all Yanks and handed the fight to a Frenchman, though I'd led him on points in every round."

It was not until the first week in November, 1918, that his regiment moved into the front lines. The division was ordered into action against the Germans manning their last defenses along the Lys-Scheldt Canal, in Northern Belgium, and it turned out to be a muddy morass of wrecked and abandoned vehicles and guns, debris left behind by the retreating and demoralized German troops. The soldiers of the Buckeye Division* could hardly wait to go in and clean them up. But just after the order came for their advance, they were called to a halt because a "false armistice" had been announced. By the time the confusion was resolved and they were ready to attack again, the genuine armistice intervened and it was all over. They never did reach German soil.

Nor did he ever "kill a Hun," which had been his great ambition. He came back to America to be demobilized as a private first class in the U.S. Army (and still the youngest), and he wore two wound stripes on his chest. Neither, however, had been incurred in enemy action. One was from falling on a rock and tearing his knee while carrying dispatches between units, and another was from the debris of a rifle that had exploded during target practice. He was still only sixteen years old when he got back to an army base on Long Island in the summer of 1919, and he reached Omaha just in time to celebrate his seventeenth birthday in September of the same year.

He may not have killed a Hun but, as he said later, "I had grown up, learned a helluva lot, and fought for my country."

But nobody in Oakdale, Nebraska, wanted to know.

"Most of my contemporaries were still in school," he said later, "and everybody else in the Middle West had long since got bored with the war in Europe. When I spoke of it, they either didn't know what I was talking about or just didn't want to listen. Soon I said to hell with it and kept my mouth shut."

In truth, only one man would have been overjoyed to see the return of "this battle-scarred boy," as Zanuck wryly referred to himself, but while he had been away at war Grandpa Torpin had fallen ill and had been shipped to a hospital for an operation. Meanwhile, a "passel of

---

*Into which the 34th had now been absorbed.

cousins" were fighting over who should manage his grandfather's assets in the Oakdale Land and Property Company while he was sick. The young veteran was curtly informed that if he wished to participate, he would have to buckle down and work — and start at the bottom. He was both hurt and irritated by their attitude, and said he was damned if he would be beholden to any of them.

Four days after arriving back in Oakdale, he shipped out again. The only person to whom he said goodbye was his grandmother, to whom he lied that he was going to rejoin his mother and stepfather in Glendale, California. As if she sensed that he intended to do no such thing, Mrs. Torpin dug into her savings (the existence of which she had, of course, concealed from her husband, since he didn't believe women could handle money) and not only bought him a ticket for California but gave him "a little nest egg, for emergencies" of a hundred dollars.

Two days later, in the last week of September, 1919, he alighted from the train in Pasadena, and, his army kitbag slung over his shoulder, set out to make his way on foot into Los Angeles. It was a warm, sunny, gorgeous California day. Since it was long before smog began to besmirch the California landscape, the surrounding mountains stood out clear against the blue sky, the breeze was soft and scented, and the sidewalks were filled with men in shirtsleeves and girls in summer dresses. Darryl Zanuck recalled how his heart "rose and fell like a yo-yo" as he drank it all in.

He was seventeen years old, and here was a whole new world opening up before him, and he was both eager to enter it and terrified at the same time. At one moment it was a beguiling and exciting challenge, and the next it yawned before him as a vast and terrifying void. On that walk downtown, he later confessed, there were moments when he felt lonelier than he had ever been before in his life, and he was strongly tempted to make his way to the only person he knew in the vicinity — his mother. But then he thought of his stepfather and he resisted. Instead, he began to look around for a cheap hotel.

# THREE

# UP THE LADDER

GRANDPA TORPIN was about the only person in the world who knew Darryl Zanuck cherished a secret dream, and that was to become a writer. It was he, in fact, who had first sown the seed of the ambition in his grandson's mind by sending one of the letters he had written, about his first train journey to California, to the local Oakdale newspaper, which had printed it in full. He had done the same thing with the letters Darryl wrote him from France while he was in the army, and at least a couple of these had been picked up and used in the armed forces newspaper, *Stars and Stripes*. Young Zanuck was very proud of them. He liked seeing his name in print over something he had written, and one day, he resolved, he was going to see the same thing printed between the covers of a book.

It was by his writing that he intended to maintain himself once he established himself in California, and one of his first purchases with a portion of Grandma Torpin's hundred dollars was an Underwood typewriter, which he lugged up to the room he rented in a cheap lodging house in downtown Los Angeles, just around the corner from the hotel where his father had once worked. It was a hot, stuffy, fleabitten lodging ("altogether a lousy dump," was how he described it himself), but he had decided he must pinch pennies until he could start earning money, and he decided that before he started putting on paper the stories already buzzing around in his head, he would have to go out and find himself some work to pay his food and rent. Someone told him there were riveting jobs going in the shipyards at Wilmington, near Long Beach, and the pay was $45 a week, which was extremely good for those days. So he took a long trolley-car ride down to the coast, lied to the employment office that he had done similar work in Omaha, and was taken on as a "rivet catcher."

It was not until he signed in on the job that he learned why rivet catchers were paid the handsome sum of seventy-five cents an hour, and earned every penny of it. Told to climb onto a scaffold roped to the side of a ship's hull, he stationed himself on the platform, amid an inferno of acrid smoke and appalling noise, and suddenly found that a mate down below him was hurling in his direction red-hot lumps of metal, which he was supposed to pass on to a riveter standing by his side.

"It was like being a catcher in a kind of lethal baseball game," he said later. "Miss one of those rivets and it could burn a hole right through you. The first day I had no protective clothing and thought I was going to get fried every time one of those flying bullets came in my direction. Even when I bought the heavy reinforced apron and gauntlets that the job called for, I was in a constant muck sweat thinking I was going to fumble a red-hot rivet and get my balls burned off."

He caught on to the knack of it by the end of his first week, and might have stayed on the job had not the physical conditions proved to be too arduous even for his wiry, whippetlike body. He had to get up before dawn in order to ride the trolley car down to Wilmington and clock in by 6 A.M., and it was long after dark by the time he got back to his hotel room, too exhausted to do anything but grab a quick meal and fall into bed. At the end of a couple of months the first rains of winter hit California, and he came down with a virus. It was probably a delayed version of the influenza epidemic that swept America at the end of World War I, and it took him a long time to shake off the debilitating effects. By the time he was up and about again, he could not even contemplate the thought of going back to Wilmington, and he looked for another job nearer his hotel.

He found one a few blocks away in a warehouse making shirts and blouses for mail-order houses. Except for the boss, he was the only male on the work force, which consisted mainly of immigrant Polish and Irish seamstresses, plus a few Mexican and Chinese. They were paid piece work for turning out a certain number of garments a day. His job (for which he was paid $12 a week) was to keep his eye on the girls, make sure they wasted no time on idle chatter, kept up their quota, and did not steal bolts of shirt-cloth.

"It may be hard to believe," Zanuck said later, "but I was sacked for selling the girls' hair!"

One day a young Chinese was waiting for him when he left the factory, and had a proposition for him.

"It seemed his fiancée, a Chinese chick, worked for us as a seamstress

and had noticed that all the girls, including herself, had nice long, lux-
uriant hair, as most females did in those days," he said.

"What he proposed was that I persuade the girls to sell their hair for
$50 a head, which was a pretty impressive sum then. He would then sell
it at $100 a head to his Chinese cousin, and cut me in at ten percent of
the profits after expenses. I calculated that if only half the girls consented
to be clipped, I stood to make around $500 as my share of the profits,
and that would stake me for the next six months. He would send in a
hairdresser to do the cutting, and I would provide a corner of the factory
where the girls could go to be clipped."

Unfortunately, Zanuck convinced the girls, even the ones most reluctant to sell what they considered "their crowning glory," that they would
only lose a few inches of their locks. The hairdresser, however, had been
instructed to go for quantity, and he proceeded to crop as close to the
head as possible.

"When the first girls looked in the mirror and saw what had happened
to their locks, they began to scream the place down," Zanuck remembered. "I have to admit that what had been done to them was pretty
drastic. We'd invented the Eton crop and the short-bob hairdo years
before its time."

The ensuing row attracted the attention of the boss. "It was a question
of choosing between me and his irate work force, and since I had made
the mistake of not cutting him in on the deal, he chose them over me. I
was kicked out on the spot, with no payoff. Worse than that, I never got
a cent in commission from that goddamn Chink."

For the next few weeks, he stayed in his room, typing out stories on
the Underwood, and sending them off to magazines around the country.
They were called "pulp magazines" in those days, and most of them
specialized in he-man, hair-on-the-chest heroes who were either tempted
by the demon drink, seductive female sirens, or dope-dealing, wily Ori-
entals, and were finally redeemed by masculine strength, fighting skills,
courage, bravery, and the love of a beautiful but upright woman. Zanuck
could turn out a couple of these fictions every day, but he lacked — at
least to begin with — the talent for combining the ingredients in the right
proportions to be salable, and until he found the knack of it the manuscripts kept thudding back on his doormat with the same old rejection
slips. Luckily, he still had some money left from Grandma Torpin's going-
away present, and this paid for the immediate demands of food and
lodging. But in the winter of 1920/21, he began to face up to the prospect
that if he did not want to starve to death while waiting for one of his

stories to be accepted, he would have to find some other way of making a living.

It was about this time that he decided to leave Los Angeles and try his luck in Hollywood. Maybe he might even get a job in the movies.

Way back in those disastrous days when he was still living in Glendale with his mother and stepfather, he had, in fact, once been given work on a movie set and had never forgotten it. After one of those stormy scenes between his parents, he had rushed out of the apartment and, after miserably wandering the streets for several hours, found himself on Hollywood Boulevard. He was still only about seven years old at the time, and, on the corner of Vine Street, a passing movie scout had picked him up and asked him whether he would like to earn $2 by playing in a film.

Since he was already saving money for the day when he could run away from home, this was like manna from heaven. Taken to a studio around the corner (he could never remember which one it was), he was led to the wardrobe department and fitted out in feathers and a leather jerkin, and told he was to play an Indian child in a scene in a Western. He remembered that the casting director decided he was not swarthy enough to play an Apache boy, "so they dressed me up as a little Indian squaw instead." He was so disgusted at having to pretend to be a girl that not even being given $2 at the end of the day made up for the humiliation he felt.

But it had been an enlivening and promising experience, all the same. He had kept his eyes open as he waited to be called, and the atmosphere of a movie set proved to be exciting in the extreme. Real live stars smiled and leaned down to pat him. He relished the noise, the bustle, the lights, the smell of sweat and makeup, the air of expectation, and he came away vowing to himself that one day — when he was grown up — he would come back here, and go to work in the movies.

So now, carrying his clothes and manuscripts in two new suitcases (he had long since thrown away his kitbag), he took the trolley car from Los Angeles to Hollywood. Getting off at Franklin, he began walking up and down the streets off Hollywood and Sunset boulevards, looking for a rooming house. There were plenty in the neighborhood, for this was the area where several small movie studios were in operation, mostly on a shoestring, which was probably the reason why it was locally known as Poverty Row. He finally picked a place on Gower Street because it was close to Christie's Hotel, where, he had heard, a lot of "movie people" lived. A large Cadillac pulled up outside Christie's early each morning and all kinds of bizarre and spectacular characters piled into it, with many shouts, laughs, and kidding, and young Zanuck soon learned that these were technicians and small-time players who worked at the Metro Studios in Culver City. They got one day off a week, Sunday, and on that day he would put on his best suit and bow tie and stroll past on the sidewalk outside, listening and envying them as they lolled about on the stoop of the hotel, gossiping in easy comradeship. To begin with he was a spectator on the fringe, following them at a distance as they strolled down to the cafés, bars, and restaurants along Hollywood Boulevard for their Sunday brunch. But one day he managed to fall into conversation with one of the Christie's residents, who turned out to be a Frenchman who was an art director at Metro. His name was Ben Carré and he was a Parisian who spoke English with a delicate Gallic accent, and at first he pretended to be deafened by Darryl Zanuck's nasal Nebraskan twang. But he was a sympathetic and attractive character, and he was amused by Zanuck's gaucheness, his goggle-eyed infatuation with movies and movie people, and, when he got to know him better, fascinated by his tales of wartime adventures on the battlefields of Flanders and in the bordellos of Armentières.

He began taking him around as a kind of mascot, and finally, a memorable day for the star-struck youngster, invited him onto the Christie's stoop one Sunday morning and introduced him to some of the others already sitting around there. Zanuck remembered meeting a florid character named Wallace Beery, whom he had seen in films but didn't like because he was a greasy and loudmouthed character; a shy and diffident young man who turned out to be the already famous John Gilbert; a French director named Maurice Tourneur; and a cropheaded, assertive German named Josef von Sternberg, who walked around brandishing a gold-headed cane. Then, a big, chauffeur-driven car came to a halt outside the hotel, and from it stepped two exquisite young women. Both were brunettes. Both were wearing similar outfits: tight, midcalf skirts slit up the side and low-cut blouses, except one's skirt was red and the other's green. And Zanuck recognized them! One was a rising star named Gloria Swanson, and the other was none other than his boyhood heartthrob, Clara Kimball Young. They had come to collect Beery (for Swanson) and Gilbert (for Young) and take them away for a picnic in the hills. Zanuck was so thunderstruck at these miraculous apparitions that he could do nothing but gaze at them in silent adoration, much to the amusement of Ben Carré, who whispered to Young that she had made a conquest. When the quartet finally rose and departed for their date, Young came across to the young man and ran her cool fingers softly across his cheek as she smilingly said goodbye, "and it produced the most arousing sensation I ever remember," he said later.

From these Sunday meetings at Christie's Hotel came many other encounters that were to stay with Darryl Zanuck for the rest of his life. He remembered that usually in midmorning they would stroll down to the barbershop on Hollywood Boulevard, which seemed to be a popular meeting place for film types at the weekend. They would all mill around in the street while waiting to get a shave, and watch the passersby.

"It was not crowded at all in those days," said Ben Carré later. "There were no cars at all along Hollywood Boulevard, only streetcars, and when they weren't passing you could quite easily carry on a conversation between the north and south sides of the boulevard." Everything was relaxed and casual. "No one really bothered to mob stars and you could do business as simply as you could exchange greetings. I met Tom Ince once in the barbershop and signed a film contract with him right there on the cigarette counter."

The favorite brunch place was a choice little Continental restaurant called Musso's (now Musso and Frank's), and it was here that Zanuck had his first meeting with Gentleman Jim Corbett, retired boxing champion of the world, and Charlie Chaplin, the most famous comedian of the day. Chaplin he conceived an antipathy for which never left him, mainly because he thought he was "nothing but a show-off." He usually came to Sunday morning brunch in his Little Tramp costume and would clown on the street, twirling his cane and doing his famous walk, before going into the restaurant, a little act his entourage always dutifully applauded. But what irked Zanuck, one suspects, was that he was always accompanied by a beautiful girl and treated her so shabbily.

"I once saw the maître d' bring a bowl of strawberries to their table," he said, "and this gorgeous blonde took them one by one by the stalks, dipped them in a cream bowl, bit off half, dipped the other half in cream, and put it in Chaplin's mouth. And at one point, he took a drink of wine and then spat the whole thing, wine, strawberry, cream, the lot, down her dress. She should have thrown the bowl of cream right back in his stupid face, but she just laughed and wriggled and went back to feeding him berries. Somebody should have kicked his balls in."

What Ben Carré could not, or did not choose to, do for his young follower was find him a job in films. Zanuck revealed to him that he had a talent for sketching, in the hope that the Frenchman might take him on as an assistant in the art department, but was told that the field was overcrowded and advised to stick to writing. When the boy asked Carré to show some of his stories to the studios, he promised to do so, but nothing seemed to come of it.

In the meantime, Zanuck still had to eat. He scrounged around Hollywood for all sorts of jobs to pay his room rent, washed dishes at the Round Table Restaurant, washed and polished cars, and even swept up at the barbershop. One weekday morning there, he ran into Gentleman Jim Corbett and was taken across the way by the ex-champion for a coffee and a slice of Musso's famous shortcake. After Darryl told him about his boxing career in the army, Gentleman Jim gave him his card and the names of some boxing promoters in the Los Angeles area. He got quite a few bouts as a result, but soon decided that professional boxing was not for him. Up against experienced pugs and the dirty tricks they had learned, he did not shape up half so brilliantly as he had done fighting amateurs, and what purses he did win were too small to make the pain and suffering worthwhile.

He was a resilient kid, though, and he did not regret that phase of his life.

"By the time I was twenty," he said, later, "I could kidney-punch a sucker with the worst of them, and by the time I retired, I had the slickest rabbit punch in the business."

But he also later confessed that "it was a black period in my life, and there were times when I just couldn't figure out where I was going. Nobody seemed to want anything I was doing. I'd even gone into the advertising business, drawing posters for restaurants, garages, shoe shops, you name it, without anyone showing the slightest interest in what I was doing. I was pretty downhearted, because I knew I was a bright kid and I had merit and talent, but nobody wanted to know."

It was about this time, while disconsolately wandering the streets, that he saw his mother coming out of a movie house on Hollywood Boulevard. She was alone, and his instinct was to rush across the street and embrace her. But something prevented him from doing so. He saw she was looking much sprucer and more fashionable than he had ever seen her before, and with her ash-blond hair and clear complexion, she looked to him more beautiful than ever. But when he put his hands in his pockets he realized he didn't even have enough there to take her into a drugstore and buy her a cup of coffee. So after following her discreetly down the treet, he let her board a streetcar without making himself known.

*        *

All this time, Zanuck had been spending hours in his room grinding out (and the phrase is appropriate) short stories for the pulp magazines, and not having much luck in placing them. Then one of them scored a hit. It was a short story he had written called "Mad Desire," the sorry history of a rich young playboy named Malcolm Dale who falls in love with a virtuous young girl named Loma. But then he is tempted into a life of degradation, complete with loose women and dope. At last, penniless, wasted away in body, he is rescued from suicide by the faithful Loma, who sets out to restore his health with good food, regular exercise, and a good woman's love. The story is told by Loma herself, with many desperate sighs, secret sobs, and cruel disappointments, until Malcolm is finally rescued, the two lovers, now sparkling with health, are in each other's arms, and the hero says proudly to his beloved:

"Yes, Loma dear, it was happiness and you — or grief and dope. I chose the first."

"Mad Desire" had been rejected by at least half a dozen pulp magazines but then was unexpectedly accepted by Bernarr Macfadden's *Physical Culture* magazine, which liked the combination of sex, dope, moral principles, and physical fitness. The editors not only sent Zanuck a check but presumed he would soon be selling the story to the movies. For this reason, they proposed to hold on to the story for some months until, they hoped, the film came out.

Nothing would have been more pleasing for the young author than to have someone make a movie out of his story, but how did one go about making a sale? It was before the days of agents. He had long since decided that Ben Carré and the Sunday-morning barbershop crowd were no help to him, since most of them were too afraid for their own jobs to risk introducing a potential competitor. He did think his idol, Clara Kimball Young, might be interested in the part of Loma, since he had some steamy scenes, in both opium dens and boudoirs, in which she struggles to resist Malcolm's attempts to get her to take dope and climb into bed with him. He therefore waylaid John Gilbert one day at Christie's and asked him if he would pass a copy of his story on to Miss Young. He waited for word for an anxious week, but heard nothing. Then he read in the *Hollywood Citizen* that Gilbert had a new girlfriend, and Gilbert said he had "mislaid" the manuscript when Zanuck asked for it back.

"If the bastard had only read it himself," he said, years later, "he might have found there was a good part for him in it too. But that was Gilbert's trouble. He not only couldn't speak — which was why he faded out when the talkies came — but he couldn't read, either."

It so happened, however, that Zanuck had by now found himself a girlfriend and she came up with a suggestion. Edna Freund was a red-headed stenographer who worked in the offices of the Los Angeles Athletic Club. She was a hardheaded, sexy girl who had concluded that no one got anywhere in Hollywood without good "contacts."* Where better to find those contacts, especially among movie people, than in the Athletic Club, which had a large number of film types among its members? Pro-ducers like Mack Sennett, Winfield Sheehan, and William Fox (of the Fox Film Company), directors like Raoul Walsh, Frank Lloyd, and Lloyd Hamilton, stars like Charlie Chaplin, his half brother, Sydney, Oliver Hardy, Fatty Arbuckle, and Tom Moore all belonged. Edna promised to find him sponsors within the club if he could come up with the money for his subscription and entry fee. He wrote to Grandpa Torpin (who was now back home and retired) asking if he could use his name as an additional sponsor, since Torpin was a prominent member of several clubs in Omaha, Chicago, and New York. His grandfather was so pleased that Darryl was moving up in the world that he sent him his subscription and fee as a birthday present, and the application went in. But then, to Zanuck's dismay, he learned that the members had turned him down, without any explanation of why he had been blackballed. It was Edna who finally found out the reason.

"It's just one of those clubs," she told him. "I should have remembered about you. They don't admit Jews."

"But I'm not Jewish!" Zanuck declared, and when he saw Edna's look of surprise, he added: "You of all people should know that."

Meanwhile, Grandpa Torpin wrote to inquire why his grandson no longer mentioned the Athletic Club in his letters, and Zanuck wrote a bitter reply explaining the reason. Torpin immediately went to work behind the scenes. The result was a discreet indication to the young man that if he renewed his application, he would probably not be turned down this time. To his credit, he hesitated. As he said later: "Did I really want to belong to a club where I couldn't take half the people I knew in Hollywood?" Even Edna confessed that she would quietly be let go if it was found out she was half Jewish. On the other hand, she was practical enough to point out the advantages of belonging, and urged him to forget

*As she later proved by running one of the most successful call-girl operations in Hollywood.

any scruples he might have. So he renewed his application and this time
was welcomed into the club.

Not only that. Within a week or two of joining the club, he had made
a sale to the movies through the influence of a couple of its members.
One of them was William Russell, a top star of the Fox Film Company,
whose studio chief, Winfield Sheehan, was also a member. Russell took
a shine both to Zanuck and his stories and they did not even need to
leave the steamroom to make an agreement with Sheehan. But when
they went to see the story chief at Fox, a shrewd operator named Sol
Wurtzel (who, being Jewish, was not a member of the club), they ran
into trouble. Russell liked "Mad Desire" and handed it to Wurtzel to
read, who not only told him he would be mad to play a dope addict and
a weakling, but added:

"Besides, as a story it stinks."

Zanuck quickly came up with another idea that Russell also liked, called
"The Scarlet Ladder," about a young man who is shanghaied out of San
Francisco by a rascally captain, and falls in love with the captain's daughter, who happened also to be named Loma, like the heroine of "Mad
Desire," since Loma happened to be Zanuck's favorite name for a girl at
that moment. Wurtzel listened, stared balefully at this cocky little Wasp,
and snarled:

"I think that one stinks too."

"In that case," said Russell, drawing himself up, "I shall go right back
to the club and tell Mr. Sheehan I have made my last film for the Fox
Film Company."

Wurtzel sighed. "Then let's by all means make the stinker," he said,
and then to Zanuck: "What did you say its name was: 'The Scarlet Letter'?
That sounds familiar."

"Ladder — 'The Scarlet Ladder,' " said Zanuck. "It's yours for a thousand dollars."

"Five hundred," said Wurtzel, "and that's more than it's worth."

It was the first of several sales he made to the movies, and soon he
was offered a job at one of the studios. He was well aware that none of
it would have happened had it not been for his membership in the Los
Angeles Athletic Club, and for that reason he congratulated himself for
having been hard-nosed enough to ignore the bigoted rules of the club.
But the incident of his initial rejection and the reason for it offended him,
and he did not forget it. He squirreled it away in his mind, in fact, and
later on, when he had more power, when the climate was more suitable,

he dragged it back as an idea for a film. What would happen if a snooty, anti-Jewish club elected a highly respected member of the community as a member in ignorance of his ethnic background, and only afterwards found out that he was Jewish? It was one of the plot-lines he thrashed around when he decided to make Hollywood's first film about anti-Semitism, *Gentleman's Agreement*, in which he cast Gregory Peck as the upstanding Jew.

# THE BEST REVENGE?

*H*OLLYWOOD was an exciting place to be in the early 1920s and young people were swarming in from all over the nation. In the decade between 1910 and 1920, Hollywood's population had jumped from 5,000 to 36,000, and was now rising at the rate of nearly 20,000 a year. Every train from every small town in America deposited young newcomers every day, all hoping for one thing — to make themselves rich and famous in the movies. In fact, by 1921 so many eager seekers after film fame were arriving that the Hollywood Chamber of Commerce held an emergency meeting and voted to start a publicity campaign. It was designed to discourage newcomers to the movie capital, and advertisements were taken in newspapers all over the country showing a mob scene outside the employment office of one of the big studios. Underneath was a caption saying:

> Thousands buck the line on every call for a few movie picture extras. This is a sample of the customary massed assault on the employment bureaus resulting from an ad for a very few men and women to work in an insignificant scene. The wage is meagre for a day and night of hard work.

The message went on:

> DON'T TRY TO BREAK INTO THE MOVIES IN HOLLYWOOD until you have obtained *full, frank and dependable information* from the Hollywood Chamber of Commerce. It may save disappointments. Out of 100,000 persons who started at the Bottom of the Screen's Ladder of Fame ONLY FIVE REACHED THE TOP.

It didn't say who the five were, either. But the young hopefuls knew their names — and others — and they were convinced that, with looks, talent, or sheer nerve, they could achieve the heady triumphs of Gloria

Swanson, Mary Pickford, Douglas Fairbanks, Charlie Chaplin, Wallace Reid, Ruth Roland, Lillian Gish, Jack Holt, Antonio Moreno, the Talmadge sisters, and Blanche Sweet. There were mothers arriving with their tiny children, hoping to turn them into Jackie Coogans or Baby Peggys. There were young men who slicked back their hair like Rudolph Valentino and Ramon Novarro, young women who dressed up like dime-store editions of Pola Negri, Nazimova, and Pauline Frederick. And there were dozens of young men, carbon copies of Darryl Zanuck, who came into town more furtively, manuscripts hidden in their suitcases, but with no less perfervid determination to make it someday in the movies, as writers, directors, and maybe heads of studios like Sam Goldwyn, Jesse Lasky, Harry Cohn, or Carl Laemmle.

One of the joys for Zanuck, who was always truly at home in Hollywood, was living in or around Christie's Hotel because you were literally surrounded by the trappings and paraphernalia of movie-making. The hotel was within a hundred yards of at least two dozen film studios, among them the L-Ko Motion Picture Company, Loftus Features, Waldorf Productions, Quality Picture Corporation, Century Film Company, Wilnat Studios, Wade Productions, Bischoff Comedies, Snub-Pollard Productions, and Goodwill Studios. Admittedly they were hole-in-the-corner operations which were apt to disappear overnight, but they churned out a succession of one- and two-reel comedies, Westerns, and cliff-hanging serials. They were always likely to send out a sudden call for extras, and so many of them were for Westerns that the sidewalks around the area were apt to be dotted with groups of young men in cowboy hats, boots and breeches, suntanned Indian types in leather pants and jerkins (some with tomahawks tucked into their belts), and girls in sequins and slit skirts, which they could whip off for dance-hall scenes. It was a reason why another name for the area was Gower Gulch, and why drugstores and eating houses sprang up around the studios. Most of the extras stayed on the corners, probably because they couldn't afford the price of a meal or a cup of coffee, but the more affluent "drugstore cowbows" went inside to eat, drink, and wait, and soon the places became recognized ports of call for talent scouts, looking for some likely type for a small part in a movie. When word of this spread around the rooming houses of Hollywood, half the would-be film stars padded their bosoms or slicked up their hair and went every day to the drugstore counters, hoping to be picked up by a talent scout.

"The whole place was lousy with pretty girls," said Zanuck later. "You didn't need to walk half a block to get any type of chick you wanted."

By the end of 1920, over forty million Americans a year were going to the movies, and the men who ran the nation's cinemas were clamoring for product to show their customers. Since they often changed the program twice a week, and again over the weekend, movies were in short supply, despite the fact that these were the days of silent films and Germany, France, and Britain were busy churning out pictures for the market. So, in addition to the fly-by-night operations around Poverty Row, there were already some bigger studios catering to the growing public appetite for film entertainment.

Some of them were within easy walking distance of Christie's and Zanuck passed them several times a week. Chaplin had his own studio on La Brea Avenue, which he had built in 1919, the year he joined with Mary Pickford, Douglas Fairbanks and the director D. W. Griffith to form United Artists Corporation, by which they would henceforth produce and distribute their own films (and keep their profits). Pickford and Fairbanks, shortly after their marriage, bought a studio of their own from Jesse D. Hampton and began making films on Santa Monica Boulevard, two blocks from La Brea. Subsequently, the three stars and the director, finding that they were being cheated by wilier hands in the business, brought in Sam Goldwyn to coordinate their activities, but at the moment he was still making his own films at Culver City, from which, being a fitness buff, he could be seen walking home every evening — ten miles back to his hotel in Hollywood.

The man who subsequently became the most influential and ruthless studio chief of them all, Louis B. Mayer, had not yet established himself. But he was already in Hollywood, and he had taken an apartment at a new block called Garden Court, on Hollywood Boulevard — one of ten new blocks in the area — from the window of which he could look down on most of the major studios and plot which one he was going to take over. Meanwhile, the studio chiefs whose names meant something were still the old-timers. There were Adolph Zukor and Jesse Lasky, who controlled the fortunes of Famous Players–Lasky (soon to be renamed Paramount). There was a quadrumvirate of quarrelsome brothers named Harry, Jack, Sam, and Albert Warner, who had made a fortune out of anti-German propaganda films during World War I, and had built a new studio with their profits. Standing at the corner of Sunset Boulevard and Bronson Avenue, its back lot contained the biggest stages ever seen so far.

A little farther out was Universal Studios, owned and run by a former New York fur salesman named Carl Laemmle, who was probably the shrewdest operator of them all. He had not only built up a roster of successful male stars (Rudolph Valentino, Elmo Lincoln, House Peters, Erich von Stroheim), but had begun to attract the kind of behind-the-scenes talents who create both good movies and stars. He had let it be known among writers, directors, cameramen, and artistic directors that he was in the market for ideas and ready to experiment, and although he paid less than the other big studios for the talent he attracted, they still came to him in the hope of making something better than the soapy trash or easy slapstick that Hollywood was grinding out for its customers at the moment.

One of the young men who had joined him at Universal was an ambitious and enthusiastic ideas-man named Irving Thalberg, who was prepared to work for a pittance for Laemmle so long as he allowed him to experiment with new ideas in films. Pittance was what his boss paid him, but he stayed at Universal until marriage (to Norma Shearer) increased his needs and Louis B. Mayer, having made up his mind, looked around for talent to join him at Metro-Goldwyn-Mayer. He tempted Thalberg with a salary the size of which he found it impossible to resist. But that was in the future, when, by combining his creative genius with Mayer's organizing abilities, he would build up the most brilliant movie-making operation the world has ever known — until Darryl Zanuck appeared, that is. In the meantime, Universal under Laemmle gained a reputation for operating the best school in the business for teaching would-be filmmakers the know-how of motion pictures, and the former fur salesman did a nice little trade in training his former rivals and competitors how to become motion picture tycoons. For a price. They had to buy their way into the studio, of course, and got no salary. But some of the toughest tightwads from the Bowery ghettos queued up for the opportunity, and among the graduates from Universal who never regretted the experience were three of the meanest — but subsequently the most financially successful — of the Hollywood moguls, Jack and Harry Cohn and their rapacious cousin, Joe Brandt. Just about this time they bought a studio on Gower Street and started making two-reel comedies, having decided that Universal had taught them enough to take the plunge on their own. They called themselves CBC Films, but because Harry Cohn later said it made people think it stood for "Corned Beef and Cabbage," they changed the name to Columbia Pictures. They were a ruthless and double-dealing (or should it be triple-dealing?) trio, and, as someone said of them subsequently:

"You knew where you were with those boys — they *always* let you down."

No would-be female star ever got out of Harry Cohn's office with her underwear intact. Even when Jack Cohn swore on the Talmud that he was telling the truth, you could be sure he was lying. And whatever a contract said about money, Joe Brandt always took an extra ten percent. But they knew how to produce money-making films, thanks to the tuition of Laemmle and Thalberg, and they went on to make a fortune molesting, cheating, and exploiting some of the most beautiful and famous stars in the business.

It was through Irving Thalberg that Zanuck got his first serious film into the movie houses, and it came about through the good advice of his newfound friend, William Russell. The Western star, wise to the ways of Hollywood, told Zanuck he could never make his fortune by writing stories for pulp magazines and hoping to sell them to films. The way to success as a scenarist, he said, was through adapting ready-made hits into screenplays, and advised him to look around for a successful play and gamble on buying up the rights and selling it to the studios.

Zanuck used the $525 he had made out of selling "The Scarlet Ladder" to stake himself to a brand-new suit in lightweight checks (he was always a dapper dresser) and, dressed to kill, he took the train to New York, where he intended to look over the current Broadway hits. The first one he saw was a drama called *Storm* and he was so overwhelmed that he went backstage, introduced himself as a scout for the studios in Hollywood, and subsequently found himself talking to the screenstruck author of the play. Although at this stage Zanuck looked even younger than his nineteen years ("Someone tried to cast me as Oliver Twist when I was twenty-one years old," he once said ruefully), the playwright was impressed by Zanuck's enthusiasm and air of authority, and when he was asked what he would take for an option on his play, he agreed to give the young man from Hollywood a free ride with it for six months, provided he paid $10,000 if and when a film of it was made.

Zanuck hurried back to Hollywood, not waiting to see any more plays, and went to work. Forty-eight hours later he had drafted a rough screenplay of *Storm* and took it out to Universal, where he bluffed his way into Irving Thalberg's office with it. He had heard that Thalberg was anxious to find a story for one of his hottest star properties, House Peters, and he was convinced the Universal chief would think it just what he was looking for.

He was quite right. A week later, Thalberg called him to the studio and asked him how much he wanted for the film rights of *Storm*. Zanuck swallowed hard and asked for $15,000.

"When Thalberg said, without any hesitation: 'It's a deal,' I could have kicked myself to Frisco and back," Zanuck said later. "I realized I could have asked for three times as much — and got it."

But, in fact, he was so exhilarated at having made the sale — which, of course, meant a $5,000 profit for himself after the playwright had been paid off — that he failed to react when the door of Thalberg's office opened and two women swept in. Then he realized who one of the women was and his eyes almost popped out of his head.

"The other girl didn't matter," he said later. "She was just another pretty kid, perhaps a little prettier than most, but they were a dime a dozen in Hollywood. She had her hair dropping over one eye, and when she tossed it back I saw she wore it that way because she was slightly cross-eyed. When I was introduced, I knew all about her, of course. She was a small-time actress named Norma Shearer, and, of course, Irving Thalberg later married her and made her famous in the movies, and you never saw that squint again. But I only had eyes for the other one. It was none other than Nazimova, who was always my idea of the quintessential Queen of the Movie Whores and the nearest Hollywood ever got to showing a star having an orgasm on screen. If you ever saw Nazimova in her own movie production of *Salome*, you'll know what I mean. She looked and acted with such abandon that when she did her love-dance with John the Baptist's head most of the males in the audience came in their seats."

It may have been an extraordinary coincidence, but in several of the more erotic scenes in *Salome*, Nazimova, who was normally a brunette, wore an ash-blond wig, which made her look remarkably like Zanuck's mother, Louise. Nazimova already had a reputation for being one of the few women stars in Hollywood who dared defy the puritanical rules of the day and insisted on acting as uninhibitedly off screen as on. When the prudes protested about the "shamelessness" of her behavior, she was known to flick her fingers in scorn and declare:

"Poof! If they don't like me as I am, I can always go back to Europe."*

Nazimova had come to ask Thalberg to a party. By this time she had made so much money in films that she had begun investing in real estate, and among the enterprises she had backed was a new and lavish complex

---

*Where she enjoyed a great *succès de scandale*. While he was in the army in Belgium, Zanuck heard British troops singing a coarse and rollicking ditty about her which began with the lines: "I'd like to sleep with Nazimova / I'd slap her bum and turn her over . . ."

of bungalow-apartments at 8150 Sunset Boulevard, which was about to open. She had named it the Garden of Allah, and she planned to launch it in a few days' time with a grand banquet. Running her avid eye over young Zanuck, whose adoration of her was apparent, she loftily invited him to come too, and when he could get his breath back he accepted.

It was, of course, one of the most extravagant, spectacular, and longest parties in the history of Hollywood, and it launched the Garden of Allah on its unbuttoned and notorious career as "an Oriental harem," "Sin Palace," and "perfumed den of vice," which was how its critics described it in the years to come. The official history of Hollywood put it like this:

> In the thirty-two year span of its life, the garden witnessed robbery, murder, drunkenness, despair, divorce, marriages, orgies, pranks, fights, suicides, frustration and hope. Yet intellectuals and celebrities from all over the world were to find it a convenient haven and a fascinating home. Among those who frequently stayed at the famous garden were Ramon Novarro, Errol Flynn, F. Scott Fitzgerald, Sheilah Graham, John O'Hara, Robert Benchley, Gilbert Roland, Tallulah Bankhead, Clara Bow and Leopold Stokowski. It was not uncommon to see tourists and movie fans lining the sidewalk just to get a glimpse of their favorite star.*

For her opening party, Nazimova had invited everyone who was anyone in Hollywood in 1921, and since she had asked them to wear Oriental costumes nearly all the men came as caliphs, sultans and desert sheikhs, and nearly all the women as houris of the harem. This, for instance, gave Betty Blythe the opportunity to wear the costume in which she had been seen in her latest film, *The Queen of Sheba*, and, because it consisted mostly of beads, this created a great sensation. Even her spectacular entrance, however, and that of Gloria Swanson in a huge tiara of real diamonds and emerald earrings long enough to snake over her shoulders, was topped by the arrival of the new young male star, Rudolph Valentino, in the costume he was wearing in his latest film, *The Young Rajah*, which consisted of strings of pearls draped about his body.

The party lasted from ten o'clock at night until twilight next day, nineteen hours in all, and those who sat down at the banquet included Norma and Constance Talmadge, Wallace Reid, Charles Ray and Harold Lloyd, Anita Stewart, Dorothy Gish, Mary Miles Minter, Clara Kimball Young, Tom Moore, Douglas Fairbanks and Mary Pickford (he came as one of the Three Musketeers, she as Little Lord Fauntleroy), Alice Terry, Pearl White, George Arliss (he came in white tie and tails), Richard Barthel-

*Hollywood: The First 100 Years* by Bruce Torrence (Hollywood Chamber of Commerce, 1979).

mess, Colleen Moore, Conrad Veidt, Francis X. Bushman, Lil Dagover, Thalberg, Lasky, Zukor, and Cecil B. De Mille. The tables were ranged around the swimming pool in the courtyard, and for the beginning of the evening, while food was being served — caviar, venison, flaming shashlik, exotic desserts, vodka, Mosel, claret, and champagne —a small chamber group floated on a raft in the middle of the pool and played Elizabethan and Oriental music. And decorum reigned.

Nazimova had attired herself in a swath of diaphanous veils, including a yashmak over her face, and that might have been awkward to handle while she was eating and drinking, but she decided to do neither. Instead she flitted back and forth among the tables, and finally emerged from one of the bungalows wearing the startling, straight, ash-blond wig she had worn in *Salome*. Slowly everyone realized she was clad in the costume from the film in which Salome had performed her seductive dance of the seven veils, and guests began to speculate at what point in the evening she would repeat this exercise in eroticism. In fact, if she ever had the intention of doing so, her plans were interrupted by the arrival of a flood of scantily clad extra girls from the studios who transformed the evening from a sumptuous dinner into a splashy orgy by plunging into the pool. Since the musicians had departed and the raft had been removed, several intoxicated guests immediately jumped in and joined the girls.

Nazimova retired to a bungalow and was not seen again. Whether Zanuck, who had come as an emir but removed his turban early on, followed her or went after the girls in the pool is not on record. One speculates that the voluptuous Nazimova in her ash-blond wig must have proved irresistible to him.

In any case, he afterwards admitted that he was one of the last to leave the Garden of Allah and did not arrive back at his rooming house until the evening of the following day, much the worse for wear. Though at whose hands he never did say.

The film version of *The Storm*, as it was now called (the definite article was added by the studio) was sneak-previewed in Santa Monica in the fall of 1922. It starred House Peters and Virginia Valli and subsequently got good notices from the critics. At the Hollywood premiere, Zanuck, at the suggestion of the publicity department, partnered Valli and she seemed strongly attracted to him until, at the reception, someone asked her whether her companion was her son or her younger brother, and she dropped him abruptly.

"That was always my trouble in those days," he said later. "I looked so incredibly young. I was twenty years old, but no matter how I did my hair or what I wore, everybody seemed to think I was just out of knick-erbockers. Most guys when they get to a certain age try to pretend to be younger. They forget there was a time when they would do anything — fake their birth certificates, alter their driving licenses, even change the way they smiled or arranged their faces — in order to look a couple of years older than they really were. In my case it was worse. No matter what I did to myself, I always looked younger than I really was. Except for the real whores, who went after my type, most girls wanted to mother me, and that was the last thing I needed from them."

While waiting for Universal to pay him for his screenplay, Zanuck had used his contacts at the Los Angeles Athletic Club to get himself a job at the studios, and it was one of his fellow members, Mack Sennett, who finally hired him as a gag-writer for $150 a week.

"It was a good salary in those days," Zanuck said, "and you could live on it. But working for Sennett was murder, because he was a real slave driver and he could be a son of a bitch if he thought you were wasting a minute of the time he was paying you for. He had about a half-dozen gag-writers on his permanent payroll, and we never put anything down on paper — because I suspect the bastard couldn't read. Instead, we used to pass ideas around and just build them up as the gags occurred to us. 'There's this girl who comes out of a shop in her brand-new dress,' I would say. 'And along the street is a guy carrying a big birthday cake for his mother,' someone else would add, and then all the others would take it from there. When we had got it in sequence, and settled just where the big laugh came, we would call in Sennett and tell it to him, and he would okay it and down on to the set we would go and get it right on film. They were all sight gags, and you had to make sure there was a laugh at least every minute, and it was hard work thinking up enough to keep them rolling in the aisles for two whole reels."

The job taught Zanuck a lot about films, and the need to keep up the attention span for every minute, and never let the audience's concentration stray.

"Sennett taught me two things about movie-making that I never forgot," he said later. "One was that no matter how serious your picture is, no matter what momentous things you're trying to say or show, the moment you forget to keep the action going, you've lost them. Put in anything, any old gag, a girl's leg, a big explosion, a sudden scream, rather than let the audience's mind wander, and that goes for any kind of film, whether you are making *Heartbreak House* or *Charley's Aunt*. As for comedy,

Sennett taught me that using words to get a laugh is a confession of defeat, and that remained true even when the talkies came in and you could substitute actual speech for subtitles. A laugh you get from what someone *does* to someone else is always ten times more effective than a witty remark or a wisecrack. Sennett knew that comedy is not words but action, and action is what movies are all about."

Darryl Zanuck stayed for nearly a year as a gag-writer for Sennett. It was a period in Hollywood's history when new and exciting developments were happening, when it was filled with hopeful and eager young people, and it was a glorious place in which to work and play and succeed. Hollywood was a surprisingly friendly, neighborly, and democratically-minded community. Most studio workers were getting very much less than Zanuck's $150 a week, whereas the big stars and directors were making vast fortunes, anything from $2,000 to $6,000 a week. On the other hand, the stars had not yet cut themselves off from the people who helped to make them famous, and although Clara Bow and Swanson and Novarro were mobbed by the public when they went on tours to New York or Philadelphia or Chicago, when they got back to Hollywood it was just like coming home, and they were treated and acted like neighbors, walking the boulevards unchivvied and undisturbed, patronizing the same restaurants and bars as the grips, cameramen, and dressers; and they neither cringed back in fear nor expected to be asked for their autographs when someone approached them.

It is true that Hollywood morals were what the rest of the country at that time would have described as loose, and for young professionals in the industry life was liberated in a way that only became possible in the rest of America a half-century later. Ironically enough, it was only the stars themselves, particularly the female stars, who were inhibited in this regard. "Foreigners" like Nazimova or Pola Negri or Lil Dagover could behave as they wished, because that was what was expected of "Continentals," but more rigid standards were imposed upon native-born stars, and in order to indulge in emotional freedoms (or "illicit sex" as it would have been described in their case) they had to adopt all kinds of elaborate stratagems. When Gloria Swanson found herself part of a failing marriage and fell in love with someone else, she was warned by her studio — on pain of suspension — not to be found in too close proximity to the new man in her life, in case the local press — which was not liberated at all — should cry scandal. Swanson, like most female stars, had a so-called Morality Clause in her contract forbidding her any activities whatsoever that might shock the public and stimulate the wrong kind of publicity. In consequence, if you were rich and famous in those days in Hollywood, and you couldn't wait to have an affair with your man, it was much easier and quicker to grab the nearest justice of the peace and have him perform a marriage ceremony. Which is why the stars in those days used to get married so frequently.

But for most ordinary members of the film colony, these frustrations did not have to be endured, and Hollywood was a liberated, free-and-easy place in which to live, love, and work, especially if you were young. Unfortunately, there were inevitably those who took advantage of this unbuttoned situation.

At a period in his life when so many things were happening to him, Darryl Zanuck needed someone to talk to about them, but the fact was that he had no one — and that, at the age of twenty, is hard. It must have been particularly galling to him that his mother was so geographically close and yet so emotionally remote, because there was no doubt that she was the one he loved more than anyone else in the world. He must have longed to confide in her. On the other hand, so long as she remained attached to his stepfather, he could not bring himself to accept the situation. It was a vile dilemma for him, and it caused him many unhappy moments and sleepless nights.

At the urging of Grandpa Torpin, to whom he wrote regularly every week, he had made one attempt at a reconciliation. Torpin had long since swallowed the fact that his daughter was fallible and unreliable, but on the other hand, he was well aware of the tug of the umbilical cord, at least in his grandson's case, and he urged him to try to renew the contact. So when *The Storm* was being sneak-previewed, Zanuck sent his mother a couple of tickets for one of the showings. She turned up alone, and that pleased him: he thus had her all to himself. It was a happy evening. The film went well and the cards coming in were almost wholly favorable. He swelled with pride when he introduced her to the Universal crowd and they seemed to find her pleasant and attractive.

They had got along wonderfully until he made the mistake of accompanying Louise back to her home in Glendale, where his stepfather was waiting for them. And it had all ended in tears and degradation, because, in the squalid quarrel that followed their arrival, Zanuck had finally done what he had longed to do for years and lashed out at his mother's hated husband, and drawn blood from an uppercut to his nose and mouth. Down went his mother in acute distress, to weep and grovel beside her husband, bathing his face, stroking his hair, begging him not to blame her for what her ungrateful son had done to him. When Zanuck curtly ordered her to get off her knees and leave the drunken bastard to fend for himself, she had turned on him and exploded on him a torrent of wrath and resentment that had driven him from the apartment.

Nothing, in fact, had changed. He knew only too well that the moment he was back on the street, his mother, up there, would once more be making a spectacle of herself, sprawled shamelessly beside her husband, plunged into one of those disgusting reconciliation scenes that had always nauseated him so much when he was a boy. How could anyone, particularly *his* mother, stoop so low and act so whorishly?

Why did she always have to let him down?

But if he did not have parents to fall back on, in whom could he confide? In his letters to Grandpa Torpin in Nebraska he undoubtedly poured out some of his feelings, but that was secondhand therapy and the replies took so long to come back. He had to look elsewhere for a confidant. It is unfortunate that the only one he found in Hollywood at that time, to whom he felt able to unburden himself, was totally incapable of providing him with the balanced view of life, parents, sexual relations, and, in particular, women, which he so agonizingly needed at that time.

The friend to whom he turned for counsel was yet another fellow member of the Athletic Club, and he was a notorious Hollywood actor-playboy. Sydney Chaplin was the brother of the more famous comedian, Charlie Chaplin, and the sad thing about him was that he had been through all the same traumatic experiences as his brilliant half brother — early poverty, a brutish childhood, persecution, and abuse — but had failed to shape them into anything because he lacked Charlie Chaplin's comic genius. He tried to imitate Charlie, even to the extent that he penciled a Chaplinesque mustache onto his upper lip, and he did not lack for parts in films. But he suspected he only got them because he shared a famous name and Charlie's reputation was rubbing off on him. In many ways he was better read and handsomer than his younger half brother, and if a shrewd or sensitive director had only taken him in hand, probed his real character, soothed his resentments, calmed his phobias, he might have developed a quality in him that could have changed his career. But nobody took the trouble to do so, and Sydney Chaplin had become one of the most outwardly confident and cocksure, and inwardly embittered, personalities in Hollywood in the twenties. His philosophy in life could be summed up in the words: "Fucking is the best revenge." He had become a dedicated womanizer. It was true that his half brother already had a reputation in Hollywood for liking women, but at least he confined his amorous activities to those females to whom he was strongly attracted. Sydney Chaplin, on the other hand, went after anything in skirts, the younger the better. He was a predator, a hunter of vulnerable females, and his appetite was practically insatiable.

"Sydney Chaplin was the greatest cocksman that ever lived, greater even than Errol Flynn," Zanuck said later.

Years afterwards, he continued to be amazed at Chaplin's persistence, boldness, self-confidence in hunting the opposite sex. He drove with him to Hollywood High School, on Sunset Boulevard, and watched him pick out a likely looking kid from among the girls streaming out after classes. He had an unerring instinct for the one who was willing.

"He would go up to them and even use his own name," Zanuck said. "Ruthless!"

Once in the car, they would drive up into the hills and Chaplin would have the kid on the back seat while Zanuck uncomfortably stayed in the front with his eyes glued to the road, or climbed out and uneasily walked around until they were finished. Except that his target had to be female, Chaplin set himself no limits, and any woman was fair game. Zanuck remembered the time when they took a trip to Yosemite and stayed at a hotel that was a favorite for honeymoon couples. Chaplin had boasted that any woman in the hotel could be had, even the newlyweds honeymooning with their husbands. He challenged his young companion to point out a new bride and swore he would get her.

"And he did," Zanuck said. "She was on her honeymoon, and he got her, he laid her!"

It was Zanuck's misfortune that he chose this embittered satyr in whom to confide his anguish about his mother, and instead of the solace and sober advice that, no doubt, he expected, what came back was a sour and cynical diatribe about the unreliabilities of parents and the fallibilities of women, mothers in particular. To Sydney Chaplin, all of them were a bunch of whores and the only way to get along was to treat them that way.

It was a period when Zanuck was still seeing the girl who worked at the Athletic Club, Edna Freund, but Chaplin quickly mocked him out of that. Had he laid her? Then why was he hanging on? The most boring thing in the world was a girl he had already had.

"There's all the skirt in Hollywood waiting out there for a bright kid like you," he told him. "Pretty girls just aching for it. Do what I do. Give it to them and then get out before they put their hooks in you. There's always plenty where they came from."

In Zanuck's case, there certainly was. It may be remembered that at the studios where he was working, they not only made two-reelers featuring Ben Turpin, Larry Semon and the irrepressible Keystone Kops, but also made shorts about the misadventures of a bevy of females known the world over as Mack Sennett's Bathing Beauties.

Most of the girls had scant acting ability, but they were all fit, healthy, and, of course, extremely attractive, despite the rather prudish swimsuits in which they had to cover themselves for most of their working day. Since they were not so prim and proper and simpered much less behind the cameras than they did in front of them, they were extremely popular with the crews, and many of them subsequently married grips, cameramen, and assistant directors, and went on to become contented wives and mothers.

Zanuck had no intention of giving them that smug satisfaction. Fired by Sydney Chaplin's example, he set out to bed them, and no doubt every successful seduction from now on was a small triumph over his mother.

"I had them all," he said later.

But he didn't. One of the Bathing Beauties held out on him, with fascinating consequences.

*FIVE*

# POLO MATCH

SUCCESS WITH the girls and a growing reputation as a gagman
made him restless, and he was filled with a fierce ambition to
show everybody that nothing could stop him from rising to the
top of the movie world. By the time he celebrated his twenty-
first birthday, he was almost as cocky as Sydney Chaplin himself. He had
his suits made to measure at an old-fashioned tailor in downtown Los
Angeles, but forced them to cut them sharply to fit his slim and wiry
figure and make them in striking colors instead of Big Business blues and
browns and blacks. He was the first character around Hollywood to be
seen in a sports jacket of brilliant green silk. He had always been a good
rider, thanks to Grandpa Torpin's tutoring, and now he joined a polo club
in Pasadena and amused the patrician members by turning up in white
silk breeches, a scarlet shirt and helmet. But then they saw him outride
and outsmart most of their regular players, though he brought only two
hairy little ponies with him, and they quickly stopped patronizing him.
He could stop his mount on a dime and speed it like a bullet to the
opposite end of the field, and woe betide anyone who got in his way.
When one of the members' wives congratulated him on how well he rode,
he grinned at her impudently and said: "You haven't seen anything yet."

It was just about this time, when he had been with Sennett for the
best part of a year, that he received an offer, with a considerable raise in
salary, to transfer to a studio just around the corner and go to work for
Charlie Chaplin, and it was a challenge he could not resist. It was a
mistake, as he quickly realized. He had done extremely well at Sennett's
studio and not just because of the Bathing Beauties, either. He had, in
fact, formed a close working association with a young director there named
Mal St. Clair, which had resulted in some funny, even sparkling two-

reelers that had gone beyond the usual slapstick in which the studio specialized.

All the same, the opportunity to work alongside such a world-famous star as Charlie Chaplin, and to watch him turning out those inspired short movies of his, was too good to miss.

Ironically enough, brother Sydney had nothing at all to do with Zanuck's new job, and it was, in fact, Chaplin's chief gag-writer, Charles (Chuck) Reisner, who was responsible for bringing him over. He had seen some of Sennett's recent films and gone to the trouble of finding out who had written and directed them, and an offer of $250 a week to Zanuck on a renewable four-week contract was the result.

Zanuck went over not expecting to like his new boss, because Sydney had already filled him with stories of Charlie's meanness, jealousy, and arrogance, but once he arrived on the lot and was introduced, he was surprised to find that the antipathy was mutual.

"Charlie took an instant dislike to me," he said later, "I think because of my youth more than anything else."

It may, on the other hand, have been because of Zanuck's association with Sydney, his expensive and fashionable clothes, his assured and self-confident manner. Whatever the reason, he quickly found himself being made the butt of Chaplin's jokes, and was always being patronized or sneered at when he failed to know the meaning of certain words.

Several times in a day, Chaplin would stroll over to him, and then say, challengingly, something like: "Can you define the meaning of *onomatopoeia?*" When Zanuck hesitated, Chaplin would rap out: "It means a word that imitates a sound, you cuckoo!" Then he would burst into high-pitched laughter, in which the rest of the crew would dutifully join.

"He would love to use words he looked up in the dictionary — to crush us," Zanuck said later. "Words like *outré*. He would say something was 'uttra' and then say, 'You understand what I mean?' Very superior, you know. But if Reisner deliberately used a word Chaplin didn't know, Charlie went immediately to the toilet. He kept a dictionary there. Sometimes he would sit in the toilet for an hour at a time."

There was only one rule around the studio, Zanuck discovered, and that was that Chaplin was the resident genius, the wellspring and inspiration of everything that went on; no matter what anyone else's input had been, he was to be credited with having thought it up.

"We would sit around working up gags among ourselves," Zanuck said later, "and Reisner's job was to invent gags but not reveal them to Chaplin. He would place all the props and then let Chaplin 'discover' the gag.

We'd sit in the background, holding our breath waiting for him to fall on it. If you made a suggestion — you're dead! He would always find the gag and damn near on every occasion he would bawl the hell out of us for not discovering it."

One day, according to a story told around the studios later, Zanuck lost his patience with the comic genius. It followed a morning when Chaplin had been particularly offensive towards his gag-writers for not having seen the comic potentialities of the set — when, in fact, they had spent a lot of time setting up the scaffolding, the pots of paint, the loaded table, the vases of flowers, for just the accidents and pratfalls that Chaplin was allowed eventually to discover for himself. Then he rounded on them and savaged them with high sarcasm for their stupidity, wondering why he went on paying them when he was forced to work out all the good routines for himself. At which, while he paused for breath, Zanuck is said to have stepped forward and declared in a tone of mild protest:

"But, Mr. Chaplin, I'd like to point out that there is an addendum to this routine which we planned and you seem to have missed. You will notice that although there are plenty of full cans of paint on the scaffold, and you have come to do a job on the walls, there are no paint brushes. We figured you would look around for them, and finally go to that closet there" — he pointed to a door in the corner of the room — "and look inside."

Whereupon Chaplin is said to have gone to the door, opened it, and received a dozen brushes, two cans of paint and a bucket of water full in the face.

In the deadly silence that followed, Zanuck could be heard to add:

"They'll laugh all right when they see it in the movie. *And* if you want to know what *addendum* means, you won't find it in your dictionary. I wiped my ass on that page in your shithouse earlier this morning."

He then walked off the lot and went to work for Harold Lloyd and Carter DeHaven.

Though he had long since moved away to work for other studios, Zanuck went back frequently to the Mack Sennett lot, and it was not simply to pick up Bathing Beauties, either. He had grown to like and admire Mack Sennett, despite Sennett's dictatorial ways, recognizing in him an instinctive movie-maker from whom he had learned a lot. Sennett had an acute sense of what makes people laugh and of the kind of gifts that were needed to make a good comedian. Sennett once confided to his young gag-writer that he had one sure test to discover whether he had a really great comedian on his hands.

"I watch him fall down," he said. "He'll get a laugh for that, of course. Anyone in the business can make an audience laugh by falling down. But getting back on his feet — that's the test. If he can make people laugh while he's getting up again, I sign him up for a long term, because that man is a comedian."

He maintained that there were only two comics in Hollywood who could do it — Chaplin and Buster Keaton — and he could no longer afford either of them.

Later on in life, when Sennett faded out and Zanuck became a big movie tycoon, he put the old man on his payroll and looked after him. He would take him with him to film festivals overseas, and wheel him on, at Cannes or Venice or Punta del Este, for interviews with the press, staying in the background while Sennett talked fond reminiscences about Chester Conklin, Ben Turpin, the Keystone Kops and the Bathing Beauties in the great days of slapstick comedy.

In 1923, however, it was Sennett who was still king, and he had become fond of this brash young writer.

"But naturally," said Zanuck, jocularly, later. "We had something in common. He recognized that I was a bit of a bastard too."

But it was of course more than that. Sennett obviously sensed that behind Zanuck's flashy appearance and cocksure manner, there was a movie enthusiast with a passion for making pictures; that here was a youngster who had an inborn sense of showmanship and a clear conviction that the quality of motion pictures as they were being made in Hollywood at that time had nowhere to go but up. He suspected that when forty million Americans grew tired of lining up at the box office to see nothing but trash, it would be Darryl Zanuck who would be waiting in the wings to wheel on movies with class. That was the reason he had been quite distressed when Zanuck announced he was leaving to go to work for Chaplin. Sennett tried hard to keep him on the payroll, even offering to give him screen credit for his contributions (something he had never done before, and, in fact, never did at all after Zanuck turned him down). For a time, there was a rift between the boss and his former employee, and Sennett, knowing how fond Zanuck had become of his Bathing Beauties, even banned him from the lot when he came around to collect one or another of them. But then he relented and let it be known that the young man was welcome back any time he liked, and could walk straight into his office.

It was, in fact, Zanuck's former collaborator, the young director Mal St. Clair, who suffered as a result of his partner's defection. Sennett took it out on him, curbing his directorial activities and finally making life so miserable for him that he too decided to leave, despite pleas to stay from his fiancée, who was one of the Mack Sennett Beauties. Afraid her betrothed's departure and his consequent unemployment might mean the postponement of their marriage, she sought the help of her friends in finding him a new job. Over at the studios where Buster Keaton made his comedies, she struck lucky. It so happened that Keaton's newest leading lady was a young woman named Virginia Fox, and she had once been a Mack Sennett Bathing Beauty too. With true esprit de corps, she let it be known that Keaton was looking around for a new director, and offered to mention to him that Mal St. Clair was both talented and available. The result was that St. Clair moved over to the Keaton lot and was soon directing some of his legendary two-reelers.

Both he and his fiancée were duly grateful for Virginia Fox's help, and wondered how to show their gratitude. They finally decided to give her an expensive night out at one of the smartest dinner-dance restaurants in town, the Coconut Grove. When the fiancée had one last hesitation, pointing out that Virginia did not possess a current boyfriend and that they really ought to invite someone else to make up a fourth, St. Clair said:

"Leave that to me."

And called up Darryl Zanuck.

The *Hollywood News* once called Virginia Fox "a pocket Venus," and it was a not wildly inaccurate description of her. She was slim, pretty, auburn-haired and tiny — only just over five feet tall. She was unusual in other ways, too. Unlike most of the other starlets working around Hollywood at that time, she was in the movies not because she had won a beauty or a talent contest, nor because she was consumed by a driving ambition, but purely by accident.

Virginia's father was a coal-mine owner in West Virginia, and the family was wealthy enough to send their daughter to an expensive finishing school in Sarasota, Florida, and to spend part of every year in a house they rented in Santa Barbara. On a trip to Hollywood one summer with a friend who knew Mack Sennett, they paid a visit to his studio and met Sennett himself, who took one look at Virginia, found her attractive material, and asked her if she would come back the following day and show him how she looked in a swimsuit. He offered her a job at once, and she was sufficiently strong-willed to overcome her parents' objections.

"It was fun," she said later. "I like movies and movie people, and the girls were great, Sennett was always a gentleman, and if you knew how to take care of yourself — and I did — you got along fine with everybody."

Virginia never claimed to be a great actress, but she was photogenic, friendly, and everybody liked her, particularly other actresses, who never seemed to be jealous of her. She made friends with several of them, including Mary Pickford, May McAvoy, Lois Wilson, Patsy Ruth Miller, Lillian Davis, and Colleen Moore, and subsequently they formed a club, which they called The Girls. Since most of them had, at one time or another, worked as Bathing Beauties, they were affectionately known around the Sennett lot as The Keystone Cuties or Mack's Smacks. The girls poured out their secrets to each other, and Virginia was soon aware that most of her friends were "having affairs," as they called them, mostly with young men they knew around the studios. She was strongly tempted herself once or twice, she later confessed, but always at the last moment decided not to go "all the way."

It so happened that she had never met Darryl Zanuck while she was working for Mack Sennett, because, by the time he was hired, she had gone on to play small roles for Buster Keaton. But she had kept in touch with the girls still working on the Sennett lot, and they told her all about his reputation as a "lady-killer" while he had been there. And, from what she heard, a change in jobs had not altered his amorous habits. If she thought about him at all, it was probably to decide that he did not sound like her type at all.

Nothing that happened on the evening of their blind date altered that opinion of him. It was not, in fact, one of the most romantic Hollywood evenings for either of them. Mal St. Clair owned an automobile, but it was a two-seater with a rumble seat, and it quickly became obvious that Virginia was used to grander things. She sportingly refused to cram into the front with St. Clair and his fiancée, but climbed into the back with Darryl Zanuck.

"I remember I wore a little white organdy dress, and a new hat with lilies of the valley on it," she said later. "By the time we got to the Coconut Grove, my hair was all blown apart."

She might have added that other things had come apart too, and caused her even greater discomfiture. Despite a warning from his director friend that Virginia was a "nice" girl, Zanuck, who didn't believe such girls existed, persisted in trying to put his hand up her organdy skirt, and went on trying the more Virginia repulsed him. The journey home to the Studio Club on Carlos Avenue (where she was temporarily staying) was more like a wrestling match than the end of an evening out, and the disheveled starlet resolutely turned away from Zanuck when he tried to kiss her goodnight. She told Mal St. Clair next day that she hoped never to see or hear from such a rough, rude, and brash young man again. St. Clair, who was deeply fond of his former collaborator, stoutly defended him, and pointed out that Zanuck was a brilliant scriptwriter and would one day make a name for himself in films. Virginia was not impressed.

Darryl Zanuck, on the other hand, had never met a girl like Virginia Fox, and still did not believe she was genuine. She was just "playing hard to get," he decided, and that only added zest to his determination to have her, and the sooner the better. During the next two or three weeks, he seldom let her alone. He sent her flowers. He waited outside the studio and was chagrined when she was driven away in Keaton's car and did not even deign to recognize him. He once went to the Studio Club and sat on the steps for several hours, waiting for her to come out, until two of Virginia's fellow boarders, ZaSu Pitts and Carmel Myers, persuaded him she had gone home to her parents in Santa Barbara.

"He was always on the phone, or at the door, or underfoot, or overhead," Virginia said later. "He would always hire cars. On his salary! There was never a boring moment."

By that she meant that when she did finally sneak away to her parents, he would hire a car and drive out on the off chance of seeing her. Her brother, Freddie, was deputed for the job of telling him she wasn't well or was otherwise engaged, and was once astounded when he saw Zanuck pay off the hired car with $150. Why, it was a fortune! How could she be so mean to the fellow? He seemed to be quite a decent chap, after all.

But when Virginia relented and went out with Zanuck, it was the same thing again, yet another struggle for her virginity, with her companion almost desperately determined to make her pay for dinner or supper or an evening at a nightclub with her virtue on the way home. Only it was more difficult now, because she did not dislike him so much; was, in fact, already half in love with him, dearly tempted to give in to his almost agonized, sometimes physically painful, struggles to do everything short of rape in order to have her; and, in truth, half hoping that he would succeed. And yet some instinct told her that if she did indeed give in and let him have his way, she would lose the battle for both of them.

The situation reached its boiling point, if not its climax, when Mal St. Clair's fiancée discovered that Zanuck was cheating on her friend with one of his old flames among the Bathing Beauties as a solace for his frustrations, and threatened to tell Virginia about his "disloyalty." The same evening, he proposed marriage to her. By this time convinced that he was the only man she really wanted, Virginia tumbled into his arms, but instinct still kept her from tumbling into his bed. It was not, indeed, until the night of January 24, 1924, in Coronado Beach, near San Diego, that he finally got into bed with her.

"It came at the end of a very long day," Virginia said later. "First of all, my mother refused to come to the wedding, and only Freddie and my father turned up. We had no other witnesses from Darryl's side, and had to make do for a third witness with a Negro janitor who came into the room, where the justice of the peace was marrying us, carrying a pail and a mop. Then, at the depot, a great crowd was waiting for us. Mal St. Clair and a lot of the girls from Mack Sennett. He, incidentally, sent Darryl a baseball bat as a wedding present! Suddenly all The Girls were there, bombarding us with confetti and roses, Mary Pickford lugging in a great bouquet and hanging it around Darryl's neck, May McAvoy flinging rose petals, Billie Dove embracing us and weeping buckets."

What Virginia did not know was that several of the girls who came to the send-off knew her husband better than she did, and were, in effect, saying a renewed goodbye. It may have been because of this that The Girls arranged for one mischievous gesture after the train for San Diego pulled out. As if sensing how Zanuck might be feeling, they allowed the newly married couple to settle into their private car and then — having previously discovered that John Phillip Sousa's band was on the same train — fixed it for a section of the brass, led by Sousa, to burst into the compartment and loudly serenade them to their destination.

"It was a long and very loud journey," said Virginia later. "Even Darryl, who loves brass bands, could hardly stand it. By the time we got to Coronado, we were very tired indeed. But he was very sweet."

There was a lot to be learned about the technique of making movies by working alongside the great stars of the day — particularly such brilliant comedians as Chaplin, Keaton, and Harold Lloyd — but for ambitious young men like Darryl Zanuck and Mal St. Clair there was a drawback attached to it. They never got any screen credits. So long as they worked for the masters, they stayed anonymous, and all the credit for the great

gags they thought up went to the star, and to him alone. None of the
great comedians in those days allowed it to be thought by their public
that they were being helped behind the scenes by talented writers, directors, cameramen — and stuntmen.* Yet screen credits, public rec-
ognition, were what youngsters like Zanuck most desperately needed if
their talents were to be developed and they were eventually to have the
opportunity of "galloping up them golden Hollywood stairs," as one
writer later put it.

It was for this reason that Zanuck, after quitting Chaplin, stayed only
a few weeks working with Harold Lloyd. He left after Lloyd flatly refused
him credit on a movie for whose story-line, situations, and gags he had
been almost entirely responsible. Meanwhile, St. Clair walked out on
Buster Keaton for the same reason. Both of them belatedly realized what
a magnanimous gesture Mack Sennett had made by offering them screen
credits if only they would stay on, and they were strongly tempted to go
back and humbly tell him they had changed their minds.

They refrained from doing so because they suspected, almost certainly
correctly, that it was a one-time offer Sennett was not likely to repeat.
So instead they began scratching around the studios to find themselves
new jobs, only too well aware that their track records were strictly unofficial and they had no screen credits to wave in front of prospective
employers. Finally they found themselves a berth with FBO Studios on
Gower Street, writing (Zanuck) and directing (St. Clair) a series of two-
reel shorts called "The Telephone Girl," for which they took a cut in their
salaries in return for screen credit. FBO stood for Film Booking Office,
and was so named because it had been founded by a former Universal
movie-booker and salesman named Hyman Berman. Berman had a reputation in movie circles as being one of the sharpest salesmen and
promoters in the business. He was usually considered to be responsible
for selling such box-office personalities to the public as Laura La
Plante, Priscilla Dean, and Erich von Stroheim, and while at Universal
had worked in close collaboration with Irving Thalberg, being described
by their studio boss, Carl Laemmle, as "the brains and the muscle of my
operation." But Laemmle grossly underpaid them (they called him Uncle
Shylock), and when Thalberg left to join Louis B. Mayer at M-G-M, at
double his former salary, Berman had quit too and formed his own organization.

*Harold Lloyd's stuntman waited until the comedian's death before revealing he had "dou-
bled" for him in several stunts.

But, as Zanuck and St. Clair soon discovered, he had learned some bad habits at Uncle Shylock's knee, and was a dedicated budget-cutter and penny-pincher. Perhaps that was why, later, FBO became a big and profitable studio (under the new name of RKO), but, when they joined it, the whole place was run on a shoestring, and, unlike Universal, quality was never insisted upon when it was likely to cost money. The lot was actually run by a mean-minded Frenchman named Emile Offerman, who watched expenditure to the last sou, but there were also a great many lowly paid deadheads around, most of them relatives of the Berman family or cousins and nephews of other shareholders; few of them had any knowledge of film technique nor any real interest in making interesting movies.

There was one notable exception among the deadheads. He was an eighteen-year-old named Pandro Berman,* who turned out to be the son of the owner, and he was attached to the Zanuck–St. Clair crew as what he himself later described as "flunkey or third assistant director." He was as enthusiastic about movies as Darryl Zanuck, and as eager to learn, and though his salary at that time ($25 a week) was low, even for those days, it did not stop him from working an eighteen-hour day or from later describing life on the set of "The Telephone Girl" as "the best job I ever had."

"They hadn't invented the word whizz-kid in those days," he said later, "but if anyone ever merited that description, Zanuck was the one. He was only three years older than I was, and he looked even younger, but he had such an air of authority, such self-confidence, that without worrying about it I found myself looking up to him. He oozed talent and know-how."

He didn't mind hard work either, Berman remembered. He arrived at the studio every morning at 7 A.M. with a new script in hand, "and he must have worked all night at it." Yet he stayed on the set all day long, sometimes until late in the night, helping St. Clair with set-ups, rewriting scenes, rehearsing the actors, working out new gags.

"Productions were rather simple, schedules were tight, and in those days we worked the equivalent of a seven-day week," Berman said later. "All day Saturday and on into Saturday night, because Sunday morning we didn't come in. We got in an extra day by working Saturday night. There was of course no overtime paid to anybody. We used to make pictures in a week, and often we would work through Saturday until dawn."

*He later became head of RKO Studios and one of the most famous producers in Hollywood.

He added: "That was the method in those days. The tycoons were milking everybody for the odd dollar. Pictures had to be made very cheaply, and any artistic quality in the film was left entirely up to the director."

He liked the Zanuck–St. Clair combination because, despite a tight budget, they tried to get some kind of different quality, a special touch, into their two-reelers, and they never lost their enthusiasm or their verve, even when the studio accountants were around, watching to see they didn't waste a minute or a penny.

"Of course," Berman said, "they had quite a good cast, much more talented than some of the slobs we had around the studio at that time. We had George O'Hara, Kit Guard, and Albert Cook, and the Telephone Girl, around whom Zanuck spun his plots for the series, was a wonderful person named Alberta Vaughn, who had the roundest eyes in the movies and always looked as if she had been startled out of her wits — which was what she was supposed to be over the shocking things she heard at the telephone switchboard."

So successful did "The Telephone Girl" series prove to be that Zanuck and St. Clair were tempted over to Universal and asked to take over a new series of two-reel boxing stories called "The Leather Pushers."

The original story about an honest young boxer fighting his way through the crooked world of professional pugilism had been written by a magazine writer from the East named J. C. Witwer, but he had proved to be an amiable and unreliable drunk who never delivered his scripts on time. Zanuck was hired to sober him up and get his ideas down on paper, but he quickly discovered that when Witwer had no alcohol inside him he also was empty of ideas. Tanked up, however, he was flowing with good gags and situations, but too drunk to write them down. This did not dismay Zanuck, who felt he knew much more about professional boxing than Witwer ever would. Scribbling busily as Witwer babbled on, he dashed back to his typewriter and added liberal atmosphere and plot-lines of his own. Meanwhile, St. Clair had found a young actor named Reginald Denny who fitted the requirements of the leading role — a sort of gentleman-adventurer of upstanding honesty who has to fight the pugs and the thugs of boxing. The first thing Zanuck did when he met him was to tell him to strip to the waist, which he hesitatingly proceeded to do. Then Zanuck took off his own shirt and began dancing around the actor, sharply slapping him about the chest and neck but keeping his hands carefully away from his face.

"Go on!" he shouted. "Hit me! Hit me back! Let's see you make me bleed!"

The good-natured Denny had no intention of doing any such thing, but merely made some feeble gestures until one of Zanuck's slaps stung and angered him, and he lashed out with his fists, landing a haymaker that felled the writer. Standing over him, deeply distressed, all the actor could say was: "Oh, dear, oh dear, oh dear. I say, I am most frightfully sorry. But you did provoke me, you know."

Meanwhile, on the floor, dabbing at a streaming nose, Zanuck was delightedly shouting across to the watching St. Clair:

"He can do it, Mal. This is our kid! He knocks a bully down and then feels sorry for him. Why, every mother in America is going to love this kid!"

They did, too, and mothers in other countries as well. "The Leather Pushers" proved to be one of the most financially successful series ever made by Universal, and promoted the charming Reginald Denny into full-fledged stardom. But when, at the end of a year and twenty-four box-office hits in the series, Zanuck and St. Clair went to ask Carl Laemmle for a raise, they were told that Denny was being promoted to full-length films "and we're going to put real writers and a real director on this one." When they began to argue, Laemmle fired them on the spot.

As they emerged from Laemmle's office, they were confronted by a small boy, smirking at them. He was the most obnoxious child on the Universal lot, but everyone was forced to tolerate him because his name was Carl Laemmle, Jr. and he was the boss's son and the apple of his eye. He went around the studio sets followed by a German schnauzer, which some visiting star had unfortunately given him as a birthday present, and it had the habits of peeing on the scenery, biting actors' ankles, and sniffling up actress's skirts.

Gazing at the two dismayed and disgusted collaborators, Laemmle Jr. said with contempt:

"You know why you two goys have been fired, don't you? My dad says you've got too big for your britches."

It was too much. Zanuck, already bursting with anger over the treatment he and his collaborator had received, rushed over to the sneering scion of the Laemmle family, and, now having nothing to lose, raised his hand to clip him smartly over the ear. However, before he could do so he found his wrist gripped by a sharp set of teeth, and the schnauzer proceeded to shake his hand as if it were a rat. In pain and rage, he wrestled with the furious animal and finally succeeded in flinging it to the ground, where it yapped and growled around his ankles and defied him while its master beat a hasty retreat.

As Zanuck was wrapping a handkerchief around his bleeding wrist and loudly saying what he thought about the Laemmles, he noticed that his companion was staring at him with a thoughtful rather than sympathetic look on his face. In fact, the whole incident had given St. Clair an idea for a film. About a dog, of course. It was to change the course of Zanuck's career.

Virginia Zanuck soon discovered that her new husband treated married life in exactly the same way as he played polo, and she meant that in the literal as well as the metaphorical sense of the words.

"He treated his wife as if she were one of his ponies," she said later, "except that at the end of each game, if not at the end of each chukkah, he tended and cooed over his exhausted pony as if he or she were a baby, and he didn't always do that with me. I was ridden hard" — and she didn't mean that in the purely sexual sense — "every moment of the day or night when he was with me, and it was like being married to a whirlwind. It could be fun, though not always, and it was never less than exhausting."

She revealed later that there were several times during the first few months when she was tempted to leave him and go back to her parents. Her mother, who had been against the marriage from the start, was not sympathetic and made it plain to her daughter that, "having made my bed, she expected me to lie in it. Once, when I went back, and said I couldn't stand his tantrums and his temperament any longer, my mother said what else could I expect from a genius? 'A *genius*? Darryl?' I said. 'Don't make me laugh!' "

At first, she gave up her room at the Studio Club and came to live with him in a small apartment he had taken near Melrose Avenue. He spent most of the night pounding out scripts on his Underwood or restlessly pacing up and down their bedroom, searching for ideas, and when she pleaded with him to come to bed and think there, he said: "There's only one thing I think about in bed, and it isn't about films." And though he could be tender and thoughtful after making love, and she grew to be desperately fond of him, he was even more of a problem when he did fall asleep, because he was subject to violent nightmares. He tossed and turned so much that later Virginia confessed she waited until he was asleep and then took large safety pins from under her pillow, with which she securely fastened his pajamas to her nightgown, "to keep him from falling out of bed."

She suspected that the cause of his nightmares was his mother, and that there was some deep Freudian reason why he never mentioned her name except in his troubled dreams. He would often grab his pillow and squeeze it until she expected the feathers to burst out, and she could hear him grinding his teeth and moaning that he was going to "kill her, kill her!" She never mentioned these incidents to him the next day, and he never spoke of them, though she sensed that he was grateful at the way she gently soothed him in his distress and wiped away his night sweat.

Then, one day when she returned from driving her husband to the studio, she found a woman waiting for her on the doorstep, and knew at once that it was Darryl's mother. She took her inside and made her coffee, and learned that Louise was now living alone, her husband having been sent away to an upstate home for inebriates. Grandpa Torpin was dead, and with the money he had left her, Louise had bought a motor court in Beverly Hills. She took a critical look around Virginia's tiny apartment and remarked that they seemed a bit cramped. She added that she badly wanted to give her son and his wife a wedding present: how would it be if she gave them one of the lodges at the motor court — for a year — rent free?

Virginia said she thought that was a wonderful idea, and she would tell Darryl all about it when she collected him that evening. She thought Louise looked lonely and rather pathetic, and that it might be good both for her and her son if they were reunited.

"But it was a big mistake," she said later. "I should never have allowed it."

# SIX

# DOG DAYS

HOLLYWOOD movie-makers have long been aware of the fact that there is much money and easy popularity to be secured if they use pets or animals in films, whether they be fawns (as in *The Yearling*), horses (as in *The Black Stallion* and *National Velvet*), or monkeylike creatures from outer space (as in the phenomenal box-office success, *E.T.*). Dogs, however, have always been the favorite animals of directors, since they don't have to be cosseted, they are almost always highly trained, and are quick to respond to almost any demand made upon them, from rescuing a struggling child from drowning to defending a mistress from rape. Moreover, since millions of households have dogs as pets, most of the audience quickly "connects" the moment they see a dog on the screen.

It was as long ago as 1911 that an actor-writer in the movies named Larry Trimble picked up a bright collie bitch named Jean, from a strays' home, and turned her into a meal ticket by persuading the studios to use her in films. He trained her well, and she was full of winsome tricks, including feeding a bottle of milk to a baby in a crib. Trimble lived well off her earnings until she caught distemper and died in 1917, and he had to go back to acting.

Early in the 1920s, however, some time after age and illness had forced him out of acting and into retirement, Trimble heard about another dog that had been picked up by a U.S. doughboy on the Western Front during World War I and brought back to America. It had been trained by the German Red Cross to search for casualties on the muddy battlefields, and the doughboy had found it faithfully standing by a badly wounded but still living soldier, and when he was shipped home to California he had brought the animal with him. Trimble knew a young Hollywood script-

writer named Jane Murfin and persuaded her to track down the ex-
doughboy, buy the dog off him, and write a series of films around it. She
did so. She named the dog, which was a German shepherd, Strongheart,
and made it the central figure of a successful series which ran in the early
twenties. Then the dog grew old and died, and Jane Murfin went on to
other things.

Strongheart's success had not, though, gone unnoticed in Hollywood
and soon other German shepherd dogs began turning up at the studios.
Nearly all their owners claimed they had once worked for the German
Red Cross on the Western Front and had been rescued from death from
starvation by animal-loving soldiers in the U.S. Army. Among the most
talented of the dogs was a German shepherd named Rinty, and he had
been featured in a minor role in a Warner Brothers movie called *Where
the North Begins*. It was this film that had stimulated Mal St. Clair's
interest in dog films. He had caught *Where the North Begins* at a sneak
preview in the Hollywood suburbs, and thought the film was awful but
Rinty quite wonderful.

Shortly after they had been kicked out of Universal, he persuaded
Zanuck to accompany him to another showing of *Where the North Begins*,
and when they emerged he was delighted to discover that his partner
was as impressed by Rinty's performance as he had been. Rinty was indeed
a splendid performer, fighting off wolves in the snow, standing guard
over its wounded master, and finally dragging him and his sled to safety
across a river full of treacherous ice floes. St. Clair had made discreet
inquiries about the cards the audience had turned in at the sneak preview
he had attended, and as he had calculated almost all of them hated the
film but every one of them loved the dog.

Quite obviously, what Rinty needed was a good script. Neither Zanuck
nor St. Clair had ever made a dog film before, but both of them had
wives to feed (St. Clair had now married his Sennett Bathing Beauty)
and were eager to try. Moreover, Zanuck was quickly full of story-lines
and situations. They fixed up an appointment at Warner Brothers studios
and got ready to sell themselves as the ones who could turn Rinty into a
star and make a fortune for the studio out of his pictures.

It could hardly have been a more propitious moment to promise box-
office returns to the brothers Warner, for they badly needed them. Once
upon a time they had been notorious in Hollywood for their meanness,
and among a confraternity of studio chiefs who were once described as
"an oligarchy of rapacious vultures," they had a reputation for getting the

last strip of flesh from the most inaccessible area of the bones. But then in the years of World War I they had made some cheap anti-German films that had succeeded at the box office beyond their wildest dreams, and the resulting affluence had gone to their heads. With their excess profits they had built themselves a brand-new studio containing one of the biggest backlots in the movie capital. But now they couldn't seem to make a hit and were so badly overstretched that they had been forced to revert to their old penny-pinching habits. They soon had a reputation for being the worst payers in Hollywood, and all the higher-priced, and most popular, stars stayed away from them. Their failure was compounded by the fact that the brothers began blaming each other for the change in their fortunes, and the two most important had begun a bitter feud. Jack Warner, who was the creator and visualizer among the brothers, was constantly being sabotaged — or, at least, so he claimed — by Harry Warner, who controlled the moneybags. Sam Warner tried to act as a peacemaker between the two but only seemed to make things worse, while Albert Warner, the fourth brother, kept to himself and quietly waited for whatever dividends might trickle in. There wasn't even a trickle in 1923, and by the end of that year the specter of bankruptcy was looming.

It was at this moment that Zanuck and St. Clair appeared at the studio. They went right to the top, thanks to Virginia. She used her old association with Buster Keaton to have him call up Warners and recommend the writer-director team, and he did it at a moment when Jack and Harry were talking to each other. Otherwise, he warned them, anything Jack promised would most likely be shot down by Harry. As it was, the two brothers were together in the office when the pair were shown in. Zanuck and St. Clair had worked hard at rehearsing the plot-lines they had worked out for at least three Rinty films, and as Zanuck set the situation and explained the gags, St. Clair went down on his knees and acted out Rinty's performance.

The brothers were so impressed that they hired both scriptwriter and director on a six-picture contract at $250 a week.

"That was on a Friday," said Jack Warner later, "and Zanuck was back in the studio on Monday morning with a script ready to shoot."

The first film starring Rinty to be written and directed by the Zanuck–St. Clair team was called *Find Your Man* and starred the German shepherd as a lumberjack's faithful pet in the pine forests of Oregon, and it was almost entirely devoted to the dog's incredible feats in rescuing its master from drowning, freezing, attacks by polar bears and wolves, ambushes, and forest fires. To launch the promotion of Rinty to stardom, the budget was inflated enough for them to shoot it on location at a lumber camp named Klamath Falls, in Oregon. Zanuck took Virginia along with him as a reward for getting them in to see the brothers Warner, which gave the rest of the company a chance to listen in — they stayed in a very small hotel — to some of the tempestuous rows that the couple were having at the time.

Virginia was a strong-minded character who knew only too well how boring filmmaking can be when you are not part of the cast or crew, so she stayed in the hotel while the shooting was taking place. But she did expect her husband's company when the day's work was over; instead, he never seemed to be around. Fearing that he might be cheating on her, she snooped around and found that he was, but not with another woman. There was a river at Klamath Falls into which the timber from the forests was assembled, ready to be floated downstream to the mills. Zanuck had watched, pop-eyed with wonder and admiration, as the lumberjacks walked across the logs and got them together so that they would float easily, and the sight of the perfectly balanced equilibrists was an instant challenge.

"He obviously regarded it as magical as walking on water, and as rewarding," Virginia said later, "and Darryl saw personal fulfillment in performing it. Every day, after shooting finished, or whenever he wasn't needed on the set, he was out there on the water, trying to walk the logs."

It turned out to be more difficult to achieve than he had calculated, and he took a ducking more times than he liked to remember later. The lumbermen loved the spectacle, of course, and began taking bets on how long he could keep his balance. The more they jeered at him, the more he became determined to acquire the skill before he left Klamath Falls; and despite pleas from Virginia, and then some very loud objections, he neglected her in favor of long hours out on the river "log-rolling," as she sarcastically put it, "like a would-be Harold Lloyd."

When the last day of the shooting was reached, the usual wrap-up party was arranged and Virginia dressed herself in her best ballgown in preparation for the celebration. But then she had to wait for Darryl's return, and time passed. The party began on the set across the river, but there was no sign of her husband. Finally, after several hours had gone by, he came in to their room. He was soaked to the skin and gray with fatigue. He had been out on the logs making one last try to walk them like a lumberjack — and, as before, falling into the water time and again. Now he was cold, exhausted, and in no mood for a party. Tearing off his clothes, his wiry body shivering with both a chill and a sense of defeat, he was about to sink into a hot bath when Virginia burst in and announced she was going to the party alone.

"Over my dead body!" he shouted, following her to the door and down the corridor, still naked. He continued to chase her to the head of the stairs, "ordering me to come back, screaming that I mustn't go there by myself and listen to them jeering at him. Undoubtedly, he would have followed me right into the crowd, stark naked as he was, had I not looked back at him and laughed, still challenging him to stop me. Then I saw him suddenly look down at himself, and I think what happened was that he realized all that cold water had frozen his manhood to the size of an acorn, and what would people think when they saw it — not him — looking like that? So he turned and ran back to our room."

When she returned later that night, he was fast asleep in bed, or pretending to be. And when she opened her wardrobe to prepare to pack for next day's departure, she found he had cut all her dresses to ribbons. She slept on the sofa and would not come back to bed until he apologized, which he did, handsomely. And more than made up her damaged wardrobe once they returned to Los Angeles.

If Darryl Zanuck never succeeded in log-walking while they were in Oregon, Rinty, the dog-hero of the movie, certainly did, and a chase across the logs was one of the big scenes of the film. In fact, Zanuck had crammed every kind of stunt into *Find Your Man*, and the dog was seldom out of action. It soon became apparent, however, that not even the talented Rinty himself, a bright, agile and willing animal, could perform all the stunts the scriptwriter had thought up for him. So first a double, then a third and then a fourth stand-in for Rinty had to be summoned to carry out all the scenes. Luckily, Rinty's owner had several other German shepherds in his kennels, all of them, he claimed, direct offspring of the original, and luckily in long-shot most of them were indistinguishable from each other. It was this tripling and quadrupling of Rinty's doubles that gave Jack Warner the idea of changing the animal's name on the cinema marquees. Jack Warner was a joker who liked to have fun with his staff, and one of his habits was to gently mock their names. He referred to Mal St. Clair as "our seasick friend, Mal de Mer," and to Darryl Francis Zanuck as "three most charming gentlemen." After the third German shepherd was called in to double for Rinty in the film, he announced that the dog-star would henceforth be known as Rinty-Tin-Tin. But both Zanuck and St. Clair thought that looked wrong above the title, and just before the sneak preview the name was changed to Rin Tin Tin. That was how the world knew him from then on.

Not only was *Find Your Man* a great success at the box office, but fans started writing in from all over the world, asking for photographs of Rin Tin Tin, and thousands were mailed out to them, complete with a paw-print.

In the next six months, Zanuck produced six more Rin Tin Tin scripts, and they were almost the only reason why the fortunes of Warner Brothers began to turn around. Jack Warner found nothing special about Mal St. Clair, whom he regarded as a reasonably talented director, but Darryl Zanuck dazzled him, with his youthful energy and skill.

"He could write ten times faster than any ordinary man," he said later. "He worked Saturdays, Sundays and nights in those days, and he was a very professional scriptwriter. Once he came in with the screenplay on a Monday morning, we knew we were ready to shoot and that in a month's time or less we would have another Rin Tin Tin movie."

By 1925, Rin Tin Tin was famous the whole world over and the best known dog-star of them all. Not only were brothers Warner profuse in their gratitude, but they stifled their miserly instincts and first doubled and then trebled the paychecks of Zanuck and St. Clair. As for the owner of the dog and his doubles, he became a rich man as Rin Tin Tin's value increased — especially for newspaper endorsements — and in gratitude he gave one of the dog-star's sons to Zanuck as a Christmas present. It became his special pet for a time, until it started snapping at the fetlocks of his precious polo ponies.

Virginia hated the dog because Zanuck had so trained it that it took no notice of her when she called it, but, the moment she turned her back, would come up behind her and goose her. She was not sorry when he passed the animal on to his mother as a guard-dog for the motor lodge, and they did not take it with them when they eventually acquired a house of their own.

In the beginning, Virginia convinced herself that the reunion of her husband with his mother had been a good idea. So long as Zanuck's salary check from Warner Brothers continued to be a modest $250 a week, the rent-free lodge to which Louise assigned them was convenient and economical, and it was an easy drive each morning and evening to the studio on Sunset Boulevard. (Zanuck did not drive, and Virginia took him and collected him in their Packard, a wedding present from her father.) It was true that sometimes she detected an atmosphere of strain between

mother and son, and it made her uneasy. He had still never more than
hinted at the circumstances that had estranged him from Louise, and
accustomed as she was to the placid family relationship that had always
prevailed in her own home, she could not guess at what might have
disturbed him. But sometimes she got the feeling that Darryl treated his
mother rather like a family might treat a son or daughter just home from
a long spell in a mental home. She often caught him watching warily as
Louise pottered around the lodge, "as if she were going to burst out, or
something." But certainly, at first, Darryl seemed to calm down, especially at nights, and the nightmares ceased for a time.

Then one day, when Virginia came back from shopping, she was startled
to hear the German shepherd dog — they had called him Randy — bark-
ing loudly, and when she walked around the pool to find out what the
fuss was all about, she heard voices coming from Louise's office, where
she kept the motor lodge books and records. To her astonishment, she
realized that one of the voices was that of her husband, and that he was
angrier than she had ever heard him before. When she peeped through
the window, she saw Louise sitting behind the counter, tears running
down her face and carving rivulets in her heavy makeup. Darryl was
standing over her, his face writhing with fury, and the words he was using
amazed her, because she could see no relevance to them. He kept shouting that he was "not going to be treated like a fucking night clerk, and
never would be" and then she saw him take Louise by the shoulders and
shake her, screaming that "she had better get that drunken Joe Norton
back again" because he wasn't going to be "one of her fancy help." At
that moment Louise lifted her arms as if to put them around her son,
and with a violent gesture he pushed her away — and then slapped her.

She beat a hasty retreat at that point, feeling, as she told her son later,
"like Bluebeard's wife, opening a door she was not supposed to enter."
It was some time later that Darryl came back to their lodge, helped himself
to a large bourbon, and then took her downtown to dinner at a new
restaurant called the Brown Derby, where they spent a happy evening
joking and reminiscing with one of Zanuck's new friends, a suave and
amiable character called Prince Mike Romanoff.

But that night Darryl had the sweats again, and he practically murdered
his pillow.

The next evening, when Virginia picked him up at Warner Brothers,
he told her to take another route home, and finally ordered her to halt
on a Hollywood street far away from his mother's Beverly Hills lodge.
Slipping round the back of the car, he opened the door for her, took her

by the hand, and led her through a small, well-kept yard, to the door of a house, which he opened with a key he was carrying. Suddenly grasping her round the legs, he carried her across the threshold, and when she gasped and asked whose house it was, he kissed her and said:

"Ours. I bought it."

For the next thirty minutes, he followed her from room to room, as she made a tour, looking at it from a woman's eye. All the furniture was there, even the pictures on the walls, the ashtrays on the tables, the drapes across the windows, the carpets on the floor.

"Ours too," he said, in response to her silent inquiry. "Change anything you wish — but this is what I bought. There should be everything. Including," he added, "food and drink."

He took her hand again and led her into the kitchen, showed her the cupboards, replete with dishes and glassware, and then opened the door of the refrigerator, which was packed with food and drink.

He took out a bottle of Krug champagne (Virginia always remembered that bottle) and as he popped the cork and poured two glasses, he said:

"Let's not go back to the lodge tonight." A pause. A grimace. A sip of champagne, and then: "Or ever. This is our new home. Let's stay here."

Virginia would rather have bitten off her tongue, but she couldn't help it.

"Have you told your mother?" she asked.

He shook his head violently. "I wouldn't have done that," he said. "Not tell her first, before telling you. I'll go and see her tomorrow."

He came over to her, kissed her, clinked his glass with hers, and, as she remembers, they got some caviar out of the refrigerator and some crackers, and they finished the bottle. "It was a very happy occasion," she said later, "and I got quite tipsy."

But though he did not try to strangle the pillow that night, he got very restless in the early hours of the morning, and she wished she had had her safety pins with her.

# SEVEN

# THE MUSIC OF MONEY

NOT ONLY DID Jack Warner humorously refer to Darryl Francis Zanuck as "three charming gentlemen" but he was soon heard to add that "if only one of them were Jewish, I'd make him a partner in this studio." His brother Harry shared his admiration for the young writer — about the only subject they ever agreed upon — and both of them admitted (though not in the hearing of the shareholders) that not only was he a true discovery but the savior of their operation. His energy and enthusiasm were just what was needed to galvanize flagging strengths around the studio and spur deflated spirits back into action. Within a year of his arrival at Warners, the organization was back on track — and not just in the money, either. It was also starting to make the kind of movies that stimulated the interest of other studios, and let them know that Warner Brothers was back in business as serious competition.

Zanuck always remembered his spell at Warners as one of the happiest and most productive periods of his life, "and probably the time when I learned most about how to make films," he said later. As soon as he realized what kind of a tempestuous type he had hired, Jack Warner set out to harness his phenomenal energy and flow of ideas by taking him off the Rin Tin Tin films, for which he considered anyone could grind out satisfactory plots,* and put him to work on program features with bigger budgets and human stars — such ones as they had left, that is, which did not go much beyond Monte Blue, Marie Prevost, and a new young actor from the New York stage named John Barrymore.

Zanuck always gave the impression to his contemporaries and his peers

---

*Though the box-office receipts dropped after Zanuck left.

that he knew everything there was to be known about making movies, since he had long since decided that a bold front, a cocksure manner, and an air of self-confidence would get him everywhere and an admission of ignorance would be taken as a confession of weakness. But he was rather more honest (and modest) with himself than he was with outsiders, and he acknowledged that so far as motion pictures were concerned, he still had much to learn. He used Warner Brothers as his university, and the professors from whom he learned most were the film editors in the studio cutting rooms. He spent hours watching the cutters at work, reducing spools of film down to reasonable size, splicing, chopping, changing sequences to eliminate boring pauses and highlight certain moments. It was a revelation to him how deft editing of a film after the writer, the director, the actors, and the cameraman had finished with it could change its whole nature, and, in particular, "turn a turkey into a sleeper, just by cutting, editing, and rejigging."

"I practically lived in the cutting room," he said later, "and it was a great education. I could see the errors and how to get out of them. I realized that all isn't lost when the script is a dud, the director is a deadhead, and the actors don't know their asses from their elbows. Unless it is a complete and utter disaster, there is no single film that can't be rescued and turned into a seeable movie, even if it doesn't turn out to be an epic."

Zanuck always admired craftsmen and skilled professionals, and he did not conceal his admiration for the way the film editors at Warners time and again, by a slice here, a transposition there, saved a movie from sudden death at the box office. He was obviously so eager to learn that they taught him all their tricks, and at the end of six months he had skill enough to have made a good living as a first-class cutter. Allowed the run of the editing rooms, he was able to do cutting jobs of his own on films that were already in the can and awaiting distribution. He had his greatest moment of revelation about the nature of film producing when he came away from a studio showing of one of the latest Warner films, and everyone knew they had a disaster on their hands. It was called *Tiger Rose*, and it included some scenes that were so ridiculously mawkish that the audience was more likely to be rolling in the aisles with laughter than reaching for their handkerchiefs to weep over the predicament of the movie's stars (Lenore Ulric, Theodore von Elz, and Forrest Stanley). Zanuck confidently told Jack Warner to let him have the film for a couple of days, and forty-eight hours later showed it to him and the studio executives again. It still wasn't the greatest film of all time, but its thrust had changed, as had its story-line, and it had become a viable and plausible weepie instead of a laughable disaster.

"I just wrote a new and better story-line," Zanuck said later, "and then I called in Archie Mayo, one of the best caption writers in the business, and told him to write a new set of subtitles. I had cut and rejigged here and there so that the whole thrust of the movie had been altered — and unless you were a lip-reader, you couldn't have told that what you were reading on the screen and what the characters were saying were two entirely different things."

It was a revelation of how smart editing could make — or break — a film, and Zanuck never forgot it.

In 1925 Darryl Zanuck wrote nineteen films for Warner Brothers, and at least a dozen of them were box-office successes. He also had dozens of other ideas for movies buzzing around his head.

"Each year we made between fifty and seventy pictures," Jack Warner said later, "and at our annual convention our sales department always wanted to know what they were. But often we didn't know. When you know you can make a movie in four weeks, you don't set out your program too precisely. So just to satisfy them and to have something down on paper, I would call on Darryl, and he would sit down and pour out synopses of upcoming movies. Some of the ideas were genuine, from plays and books we had bought, but others we would just make up. I would find out they wanted stories about prize-fighters. Boom! Darryl would make up 'The Prize Fighter and the Lady.' He could do all sorts of things ad lib. He would jump up and scream, 'I've got it!' and do it. Then we'd fake up some title."

Warner added that "many of the stories were revamped after the films were finished," by which he meant that Zanuck got to work on them in the cutting room, sliced out their faults, and sometimes completely changed the plot-line. His name began to appear so frequently on the credit titles that at one of these Warner conventions one of the shareholders rose up to grumble, as usual, about the studio budget, and picked out the expenditure for the story department, wondering why they had to spend so much money there "when you've only got one writer, this guy Zanuck." Harry Warner sent for Zanuck at the end of the convention and told him that they didn't want him to stop writing scripts for them, but that henceforth he would have to do so under different names. He chose three pseudonyms in addition to his own: Mark Canfield, Melville Crossman, and Gregory Rogers, and he was shrewd enough to persuade Harry to

draw up separate contracts for each of them. It swelled his weekly pay-
check to $1,000. Each of the writers specialized in certain genres, Canfield
concentrating on melodramas, Crossman on the bigger-budget epics, Rogers on comedies, and Zanuck saved himself for light comedies starring
his friend Sydney Chaplin and specialized films by potential stars around
the lot who took his fancy, like Dolores Costello in *The Little Irish Girl*
and a winsome little girl named Myrna Loy in *Across the Pacific.*

Ironically, it was Crossman's films that always seemed to get the most
attention, and one day the telephone rang and it was Louis B. Mayer
from Metro-Goldwyn-Mayer. He had just seen Crossman's latest, and
was prepared to offer him a writing contract.

"Crossman isn't available," said Zanuck, "but I think I could get Darryl
F. Zanuck for you. He's just done *Old San Francisco*, which I believe
you saw at the sneak last night."

"Not interested," said Mayer, and slammed down the telephone.

At the end of two years, in 1925, Jack Warner summoned Darryl Zanuck
to a conference of the four brothers and informed him that they had made
a decision.

"We fired Schrock this morning," Jack said, "and from now on, if you
want it, you're it. The only thing to be settled is how much are you asking
to take on the job?"

He was referring to a veteran movie-maker named Raymond Schrock
who had joined Warners some years earlier after working for Pathé in
Paris and UFA in Berlin. He had risen to become head of production
and had got on well with his bosses until the arrival of Zanuck. Since that
time he had been throwing fits of temperament, especially when Jack
gave the newcomer the freedom of the lot and consulted him over what
kinds of movies they would make and who would star in them. He called
it "favoritism" and in one row with Zanuck had characterized him as "a
smart-aleck upstart." Rumor had it that Schrock had finally delivered an
ultimatum — and lost.

"You were paying Raymond three thousand dollars a week," said Zanuck. "I can do twice the job he was doing, and I'll do it for five thousand
dollars a week."

Jack Warner looked shocked; Harry, Sam, and Albert put their hands
to their cheeks as if they had never heard of such a sinful demand in their
lives; and three minutes later it was all settled. Darryl Zanuck, twenty-
three years old, was head of production for Warner Brothers.

That night Jack Warner and his then wife, Irma, gave a small dinner

party for Darryl and Virginia to celebrate his protégé's promotion. All
the other brothers and their wives were present, and applauded emotionally as Jack welcomed Zanuck as "the newest and brightest member
of the Warner family." Later, when the men retired to the billiard room,
Jack took the young man to one side and said:

"You stay with me, kid, and I'll have your name up there as a Warner
partner." He looked him over and sighed. "If only you were one of us.
That would make it so much easier."

"What do you want me to do, Jack?" Zanuck asked. "Circumcise myself?"

For the first time in his life, Darryl Zanuck now had money, and he
liked the feeling. Not that money was ever all that important to him,
except when he needed it to finance or finish a movie, and the ambition
to make big pictures of his own was already more important to him than
money in the bank. It was one of the main reasons why he was happy to
be at Warners. He was convinced that the fraternal feud between Jack
and Harry would one day end in a rift which only he would be able to
bridge, and that would mean a partnership of the kind Jack was already
hinting about, with, maybe, his name up there on every studio picture:
WARNER BROTHERS & ZANUCK PRESENT. If the feud became too bitter,
perhaps control of the studio's program might even pass over entirely to
him. The driving ambitions that had consumed him ever since he had
written his first script were growing stronger every day he worked in
Hollywood, and those ambitions would always be more important than
the size of his weekly check, except as a measure of his importance.

"Darryl always acted like a millionaire, even when we had next to
nothing," Virginia said later, "and I can't say there was any difference in
his attitude when he was making two hundred and fifty dollars a week
and when he was earning twenty times that much. Right from the first
time I ever knew him, he always acted in the grand manner. He was the
only man who ever *swept* me into Schwab's Drugstore for a milkshake
and got us instant attention, just as, later, he swept me into the Beverly
Hills Hotel or the Academy Awards dinner or a banquet at the Paris Ritz.
He had something about him, even when we had nothing in the bank,
that only millionaires and crowned heads have, an electricity that sends
waves across a room and even affects the snootiest maître d'."

All the same, having real money was convenient, and it enabled the
Zanucks to indulge themselves. Virginia went out, replaced the wardrobe
Darryl had ruined at Klamath Falls with designer gowns, and then com-

pletely refurnished the house her husband had bought, just for the fun
of making its atmosphere her own. She had other plans, too, that would
await the moment when Darryl could take time off from his new responsibilities at the studio.

In the meantime, he went out and bought new polo ponies, increasing
his stable to six. He was riding harder than ever, but more skillfully as
he learned more about the game. One of his most dangerous opponents
was a murderously reckless giant of a man named Big Boy Williams, an
actor who was suitably deferential to Zanuck when he met him at the
studio as head of Warner productions, but became transformed on the
field into the wrath of god, bumping, boring in on, and sometimes bat-
tering Zanuck and his mounts literally into the ground. Williams, who
weighed around 280 pounds, was so heavy that he all but broke the hearts
of his tough but gallant ponies, whose size was limited by the rules of
the game. He used his mounts like bulldozers, and woe betide anyone
who got in his way. Zanuck, who made it plain in both attitude and remarks
that he despised the way Williams wasted his brave little ponies, was
learning how to drive his adversary apoplectic with rage, by running rings
around him, avoiding collisions by a hair's breadth, stealing the ball from
practically under Williams's nose, and becoming a dazzling and stinging
gadfly. Every Sunday crowds poured onto the ground from Hollywood
to watch the weekly duel, waiting for the day when the wrath of god
would exact revenge for his continual humiliation. As indeed, one Sunday,
he did. But not yet, and the crowds roared with pleasure week after week
as they enjoyed the spectacle of the bully being humbled.

One other thing the new affluence made possible was travel, and it was
this for which Virginia was planning, just as soon as she could get her
husband away. On their first foreign trip together, he took her skiing in
Switzerland, and there were side trips to Paris, Vienna, and the South
of France. But the biggest thrill for both of them was the time in 1927
when they went on their first big-game safari in Kenya. For Zanuck,
Africa, with its rolling plains, its spectacular mountains, its wildness, and,
above all, its rich animal life brought him a sense of happiness and fulfillment such as he had not experienced since his boyhood out hunting
in the woods with Grandpa Torpin when everything had been so simple.
Kenya was an opulently exotic re-creation of Nebraska as he had once
known it, when you fished or shot for your supper, and matched wits
with the forces of nature. Those were the days before camera safaris, and
it would not, in any case, have occurred to him to take photographs of
the quarry he stalked along the shores of Lake Rudolf. He was a hunter.

Grandpa Torpin had taught him to be a hunter. You took the risks. You matched your skills, stalker against quarry, and then you faced up to the confrontation.

"The first time this big, ornery rhino came charging at me," he said, later, "was the biggest thing that ever happened to me. No fuck in the world ever equaled it. It was him and me, and him *or* me. He burst out of a thicket with his tusk down, his piggy red eyes half closed, but he knew just where I was from the smell of me. And I had to let him come on until just the right moment. If I fired too soon, the bullets would just splat against his armor-plating and he'd run me down like a tank. If I fired too late, we'd both die, because sheer momentum would keep him coming. I had to hit him just at the right moment, right through one of those pig-eyes."

He held his ground and his fire, and put the bullet into the right target at the right moment, and the rhino collapsed almost at his feet.

"God, what a moment," he said. "I found I'd peed in my britches and probably done other things as well, but there he was, dead at my feet, and if the bearers hadn't been screaming around us with their knives already out, I'd have leaned down and kissed the brute for dying such a beautiful and noble death."

Someone took a picture of Virginia and Darryl immediately after the kill, and it is eloquent of the moment. She looks as if she has come through something of an ordeal, but he has the wide-eyed, triumphant look of someone who has enjoyed the ecstatic experience of a lifetime.

It was still not a calm and stable marriage, and sometimes their quarrels were so sharp and bitter that she would go home to her parents and threaten not to return — but, of course, she always did. He had such a febrile temper and made such scenes in public, and these embarrassed her because she disliked open displays of temperament. She also resented the way he bullied people and scolded them in front of others for being stupid, and she felt particularly angry when he reacted to the sight of a beautiful girl in such an overtly sexual way. From the manner in which he treated the younger actresses at the studio, contemptuously slapping them on the butt, stroking or caressing them, curtly silencing them when he was not in the mood, pushing them around, she became convinced that he really regarded all females as a lesser breed, sexual objects with no reason to be respected. And it was true. In later years, one of his children recounted how an opportunity had arisen to listen in to one of the parental quarrels, which had, as usual in those days, concerned Virginia's anger at Darryl's casual infidelities.

"Why do you get so mad about them?" the child heard Zanuck shout. "They're just tarts — girls to be fucked and thrown away. Why get so worked up?"

"Because it's an insult to me!" Virginia shouted back.

"But why?" asked Zanuck, in obvious perplexity. "What have they got to do with you? They're just tarts, I tell you. You're different. I respect you."

"Thank you for nothing," she said.

And yet, she did love him, and not only that, she admired him for the way he was making his way through the Hollywood jungle. She had sensed from the first days of watching him at work in the studio that here was someone with talent and flair far beyond the ability to write Rin Tin Tin scripts and program movies for Warners. She had kept her eyes open while she was playing with Buster Keaton over at First National studios, and she knew the difference between a real man of the movies and a grinder-out of quickies. She knew that her husband had something special in him, and that one day he would leap the chasm between trash and serious movies, and that the reason why he was such a taut ball of tempers, tensions, and frustrations was that pent up inside him were large ideas and yearning ambitions which he had not yet learned how to fulfill. But he would, he would, she felt sure.

During their second trip to Europe, in 1926, she got a new insight on her husband, because at one point, while they were in Berlin, he had taken her to the UFA studios and asked to see the German actor-director Ernst Lubitsch.

Virginia was surprised that Darryl had even heard of him, because at that time he was not generally known for his movie talents outside Germany, not even in film circles in Hollywood. She herself knew Lubitsch's name and work only because one night, by accident, she had found herself at a showing in First National's studio projection room of two new films from Germany. One starred a dark dramatic beauty named Pola Negri, and both had been directed by the same man, Ernst Lubitsch.* Mainly because of rumors of Negri's potent attractions, word seemed to have

---

*They were probably the last two films Lubitsch made in Germany for UFA–Famous Players–Lasky, *Passion* and *One Arabian Night*.

spread among the cognoscenti in Hollywood, and an unusual number of
film people from outside the studio had turned up for the showing.
Virginia had noticed Charlie Chaplin, Erich von Stroheim, and D. W.
Griffith among them, and Buster Keaton had personally invited a new
and intriguing Swedish actress to accompany him. Her name was Greta
Garbo, and she had just arrived on the strength of her Swedish film *The
Story of Gösta Berling.*

What Virginia had not realized, because she did not know him at the
time, was that Darryl Zanuck had also been in the audience. The two
films were not the best work Lubitsch had ever done, but Zanuck had
been impressed by them, and when he reached Berlin all he could think
of was that here was an opportunity to meet the director in the flesh.
Luckily for the two Zanucks, Lubitsch, who was always the most charming
and friendliest of men, immediately invited them to dinner that night at
Horsch's, and there not only talked about his own work but seemed keenly
interested in Zanuck's stories of what he was doing in Hollywood. They
parted with expressions of mutual esteem, and Virginia was touched to
note what store her husband put in the encounter, plainly much flattered
by Lubitsch's reception of him.

Shortly after they returned home, Zanuck was galvanized by news that
Lubitsch had arrived in Hollywood to direct a film. He had, in fact, been
loaned by Famous Players–Lasky to United Artists to direct a new Mary
Pickford film called *Rosita*. What Lubitsch apparently did not know —
but Zanuck discovered from Hollywood gossip — was that UFA and Famous Players–Lasky did not want him back in Germany, where his contract was the most generous ever given to an actor-director and stipulated
that he was to have control of all aspects of his films, from casting to
marketing. This conflicted with UFA's new studio chiefs, who considered
him too capricious in his choice of subjects, stars, and the amount of
money he spent on them, and they had secretly asked Jesse Lasky, who
controlled the American side of the company, to make sure Lubitsch
remained in Hollywood.

But, Zanuck had heard, Lasky didn't want him either, having learned
that he had clashed with Mary Pickford on the making of *Rosita* and was
reputed to like throwing his weight around in the studios. Lasky preferred
to be the only one to do that on his home lot, and feared the clashes that
might ensue.

To Zanuck this seemed a golden opportunity for Warner Brothers to
secure the services of a great director, and he went to see Jack and Harry

at once and urged them to get Lubitsch on the Warner roster of directors. Neither had ever seen a Lubitsch film (or even heard of him, for that matter), but they were sufficiently stirred by their young scriptwriter's enthusiasm to agree to approach the German director with an offer. Not only that. To their astonishment, because they never thought this cocksure young man would ever be in awe of anyone, they found him quite put out when Jack suggested Lubitsch might direct the latest script that Zanuck had written.

"Oh, I don't think we could suggest that," the young man said. "Herr Lubitsch likes to choose his own scripts. Don't, for God's sake, try to foist one of mine on him. And don't think he's going to be easy to snare. This is a great director, and a straightforward approach isn't going to work. We've got to think up a strategy."

He was quite right. Lubitsch had hated his directing chore with Mary Pickford, disliked Hollywood studios and their methods, and was homesick. Unaware of the machinations that were going on back in Berlin, all he wanted to do was get back to Germany and go on as before at UFA–Famous Players–Lasky. He had brought his young assistant director, Henry Blanke, with him from Berlin, and he too had found making movies in America uncongenial. So when the filming of *Rosita* was finished, the two of them went round to see Jesse Lasky at the Famous Players studio on the corner of Vine Street in Hollywood, which was then still an old dirt road lined with pepper trees. The rural scene summed up what the two Germans felt about Hollywood, and they yearned for the theaters, concerts, restaurants, and bright lights of the German capital.

So when, on being shown into Lasky's office, they heard him say: "What do you want to do now, Mr. Lubitsch?" it was only natural that the director should reply:

"I want to go back to Germany. I have a wonderful contract there, and I don't want to stay in Hollywood and work with this factory style of making films."

At which Lasky said: "But we don't want you to work in Germany anymore."

He then proceeded, in terse and uncomplimentary language, to enumerate Lubitsch's faults and extravagances, and to make it plain that Berlin didn't want him back. If he wanted to stay on, all right, he could make quickies for Famous Players–Lasky, provided he toed the line and did what he was told. Or he could quit entirely.

"How much do you want for your contract?" he asked.

Lubitsch was astonished and outraged at this unexpected turn of events. It confirmed everything he had suspected about Hollywood's method of dealing with artists. He still did not realize it was his home studio in Berlin that had grown tired of his temperament and extravagant ways, and was using its Hollywood partners to get rid of him. Knowing his contract with Berlin still had several years to run, he named the first sum he could think of off the top of his head, and it was an astronomical one. That would show these Yankees how much he was worth, and how expensive it would prove to dispense with him. But instead of being fazed, Lasky reached across his desk and pressed a bell. When the secretary came in, he said:

"Make out a check for Mr. Lubitsch for two hundred thousand dollars."

Five minutes later, the check was handed over, and, as Henry Blanke put it later, "We were free — free to leave this terrible place and go back to Germany."

Lubitsch still did not fully realize what had happened to him, and still did not seem to be aware that it was UFA that had turned against him. So all he could think of was to cash his fat check into German marks and get back to his native land, there to carry on as before.

He and Henry Blanke had been staying in a rooming house on Norton Avenue in Hollywood, and they hurried back to pack and take the first train to New York and home. But Darryl Zanuck had kept in step with all the developments, and been in touch with Warner Brothers. Within ten minutes of Lubitsch's arrival on Norton Avenue, there was a knock on the door of their rooms, and a most beautiful woman walked in upon them.

Her name was Irene Rich, and later she would become a famous Hollywood star. For the moment, however, she was still a member of Mack Sennett's Bathing Beauties, and she had once had among her lovers Darryl Zanuck and Mack Sennett himself. Now she was the paramour of Jack Warner, who had just begun to cheat on his wife, Irma. Jack had reluctantly consented to Zanuck's suggestion that Miss Rich and her considerable charm be used as a go-between with Lubitsch, whom he knew to be susceptible to attractive women.

Assuming a deliciously conspiratorial look and putting a scented finger to her admirable lips, Miss Rich whispered:

"I have come to warn you that in five minutes a man is coming to see you, and his name is Harry Warner. He and his brother make the greatest films in Hollywood, and they would love to have you stay here and make the kind of films you want to make, the way you like to make them. So do please listen to what he has to say."

With that she blew a kiss at the astonished Lubitsch and his assistant and disappeared the way she had come. Five minutes later, Harry Warner arrived, clasped Lubitsch by the hand, called him "Master," and added:

"You and I have never met and you do not know me, but I know all about you. My brother and I have just built the most modern film set in Hollywood on our lot on Sunset Boulevard, and we would like you to have it for your special use. Do please come and join us."

At the same time (Henry Blanke later remembered) he mentioned a long-term contract for a sum of money that made Lubitsch's eyes sparkle for the second time in the day. It was too big a sum to turn down, he was to say later, even for a homesick German, especially since Warner casually turned and hired Henry Blanke too.

So shortly thereafter, Lubitsch and Blanke arrived at Warners and began work on their first Hollywood comedy, *The Marriage Circle*, with Florence Vidor and Creighton Hale. It was one of the successes of the year and helped to consolidate the recovery of Warner Brothers, already in profit thanks to Zanuck's Rin Tin Tin films.

The whole incident threw an interesting light on Zanuck's character. He renewed acquaintance with the German director the moment he arrived at Warner Brothers, and reminded him of their earlier encounter in Berlin. But he never did mention to Lubitsch that if it hadn't been for his intervention, he would have gone back to Berlin — probably to obscurity; maybe, since he was Jewish, to his humiliation and death at the hands of the Nazis. It was only years later that Irene Rich revealed to the director the part that Darryl Zanuck had played in the resuscitation of his career.

There was one other sidelight on the incident that deserves to be mentioned. Zanuck was now so sure of himself that, once he became head of production at Warners, he demanded screen credit on all productions made by the studio — with notable exceptions. Henceforth, all films made on the lot announced on-screen: WARNER BROTHERS PRESENT A DARRYL F. ZANUCK PRODUCTION. But not Ernst Lubitsch's films. On those Darryl Zanuck took no credit at all, even though none of them could have been made without him.

On September 2, 1925, visitors to the office of the head of production at Warner Brothers noticed something different about Darryl F. Zanuck.

He had, in fact, grown a mustache for his birthday, taken to wearing gold-rimmed glasses, and smoked a big fat cigar. It was the disguise he had adopted to make himself look older, and, as Jack Warner later remarked, "It certainly put about eight years on his appearance. He no longer looked like a kid, but all of twenty-five."

He was still, however, only twenty-three years old, and he was earning $260,000 a year.

# EIGHT

# THE MUSIC OF SOUND

INETEEN TWENTY-SIX was one of the most prosperous years in the history of Hollywood, and almost all of the four hundred films made in the studios were box-office successes. Movie-going had become a national habit and there were now 14,673 picture theaters in the country and receipts at the end of the year came to more than 120 million dollars. Though the big box-office stars were still Pickford, Fairbanks, Chaplin, and Harold Lloyd, there were others already on the rise to stardom and to the dizzy-making riches and fame that this ensured in the last year of the silent films. Mae Murray had had a stunning success in Erich von Stroheim's uninhibited and lavishly rich version of *The Merry Widow*, and the hit of the year was undoubtedly King Vidor's rough and roistering film about World War I, *The Big Parade*, which starred John Gilbert and a delectable-looking French dish named Renée Adorée. Both of them broke the hearts of moviegoing America in their passionate love scenes, but were destined to make the same audiences break into embarrassed giggles once the sound of their voices was heard a little more than a year later.

On the rung of the golden ladder just below the four superstars were such potent sirens as Pola Negri, Nazimova, Dorothy and Lillian Gish, Colleen Moore, Corinne Griffith, and the most lubricious of the screen vamps of the day, Nita Naldi. Big bosomy stars were fashionable in 1926 and there was no suggestion whatsoever that well-endowed personalities such as Betty Blythe should slim. Expert cameramen like Karl Struss were told to emphasize the broad shoulders and even broader hips of such coming personalities as Joan Crawford, and desperately sought camera angles that would put more flesh on Vilma Banky and Barbara La Marr. The most popular male stars in 1926 were Ronald Colman, a suave,

mustachioed Englishman whose silky tones would win him even more
fame once talking films arrived, Richard Barthelmess, Reginald Denny,
Rod La Rocque, Lew Cody, and Conrad Nagel. But none of them set the
pulses racing among film fans quite so palpitatingly as the biggest male
heartthrob of them all, Rudolph Valentino. When he suddenly and unexpectedly died in August of that year, the nation mourned him. Valentino's funeral train was mobbed by sobbing crowds at every station where
it halted on its passage across the land to the burial ceremonies in New
York. Even Virginia Zanuck felt compelled to wear black in mourning for
the departed star.

It was a busy year for Darryl Zanuck. He made six movies under his
own name and seven others using his studio pseudonyms. Most of them
were directed by well-tried veterans (seven of them by Roy del Ruth)
and starred such contract players as Patsy Ruth Miller, Ben Turpin, Tom
Moore, Louise Fazenda, Myrna Loy, Monte Blue, and his old friend
Sydney Chaplin. If none of them showed any particular flair or brilliance,
that may have been because he was spending most of his time between
writing chores on the responsibilities of his new job as head of production.
Jack Warner had given him a free hand to hire and fire whomever he
wished, in addition to which he sat in on some complicated negotiations
that resulted in the purchase of a rival studio named Vitagraph Films;
this did not bring in any particularly valuable stars or properties, but it
did add a considerable library of films and an additional booking circuit
to that already possessed by the brothers Warner. And, even more important than that, it brought to the studio some new developments in the
techniques of movie presentation, which were destined to change the
nature of motion picture production.

Nineteen twenty-seven is generally accepted as the year when talking
pictures arrived in Hollywood, but most of the big studios were aware
that the advent of sound was looming long before that. It was one reason
why, in 1926, they were so prolific in their production schedules and so
determined to cash in on the box-office value of their established silent
stars. They saw trouble ahead once the movies began to talk. For what
would the cinema become? Nothing more than a photographed copy of
the live theater, in which their high-priced stars, untrained in speech
dramatics, would draw attention to their feeble voices and outlandish
accents and lose the impact of the very qualities that had made them
popular with the public — their looks and their physical expressions. To
the men who had made Hollywood the movie capital of the world, speech
was anathema. Verbally inarticulate themselves, and not just in the En-

glish language, they had grown accustomed to a universe of mime, and regarded the advent of sound in films as a threat and an intrusion. To many of them, sound was already the enemy that they heard each night on the national networks, where, their bookers informed them, popular radio programs were cutting into their box-office receipts.

As purveyors of entertainment to the masses, they were in business to give the public what it wanted, and if what it wanted was sound, then sound is what they would provide. But sound, not speech. For the moment, they thought of it as no more than a gimmick, and although Vitagraph Films had gone far beyond gimmickry in their experiments over the past few years, it was simply as part of the assets of the company that Warner Brothers had taken over their results and equipment. No one expected the experiments to have produced anything but a cacophony of noise — and it was with noise rather than actual speech that the brothers Warner hoped that moviegoers might be satisfied for the time being.

They were wrong. Vitagraph had progressed far beyond mere sound accompaniment and ventured into the dread territory of spoken language. Shortly after the studio technicians had assembled Vitagraph's equipment, Zanuck announced a showing of a number of its short film subjects, all of which, his experts informed him, had been given "sound" accompaniment. But when the two-reelers were actually run through for him and the brothers Warner, they discovered that the characters actually "spoke." And the noise was terrible.

"It stinks!" said Zanuck, when Jack Warner asked his opinion of what he was hearing on the screen. And certainly it was not very good. The process on which Vitagraph's experts had been working was a sound-on-disc system developed by the Bell Telephone Laboratories, and in the shorts screened that evening, characters on the screen talked, dogs barked, animals roared, trains and cars whizzed by, all with additional background noises. It would have been impressive had not the noise of the whirring camera been so conspicuous on the sound track, for in order to synchronize sound and motion the sound system was built into the camera itself.

Zanuck and the Warner brothers found it tolerable in one- or two-reelers, and they subsequently sent out some of the Vitagraph shorts to accompany the showing of their main features. Ten or twelve minutes of the horrendously scraping noises were about as much, they found, as movie-house audiences could stand. As word spread around Hollywood of what had been achieved, everybody, particularly the big silent stars, was relieved. No one would ever be able to stand a full-length feature with such a noisy accompaniment, which meant that silent film production

could continue as usual. Jesse Lasky and Adolph Zukor, over at Famous
Players–Lasky, were particularly relieved at the poor results Vitagraph
had achieved, because their organization had most to lose from talking
films. Famous Players, now in process of renaming itself Paramount, still
earned hefty profits from importing films from its Berlin operations. Once
talking films were achieved, these German stars would have to start
speaking English or lose their American market.

"And who the hell wants that?" asked Lasky. "Have you ever heard
Emil Jannings speaking? Even in German, he sounds like someone's
taking a shower. In English, he'll make it sound in every scene as if it
had been shot in the bathroom."

"And who wants to hear a star talking, anyway?" echoed Jack Warner.
"The moment he opens his mouth, the public will think Jack Gilbert's a
fairy. They'll hoot every time he kisses a girl on the screen and squeals
that he loves her."

It was for this reason that when, late in 1926, the Western Electric
studios announced they had invented a movie sound system that operated
*independently* of the cameras, few studio chiefs showed any interest or
enthusiasm. When Western Electric technicians began hawking their new
invention around Hollywood, they were successively turned away by
M-G-M, Goldwyn, Famous Players/Paramount, United Artists, and Fox.
Finally, and only as a last resort, they asked Jack Warner if he would like
to attend a special showing of the new system. Jack said he was busy but
sent his brother Harry in his place.

Harry was shown a series of shorts in which an orchestra played, Dame
Nellie Melba (one of the great divas of the time) sang, and John Barrymore
recited Shakespeare. Harry sat down a skeptic and rose an enthusiast.
The words and the songs didn't make much impression on him, but he
was particularly struck by the sound and quality of the musical effects.
He tried to keep his opinion to himself, but in the end could not stop
himself from telling the Western Electric experts that he was completely
sold on their system and determined to get the exclusive rights of it for
Warner Brothers. He went back to enthuse to his brother Jack and Zanuck, and his keenness was so obviously genuine that they agreed to attend
a second showing that he had arranged especially for them. He spent
most of the time in the projection room watching their faces, and knew
long before the end of the presentation that they had been won over too.

So far as Harry was concerned, the value of the system lay solely in its
sound effects. "He didn't care a damn what the characters were saying
on the screen," said Zanuck later, "and I have to say that I didn't bother

about it much either. We all thought Harry had a point when he said: 'Do you realize what this means? From now on we can give every small town in America, and every movie house, its own 110-piece orchestra!' "

Orchestras didn't mean much to Zanuck. Except for brass bands, he had a tin ear. It was the reality of all those sound effects that excited him. "Just think," he said. "A guy points a revolver and fires and the bullet hits the wall behind the other guy. *Boom! Splat!* Next time he fires, it hits the other guy and goes right through his chest. *Phloomph!* Everyone in the audience will be sucking in a gut at the impact."

A few weeks later, Zanuck called in John Barrymore, who was one of the Warner contract stars, and told him they were going to try out an experiment with the Western Electric system. Zanuck had collaborated on a script that was, in fact, a shortened version of the Mozart opera *Don Giovanni,* and Barrymore was told to simulate songs from the score and pretend to be singing them. Then, under Zanuck's supervision, Western Electric technicians set to work to dub the music and words so that they synchronized with Barrymore's lip movements. The result was impressive, even though few people actually heard the sounds (it was later released as a silent film).

Among those who heard the sound version were Ernst Lubitsch and his assistant, Henry Blanke, now working at Warners. They were considerably impressed.

"They used the whole score," said Blanke later, "and they had somehow managed to separate the sound from the camera and get all the noises out, and they had perfected it. It was quite something to see and hear. Very exciting."

As they came out of the projection room, Jack Warner said to Zanuck: "What do we do now?"

And that was the problem. Zanuck's nights were more troubled than ever as he paced up and down the bedroom and tried to work out a way of exploiting the new system. It was Virginia, anxious to get some sleep, who eventually ventured a suggestion. At least twice a week, the two of them dined out with the Jack Warners, and on the last occasion they had been joined by the eldest member of the Warner clan, Sam, who had just returned from a trip to New York. There he had gone the rounds of all the Broadway shows, looking for prospects for Warner pictures, and he was enthusiastic about only one of them. It was a musical about a rabbi's son who becomes a popular singer, and its star, George Jessel, had turned it into a smash hit.

Sam was so enthusiastic about the play that he had purchased an option on it on behalf of Warner Brothers, and Zanuck had made the trip to New York in order to look it over, taking Virginia with him. Neither had raved over what they had seen, and, at the time, Zanuck saw no way of getting over the music and the songs to a movie audience, and those were the ingredients that had made the play into a hit. But now Virginia said:

"What about that play Sam liked so much in New York — and we thought would be ruined if it was made into a movie? Couldn't you use the new system to actually put the songs on the sound track, so that when the guy opens his mouth to sing, you actually let him sing — and the movie audience hears him?"

"Jesus!" said Zanuck, as he thoughtfully climbed into bed.

"Jesus, wouldn't that be something!" Jack Warner exclaimed when Zanuck repeated Virginia's suggestion at the studio the following morning.

"I warn you, it's a real piece of schmaltz," Zanuck told Jack, "but what makes it go is the music — and the songs. Without them, the whole thing is pure corn. But if we can only get the guy to sing on the sound track, we'll have them bawling in the aisles."

With Jack Warner's approval, it was decided to go through with the purchase of the play, and Zanuck dispatched one of their most reliable studio directors, Alan Crosland, to New York to look it over. A scriptwriter named Alfred A. Cohen was sent with him and told to come back with a draft screenplay. A month later he was ready with a shooting script, and production was scheduled for that summer on location in New York.

The name of the movie was, of course, *The Jazz Singer*, and though it was not by any means the first talking film in the history of motion pictures, it was certainly the one that brought the era of silent films to an end and changed the nature of the industry.

Darryl Zanuck was always sensitive about two things concerning himself — his size and his youthful appearance. He compensated for the first by keeping in such good physical trim that few men with twice his girth possessed his strength and endurance. He could arm-wrestle a world champion boxer and beat him (as he did several times with Jack Dempsey and Gene Tunney). The moment he had enough money, he hired the black lightweight champion boxer, Firpo, to go five rounds with him in the ring every morning, and warned him, on pain of dismissal, not to pull his punches. He could perform on the high wire, the vaulting horse, and the trapeze to well-nigh professional standards.

Polo, big-game hunting, running, and swimming were all pursued not so much because he enjoyed them but because they proved his virility, and demonstrated to the world that size was not everything, that small men could be strong, inexhaustible, and just as enduring as the average hunk of American male. Sex was important to him, too, for the same reason. His mother's behavior had long since proved to him that women were weak, fallible, and treacherous — and whores in the bargain — but it gave him some satisfaction to be able to use their weakness to demonstrate his own strength. Each female conquest not only proved that women were all alike — with the possible exception of Virginia — but also enabled him to demonstrate that in sexual matters he had the muscle and the prowess to show he was that much bigger and stronger than his appearance indicated. Sex, in fact, was just another form of pugilism or arm-wrestling, and part of the crusade to prove he was as big as any six-foot hulk on the team — and more successful with the girls, too.

He found it more difficult handling his youthful appearance. In truth, growing a mustache, wearing glasses, and smoking a big cigar only made him look more youthful. He was not the only character in Hollywood at that time who suffered from the same drawback. Irving Thalberg and David Selznick, two other cinematic geniuses who were around just then, shared Zanuck's inability to shed their schoolboy looks, but it didn't seem to bother them so much. Thalberg and Selznick once turned up on the Warner lot wearing the shorts, blazers, and caps of English schoolboys, and suggested Zanuck should join them in a Maskers Club sketch bemoaning the drawbacks, especially with girls, of always being mistaken for a kid from grade school. Selznick had even written a song they would all sing bewailing the fact that "girls never get the hots for kids in shorts" and included a bedroom scene in which a scantily clad female asks, suspiciously, of one of them:

> I know you're a knave
> From the way you behave —
> But do you SHAVE?

Zanuck lit another cigar and turned them down.

Youth was, in fact, a touchy subject with him and would continue to be so long as he remained looking years younger than his age. He had never really forgiven Charlie Chaplin for making fun of his babyish appearance when he had worked as a gag-writer at the Chaplin studios. What may have been intended as no more than gentle ridicule on Chaplin's part cut deeply into Zanuck's amour propre when he was particularly vulnerable, and he resented it and held it against the great comedian for the rest of his life. So much so that many years later he said: "I used to

go to Chaplin's films to hiss him in the places where he was making other
people laugh. I hated the bastard. And I didn't think much of him as a
comic, either. That crappy walk and simpering manner never got me the
way it did others."

But if he never forgot a slight, he never forgot a favor either, and he
always paid off both, usually with dividends. In a city where gratitude is
hard to come by and good turns are only too easily forgotten, he paid his
debts once he began to be established at Warners. It would be many
years before Mack Sennett would need his help, but when the time came
he remembered that it was Sennett who had given him his first studio
job, and rescued him from penury.

William Russell, the Western star who had threatened to walk out of
Fox if the studio didn't buy young Zanuck's script, never needed to look
for a part now that his protégé had taken charge at Warners. And then
there was Sydney Chaplin. By this time Sydney's sexual hangups had
become a favorite topic of Hollywood gossip, and as the targets of his
satyriasis grew younger and younger, there was a constant threat that
arrest and scandal would break over his head. In consequence, many of
the studios had begun shunning his services, bright actor though he might
be, in fear that he might suddenly find himself in the hands of the police
during the making of a film.

Zanuck, on the other hand, never allowed Sydney's obsessions to interfere with their friendship, even if married life did change the pattern
of their association. There was no more cruising around the bars, brothels,
and burlesque houses of downtown Los Angeles, nor embarrassing pickups among the schoolgirls at Hollywood High. And in a way this was a
relief, because he had always considered it dangerously juvenile behavior.

But as a result of his friendship, Sydney Chaplin always had a picture
to make at Warners, and entirely as a result of Zanuck's efforts on his
behalf, his salary and his status in Hollywood had been raised to stardom.
It was Zanuck who wrote the scripts for two of Sydney's greatest hits,
*The Better 'Ole*, based on the wartime hit play by Bruce Bairnsfather,
and another World War I comedy called *Oh! What a Nurse!* written as
an original story by a staff writer named Robert E. Sherwood (who would
go on to greater things).

As usual, Sydney Chaplin had an unfortunate way of repaying Zanuck's
favors, and his behavior around the Warner set time and again aroused
the ire of Jack and Harry Warner, neither of whom was particularly
scrupulous in his behavior towards the opposite sex but were much more
circumspect in the way they went about it. Charles Reisner, who directed

*The Better 'Ole*, had once worked for the San Francisco Opera when
Caruso, the great tenor, sang there, and had been much amazed at the
method the singer used to "clear his voice" by having a different sexual
encounter with a female singer in the company in the intervals between
the acts. But even he was never quite so active, he revealed later, as was
Chaplin between takes of *The Better 'Ole*. He calculated that the star
collected four different female scalps a day during the fifteen days of
shooting, and each time he disappeared into his dressing room with a
new starlet there were heavy jokes involving the title of the movie. Jack
Warner flew into a fury when he found one of the crew hanging a clapper
board on Sydney's door with his name on it, the title of the film, and
"Take 4" written underneath. He had Louella Parsons, the Hollywood
gossip writer, with him, and he feared a scandal that might rebound on
the studio.

Zanuck had to plead with his friend to curb his appetites until the end
of the working day, and Sydney promised to do so. "The trouble is, I get
so horny," he said.

Unfortunately, Sydney Chaplin's attitude towards women, and his
treatment of them as nothing more than objects to be used, did not leave
his friend unaffected. Ever since his marriage to Virginia and his es-
trangement from his mother, Zanuck had lived what, for him, could be
considered a celibate life, and his days of dalliance with the Bathing
Beauties from Mack Sennett were definitely over. It was not that his
hunger for sex was by any means appeased, and it is true that there was
opportunity at Warners; but for the moment he had scruples about that,
and he had carefully avoided "fouling his own nest," as Grandpa Torpin
would have put it.

But he was still young enough to be influenced by his friend, and
Sydney Chaplin mocked his new respectability.

"All this talent around and you're letting it go to waste?" Sydney exclaimed one day, waving his hand at a bunch of pretty extras. "What's
happened to that kid I used to know at Mack Sennett? Why, in your
position I'd be screwing the ass off of every star on the lot. What's the
matter, kid? Has marriage debollicked you? Can't get it up any longer?"

Nothing was more calculated to make Zanuck angry and feel challenged.
If Sydney Chaplin hadn't been his friend, he would have taken him around
the corner and beaten him into a pulp. No one — ever — called Zanuck's
virility into question and got away with it, and the very suggestion made
it vital to prove that the opposite was true. Otherwise, he couldn't claim
to be a man any longer. It was his father's lack of virility that had caused

his mother to walk out on him. Without virility, muscle, masculinity, you might as well be dead. He had to show his friend Sydney that he was nowhere near dead yet.

It so happened that just about this time, on the Warner lot, Zanuck was keeping a more than usually close eye on a movie being made from one of his scripts. It was called *The Little Irish Girl*, and its production marked the debut at the studio not only of an up-and-coming director, Roy del Ruth, but of the female star of the film, an attractive blonde named Dolores Costello. Dolores and her sister, Helene, were the daughters of the well-known Irish-American actor Maurice Costello. Even though Dolores was still under twenty, she was already a veteran around the movie colony, since both she and her sister had often played child parts in their father's films.

This was her first grown-up role, and Zanuck could plausibly have claimed that it was for purely professional reasons that he spent so much time watching her performance on the set. In truth, however, he was strongly attracted to her, and every encounter he had with her, whether on the set or in the projection room when they viewed the day's rushes together, convinced him that not only was she going to be a great star, but that she was also one of the most charming young women he had ever met. His feelings towards her were not exactly diminished when she showed every sign of reciprocating them. As he said many years later: "Dolores Costello was the most delightful movie star I have ever known. Beautiful, charming, willing, malleable, intelligent — and a splendid actress as well."

Was it the influence of Sydney Chaplin, and his mockery of his friend's newfound respectability, that moved Zanuck to carry his feelings a stage farther? Or was Dolores Costello to blame not just for being so seductively attractive but for responding so willingly when she discovered that the young head of production was smitten with her? At any rate, one thing led to another, and the liaison was soon the talk of Warner Brothers and then an item in the gossip columns. Sydney Chaplin walked around the studio with a knowing smirk, and the crew began whistling "When Irish Eyes Are Smiling" whenever Miss Costello came onto the set.

Fortunately, Zanuck's affairs never lasted long — not in those days, anyway — but the end of this one came in an unexpected fashion. One night, while waiting outside the studio in the Packard to drive Darryl home, Virginia was confronted by an agitated man who slid into the front seat beside her. She recognized him from his profile and from his shock of gray hair as the actor Maurice Costello. Taking her hands in his own, he began pouring out an angry torrent of words, relating in detail — with places, hours, and dates — what her husband had been doing with his daughter. He was shocked and disgusted, he said. How could her husband use his position to seduce such a nice, simple, and innocent girl? Was he going to get a divorce and marry her? Or was he going to cause a scandal and ruin Dolores's career? If he did that, Costello promised, in rising passion, "I'll kill him! I'll kill him! You tell him that. I'll kill him!"

He departed then, as the studio workers began coming out of the gates, leaving Virginia embarrassed and appalled. She knew her husband's reputation well enough to suspect the story of the liaison was only too true, that Darryl really had been sleeping with the girl. It wasn't surprise she felt, therefore, but humiliation — humiliation, particularly, over the way she had had to learn about it. To have the father of the girl spill out the sordid details about his daughter and her husband — it was really too much! Her pride was hurt, and so, literally, was her amour propre.

That night was a stormy one. Virginia Zanuck always seemed to know instinctively that her only hope of holding on to her marriage to this strange, vulnerable, prickly young man was to stand up to him. If she behaved like all the other wives in Hollywood and allowed him to think for one moment that she would complaisantly accept his little affairs, she sensed that she would lose both his respect and her marriage. She suspected that she would never turn him into a faithful husband, since there was something in his character that forced him to challenge the virtue of every attractive female he encountered. But she was determined from now on to make him feel guilty every time he betrayed her with another woman, force him to feel a sense of sin, make it seem furtive and shabby, and, above all, make him do it in such circumstances that she would never be shamed again as Maurice Costello had shamed her. And though she did not succeed, at least she made it plain she was determined never to be so humiliated again.

She put her marriage on the line by informing him she was leaving next morning for her parents' home in Wheeling, adding that her erring husband need not expect her back until he had learned to respect her. Meanwhile, she did not just throw him out of her bedroom, but out of the house as well. He spent some hours wandering the streets, feeling like a little lost boy again — but then again, not quite. For in those days when he had wandered, sad and miserable, around Los Angeles it was because a woman had let him down — his mother. But who was to blame this time? Certainly it was not Virginia who had let him down. Finally, he turned up at Sydney Chaplin's bungalow and poured out the whole story to him. It was not a situation likely to arouse his friend's sympathies, and Chaplin's reaction was both cynical and glib.

"But kid," he said, "haven't I always told you never to waste it on one woman? Play the field! There's safety in numbers. Why confine yourself to one broad, especially in Hollywood? And always remember to keep your exits covered, and make sure the boyfriend — or the father — isn't waiting for you when you come out. Or, in your case," he added, smirking, "your wife."

The only good advice Sydney gave him was to go back to Virginia and grovel, but when he returned home, prepared to throw himself on her mercy, he discovered she had already departed for West Virginia. He bombarded her with flowers, telegrams, letters, bracelets and necklaces from Cartier, all to no avail. Finally, he had to make the journey to West Virginia and woo her all over again before she finally promised to return home.

He had an extra surprise waiting for her when they got back. For some months, ever since he had become head of production at Warners, they had been building themselves a beach house at Santa Monica, and it was to this splendidly lavish abode that he drove her from the railroad depot.

Once more, he had furnished most of the rooms himself, but at the door of each one of them he had hung a notice announcing that "these furnishings are strictly temporary, and will shortly be replaced by the expert (Virginia Zanuck)."

Meanwhile, so far as Dolores Costello was concerned, he had made the great sacrifice and informed her that their association was at an end. Since she was never quite as virginally innocent as her father appeared to believe, she did not seem to be unduly dismayed by the end of the relationship and soon established a new liaison, once more confirming Zanuck's feelings about the fickleness of women. She became romantically involved with one of the most successful male heartthrobs of the day, Conrad Nagel, with whom she starred in a number of very popular films. The teaming up of Costello with Nagel was, in fact, Zanuck's farewell present to his lovely mistress. He cast them together at Warners in a movie he had written himself, called *Tenderloin*, and it was such a success that they starred together from then on and were soon causing romantic palpitations in the hearts of millions of film fans. Even professional actors and actresses were not immune to the seductive quality of their screen relationship, and Joan Fontaine wrote later:

Conrad [Nagel] had made a strong impression on me [playing] opposite Dolores Costello. So had she. I often put myself to sleep at night replaying their scenes, weeping into my pillow at unrequited love, or clutching it passionately during imaginary embraces. He was a dashing, romantic figure and Miss Costello the epitome of blonde femininity.*

Zanuck might have been forgiven if he had viewed Costello's fevered response to Nagel's embraces with a certain cynicism, but the public reaction to the new couple (plus the considerable box-office receipts) was probably adequate balm for his wounds. And he was still professional enough to be pleased with the critical reception *Tenderloin* received at its premiere in New York, even though he had been careful to write the script under one of his studio pseudonyms. It has gone down in the film records as "story and screenplay by Melville Crossman." He felt, in the circumstances, that Virginia would prefer it that way.

*The Jazz Singer* was originally written as a short story called "The Day of Atonement" by the New Yorker Samson Raphaelson, who then adapted it as a Broadway play for George Jessel. It told the story of a rabbi's son who turns his back on his father and his Orthodox Jewish faith and makes a career as a singer of jazz in nightclubs. On the night of his big debut, he receives news that his estranged father is dying. It is the Day of Atonement, which does nothing to assuage his religious guilt. Torn between this, his filial piety, and his soaring ambitions, he finally listens to his heart and his upbringing and rushes to his local synagogue to sing the Kol Nidre to his dying dad, and then returns to score a triumph with his nightclub act.

As Zanuck had already indicated to Jack Warner, it was a mawkish, treacly, and oversentimental story even for those times, and schmaltz was a good description of it. But since it was written with great skill and sincerity by a man who would become one of America's best-known playwrights, it had great gripping power and it was effective in appealing to gut emotions. Sam Warner, a devout Jew himself, genuinely believed that *The Jazz Singer* provided him with the most moving experience he had ever had in the theater. And even Zanuck was convinced that, with sound, songs, and music added, it would have enormous impact on the moviegoing public.

The idea in the beginning was to give the main role to the actor who had played the star part in the stage play, George Jessel. Jessel was

*No Bed of Roses by Joan Fontaine (William Morrow and Co., 1978).

enthusiastic at first, but when he heard he would be expected to sing in the movie, and on a sound track, he asked for $100,000, which was double his usual film fee. Zanuck was forced to turn him down on Harry Warner's orders, because Harry had now begun to get cold feet and thought they were already paying out enough for what might turn out to be the biggest film disaster of all time.

They then turned to another well-known stage star, Eddie Cantor, but he too was afraid and turned down the part because he feared for his reputation if, as he forecast, the experiment failed. Finally, the role was accepted by a so-called Mammy singer who specialized in performing in blackface. His name was Al Jolson and he had a reputation in show business as a good singer with an excellent stage presence, but a reputed tendency to supplement his lines, when the opportunity presented itself, with some exuberant ad libs. Zanuck was not worried about that. As he and the brothers Warner had envisioned the production of *The Jazz Singer*, most of the film would be silent, except for offscreen sound effects. Only the musical sequences would be done with synchronized sound, and there would be no speech.

In the late spring of 1927, director Alan Crosland entrained his company for New York, where they established themselves on the East Side and shot several sequences in the Jewish quarter around Hester Street. Afterwards they moved up to Times Square and the nightclub and theater district.

Zanuck arrived a couple of days later and henceforward was on the set every day and sat in with Crosland and the editors on the nightly viewing of the rushes.

They were about a couple of weeks into the film and were beginning the musical sequences when Jolson was called upon to sing a song called "Dirty Hands, Dirty Face." Since it would be the first time a song had ever been recorded for a major feature film, everyone was particularly nervous, especially the sound technicians, and Jolson was warned by the director, by Zanuck, and by the soundmen, that he must follow the exact directions he had been given and neither stray from his marks nor from the script. The back-up orchestra was also warned to follow instructions and to deviate neither in sound nor in movements from what they had been instructed to do.

All went well with Jolson's song, and both Zanuck and Crosland nodded at each other with delight as they listened to the words of "Dirty Hands, Dirty Face" through the earphones with which they had been provided. Catching the pleased expression on their faces, Jolson realized that he was a success, with the result that he reacted exactly as he would have done on the stage to an appreciative reception. He suddenly burst into a stream of high-spirited ad libs:

JOLSON (*staring out at the audience as applause came on the sound track*): "Wait a minute, wait a minute, you ain't heard nothin' yet! Wait a minute, I tell ya, ya ain't heard nothin'! You wanna hear 'Toot Toot Tootsie'? All right, hold on, hold on. [*Turning to the band leader.*] Listen, Louis, listen — play 'Toot Toot Tootsie.' Three choruses, you understand? In the third chorus, I whistle. [*Waving a hand above his head.*] Now give it to 'em hard and heavy! Go right ahead!"

The band, too stunned to disobey, struck up with "Toot Toot Tootsie," a well-known popular song, and Jolson began to sing. Crosland was appalled. The sound engineers clutched their ears in anguish. Only Zanuck stayed calm.

That night, as they moved uptown to the specially equipped Fox cinema where the rushes were usually shown, everyone was glum. Crosland feared the first big song sequence of the film had been ruined, but hoped that something could be salvaged from it by judicious editing. He was so worried that he did not seem to notice, when the screen showed the "Dirty Hands" scene, that it came over wonderfully and that Jolson sang and performed superbly. All he could think of were the next few disastrous minutes when the singer went beyond his script and ruined the sequence.

He watched and heard it through in ever increasing gloom, ordered it to be played over again, and then said finally, as Jolson began his ad libs: "I think we can save it — this is where we cut."

"Oh, no we don't," said a voice from behind him.

It was Darryl Zanuck. He did not look gloomy at all.

"Let's leave it in," he said. "For the time being, anyway."

Crosland looked at him in astonishment.

"What, all of it?"

"All of it," said Zanuck. "Words, song, gestures, all of it."

In the next few days, Zanuck and Crosland went through the ad libbed sequence again and again and again, and were soon convinced that it was one of the most effective scenes in the film.

The next week they shot a scene in which Jolson tries to explain to his screen mother, who has always shut her ears to the sound of it in the past, what jazz is all about. At the end of a passionate peroration, he sits down at the piano, on which nothing but religious and classical music has ever been played, and begins to accompany himself as he sings a song (it was "Blue Skies," especially written for the film by Irving Berlin). In the middle of his performance, who should walk in but his rabbi father, who lifts his hands in horror at the barbarous sounds and cries in a thunderous voice: "STOP!"

This time it was no accident that the microphones were working and picked up both dialogue and song. The scene had, in fact, been deliberately written and inserted into the script by Darryl Zanuck. By this time he had made up his mind, and decided that films should not only have sounds but should talk as well. He instructed Alan Crosland to leave the first sequence, with its ad-libbed dialogue, in the final cut of the film, and added several other spoken scenes before the shooting was finished.

Jack Warner was alarmed when he heard what was happening and bombarded Zanuck with telegrams warning him to cut out these "talking tricks." When the company returned to Hollywood and the roughly assembled film was run through for the quartet of brothers, they neither objected nor applauded. It was obvious that they were stunned, puzzled, and unsure of themselves. Even Zanuck was not quite certain how the moviegoing public would react to the actual talking sequences, and there were long studio confabulations about the risk they might be running by keeping them in.

"What if they laugh when they hear that guy talking?" said Harry Warner. "God, we'll be ruined."

Opinion around the studio was divided until the last moment before the first public showing, and only Virginia Zanuck, who had sat in on most of the arguments and projection room screenings, never had any doubts at all. She was an easy weeper at the movies (a "sob sister," as she called herself) and knew that if she didn't shed tears over a scene in one of her husband's pictures, he would cut it out of the final version. He was vastly encouraged by her reactions to *The Jazz Singer*. She not only shed tears each time the film was shown, but she told her husband after the first run-through: "I almost died when Al Jolson spoke for the first time. It was as thrilling as hearing the voice of God."

The world premiere of *The Jazz Singer* took place at the Warner Theatre in New York City on the night of October 6, 1927, and it was a memorable occasion in the history of the movies. The audience was just as thunderstruck by the sound of Jolson's voice as Virginia had been. Not only did they shed tears over the most mawkish incidents in the story, but when Jolson suddenly shouted: "Wait a minute, you ain't heard nothin' yet!" a murmur of surprise and wonder susurrated through the theater and then rose to excited shouts of approval and a veritable storm of applause. As

Jolson lectured his screen mother on the attractions of jazz and then began to demonstrate its beguilements by singing "Blue Skies," there were shouts of pleasure from the audience and then everybody was on his or her feet, wildly applauding.

The climax of the audience reactions came, appropriately enough, after the concluding scene in the film, when Jolson sings once more to his mother and falls dramatically on one knee, turning to face the camera and loudly and emotionally singing the single word: "Mammy!"

As the scene faded from the screen, the audience was transformed into what critics next day described as "a roaring, milling, battling, cheering, tear-stained mob." The atmosphere in the theater was volcanic. "Evening-gowned women," one critic wrote, "began pouring into the foyer, their hair awry, tears still glistening on their powdered bare shoulders."

Virginia Zanuck was equally moved. As she stared down at the milling crowd, she turned with shining eyes towards her husband, flung her arms around his neck, and, as he put it later, "soaked me with tears right down to my underwear."

By an ironic twist, it was a night of triumph that Zanuck did not have to share with his bosses. In normal circumstances, all the brothers Warner would have been there to accept the plaudits and take the credit for the splendid reception of the film. And rightly so, in many ways. It was they who had put up all the money and taken all the risks, and although it was Darryl Zanuck who had seen the production through to completion, they were the ones whose faith had backed the system and the venture, and now they had earned the respect, if not the gratitude, of the whole film industry for having brought it off.

But, as fate would have it, there was not a single member of the Warner quartet present at the world premiere of Hollywood's (and their) first talking picture. The reason for their absence could have provided a plot for another film with a story-line almost as schmaltzy as that of *The Jazz Singer*.

In the film, the hero's father, Rabbi Rabinowitz, dies without ever hearing his son sing and score a smash hit on his opening night. Sam Warner did likewise. Having first discovered *The Jazz Singer* and bought it for Warner Brothers, he did not live to see it score a smash hit at its world premiere. Rushed to the hospital for an emergency operation, he had a heart attack and died on October 5, just twenty-four hours before the opening of the film he had been responsible for fathering.

His three brothers were shattered by the news of Sam's death, which was telephoned to them in New York just before the premiere. In accordance with Jewish custom, they gathered up their wives and relatives and took the train back to Hollywood for their brother's funeral.

It was left to their non-Jewish studio chief, Darryl Zanuck, to take the plaudits and accept the credit for the first showing of what was probably the most momentous movie in the history of the motion picture industry.

# NO KEYS TO THE KINGDOM

H OLLYWOOD in general and Warner Brothers in particular made so much money out of talking pictures that they did not even notice the Wall Street crash of 1929 and the Depression that followed. Everything they touched in the way of movies, providing it had sound effects, turned to gold. Shortly after the success of *The Jazz Singer*, which, it may be remembered, was a talking film only in certain sequences, Darryl Zanuck set about making the "First All Talking Film," as the billboards subsequently dubbed it. He had a two-reeler on hand called *The Lights of New York*, and this he decided to expand into a full-length feature with spoken dialogue.

Fortunately, Jack and Harry Warner, who would have had to approve the budget, were away in Europe. Zanuck told the director, Bryan Foy, to go ahead and spend up to $75,000 on the remake, this being the limit he dared release without securing official Warner approval. The result was probably one of the worst films in the history of Hollywood, with an excruciatingly embarrassing plot and some of the loudest sound effects ever to come out of a loudspeaker. But it was a howling success and eventually grossed over $3 million for the company.

In the meantime, Zanuck added sound and dialogue to every other movie being made on the lot, and even his beautiful Dolores Costello had to murmur "Darling!" and "Oh, dearest!" and heavy, ecstatic sighs between her passionate clinches with Conrad Nagel. There was, not surprisingly, a follow-up to *The Jazz Singer*, with Al Jolson talking and singing and ad-libbing his head off in a trashy sentimental saga called *Sonny Boy*. It was the greatest moneymaker in the history of Hollywood until the gross receipts from *Gone With the Wind* superseded it years later. Warner Brothers became the film city's most successful studio, and Jack and Harry waxed fat on the money Zanuck was making for them. Jack continued to encourage the belief in Zanuck that one day he would be put on the board of the company and maybe even have his name up there on the billboards: WARNER BROTHERS/ZANUCK PRESENT. He became convinced that Jack, disappointed with his own son, had designated him his rightful heir, at least so far as his movie interests were concerned. Jack deliberately did nothing to disabuse him. He was only too well aware that other Hollywood companies were now trying to steal the boy wonder away from Warners, and he was ready to dangle any kind of bait in front of Zanuck to persuade him to stick around. As Wilson Mizner said of him later:

"Jack's a real bad 'un. He's the only man I know who lines his pockets with rubber so's he can steal the soup. He's mean, he's a liar, and he'll do anything, promise anything, to get his way."

What Mizner did not add was that Jack was a charmer too, and even the victims to whom he lied so smoothly never really came to dislike him. He had a beguiling manner that made his associates believe in him even when they knew in their hearts that he was conning them. He had a way of suggesting to Zanuck that yes, he did lie to all the others, that around the studio you could never depend on his promises, but that Darryl was the cherished exception and he must never forget that. He was special and their relationship was different. To him he would never, ever lie. And Zanuck, who had grown wise to the ways of Hollywood, who had watched his wily boss in operation and knew him to be a cheat, continued to believe in what Jack was telling him. *He's got too much admiration and respect to lie to me.*

In 1930, at the height of the Warner boom, Jack and his then wife, Irma, took Darryl and Virginia on a vacation to the South of France and installed them in the bridal suite at the Hôtel du Cap at Cap d'Antibes. From the loving way in which Jack treated Irma whenever they were together, few would have guessed that he had a mistress waiting for him back in America and that he was planning to dump his wife the moment he returned to the States.

Every night after dinner at some fashionable Riviera restaurant, Jack would send the wives home in his chauffeur-driven car and take Darryl to one of the gambling casinos in Cannes, Juan-les-Pins, or Monte Carlo. He was a big gambler and not a very successful one, which is one of the reasons why he didn't like having Irma along. "She bitches so much when I lose," he complained. Zanuck watched in wonder at the sums his boss lost at the chemin-de-fer table and marveled at the heady risks that even rich men like Jack were willing to take.

Gambling, win or lose, seemed to act on his companion as an aphrodisiac, and when they finished at the tables the routine was nearly always the same. Jack would introduce him to the sophisticated relief available in the expert arms of the Riviera's *poules de luxes.*

Emerging at dawn from one of these sessions, Zanuck would often notice that Jack had tears rolling down his cheeks as they strolled along the Croisette.

"You know," Jack wept on one occasion, "I sometimes feel like killing myself after a night like this. I've lost a fortune and I've been unfaithful to that dear, precious wife of mine. I love Irma more than life itself, and I feel like a bastard for taking the risk of hurting her. If she finds out, that is," he added. Then turning to Zanuck and putting an arm around his shoulders, he drew him close and went on: "You won't tell her, will you? You won't even whisper a word to your Virginia, will you?"

Zanuck assured him he would be as silent as the grave.

"Because I really love that woman," Jack said, "and I'd do anything to avoid causing her pain."

If Zanuck was given this revelation of Jack's hypocrisy towards his wife, nevertheless he did not allow it to influence his faith in his boss's sincerity towards himself. After all, Irma was just another woman, and women only got what they deserved. With men it was different, and with Jack and him it was special.

So although, by this time, all sorts of offers were now coming in from other Hollywood studios, Zanuck resisted all temptations to move to bigger things. So optimistic was he, in fact, about his future at Warners that the only person who gave him a pang of doubt during this period of euphoria was his idol, Ernst Lubitsch, who also happened to be staying at the Hôtel du Cap while the Zanucks were there with the Warners. There were, in fact, several big Hollywood names in the hotel at the time, including Gloria Swanson, Pola Negri, Ronald Colman, and the directors Lewis Milestone and George Cukor. One morning Virginia came onto the terrace, stretched out her arms, and stared in wonder across the rock pool at all the beautiful people, at the deep blue sea, and the hazy mountains of the Esterel beyond.

"Isn't this *paradise!*" she breathed.

Lubitsch, who had come up behind the Zanucks and heard Virginia's remark, sighed and said sadly: "Ah, my dear, you should have been here before the war. In those days half the monarchs and aristocracy of Europe stayed here. Then the place was filled with princes and princesses, with grand dukes and duchesses, and the hotel register read like the Almanach de Gotha." He looked around and sneered. "Now there's no one here but Hollywood bums! Fairbanks! Chaplin! Swanson and Garbo!" He snorted the names as if he were gargling them. "All these ridiculous people!"

At that moment his jaundiced eye was caught by someone else, and he pointed a quivering, indignant finger across the terrace. "Phonies and cheats, the lot of them! Do you know of a bigger fake and liar than *that* one? They should be ashamed to give him a room in the hotel!"

Zanuck was irritated to note that Lubitsch was pointing at the elephantine figure of none other than Jack Warner. He was aware that Jack had recently reneged on several promises he had made to Lubitsch, and that they were about to lose the director, despite Zanuck's efforts to keep him, to Paramount Pictures. So he put down the director's remarks to personal resentment. All the same, such condemnation from Lubitsch, whom he trusted and admired, sounded a warning bell, and its note was silenced only when Jack himself came over, kissed Virginia an affectionate good morning, and said: "How is the lovely wife of my favorite man today?"

In fact, so fond had both the Zanucks become of Jack, and so confident were they of their future at Warner Brothers, that it was while staying at the Hôtel du Cap that Virginia made up her mind. Since her marriage she had taken all possible steps against becoming pregnant, but now she decided the time had come to add an extra dimension to the union. They were now secure enough, she informed her husband, to start a family and informed him that she had thrown caution to the winds — or, rather, into the Mediterranean.

The following year, in 1931, she gave birth to a daughter, and she was christened Darrylin. Another girl was born two years later and named Susan. It was not until December, 1934, that Virginia gave birth to a son. It was unusual for the time, but Zanuck had been present at the births of all his children, and on this occasion, when the baby was drawn clear and he saw it was a male child, he gave a loud whoop of triumph and joy.

He had never made any secret of the fact that girls were not what he wanted — not as members of his family, anyway — and that all he was interested in was having a son.

"It was the most precious gift I ever gave him," Virginia said later. "He was the proudest man in Hollywood — no, in the world!"

In a land where young men increasingly take over the reins of power, American executives of tender years have learned to be cautious in flexing their corporate muscles and discreet in utilizing the privileges of their position. The *Wall Street Journal* publishes hints to young executives on how to handle "the special kind of management problems" involved in supervising people older than themselves, and advises them, where necessary, to play it cool or even humble.

That was never Hollywood's way, where a man likes to show he is the boss even if it means cracking a whip, and a young head of production who fails to make his position clear is likely to be taken for a gofer or a waiter. Darryl Zanuck did not know how to be humble, anyway, and so long as the three surviving Warner brothers were still technically his superiors, he tried to make it clear that it was really he who made all the decisions, and let no one be in any doubt that he was in charge of the studio operations.

One of the young men who joined Warner Brothers about this time (in the early 1930s) was Milton Sperling, who subsequently became a well-known Hollywood producer, and he began by believing that Zanuck was the boss, but soon came to realize that no one, not even Zanuck, really shared the power with the owners. That, however, did not prevent Zanuck from behaving as if he actually was one of the bosses.

"The atmosphere these men — Jack and Harry Warner, and Zanuck — created around them," Sperling said later, "gave you the feeling that when you went to work for them you were becoming a subject of a private kingdom. A kingdom which was, in fact, run by very young men. When I first knew Darryl Zanuck he was about thirty years old, but he seemed like a father to me because I was only nineteen. Jack Warner was nearly forty and that seemed very old. But you kind of got the feeling when you joined that you were being sworn into a sort of citizenship. These men may have been insecure themselves for all I know, but they created around themselves a sense of permanence, of security, loyalty. In those days in Hollywood, studio loyalty was a factor of your life. If you were a Warner employee, or a Fox employee, or a Metro employee, that was your home, your country. You voted en bloc for your company's films at the Academy Awards. You played baseball against the other studios. You had T-shirts with your studio's name on them. It was just like being a subject, and a patriotic subject at that. People who lived and worked beyond the studio walls just didn't belong, and you were prepared to fight them off, like the Philistines."

Sperling met Zanuck for the first time when he arrived in Hollywood in 1932, but he had seen him, admired him, and envied him from afar long before that.

"Even as a boy I was always interested in films," Sperling said later, and he had become obsessed with them, and determined to make a career of them, after he got a vacation job at the old Astoria Studios on Long Island. That was when he was still at school and living with his parents in New York.

There was a distinguished group of directors and writers making films on the Astoria lot at the time, including such future distinguished directors and producers as George Cukor, Walter Wanger, and Lewis Milestone, and such writers as Donald Ogden Stewart, Ben Hecht, and Herman Mankiewicz. Even Ernst Lubitsch had once worked at the Astoria studios. They were a friendly bunch of technicians, and they all took a shine to Sperling, who was young, worshipful, and eager, and bright into the bargain. One year, when they all went on a joint trip to Europe, they even took the kid along with them, and it was his first trip abroad. One of the places they stayed at was the Hôtel du Cap in Antibes, and it was there he had both Jack Warner and Darryl Zanuck pointed out to him, though he was not introduced to them at the time.

Not long after their return, Paramount took over the Astoria Studios and Walter Wanger was fired from his job as production chief. The others were so incensed that they decided, out of loyalty, to quit their jobs too and to move out as a team to the West Coast. Cukor, Stewart, and Milestone, who had become fondest of their young gofer, suggested that he forget his parents' idea of going to college in New York and come out with them to Hollywood, where they would find him a job in the studios.

"So I did," said Sperling. "First of all I went to work for Milly [Milestone] at United Artists, which was then under the control of Joe Schenck, but that fell apart in about six months because Milly got into a fight with Schenck and quit, and I quit along with him. I remember walking into Schenck's office that day and saying 'I quit!' and he said, 'Who the hell are you?' as I was walking out. He'd never seen me before. 'Who the hell are you to quit?' he kept yelling."

True to his promise, Milestone made it his first priority to get young Sperling a new job. He picked up the telephone and called Darryl Zanuck at Warners, and Sperling remembers him saying: "I have a very bright kid here — I think you should hire him." He arranged an appointment for Sperling to see Zanuck over at the studio. That was to be the first time the two met, and it gave Sperling a taste of the nature and quality of the man.

"I came to Zanuck's outer office [at Warners]," he said later, "and his secretary buzzed him on the intercom and said: 'Milton Sperling is here,' and a crisp voice replied: 'Oh yes, when you hear the buzzer, send him in.' So I waited for about ten minutes, and then there was a buzz. The secretary motioned to me, and I walked in through what turned out to be double doors. I opened the first and hit my nose on the second door, and opened that and walked into the room, and I saw a most extraordinary scene. There were six men sitting around the walls of this enormous office, as in a ballroom, and the desk was at the far end. My eye went to the desk, and there was no one there. All these men were looking at the desk and then turning and looking at me, then turning back to the desk, and then looking at me. As I stood there, Zanuck suddenly popped up from behind the desk and he had a short stick [it was a polo mallet] which he aimed at me and, simulating a Tommy gun, went 'tt-tt-tt-tt!' And then, as I still stood there, Zanuck shouted: 'Fall down, you son of a bitch! You're dead!' So I did. And then I heard him say to the others: 'That's the way Cagney plays the scene. The guy walks in, Cagney's behind the desk, and he shoots the shit out of the guy as he comes through the door.' Then I saw a natty pair of custom-made shoes standing near my face, and a voice said: 'All right, kid, you can get up now.' "

What Sperling did not know at the time was that Zanuck was illustrating a scene from what turned out to be *The Public Enemy*, the first film James Cagney had been signed up to do for Warners, and it signaled a radical change in the nature of gangster films as Hollywood knew them. One of the creative talents Zanuck had picked up once Jack Warner made him head of production was a bright young director named Mervyn LeRoy, who strongly believed that the time was ripe for a new wave of gangster films. He pointed out to Zanuck that Hollywood had always done well with stories about crime, violence, robbers, outlaws, and reminded him that the first big hit in the original bioscopes had been a smash-and-grab thriller called *The Great Train Robbery*.

LeRoy wanted to make a film out of a book called *Little Caesar*, a new gangster thriller written by a popular writer named W. R. Burnett, and thought a Warner contract star named Edward G. Robinson would be ideal to play the cigar-chomping Chicago gangster. Zanuck gave him his head and found he had a hit on his hands. What is more, both exhibitors and movie fans clamored for more. So he gave them more, and started the successful cycle of gangster films for which Warner Brothers became famous in the early 1930s.

LeRoy made other gangster hits for him, including *The Mouthpiece* and *Smart Money*, and they had what proved to be their greatest success of all with an attack on the Southern system of prison camp punishment, *I Am a Fugitive from a Chain Gang,* starring an actor from the New York stage called Paul Muni. But over the denouement of the film, Zanuck and LeRoy had their differences. They had deliberately made the chain gang sequences as unrelenting as possible, and LeRoy was satisfied that movie fans had been given just about as much as they could take of graphic scenes demonstrating man's cruelty to man. But when Zanuck saw the film at a preview, he came away feeling that the movie lacked a final, annihilating punch. It needed something extra.

So he went home, paced the bedroom for a few hours, and then sat down to provide a new ending. It became a movie classic. The scene he added showed Paul Muni, having escaped from the chain gang, on the run from the prison authorities and forced to live a clandestine life. One dark night he has a meeting with the girlfriend whom he had planned to marry before he got arrested and sentenced to the chain gang. They touch each other in the furtive darkness, and then the girl, trying to grasp the kind of fugitive life he is leading, asks him about it. LeRoy shot that scene and did it well, and Muni gave everything he had as an actor to make it effective. But it was Zanuck who thought it up.

CLOSE UP

(Girl's face)

But how do you live?

CLOSE UP

(Man's face. His eyes have a glint of fearful madness in them)

I steal!

(He runs off into the darkness as we)

FADE OUT

Coming at the end of a grim but dramatic movie, it hit moviegoers where it hurt the most and sent them out of the theater stunned. But LeRoy always thought it was just too much for the audience to bear and never liked the ending. Zanuck, on the other hand, was delighted by its impact. To him making pictures was just like a boxing match, and nothing went over like a final knock-out blow.

The rehearsal of the Cagney film into which young Sperling had stumbled was a good example of the type of action Zanuck was trying to insert into the new kind of movies he was beginning to make. He had long since grown tired of the sloppy sentimentalities of the first talking films, and was convinced that the filmgoing public was ripe for a dose of realism of the kind they rarely encountered in plays or movies. Why did films always have to have a happy ending? Why did the worst kind of gangsters turn out to have hearts of gold? Why did movies always sentimentalize women and spend so much time maundering on about love? When was someone going to cast an actress in the role of an honest-to-god straightforward tart?

All these questions were running through his mind at the time he read a script that had recently been submitted to Warners. It was called *The Public Enemy,* and its two authors (Kubec Glassman and John Bright) had made a valiant attempt to get away from the usual gangster movie by squeezing any drop of sentimentality out of their story. The principal character was a young punk who was so tough that when his gangster boss is killed by a fall from a horse, he goes around to the stables and puts a bullet through the horse's head "to teach it to be more careful whose neck it breaks in the future." The punk's girlfriend is a loud-mouthed blonde who talks too much.

Unfortunately, the scriptwriters had drained most of the energy out of their story along with the sentimentality, and even they could not avoid softening the ending by having the punk's weeping mother declaring that "he was a nice kid who went wrong" when her son gets his comeuppance in the final scenes.

But Zanuck still thought it could make a good, tough gangster movie, providing both the director and the principal actor could keep its quality of unrelenting and unsentimental realism. But which director and which actor? Eschewing the services of Mervyn LeRoy, who, he suspected, would blunt the impact of the story by toning down some of its scenes, he picked instead a director who, though still young, had already gained a reputation as a hardened cynic. His name was William Wellman, and Zanuck went to work with him to enliven the shooting script and began injecting new scenes.

The principal actor was a much more difficult problem, until one night, when watching the rushes in the projection room as usual, he had a flash of inspiration. The English actor George Arliss was on the lot at the time making a picture called *The Man Who Played God,* and Zanuck was particularly anxious to see how it came out. For one thing, he thought Arliss was a terrific actor and could be turned into a profitable Warner star by making use of the very qualities of breeding, culture, exaggerated English accent, and snobbishness that were usually thought to be poison at the U.S box office. He was also interested in the performance of a new young actress whom he had personally signed up a few days earlier and cast opposite Arliss in the film's principal female role. Her name was

Bette Davis, and she was doing well. Arliss thought her "a splendid little actress who will go far."

There was another of his "finds" to be seen in the rushes that night, but in him he had less hope. On a recent trip to New York he had seen performances on Broadway by two young players who had struck him as such fresh and vigorous personalities that he had signed them up and brought them out to the Coast. He had had more success with the female member of the duo, an actress called Joan Blondell, than he had with the male player, a song-and-dance man named James Cagney. Finally, in a desperate attempt to give him something to do, Zanuck had told the casting office to give him a small role in *The Man Who Played God,* and here he was in the rushes. He was awful. Miscast and obviously uncomfortable in his role.

And then suddenly, in one of the loops of film that had not yet been cut, Cagney was seen turning towards the camera. Assuming the scene was over, he was curling his lip in frustration and anger, and from him came the words:

"For God's sake, who wrote this crappy dialogue, anyway?"

Zanuck knew at once he had his man. Here was the tough young punk he was looking for.

After Milton Sperling had picked himself up and dusted himself off following that first startling encounter with Darryl Zanuck in his office at Warner Brothers, he found himself standing in front of the great man's desk and being questioned about his qualifications for a job. He remembered that Zanuck seemed in high good humor, as if the script conference that young Sperling had just witnessed — and in which he had played his inadvertent role — stimulated the production chief. He was to discover that nothing enlivened Zanuck more than to inject a new incident into a movie script and then illustrate it for his staff of writers, directors, and producers.

"He was a born ham," Sperling said later. "He just loved to act out a scene."

Now he looked across the wide spaces of his desk at the young jobseeker from New York and said: "Milly tells me you're a pretty smart kid. Is there anything you would particularly like to do here? Can you take dictation?"

Sperling couldn't, but said he could, and Zanuck thought about it for a moment. Then he went on: "Okay. You understand a story? You worked for Milly and Cukor and Stewart and Mank, so you must understand what a story is. I want you to be my conference secretary. It's a whole new job," he said, obviously having just invented it. "I want you to sit in the room with me when I have a conference, just like now, and I want you to take notes of everything I say. Then you type it all up and give it to all these other guys, so they'll know everything I say."

For the next year, that was what Sperling did, and found out by the end of it that he knew more about what makes a good scene and a good movie than anything he had previously learned from his earlier mentors at the Astoria Studios. Zanuck was a born storyteller.

"I was thrown in right at the deep end," he said later, "because all the conferences I sat in on during those first few weeks were concerned with the production of Jimmy Cagney's first big film, *The Public Enemy*, and I soon realized that Zanuck was determined to make it into a blockbuster. He was all hyped up about it, and kept repeating to Willie Wellman and his crew that they mustn't let a drop of sentimentality seep into the action. 'Everyone in this movie is tough, tough, tough,' he kept saying. 'People are going to say the characters are immoral, but they're not because they don't *have* any morals. They steal, they kill, they lie, they hump each other because that's the way they're made, and if you allow a decent human feeling or a pang of conscience to come into their makeup, you've lost 'em and changed the kind of movie we're making.' "

During one of the many morning conferences, when the director and the crew filed in, they found Zanuck sitting behind his desk with a phonograph in front of him. Presently, when they were all seated, he leaned over, put the needle in the groove, and the voice of Eddie Cantor was heard singing the words of "I'm Forever Blowing Bubbles." Zanuck looked towards the rear door of his office (which led to the bathroom he shared with Jack Warner) and shouted: "Okay!"

A voice was heard saying: "Buzz! Buzz!" as if imitating a bell, and Zanuck got up and went to the door and opened it. Milton Sperling came in. He was covered from head to foot in a sack, which was looped around his neck.

"Why, Tom!" said Zanuck, in a high-pitched voice.

Sperling grimaced as he stumbled into the room, and, looking at Zanuck, said: "Hello, Mom," and then fell flat on his face.

Zanuck stared down at him for a moment, and then turned to Wellman.

"There's our final scene," he said. "We close with the same music we opened with."

Then to Sperling:

"Okay. On your feet!"

As Sperling wrestled with the sack and clumsily scrambled to his feet, Zanuck pointed to the phonograph and said: "And turn that goddamn thing off!"

There were two main female roles in *The Public Enemy*, Cagney's mistress, played by Mae Clark, and a sinuous gangster's moll played by an M-G-M star he had borrowed from Irving Thalberg, Jean Harlow. Zanuck made it quite clear whenever she was on the set that he thought Harlow quite the most seductive woman he had ever met, and the crew sometimes sniggered at the way in which he was always putting his hands on her. Like Alla Nazimova (and like his mother) she was an ash-blonde (though in her case they called it a platinum-blonde) and he gave her some of the film's most effective scenes with Cagney. But he was too much of a professional to allow her to overbalance the action, and she was never allowed to overshadow her fellow players in the sequences where it mattered.

One of the places where it mattered a lot was the sequence showing Cagney becoming increasingly irritated by his live-in girlfriend, who was played by Mae Clark as a faded blonde with a case of verbal diarrhea. She yaks so much that she is driving Cagney to distraction, and in the original script there is a scene in the bedroom where he finally turns over to her and says: "Shut your mouth and open your legs, for God's sake!" Even in a film of this nature, Zanuck knew they would never be allowed to get away with a scene like that, especially in those censorious times, and for days they wrestled with the problem. Finally, they worked it out that the scene should be played at the breakfast table, inferentially after a night of sexual activity, with Cagney suffering from a bad case of post-coital hangover. As his mistress babbles on, he can endure it no longer. Verbal pleas to her to belt up having had no effect, he finally leans across and slaps her.

But when Cagney and Clark rehearsed it together, Zanuck was dissatisfied. The scene didn't have the impact he was looking for and he was puzzled about how to overcome it. And then at one of the script conferences, with Sperling busily taking notes, he had an idea.

"Let's make sure that the breakfast table is properly set up for a real honest-to-god American breakfast," he said, "with juice, half grapefruit and all the trimmings. Cagney has a half grapefruit in front of him, and when he can't stand her yakking any longer, he doesn't lean across and slap her. He picks up the half grapefruit and he stretches out and pushes it into her yakkety-yakking face."

It turned out to be one of the most effective scenes in a very hard-nosed film, and even those critics who called *The Public Enemy* immoral saluted Cagney and the director for that moment. "But it was my idea, the grapefruit," Zanuck said later. "I thought of it in a script conference."

He was pleased with the impact of the film, even though the critics attacked it, and was afterwards quoted as saying about it: "When I made *The Public Enemy* I was way ahead in my thinking. No love story, but loaded with sex and violence."

Not only were many of the critics shocked by it, but so were some of the exhibitors and self-appointed censors of morals around the nation — to such an extent that the Warners became alarmed and, over Zanuck's objections, followed the episode of Cagney's death in the final scene with a little screen homily saying: "The end of Tom Powers is the end of every hoodlum."

To Zanuck's way of thinking, *The Public Enemy* was the definitive gangster film, and, so far as he was concerned, the end of the cycle. He was no longer particularly interested in them after that, and began to look around for a new theme to start a new cycle.

Meanwhile, *The Public Enemy* made a large amount of money for Warners. And, of course, it made James Cagney into one of Hollywood's biggest stars.

# *TEN*

# BREAK

I N THE BEGINNING, it seemed to Milton Sperling that Darryl Zanuck was the king of the Warner studio and monarch of all he surveyed, and he was both awed at his power and shocked at the autocratic manner in which he wielded it. His behavior around the studios reminded Sperling, sometimes with uncomfortable force, of the posturings of Benito Mussolini, the dictator of Italy, who was getting a lot of publicity in the newsreels about this time. The fact that Zanuck often dressed like Mussolini, in tight breeches and riding boots, did not distress him unduly, since boots and breeches had been de rigueur as a uniform around the studios since the earliest days of films. But he was perturbed by Zanuck's swaggering manner, the habit he had of swinging a polo mallet as he strode the streets of the lot, and by the arrogance, the often thoughtless ruthlessness of his behavior.

"Shortly after I joined Warners," said Sperling later, "I was coming out of the studio commissary after typing Zanuck's script conference notes. He always ate late, and I saw him leaving the executive dining room and making his way back to his office. He was, as usual, followed by his court, assistants, producers, stooges, and others in his crowd. And he was talking away, and suddenly, while he was still talking, I was astonished to see him unbutton his fly, and, still talking, he pissed against the wall of one of the stages. The streets of the lot were crowded and there were literally scores of people around of both sexes, extras, crews, people mixed in filming. It didn't faze him one bit. He was as innocently shameless as an Italian street urchin. I was still a well-brought-up Jewish boy at the time, and I was shocked."

Zanuck had other habits that flustered Sperling, even though, as the months went by, he became more accustomed to the crudeness of studio life and somewhat coarsened by it. But there were still things Zanuck did that stuck in his craw. "I've mentioned that he used to go around the studio swinging a polo stick — or, rather, a cut-off version of one to strengthen his wrist," he said later. "But not always. Shortly after I got there, I found he had swapped the polo stick for what was known as a goosing-stick. It was like a cattle prod. He used to walk around the studio with one in his hand, and he would unexpectedly goose people whenever they turned their backs on him. Only certain people, though, his stooges. There was one man who worked for him for years and years, a man known as Pathé Nathan, a pratfall artist in silent pictures (named after the company that first hired him). When he goosed him, Pathé would leap high in the air like a ballet dancer. And Zanuck would scream with laughter."

Because of the nature of his work, Sperling found he was often a member of Zanuck's entourage as they made their way from stage to stage, and he remembers the day when they were walking along a studio street and an old actor planted himself in front of him and said, in his grand tragedian's voice: "Darryl, can I talk to you a minute?"

Zanuck said: "I told you to stay away from me, you old cocksucker!"

And then Sperling saw him suddenly lift up his boot and stamp on the old man's foot.

"He put his heel right down on his instep, and he said: 'Now don't come back — get out of here.' Well, the old man may have been way out of line and it could be that he had previously provoked Zanuck into a rage. But all the same, it was an act of bald physical violence. And Zanuck never gave it a second thought, just walked on, obviously without guilt, none whatsoever. It was a revelation to me. I watched him with discretion after that, how he behaved, how he reacted, and I came to the conclusion that he was a single-purpose machine, a filmmaking machine with predictable reflexes, and that was what he was good at and obsessed with."

That was at the beginning of their association. It seemed to Sperling during their first few months together that the tyrannical behavior Zanuck displayed around the studio came with the position, and he was acting like an all-powerful monarch because that was what he was and that was how Hollywood expected monarchs to behave. And it confirmed his conception of these Hollywood studios as being exactly like little medieval kingdoms, where the man on the throne possessed the almighty power to do with his subjects exactly what he liked. It was not until some time had gone by and he came to know both Zanuck and the studio set-up better that he formed a different opinion of his boss's authority. He still

believed that Warners was a kind of principality, a little kingdom, but
he came to the conclusion that Zanuck acted the way he did not because
he was king of the castle and monarch of all he surveyed, but because he
was beginning to suspect he never would be. He was compensating with
these petty displays of imperial arrogance for the fact that real power was
not in his grasp and would never be his. Not in this kingdom, anyway.

"Darryl had always been so sure that he was the crown prince and heir
to the Warner throne," said Sperling, "and only now was he beginning
to realize that Jack Warner had never been serious about making him his
heir. He had been conned into believing that he was the crown prince,
whereas, though head of production, he was really just like the rest of
the studio employees, beholden like them to the next ones up in the
pecking order — in his case, all the members of the Warner family, who
came first between him and Jack and him and the throne. And I think
what made him mad was the fact that he was beginning to realize that
King Jack was squeezing the last drops of loyalty out of him before denying
him the succession. It was frustration, I think, that was making him behave
the way he did." The ironic thing is that Sperling himself was not immune
to Jack Warner's blandishments. After about a year around the studio,
watching the Byzantine maneuvering that went on around the place, he
became involved himself. He became what he himself called "Jack's beard."

"Jack was dallying at that time with a woman," he said. "And Jack, of
course, was still married to Irma. Well, he needed some excuse with
Irma to stay out at night. I was his Friday-night excuse, mainly because
I was Jewish and had some Orthodox background. Jack's father and mother,
who were Orthodox Jews, had a Friday-night supper which he would go
to, and he started to take me along. The reason his father wanted Jack
there was not only for the traditional Friday-night sabbath ceremony but
because he wanted him to play pinochle with him after dinner. It was
understood with Irma, who was suspicious about her husband, and quite
rightly, that Jack and his father would play pinochle until midnight, and
that was how long he could stay out. And my task was to accompany Jack
to the dinner, then stay on with the old man and play pinochle with him,
while Jack went away and got laid."

As a result of this conspiring, Sperling felt that he was becoming close
to Jack Warner, and gradually found himself being tempted in the same
way as Zanuck must have been, by Jack's sly promises and the seductions
of power. Jack would flatter the young man and assure him that if he
stayed on with Warners and made a success of his career, anything was
possible (except a raise). It gave Sperling, young and naïve though he

was, a new insight into the way Jack Warner worked, and he began to understand what were the real chances of Zanuck succeeding to the Warner throne.

And yet he could see why, at least for a time, Zanuck persisted in believing. After all, it was not just Jack's heavy patronage that encouraged him to cling to his hopes, but the facts of the situation, too. There was not much doubt that had it not been for Zanuck, the fortunes of Warner Brothers would have been abysmal. It was he who had been the galvanizer of their activities ever since the advent of talking films, and without his energy, drive, and bubbling ideas, their economic situation could have been dire. They lacked stars, directors, stories, and technicians, and were too mean to pay money to get them. It was Zanuck who had prodded them into striking out and opening up their purse strings. In many ways, he *was* Warner Brothers, and he may have convinced himself that he would get to be boss of the whole show simply because they could not do without him. "And that was a mistake," said Sperling. "I already knew in those days that Zanuck would never be given the studio, indispensable though he might be. And Jack was prepared to cut his right arm off, or even his head, rather than hand over supreme power to anyone. Not even his brothers."

One day, in an unexpected and shameful scene, Sperling realized only too clearly the reality of the Warner–Zanuck relationship. Zanuck urgently needed some notes Sperling had been typing, and Sperling hurried to his boss's office to hand them over.

"Jack and Darryl had adjoining offices on the lot," Sperling said, "and between the offices was their own bathroom and toilet. It was accessible only to them. I came into his office with my finished notes and he wasn't there. But I heard voices in the corridor between the two offices, and I figured he must be with Jack in Jack's office, so I went through, into the sacred precincts. The door of the bathroom was open and there was Jack Warner on the toilet, taking a shit, and Zanuck, exhorting him eloquently, had his hand on the chain, ready to pull it at the appropriate moment."

One might have thought that the two men would have reacted to Sperling's presence in such intimate circumstances, and looked embarrassed. "The awful thing," said Sperling later, "was that they didn't react to me at all. Zanuck was not even aware he was doing anything unusual. I found out later he often pursued Jack there. Now he just took the pages and went right on talking."

But it was a revelation to Sperling of how the two men stood, the nature of their association. And though Zanuck was not by any means upset by the knowledge of what Sperling had witnessed, it may still have given him an insight into his relationship and reinforced the determination that was building in him at this time to strike out on his own, to abandon all hope that Jack Warner would one of these days promote him from his subservient position to studio heir.

Not that he could walk out, just like that. Zanuck was under a long-term contract as head of production at Warners, and it had some time to run. He could not break it without earning Jack Warner's wrath and the kind of reprisals that Hollywood studio bosses were capable of exacting from their contractees in those days.

While it was true that the movie industry hardly noticed the great Depression of the 1930s, thanks to the advent of the talkies and the box-office boom that followed, the studio chiefs took good care not to noise abroad the news of their splendid financial condition. No one at M-G-M, Fox, Goldwyn, Paramount, Columbia, or Warners would have admitted their prosperity or allowed anyone outside their accountants' office to look into their books. From their earliest days in the fur shops and the sweat-shops of the Lower East Side, the Laskys, the Zukors, the Goldwyns, and the Cohns had learned that it was wiser to keep a low profile where money and profits were concerned, and since arriving in Hollywood most of them had learned the art of "skimming" the top off their takings. They took great pains to make sure that only the minimum share of the vast monies they were making filtered down to the men and women who made them fat and prosperous. True, many of the stars, directors, and even some of the writers were able to command high salaries, but only if their talents were unique and their services indispensable.

Hollywood studios could exact costly penalties from those players and technicians who tried to put pressure on them and then turned out to lack the clout to back up their ultimatums. A star who stepped out of line could be put on suspension, and no other studio in Hollywood would employ him or her. The studios were run like a cartel and discipline was tight, and only when a star apologized, promised to toe the line, and came back to the home lot on the old salary, was he or she allowed to return to work. As for lower members of the hierarchy, feature players, cameramen, writers, and the like, they were simply sacked when they kicked against studio conditions, and then word was passed around Hol-lywood. In consequence, no other studio in town would offer them a job or an assignment. No one ever said so out loud, or put it on paper, but they were boycotted and were well advised to change their profession or get out of town.

Hollywood studios were well-organized in the thirties, and the rank-and-file workers who made the films there were not. Meanwhile, no matter how well their movies were doing, the owners of the studios pleaded poverty whenever a general wage increase was demanded, and took draconian measures to crush any attempt by writers, technicians, or directors to form a union and organize a campaign to alter working conditions or ask for more money.

Hollywood, in fact, was still an open town in 1933, and the only unions allowed on the movie lots were those to which the grips, electricians, engineers (IATSE), and musicians belonged, and that only because their unions were national institutions with clout across the nation. Bearing that in mind, some workers in Hollywood tried to unionize the creative side of the industry by organizing the writers, actors, and directors into Hollywood branches of the Dramatists Guild and Actors Equity of New York. But the studio bosses, thinking fast, persuaded their contract players, directors, and writers to eschew the approaches from these "foreigners." Instead they urged them to join a hometown organization called the Academy of Motion Picture Arts and Sciences, extending a warm welcome to any director, producer, writer, or technician who cared to apply. A lot of them did so. And all might have been well for the studio chiefs had not some of the greedier ones among them decided to push too hard.

On March 8, 1933, the administration of President Franklin D. Roosevelt was ushered in under a cloud of bad financial news. Worldwide depression and domestic economic instability had culminated, just before the new President took office, in a run on the banks. Many of the financial institutions from which the movie studios obtained their loans (or in which they kept their money) found themselves suddenly short of ready cash, and, claiming an emergency, temporarily closed their cash windows and eventually their doors. Their clients, several studios among them, faced the prospect of being unable to meet their payrolls for the week. Only M-G-M, which kept large amounts of ready cash on the lot, was able to pay the salaries of its employees. Universal and Fox notified their workers they would have to wait for their weekly paychecks, and next day Paramount, Columbia, RKO, and Warner Brothers announced that they were unable to cash checks at their banks and therefore could not pay anyone.

By this time Roosevelt, having taken over the White House, issued a presidential order declaring a bank holiday and ordered all banks to close down. In Hollywood the studio chiefs met in emergency session to debate whether they should close down too, and cease movie production for the time being.

They eventually came out against this, and worked out a solution more in keeping with the character of the studio bosses at the time. They decided the answer to the grim economic situation was wage cuts. Nicholas Schenck of Metro, Sidney Kent of Fox, and Sam Goldwyn of United Artists recommended that all studio employees earning over $50 a week should take an immediate cut of fifty percent, and those receiving less than $50 should take a twenty-five percent cut, the economy measures to last for at least eight weeks.

When there were murmurs of opposition from the more vocal of Hollywood's acting and writing talent, Louis B. Mayer, head of M-G-M, the film city's biggest movie-maker, announced his studio would not put the cuts into operation unless all contract employees on the lot, including stars, directors, writers, and department chiefs, first signaled their agreement. He summoned M-G-M's complete roster of hired help, no matter what their status, to a meeting to discuss the question. The discussion opened with one of the studio's best-known and highest-paid stars, Lionel Barrymore, addressing the assembly. He announced he had carefully thought over the whole question of the financial situation, and that he proposed to accept a fifty percent cut in salary immediately, adding emotionally that if every other employee of M-G-M followed suit he believed it would be "for the good of M-G-M, of Hollywood, and of the country."

At this, a screenwriter named Ernest Vadja, a Hungarian who had written some of Ernst Lubitsch's greatest hits, rose to his feet to object. He read a list of M-G-M's recent successes and figures from the latest published balance sheets, and then asked why any employees, no matter what they were being paid, should take cuts in salary from a company that was obviously doing extremely well. Yes, he agreed, the national situation was worrying. But wouldn't it be better to stick by the working conditions as they prevailed at the moment, and wait and see what happened to the economy?

Lionel Barrymore was thereupon heard to be objecting loudly to this sentiment, and when Louis B. Mayer succeeded in securing silence for him, he declared, pointing dramatically at Vadja: "Sir, you are acting like a man on his way to the guillotine who wants to stop for a manicure."

"At least it postpones the execution," Vadja was heard to remark. But

Barrymore's appearance and declaration had its effect, and his listeners were impressed by his doom-laden warnings. Another screenwriter who was present, Frances Goodrich, remembers that Barrymore's ringing declaration sent a shiver of apprehension down the spines of most of the high-priced help.

"Everybody got very pious and scared about the possibility that the studio might close down," she said later. "So we took the pay cut. Most of us had never had so much money anyway, and we preferred a few tough weeks rather than coming to the end of the pastures of plenty."

Louis B. Mayer was delighted. He quickly got the word around to the other studios, and it was announced shortly afterwards from Paramount, Columbia, and Warner Brothers that their employees, having been summoned to a meeting, had been persuaded to follow M-G-M's example and accept the salary cuts. Even the musicians union, after hesitating about whether to call a strike, finally agreed to allow its members to take a twenty-five percent cut. But then the only union with any real clout around the studios stepped in. IATSE, which was a rich, powerful, national organization representing both electricians and movie-house technicians, announced it never had and never would accept wage cuts, and that rather than accept them now, it would call its members out on strike, including its cinema projectionists.

"They'd never dare," cried Harry Warner. "Let's call their bluff."

He persuaded Louis B. Mayer and his fellow studio bosses to close down all production in Hollywood for twenty-four hours to emphasize the gravity of the financial situation, and on March 13, 1933, a deadly hush descended on sound stages from Gower Street to Culver City. But IATSE was not intimidated, and not only insisted that its own members be protected from any cut in their salaries but that all lower-paid studio workers in Hollywood, IATSE members or not, be protected from the financial axe. Otherwise, the union would call out its members and not only would Hollywood production cease but every movie house in the country showing current product would have to close down, since IATSE's projectionists would be out on strike.

The studios backed down. Instead of ordering new salary cuts throughout the industry, they announced that their economy measures would apply only to the highest bracket of producers, directors, and stars. Their pay would be sliced by fifty percent. And even then a number of stars (among them Maurice Chevalier, Constance Bennett, and Clara Bow) announced that they were deliberately going off salary rather than create a precedent by accepting a cut.

A nervous Hollywood community, shaky from the repercussions of the one-day strike and IATSE's threats, went back to work in an apprehensive mood, and their fears of further trouble were not exactly relieved when they heard that Jack and Harry Warner were planning rebellion against the decisions of the studio bosses. To show their displeasure at the way their associates were weakening, the two Warner brothers announced that while everyone else among their top-flight talent would be subjected to the fifty percent cut, they would refuse to slice their own salaries in any way whatsoever.

When this high-handed action threatened to irk IATSE once again and make the rest of Hollywood's workers angry and rebellious, Sam Goldwyn rushed in to appease them. He announced that he was not only restoring all salary cuts that had already been made, but was awarding all his studio workers a special extra bonus. It was at this moment that Darryl Zanuck got into the act. He was furious at Jack and Harry Warner for the way they had behaved in the recent crisis, especially in view of the fact that they had repeatedly made public statements without consulting him first. Not only had they failed to inform him before announcing they refused to cut their own salaries, but they had sliced his own in half without even a word of explanation.

So far as he was concerned, it was a moment when he recognized and accepted not simply that he would never make it to the top of the power structure at Warner Brothers but that he wasn't really interested in getting there with these people any longer. Jack had not just conned him with false promises, but he was now rubbing his nose in the dirt by treating him with the same contempt as he displayed towards any other of the hired help. Did he have *any* power left? Did his job as head of production mean *anything* any longer?

In a last test of what clout he had left, Zanuck made a decision. Hard on the heels of Jack and Harry's defiant announcement that they would take no salary cuts themselves, he issued a statement of his own. It concerned the policy of Warner Brothers studios towards its salaried personnel, and thus should probably have been cleared first through the studio front office — which meant, in practice, Harry or Jack Warner.

Instead of doing so, Zanuck called in reporters from the industry trade papers on his own and handed them a statement. It announced that though Warner Brothers had originally gone along with the decision of the studio bosses to institute wage cuts for a minimum of eight weeks, he, Darryl Zanuck, had now taken a personal decision to rescind these cuts and restore studio pay to its normal levels. Not only that, he was also following the example of Sam Goldwyn and handing out bonuses in certain cases to loyal employees for meritorious service.

No action could have been more calculated to demonstrate to Zanuck exactly where he really stood in the Warner Brothers pecking order. Jack Warner hit the roof when he heard about Zanuck's announcement. The emergency in Hollywood had given him great joy, notorious tightwad that he was, because of the excuse it had given him to institute wage cuts and economies. Thanks to Zanuck's production policies, the studio was in a strong position, with at least twenty-five unreleased movies in its vaults. Jack would even have welcomed a strike, since he was convinced the workers would eventually have had to crawl back and beg for rein-statement. He was determined to squeeze something out of them, and the last thing he wanted was to make benevolent gestures to them such as the swift restoration of cuts and the handing out of bonuses.

So he issued a curt statement himself, not just repudiating his studio chief's decision about the salary cuts and bonuses, but prolonging the cuts for an extra week — to nine weeks in all.

Hollywood waited, holding its breath, to see how Darryl Zanuck would react to this public slap in the face. They did not have to wait long. On April 15, 1933, he called in the trade paper reporters again and handed them another statement.

"On April 10th," it said, "as Head of Production of Warner Brothers Studios, I announced that the salary cuts decided upon on March 15 last would be restored immediately. This promise has now been repudiated, and since a matter of principle is involved and I obviously no longer enjoy the confidence of my immediate superiors, I have today sent my resig-nation to the Chairman of the Company, Mr. Jack Warner."

Milton Sperling stayed on at Warners after Zanuck's departure prin-cipally because he had married one of Harry Warner's daughters, and had thus become — or so he thought at the time — "one of the family." He took a rather more cynical view of Zanuck's resignation than the rest of Hollywood, firmly believing his chief had used the situation as a con-venient instrument for getting out of his commitment to Warner Brothers.

"Personally," he said later, "I think the resignation was a fraud. He wanted out for very different reasons. But that was the only way to break his long-term contract with Warners."

It was certainly a welcome opportunity, and one that was to change the course of Zanuck's career. But it does an injustice to him to suggest that only his pride and his personal resentment against Jack Warner were involved in the resignation. Zanuck could be brutal and unfeeling, and sometimes he treated his employees roughly, but he never went back on a promise he had made to them, and he certainly never acted like a Scrooge where pay was concerned. On the question of the pay cuts that the studios had tried to squeeze out of the studio workers in 1933, he was out of sympathy with the bosses from the beginning. It was just about this time that he had become interested enough in politics to register as a Republican. But so far as he was concerned, Republicanism did not mean squeezing the workers — as it certainly did to Jack Warner, Harry Cohn, and Louis B. Mayer, all of them Republicans in good standing. What Republicanism meant to Zanuck was getting the most out of a man on the job, but paying him enough to ensure that he was prepared to put in the effort, and was keen to help you make a profit. Not only did he object to a studio pay cut ("except for the bosses, who were the ones who should have had their salaries sliced. They weren't worth half of what they were getting") but he felt that most Hollywood technicians were worth a raise. Which is what he eventually gave them.

It was because he despised them for their meanness, and because they were too stupid to see that talent was worth rewarding, that he got good and mad at the brothers Warner in 1933 — mad enough to hand in his resignation.

## ELEVEN

# GOLD RUSH

ON APRIL 17, 1933, forty-eight hours after he had resigned from Warner Brothers, Darryl Zanuck took a telephone call from his friend Prince Mike Romanoff, who asked if Zanuck could come to breakfast at the Brown Derby restaurant in Hollywood the following morning. When he got there, he found the well-known movie impresario Joseph Schenck waiting for him at the table. The first thing Schenck did was wave a piece of paper in the air and say: "We're in business. We got it."

The piece of paper was a check for $100,000, and it could buy so much in 1933 (at least twenty times as much as today) that it — plus some brains and enterprise — was about to change the nature of the movie industry.

Joe Schenck was one of the authentic pioneers of the motion picture business in America. Unlike most of the other studio bosses, who had come into the movies from more furtive trades, he was a sunny and outward-looking personality who genuinely loved the cinematic art and would probably have been in the business even if it hadn't offered him opportunities to make a great deal of money.

Already, in the 1930s, Joe and his brother, Nicholas Schenck, were two of the oldest names in the movies. While they were still in their teens and just out of Ellis Island immigration pens — after emigrating from Russia — they had been taken up by a honky-tonk showman named Marcus Loew, who showed some of the early movies in his nickelodeons along the midway at Paradise Park, near Fort George. They were hooked from then on. Soon their enthusiasm helped persuade Marcus to diversify from fairgrounds in the sticks to movie houses in the cities, and from that came Loew's Incorporated, a chain of theaters in the big eastern centers; and this quickly expanded, once the motion picture habit spread, to a movie lot in Hollywood to keep the chain supplied with product. After Marcus's death, Nick Schenck succeeded him as president of Loew's Inc., and he appointed Louis B. Mayer to take over the Hollywood operation, henceforward called Metro-Goldwyn-Mayer.

His brother, Joe, meanwhile, decided to make his own way in the industry as an independent producer, and he had done well. He was the organizer behind such successful comic stars as Buster Keaton and Fatty Arbuckle, and he had also nurtured into profitable stardom two of the most beautiful of the Hollywood sisters who were around at the time, Norma and Constance Talmadge. When Douglas Fairbanks, Mary Pickford, Charlie Chaplin, and (subsequently) Gloria Swanson formed their own independent production and releasing company, United Artists, they had first brought in Sam Goldwyn to oversee their production schedule and then asked Joe Schenck to control all their activities as chairman of the board. In early 1933, he became president of United Artists, his position on the morning of the breakfast meeting with Darryl Zanuck. But Hollywood rumor (which for once was correct) had it that he and Sam Goldwyn didn't get on, that there had been quarrels with the temperamental Miss Swanson, and that Joe was restive and wanted to move on. Schenck was a plain, almost oafish-looking man whom women, including Virginia, adored because he had loads of charm and possessed a rich sense of humor. Like Jack Warner, he was a daring gambler for high stakes who would turn a card for $50,000 and not twitch a hair when he lost — except that he rarely did. Also, as did Warner, he had a penchant for puns, bad jokes, and the mangling of the English language. When Fatty Arbuckle was involved in the great Hollywood scandal over the death, following an "orgy," of a starlet named Virginia Rappe, Schenck called the subsequent hounding of Arbuckle by press and police outrageous and declared that "Fatty got a real bum Rappe." Both of his lovely stars, Constance and Norma Talmadge, fell in love with him, and when he subsequently married Norma and was asked why he had chosen her instead of her much more vivacious and sophisticated sister, Constance, he replied: "Because I preferred Normality to Inconstance."

It was Virginia Zanuck who had introduced Darryl to Joe, whom she had first met while filming with Buster Keaton. She sensed instinctively that the two were quintessential movie-men and might well make the sparks fly if only they could find a reason for working together. They certainly established a rapport immediately after they got to know each other, though Joe Schenck never seemed to remember that Zanuck was not Jewish and was always putting his arm around him and saying: "We Jews should stick together. It's us against the schmucks."

Now he gave Zanuck a closer view of the $100,000 check, and pointed to the signature on the bottom. It was signed by Louis B. Mayer. Using his family connection with M-G-M (his brother, Nick, was still head of the parent company, Loew's Inc.) he had persuaded Mayer to back him and Zanuck in the formation of a new independent production company, and in those days the amount they had been loaned was more than enough to begin operations. Schenck pointed out that Mayer, not surprisingly, had made one condition. "He wants us to bring in his son-in-law, Bill Goetz," Schenck said. "Can you live with that?"

Goetz, who had recently married one of Louis Mayer's daughters, was working as an assistant director at RKO Studios, a position Mayer considered much too lowly for one of his sons-in-law. Normally, he would have brought him into M-G-M and given him an impressive title, but everyone in Hollywood knew he couldn't do that. Another of his daughters, Irene, was married to David O. Selznick, who was already producing films at M-G-M and couldn't stand the sight and sound of Goetz. Was it worth $100,000 to Schenck and Zanuck between them to solve Mayer's dilemma? So far as Zanuck was concerned, it certainly was.

"We'll make him a director," Zanuck said, "and he can work for me as my assistant."

"Why would you do that?" asked Schenck, who had expected Zanuck to balk at any competition from one of the Mayer in-laws.

"Because I know all about him," was the reply. "Goetz wouldn't recognize a good script from a roll of toilet paper. So long as he keeps his father-in-law's money in our company, he can work for me as long as he likes."

He hardly needed to remind Schenck that with Goetz around, they would have an automatic entree to M-G-M and its stable of stars, which they were likely to be able to borrow at bargain rates. That could save them big money in the months to come.

As a result of that breakfast meeting, a new Hollywood production company was formed later that day, with Darryl Zanuck, Joseph Schenck, and William Goetz as its three directors, each owning a third of the shares. At the suggestion of a director friend of Schenck's, Sam Engel, who subsequently joined them as a producer, it was named Twentieth Century Films. Schenck, as his last official action as president of United Artists, signed an agreement with Twentieth Century Films under which the company would produce one film a month for the next eighteen months for UA distribution.

The new company moved onto the Sam Goldwyn lot, where, not being able to afford the outlay for equipment, they rented everything: stages, office space, typewriters, files, cupboards, even desks and chairs.

While Schenck went to work on the administrative side of the business and began drawing up a program, Virginia persuaded her husband to take off for a vacation. He needed one because the quarrel with Jack Warner had taken more out of him than showed on the outside, and Virginia was worried about him. He was sleeping even less than usual and losing weight, and, as she said later, "I knew he liked to be as lithe as a whippet, but I didn't like the way his rib cage showed." Normally, she would have gone with him on his trip, but she now had a baby and was pregnant with her second child. Having been assured by the doctor that he would be back well in time to be present at his wife's accouchement, he took off with some California friends for a hunting trip in Alaska.

There is a mystery about this trip, and no perusal of Zanuck's papers or those of his former associates seems to elucidate it. It has been indicated in this story already that Darryl Zanuck was a keen and dedicated hunter, and a collector of trophies from the chase. In this he was both a product of his generation and of his childhood upbringing. Ever since Grandpa Torpin had taken him into the Nebraska woods, he had thrilled to the challenge he always felt when he went into the wilderness. He had learned to live in and off the wilds, shoot and fish for his supper, and make money out of the skins of the wild animals he trapped or shot.

In Africa he had found that facing up to a charging rhino and dispatching him at the last moment was a thrill like no other in the world. He was living in a time when no one worried about the survival of endangered species, and though it pleased him to be able to cook and eat the game he had shot himself, it did not occur to him to worry about what happened to the wild animal he had, for instance, just dispatched with his rifle while on safari in Africa. Okay, it was fine when the bearers plunged in and cut up the elephant carcass for meat, and he was presented by the head-man with the tusks. But other than for trophies for his den, he forgot about them thereafter. He was sometimes a little rueful that in his office on the Warner Brothers lot he had kept the four feet of one of the elephants he had dispatched in Kenya, which he used as ashtrays. But he had no guilt about it. He liked to hunt. He liked to shoot. He liked to get himself in a situation where his wits, his skill, his marksmanship were pitted against an animal in the wilderness. And he had no qualms, only pride, when he survived and a beautiful animal lay dead.

"It was him or me, wasn't it?" he used to say, when an animal lover raised a skeptical eyebrow over his unabashed pleasure at the outcome.

And then, that summer in Alaska, something happened that changed his whole attitude towards hunting. All that can be gathered from the thin stories that are still gossiped around was that the hunting party went on the track of a polar bear somewhere in the Alaskan wilderness, and when the vital moment came it was Zanuck who stepped out to shoot down the charging, furious animal. His bullet, it is said, found its mark all right, but it did not kill. The polar bear came on, and Zanuck stood his ground, pumping away with his rifle.

Only this time it was not "him or me," but "him" and someone else. The wounded and enraged bear, still alive and still charging, swerved around Zanuck and swiped with his great paw at one of the men standing behind him — and only after it had killed this other man did it fall at last into the snow, and die itself. That's the story, and no one seems to be able to confirm it nor remember the name of the man who died. The only certain thing is that when Zanuck came back, he announced to Virginia that he had given up hunting. And he never went out and shot a wild animal again, not even a jackrabbit for his supper.

Virginia was rather sorry about that. Having begun by loathing her husband's enthusiasm for slaughtering wild animals, she had become hooked herself. She had taken lessons in marksmanship, and become such a good shot that on her last African safari with her husband, before motherhood intervened, she had bagged a leopard and been photographed standing proudly beside the dead animal. She had enlivened the duller moments of her pregnancy by watching the amateur movies Darryl had made of her triumph.

Now she sadly ran the film through again. From what she gathered from her husband, their hunting days were definitely over.

Darryl Zanuck left a considerable legacy of valuable films and stars behind when he left Warner Brothers Studios. For one thing, he had announced he was ending the Warner cycle of gangster films by reviving musical films instead, and Jack Warner had been furious about it and ordered him to do no such thing, since he was assured by all his bookers that musicals were a drug on the market.

So determined was Jack that Warners would never make another musical that Zanuck, having written the script for one which he was sure would be a winner, decided to make it in secret. He hired a director named Lloyd Bacon to make two films simultaneously. One of them was a straightforward backstage film about Broadway shot with dialogue only on the Warner lot, where Jack could come and watch its progress. The other was an amalgam of song and dance numbers shot clandestinely on a stage of the old Vitagraph lot, which Warners had retained after they purchased Vitagraph Films. Then Zanuck and Bacon between them married the two films together and sneak-previewed the result for Jack and Harry. Jack grumbled when he realized what Zanuck had done, but Harry Warner was ecstatic and pronounced it "our greatest film for years."

The public thought so too, for it was *42nd Street*, with Ruby Keeler and Warner Baxter, and it was not only one of the biggest box-office successes in Warner history, but it started a cycle of musical films in every Hollywood studio that year — except at Warners. Because, of course, it was after *42nd Street* that Darryl Zanuck quit.

He left behind a roster of star names, too, nearly all of them made by the movies he had created for their talents: Bette Davis, George Arliss, James Cagney, Ruth Chatterton, Kay Francis, Ann Dvorak, Barbara Stanwyck, Edward G. Robinson, Ruby Keeler, Adolphe Menjou, Lewis Stone, Warren William, and George Brent. Since all of them were under contract to Warner Brothers, Jack was determinedly holding on to them, and it seemed doubtful that Zanuck would be able to seduce any of them away to his new operation.

It was a grim prospect. He more than anyone in Hollywood knew that big stars make money at the box office, and he did not yet have the courage to decide that in future his stories would have to be his stars. He was therefore considerably heartened, when he got back from Alaska, to discover that certain of his old stars had succeeded in getting out of their Warner contracts and now indicated they were ready to go to work for him. They included one of the biggest male actors at the box office, George Arliss, and two talented and beautiful female stars, Constance Bennett and Loretta Young.

Unfortunately, he did not have scripts ready for any of them, and United Artists was clamoring for Twentieth Century Films to fulfill its contract and produce its first film. So out of a half-dozen scripts and story ideas that Joe Schenck had assembled for him, he picked one called "The Bowery," and was so pressed for time that he was not even able to polish up the screenplay himself before putting it into production.

*The Bowery* was not the greatest film of Darryl Zanuck's career, and had it not been for its cast, it could have been a disaster. It was a clumsy hodgepodge of popular American myths — about the newsboy, for instance, who jumped off the Brooklyn Bridge, about the world champion barefist boxer, John L. Sullivan, and the bottle-smashing Prohibitionist saloon raider, Carry Nation. Its chief merit was that it contained some rough scenes of life in the turn-of-century Bowery, lots of fights and bar-wrecking, and bouncy vernacular dialogue.

And good players. Zanuck decided that if ever there was a time to exploit Bill Goetz's connections with Louis B. Mayer and M-G-M, this was it. So through him, he managed to borrow, for a very modest fee, three extremely popular M-G-M stars, and one promising newcomer. The newcomer was George Raft. The three stars were Wallace Beery, Jackie Cooper (a famous child star), and Clark Gable. Zanuck was particularly pleased to get Clark Gable at a bargain rate, because he had once turned him down at Warner Brothers. He had decided that Gable's ears were too big and stuck out too far for him ever to make a romantic lead, and he had refused him a contract. He had been kicking himself ever since, especially when he noted that M-G-M had signed him on, sent him to a cosmetic surgeon to have his ears pinned back, and turned him into one of their biggest stars.

Still, he made it up to Gable in *The Bowery*, making sure he had the best lines and scenes. It paid off, too. The critics thought the movie was awful and said so bluntly, but the moviegoing public strongly disagreed. *The Bowery* was such a great box-office success that Twentieth Century Films was launched with a bonanza.

Gable was so pleased with the way Twentieth had handled him that when Mayer refused a second request from Zanuck for the loan of his services unless he paid the fee the studio normally charged, which was enormous, Gable insisted and was already too successful to be refused. So he went back to Twentieth Century to make a version of Jack London's *Call of the Wild*, with Loretta Young as his female star, and it was again a gratifying success. In its first year, Twentieth met its contract with United Artists in full, and produced twelve films, among them a New York newspaper story called *Broadway Thru a Keyhole*, starring a fresh-faced young player called Constance Cummings; George Bancroft in *Blood Money*; an actor with a verbal delivery like a machine gun, named Lee Tracy, in *Advice to the Lovelorn* (based on the novel *Miss Lonelyhearts*); Ann Harding in *Gallant Lady*; Constance Bennett and Franchot Tone in

*Moulin Rouge*; George Arliss in *The House of Rothschild*; Fredric March in *The Affairs of Cellini*; and *Looking for Trouble* with Constance Cummings and Lee Tracy.

There was only one box-office failure in that first year, and it lost Twentieth money they could ill afford. It was called *Born to Be Bad* and it was Zanuck's only attempt to shock the moviegoing public in the same way as he had at Warners with Cagney in *The Public Enemy*. In *Born to Be Bad* he cast Loretta Young as a sexy, bitchy, unscrupulous female — the kind he believed in off the screen — opposite a new star named Cary Grant, playing the naïve hero.

But Grant was under contract to another studio and Zanuck had to pay a whacking fee to get him. All for nothing, as it turned out. By the time *Born to Be Bad* started shooting, Hollywood was seriously beginning to worry about its morals, and the so-called Hays Office had been established to blue-pencil from studio scripts any suggestion of sin, especially female sexual sin. So the character played by Loretta Young had to be "purified," and, as Zanuck put it later, "it did away with the whole fucking raison d'être of the film, including the fucking." The neutered product died a dull death at the box office, and Twentieth was out Cary Grant's fee.

But otherwise, what with the help of all the stars they were able to borrow so reasonably from the indulgent father-in-law of their third director, Twentieth had a good first year. One night, close to their first anniversary, Joe Schenck came over to Zanuck's office with a bottle of champagne, and, filling two glasses, handed one across as he drank a toast to "Louis B. Mayer, from whom all blessings flow." To which Zanuck added: "Coupled with the name of Bill Goetz, without whom."

There was, in fact, only one thing wrong with that successful first year, and that was Darryl Zanuck's financial return for all his box-office hits. When he had agreed to go into business with Joseph Schenck and the production distribution deal had been signed with United Artists, he had understood he was to receive $5,000 a week, plus ten percent of all profits made by the Twentieth Century films for which he had been responsible. Which, in that first year, were all of them except the loss-making *Born to Be Bad*.

He therefore expected a handsome check at the end of that first year, with which he planned to buy himself a couple of new polo ponies, a new car, some jewelry for Virginia, and additional rooms at the Santa Monica house, since his wife was pregnant for the third time and they would soon be needing an expanded nursery.

Then he discovered that so far as the board of United Artists was

concerned — and UA, as distributor, was also participating in the profits — what he had been assigned was ten percent of the *net* profits, which
meant that United Artists took their share before he got his. He was
disgusted and angry when he heard about it, and telephoned Joe Schenck
to say that he was walking out of the company. Schenck told him to hold
his hand, and at once called a meeting of the UA board. To them he
suggested that the agreement be changed at once to the way Zanuck
wanted it. Douglas Fairbanks, Pickford, Swanson, and Sam Goldwyn
agreed at once. Only one member, Charles Chaplin, disagreed and insisted that a contract was a contract, verbal or not, and Zanuck must either
swallow it or depart. Chaplin called for a vote, and when he was defeated,
five to one, he stamped out in a rage.

The incident hardly helped their relationship, and Zanuck never felt
really comfortable from then on, not just with Chaplin but with United
Artists too.

It was during that first year that a writer came into Zanuck's professional
life who was to have a considerable influence not only on his bank account
but on his standing as a filmmaker too. His name was Nunnally Johnson,
and once Zanuck got to know and trust his work, Ernest Hemingway was
about the only other writer he came to admire as much.

"Darryl always thought of himself as a writer," Johnson said later,
"although he wasn't. He could hardly spell *cat*. He was an ideas-man
pure and simple. We would go to the Brown Derby at two in the morning
and look through the early editions of the papers, and he would tear out
a story and say: 'How about that?' And it would be a story of the suicide
of Kreuger, the Swedish match king, and he would go on: 'Let's develop
it along these lines,' and by the next morning he would have an outline
ready to be turned into a script and handed to a director."

In some ways, Zanuck ran Twentieth Century Films rather like a dynamic editor runs a newspaper. He was shrewd enough to see that the
movies would always rely on big, glamorous stars to sell their product at
the box office. But he also realized that so far as stars were concerned
Twentieth Century would never be able to compete with, for instance,
M-G-M, where Louis B. Mayer had cleverly assembled a stable of handsome leading men and polished and impeccably beautiful leading ladies.
His company just couldn't afford them. Where the really potent box-office
stars were concerned, M-G-M would always outshine him. For the time
being, anyway.

All he could do was use his brains where M-G-M used its glamour, and outmatch them in ideas. The reason he would have made a good editor was because he could see big stories shaping up, human interest news items that deserved developing because the public began asking questions about them the moment they read them. The difference was that where an editor would have sent out a good reporter–feature writer to ferret out the facts and put them into an article, he thrashed them out at script conferences or over a table at the Brown Derby, and then sent his writers away to turn them into a screenplay.

"Why did the Swedish match king throw himself out of a plane over the English Channel?" he would ask. "Those crooks in the French government who were tied in with him are never going to let the real story get out. So let's make a movie with our own explanation of the suicide. And what I think might make a good, dramatic explanation is this . . ."

He was brilliant at snatching page-one items from the newspapers and adding the background material, the behind-the-scene dramas and tragedies, that reporters could not or were not allowed to tell. Nunnally Johnson and Milton Sperling were constantly amazed at the fertility of the Zanuck brain, always sprouting with ideas, with the instinct of how a front-page story could be turned into a front-page movie, by which he meant a movie that everybody would talk about when it hit the local cinema.

Nunnally Johnson put it this way:

"It didn't have to be a hot news story, either, but just something that pricked his interest. For instance, I remember once he came steaming into a restaurant waving a copy of *Time* magazine which had carried a story about the Dry Tortugas, just below the Florida Keys, where the United States once ran a prison camp for political prisoners. That was where they incarcerated the doctor who tended the wounds of John Wilkes Booth after Lincoln's assassination. *Time* suggested that the doctor was the victim of a monstrous injustice, had nothing to do with the assassination but had merely been performing his humane medical duty. 'What a movie that would make!' Darryl cried. 'Let's dig into this and get a screenplay. Now the way I see it is this . . .' And that's how we came to make *The Prisoner of Shark Island*, which I wrote and John Ford directed."

Bubbling over as he was with these intriguing inspirations, Zanuck still envied the craftsmen who could turn his ideas into books or scripts. For him writers were the people he most admired, especially those who could bring to life the settings he loved. Ernest Hemingway, with his gift for conjuring up the fecund plains around Kilimanjaro, the streets of Mont-

martre, the excitements of a bullfight, became one of his heroes long
before he met him in Paris. Johnson he admired for his skill in fleshing
out the notions expressed at two in the morning in a Hollywood restaurant,
and bring them back as a script a few days later, filled with people, vivid
scenes, and dramatic dialogue.

Nunnally Johnson had come out to Hollywood by way of New York
newspapers, short story writing for the *Saturday Evening Post,* and some
mild successes on the Broadway stage. He had a reputation in the studios,
when he swam into Zanuck's ken, as a smooth writer of light comedy
scripts, but he was such a genial and amiable man, always ready with a
smile and a wisecrack, that no one believed he could handle more serious
matters. "Anything with froth on it, that was my métier," Johnson said
later. "I kept the bubbles rising in the champagne, and if necessary I
could even provide fake bubbles in fake bubbly. I made some stinkers in
my time, but nobody could say they didn't sparkle."

It was for this amiable expertise that Zanuck first summoned him to
Twentieth Century and paid his fee — which was always handsome —
to write a script for a film starring Constance Bennett and Franchot Tone.
It wasn't just an adaptation but a rewrite of a plot Zanuck had used several
times before in the movies.

"Zanuck, when he wasn't fizzing with new ideas," said Johnson later,
"was a nut about rewrites and redoing old film plots. He never liked to
waste old standbys. This was one of those." The plot-line he handed over
to Johnson was what he called "the Coney Island story," in which two
vaudeville artists squabble over a girl who assists them in their performance. Their quarrels reach a climax in a scene with a showdown between
the two comics, and then comes the punch line: "Ya mean ya gonna break
up the act?" That one. In this version, the movie was called *Moulin Rouge,*
and Johnson did not have to spend too much time on it in order to turn
in a highly professional screenplay. The movie naturally inspired no critical shouts of joy but did quite well at the box office, and only after they
came away from the sneak preview did Johnson realize that Zanuck had
really been trying him out to see what he could do with an old turkey,
and was now ready to give him something serious.

It has already been mentioned that among the stars who had been
persuaded to follow him from Warner Brothers was the distinguished
English actor George Arliss, who specialized in costume films. He had
great faith in Zanuck as a movie-maker, mainly because he sensed the
young man admired his cultivated background, his aristocratic appearance, and his eloquent English voice, which he could play like a musical

instrument. It seemed that Arliss for years had been longing to make a film about the Rothschild family, and without presenting Zanuck with an ultimatum — he was far too polite to do that — he had suggested that making a film on the family, with, naturally, Arliss as the star, would be a suitable act of gratitude on Zanuck's part for Arliss's loyalty to him. Zanuck saw no way out but to make such a film, and he hoped Johnson could produce the right kind of script to make the venture worthwhile. He handed the writer a book about the Rothschilds and told him to go away and read it, and report whether there was a movie in it.

"Mr. Arliss wants to play more than one part in the film," Zanuck said, and added, having already read the book: "He sees himself as old Meyer Rothschild, the father of the family in Vienna, whose five sons become the bankers of Europe. He also sees himself as the most famous of those sons, Lionel Nathan Rothschild, who establishes himself in London and becomes close to Disraeli, the British prime minister, who was also a Jew. He'd like to play Disraeli too, but I think we can talk him out of that." He looked at Johnson: "Think you can do it?"

Johnson pointed out that this was a dramatic film; had Zanuck forgotten that he was a comic writer?

"All my characters are liable to fall into flour barrels," he said.

"Never mind that," Zanuck said. "Read the book and go and talk to Mr. Arliss."

Johnson later confessed that "talking to Mr. Arliss was rather like talking to the king of England." The actor was obviously not pleased that so light, and light-minded, a writer had been assigned to the task of producing a screenplay dealing with his favorite subject, and Johnson found the atmosphere so frigid that he was often frozen by the actor's lofty manner. On the other hand, he found the task of writing a script of the Rothschild story a rewarding one. To begin with, he was awed by Zanuck's willingness to tackle such a subject at this time. It was 1933 and Adolf Hitler and the Nazis had just come to power in Germany. Not only were the newspapers and newsreels full of pictures of the Brownshirts on the rampage against the Jews in Berlin and Munich, but the smell of anti-Semitism reeked strongly enough to drift across the Atlantic and be sniffed eagerly by racists in the United States. From a purely commercial point of view, it was a controversial movie to be making at this time. But if Joe Schenck and the bookers at United Artists were apprehensive about this, Zanuck, on the contrary, was stimulated by the prevailing conditions, and felt that here was a page-one film if ever there was one, its story brought bang up to date by the happenings in Nazi Germany. He was not only enthusiastic about Johnson's script, but he believed that the controversial aspects of it would attract rather than repel moviegoers.

Johnson was always proud of what was his first serious screenplay, but he gave most of the credit for its success to George Arliss's performance (or performances). There were some other notable English actors in the cast, however, and they helped to lend a special European aura to the movie. Most of them were members of the film city's English film colony, led by the captain of the Hollywood cricket club, an august character named C. Aubrey Smith. He played the Duke of Wellington and particularly relished delivering the line Johnson had inserted in the script about wars being won on the playing fields of Eton, not least because he was an old Etonian himself. Alan Mowbray was Count Metternich. And while Loretta Young did not exactly possess the dusky sensuality needed for the role of Julie Rothschild, she certainly brought a freshness to scenes that might otherwise have been too dustily redolent of politics and money.

A new English actor named Boris Karloff was picked by Zanuck to play an anti-Semitic role. Karloff was later to win stardom as the monster in Hollywood's version of *Frankenstein* and other horror movies. Johnson used him to remind cinemagoers that anti-Semitism was not a singularly Nazi problem, and that it had often been brutally exercised and bluntly expressed in Rothschild's day. Karloff played the role of Ledrantz, a bigot who liked to rabble-rouse against the Jews.

"I wrote for him," said Johnson later, "a savagely anti-Semitic speech to which, needless to say, Arliss is called upon, as Rothschild, to reply — and tops him."

But some rough racist remarks had been included in Ledrantz's diatribe, and shortly after copies of the final script were distributed around the studio, Zanuck sent for Johnson and informed him that Joe Schenck, who rarely read anything, had read this screenplay and blown a fuse.

"Now, because my name is Zanuck, a lot of people think I'm Jewish," Zanuck told Johnson, "and one of them is Joe Schenck. So he talks more openly to me than he does to any of his goy friends. And do you know what he said to me about this script? He said: 'Look, that anti-Semitic speech that Karloff delivers, I'm a little worried about that.' I said: 'What are you worried about? People are not going to complain about its nastiness once they hear what Arliss says in reply.' And Joe said: 'That's not what I'm worried about. What I'm afraid of is that when Karloff finishes saying what he thinks about the Jews, a lot of people are going to get up and cheer.' " Zanuck laughed, and added: "It will be interesting if they do, won't it?"

In fact none of them did. Ledrantz's speech was listened to in tense silence by American moviegoers, and, much to the relief of Zanuck and Johnson, there was often applause and cheers at the end of Arliss's reply.

"Actually," commented Johnson later, "I think we may have leaned over backwards a bit too much. Certainly the general effect of the film was so pro-Semitic that a lot of Jews I know reacted the opposite way Joe had done, and were made uncomfortable about it because it was just too sweet, lacked a sense of balance. But what Darryl and I found particularly interesting, and what in the end made the film such a big success, was the fact that we were showing it in that climate at that particular time, and that for once in a way the movies were not shying away but dealing with a real touchy subject right up there on the screen."

It taught Zanuck a lesson, and he was sold on controversial subjects for the rest of his career.

*The House of Rothschild* was not just Twentieth Century's most successful film, both from the point of prestige and financial reward, but it confirmed Darryl Zanuck's growing reputation in Hollywood as its boldest and most enterprising purveyor of screen entertainment. It was a period when he was seen everywhere, at sneak previews, Hollywood premieres, nightclub openings, and, every week, playing in the Sunday game of polo at the Uplifters Club.

For the time being, Virginia was too occupied with her family to accompany him, but he was never without an attractive female companion. One of the most frequent of them was a strikingly lovely star, Ann Harding, who was making a movie for him called *Gallant Lady*. It may have been a coincidence that Harding's crowning physical attraction was a head of corn-gold if not quite ash-blond hair, in addition to which she was much less scrupulous sexually than her angelic appearance indicated. She could have been his mother's youngest sister. Zanuck found himself called frequently to the set of *Gallant Lady* because he had appointed Gregory La Cava as the director, and La Cava had a reputation not only as a drinker but also as an inveterate improviser. He liked to read a script overnight, then throw it away and invent dialogue and scenes off the top of his head on the set.

This was not something Ann Harding was used to. She preferred to learn her part beforehand and have every word and every angle laid out

Frank Zanuck, father of Darryl Zanuck. (*Zanuck Family Collection*)

Louise Zanuck, mother of Darryl Zanuck. (*Zanuck Family Collection*)

Henry Torpin, Zanuck's grandfather, protector, and mentor. He was a pioneer of the Old West and taught Zanuck to hunt, shoot, and ride. (*Zanuck Family Collection*)

The youngest doughboy on the Western Front? Darryl Zanuck in the U.S. Army, aged sixteen, just before being shipped to France during World War I. (*Zanuck Family Collection*)

Just before being appointed head of production at Warner Brothers studios, Jack Warner told Zanuck to grow a mustache to make him look older. This was his first attempt. (*Zanuck Family Collection*)

Dolores Costello was one of the famous Hollywood "sister" stars (Helene was the other). Daughter of Maurice Costello, a well-known actor, she had a brief fling with Darryl Zanuck. (*Warner Brothers*)

Rin Tin Tin and Mary Louise Miller in *Jaws of Steel*, one of the first scripts Zanuck wrote for the dog star. There were in fact several Rin Tin Tins, one for racing and leaping, one for fighting, one for affectionate scenes with little girls. The owner of the Rin Tin Tin kennels gave one of the original dog's first puppies to Zanuck in gratitude for making the dogs famous and him rich. (*Culver Pictures*)

An historic scene from the first successful talking film, *The Jazz Singer*, in which the rabbi denounces jazz and his son (Al Jolson). Zanuck wrote the words for this scene. (*Warner Brothers*)

Virginia and Darryl Zanuck return
from a European trip in 1928.
(*Zanuck Family Collection*)

Zanuck was an enthusiastic and bold polo
player, but he gave it up after an injury
forced him to have cosmetic surgery on his
face. He donated his stable of ponies to the
U.S. Army at West Point.
(*Zanuck Family Collection*)

Virginia and Darryl Zanuck on their first African safari in 1930. (*Zanuck Family Collection*)

Producer Milton Sperling in 1942 after he had joined the U.S. Marines. In Hollywood he had been assistant to Zanuck but felt he "would be safer in the Marines" than as a member of Zanuck's fire-and-brimstone photographic unit in the Army Signal Corps. (*Milton Sperling Collection*)

Zanuck, head of production at Warner Brothers, aged twenty-eight. (*Zanuck Family Collection*)

Virginia and Darryl Zanuck dancing at Coconut Grove. (*Zanuck Family Collection*)

Frank Capra, James Cagney, Zanuck, and Jack Warner at Warner Brothers in 1931. (*Warner Brothers*)

Family portrait of Virginia and Darryl Zanuck with (left to right) Richard, Susan, and Darrylin in 1935. (*Zanuck Family Collection*)

Zanuck with his son, Richard, aged two, in 1936. (*Zanuck Family Collection*)

Darryl and Virginia Zanuck skiing at Sun Valley in 1936. (*Zanuck Family Collection*)

Zanuck on location with director Henry King in 1935. (*Zanuck Family Collection*)

Zanuck interviewed by columnist Hedda Hopper. (*Zanuck Family Collection*)

Shirley Temple, Zanuck, and Darrylin Zanuck. (*Zanuck Family Collection*)

in advance, and she was often driven to tears when La Cava suddenly thought up a new line, or, when she asked about the next scene, he told her he was changing the dialogue but she wasn't to worry because "I can always spit out the words at the last moment."

She literally sobbed on Zanuck's shoulders, and one thing led to another. He did not tell her that La Cava knew exactly what he was doing, and was getting an extremely good performance out of her. He continued to comfort her for the duration of the film, after which both of them sought other consolations.

While Virginia was preoccupied either with her baby daughters or with her latest pregnancy, Zanuck spent a lot of time at the Athletic Club in the steam room, talking movies with Joe Schenck, Sid Grauman, who owned the new Chinese Theatre on Hollywood Boulevard, and Douglas Fairbanks. He maintained that it kept him fit and kept his weight down for the weekly polo, at which he still played a hard and unrelenting game. One of those who played with him about this time was David Niven, then trying to carve out a film career in Hollywood. He had been advised to cultivate the up-and-coming young impresario, and, since he had played polo in the British army in Malta, thought a good performance on the field would be most likely to impress Zanuck into giving him a job.

He impressed Zanuck all right, but rather too painfully. Lent a frisky Arab stallion named Saint George by an old English friend, Aidan Roark, Niven sped down the field in chase of Zanuck and the ball, only to have Saint George reach out and bite Zanuck in the breeches. It was years before he made it into one of his films.

The crowd still came to watch the weekly matches, since the players were almost always the same, and among them was that murderous giant, Big Boy Williams, who continued to ride his gallant ponies to the point of exhaustion and dearly wanted to do the same to Zanuck. Time and again there was a wild chase down the field and a duel for the ball between the two adversaries, and it often culminated in a juddering crash that upturned the ponies and flung both riders heavily to the ground.

Williams may have been a murderous punisher of horseflesh, but he knew how to play polo, and not only could he hit a ball with the force of a cannonball from one end of the field to the other, he could also direct the missile with deadly accuracy.

In the course of one game, he lofted a ball and it smashed into Zanuck's back with a thud that would have smashed his spine had he not been wearing a protective harness under his shirt. Almost collapsing with pain and shock, he managed to wheel his mount and galloped full tilt towards Williams and other players milling around for possession of the ball. What he intended to do is not quite certain, but before he could do any damage to his erstwhile opponent, a whistle was blown for the end of the chukkah, and Zanuck quietly slipped out of his saddle and collapsed on the field. He was carried unconscious to the dressing station, and could hardly walk (and certainly could not ride) for the next three months.

It kept him from the polo field, but not from the studio, where his reputation was still riding high. Since Twentieth Century was looking for money, and United Artists was not always prompt with its payments from rentals, it was vital to keep production going. Almost immediately after their success with *Rothschild*, therefore, Zanuck sent Johnson back to his typewriter with a request to give him a script that would cost little to make and do well at the box office — "a modest-budget blockbuster," as he called it.

Johnson did his best to oblige. The star they borrowed (from M-G-M, naturally) was Ronald Colman, and the movie was called *Bulldog Drummond Strikes Back*. It was based on a debonair British fictional private detective and was an ideal role for the smooth, sardonic-sounding Colman. One of the studio's own stars, Loretta Young, who adored Zanuck and would play any part he gave her, palpitated her admirable bosom as the heroine who waits in a succession of perilous situations until the gallant English detective rescues her. Since Johnson could write this kind of script with his eyes shut, Zanuck, who was still hobbling around in a harness for his back, left him to his own devices. Actually, the film came out reasonably well, and Johnson was satisfied with it. But it moved too slowly for Zanuck's liking, and he adjourned to the cutting room and got down to work editing the film and eliminating the yawns and longueurs.

"We didn't have them in those days," said Johnson later, "but if we had been in the atomic age you would have said that Zanuck had a Geiger counter in his head. When he read a script or watched the rushes, he knew the moment a movie got dull or a scene didn't move along. His Geiger counter would go tick-tick-tick and he would say at once: 'This is where it goes wrong. This is where the action stops.' And he would get out the script, leaf through the pages, and then point triumphantly and say: 'There!' And then he would begin to cut."

*Bulldog Drummond* was an exception in that he began slicing it up after the shooting had been done, but he usually followed the same routine the moment the writer had produced the first draft of his screenplay. He would have it copied and circulated to the director and crew directly involved, and then he would call a conference in his office with the director and his assistants present.

The director was expected to have studied the draft carefully and was encouraged to make suggestions about scenes, actions, dialogue, motivations. But those suggestions had to be made to Zanuck and to Zanuck only, and if he accepted them, they had to be written out and approved by him before being added to the final script. He never allowed any leeway to a director. He admired directors as a breed and he knew they could make all the difference to the quality of a film, especially in securing a good performance from the actors. But they were his servants and they did what he told them, and he always made it crystal clear that he was their master and arbiter of everything they filmed. A director on a Zanuck movie was still beholden to him even when on the set, and could not make a shot without his approval. Nobody had told Ann Harding, but even a maverick like Gregory La Cava was subject to the same rules, and he had been told to clear everything, even the "spontaneous" scenes, before shooting them. Every picture made under Zanuck's aegis belonged to him and he decided exactly how it should be made.

Johnson later remembered one script conference in the early days of Twentieth Century when a director named Steve Roberts had been brought over from Paramount Pictures. At Paramount directors were always treated like kings and their word was law so far as the front office was concerned. After a short discussion of the screenplay, Roberts looked airily across the room and said to Zanuck:

"I'll tell you what I'll do. I'll read the script over the weekend, and I'll kick it around."

As Johnson remembered that moment, "it was as if he had insulted everybody's mother and the United States flag." Zanuck flushed angrily and rasped out:

"What do you mean, you'll kick it around? If you have any suggestions, I'll be glad to listen to them. But remember this — I'm the one who kicks things around here."

Roberts looked shocked. He had never been spoken to like that before, and he didn't like it. He was later reported around the lot as expressing his opinion of Zanuck in rough and ready language, and when his complaints reached Zanuck's office his future at Twentieth Century was abruptly terminated.

"And as a scriptwriter, I had no complaints about that," Johnson said later. "So far as Zanuck was concerned, not even a director was allowed to treat a screenplay lightly. He knew it was upon the quality of the screenplay that a movie's chances of success mostly depended. No detail in a script was too small to escape him, and no scene was unimportant or trivial. And no one, except him, of course, was allowed to kick it around."

# TWELVE

# NEW REALM

O NCE ZANUCK had found a scriptwriter who could fertilize and cultivate his ideas, he clung to him, and Johnson was given little time to himself from then on. But Zanuck was generous in his payments, and Johnson rapidly became one of the three highest-paid writers in Hollywood and probably the most richly rewarded in the country.

With *Bulldog* successfully accomplished, he was put to work to produce another costume film for George Arliss. Zanuck had come across an article on the life of Cardinal Richelieu in the Encyclopaedia Britannica and he immediately saw a great movie in the cardinal's colorful career, and had a dazzling vision of the lordly Arliss bestriding the screen in magnificent robes. Once he started writing, Johnson became aware that he knew no more than Zanuck did about life in France during Richelieu's time at the court of King Louis XIII, so he asked his boss whether he could take on a historian of the period to help him. He suggested a friend of his, Professor Cameron Rogers, who had written a life of the poet Cyrano de Bergerac and knew the French kings as familiarly "as if he had been master of the bedchamber."

Rogers, however, was a touchy man when it came to meddling with history. At Zanuck's script conferences he had a confusing habit of always referring to Richelieu as "du Plessis," since that was his family name, and he would suddenly break into a discussion about cinematic motivations to remark: "You know, the du Plessis family were really cracked, most of them. Now the cardinal's sister in middle age became obsessed with the idea that she had a glass ass. And she took to her bed because she was afraid that if she got up, she would shatter."

Zanuck began by being impressed by the professor's remarks, for he was always respectful of experts, but then he grew irritated with his didacticism and started to play havoc with historical facts, insisting that action was more important than accuracy. Johnson remembered being at one conference when the professor became absolutely pop-eyed with rage at what Zanuck was doing to history, and at last he could stand it no longer. "If you don't mind my saying so, Mr. Zanuck," he cut in frigidly at one point, "I can't imagine any scholar accepting a falsification of history of such an appalling nature. Next thing I know, you'll be putting the cardinal on a horse at the Battle of Waterloo."

Darryl was momentarily abashed by the professor's indignation at the way he was mangling historical events. Then he shrugged his shoulders and grinned.

"Aw, the hell with it," he said. "Who cares about whether what Richelieu does is history or not. Nine out of ten people are going to think he's Rasputin, anyway."

Johnson's trouble with the screenplay of *Cardinal Richelieu* (as the film was eventually called) was that George Arliss began meddling with it, and he did so after Zanuck had approved the final shooting script, which was against the rules. The original draft had been sent to Arliss for his approval while he was on holiday in Paris, and it had been followed by a long cable — Zanuck always sent cables at least five hundred words long — explaining to the star why certain liberties had been taken with history in the script, and why incidents and sequences had been shifted around. The cable had ended with the words: "DO YOU APPROVE?" Arliss happened to be a very thrifty fellow who believed that cablegrams were a flamboyant extravagance, and it did not occur to him to send one back in reply to this inquiry. Zanuck twisted and fidgeted while waiting for a reply from his star which never came. Nor was his impatience appeased when a postcard was delivered to him from Paris on which the great actor had written: "Having rewarding and relaxing time. Wish you were here."

One day, after shooting had finally begun, Johnson came onto the set to find Arliss making a scene in which he emerges through a door connecting one room to another. A previous scene had just been shot in the other room. Arliss was dressed in full cardinal's fig, complete with an ornate amber necklace from which two huge round green semiprecious stones hung. Arliss did not trust the director (Rowland Lee) nor the script girl to keep him *au fait* with the action, but relied upon his faithful and devoted secretary-assistant, Maude Howell, to check on his costume, movements, and performance. He now looked across at her and said:

"Miss Howell, do you remember what I was doing when I was in that other room and went through that door?"

"Yes, sir," she replied, in her precise English voice. "You were playing with your balls."

The suppressed sniggers (for no one dared to laugh out loud) did not conceal from Johnson the fact that Arliss was not playing the scene as he had written it, and had been tampering with his dialogue. And when he visited other sequences, he found that the star was making considerable alterations to the script. He went at once to Zanuck to complain and informed him that if any more changes took place, he was going to insist his name be removed from the credits of the movie.

Zanuck reacted to this ultimatum as most other Hollywood producers would have done. He jumped to the conclusion that Johnson didn't like the way the movie was progressing and thought it would be a failure, the only reason he could imagine a writer would want his name removed from the credits. Johnson assured him that wasn't the reason at all; so far as he could see, the picture was going fine, but he had been told that Arliss was jotting down new dialogue and scenes on the backs of menus and bits of paper and then changing things around — "and I don't want to get credit for that if it turns out good and I don't want to be blamed if it turns out bad."

Zanuck sympathized with Johnson. He had already been told by the director what Arliss was up to, and had several times asked the star to leave things alone. But Arliss, having faithfully promised to behave, could never resist and was meddling again a few hours later. Moreover, everyone was so in awe of him, including the director, that he was allowed to get away with it. Even Zanuck realized that the only way to discipline Arliss was to threaten to take him off the film, and he certainly was not prepared to do that. On the other hand, he did not want to lose Johnson either. Both star and writer were too valuable.

"All right," he said, at last, and agreed to take Johnson's name off the script. "You're the first writer I've ever been able to persuade to work twice with Mr. Arliss, and I've *never* had a director work twice with him — because he is —" He hesitated and then added: "Well, he isn't arrogant, exactly, he just has to have it his way."

The writing credits on *Cardinal Richelieu* were eventually given to "Maude Howell, W. P. Lipscomb and Cameron Rogers." But everyone in Hollywood knew it was really Johnson's screenplay (with additions by George Arliss). Zanuck was not too bothered about that, because the movie was both a prestigious and financial success. But Arliss himself professed to be quite hurt when he heard about Johnson's action, and when they met later, he said: "Now why did you have to do that? My dear fellow, we couldn't have made the picture at all if it hadn't been for you." Johnson was not mollified. He considered his final scripts to be sanctified, and no one but Zanuck was allowed to touch them, especially not actors. He did not forgive Arliss for meddling even when, years later, the great actor described the script of *Cardinal Richelieu* as the best of his career, and added: "It was by Nunnally Johnson, for whom I have a great respect, which, I fear, is not reciprocated."

Twentieth Century Films was now so solidly established and financially successful that both Zanuck and Joe Schenck were growing increasingly dissatisfied with the proportion of the profits they were receiving from their operations. Every time they studied the books, they realized that their distributors, United Artists, were taking the major share of the receipts, whereas they were receiving next to nothing from the movies being made by the UA stars themselves, most of whom, in their opinion, were a bunch of prima donnas.

"While Chaplin was still brooding over the future of talking films and doodling around with politics," said Zanuck, sourly, later, "and while King Fairbanks was worrying about how best to dump Queen Pickford, there was no one around the place making films but us. Meanwhile, they were helping themselves to our profits and socking us for their expenses."

Zanuck was now a family man with a baby son and two growing daughters, and he liked to indulge them. He also liked to spoil his wife. He would never be sexually faithful to Virginia, because Hollywood was too full of attractive girls, and he got a triple satisfaction out of sleeping with them — it proved he was attractive enough to get the most beautiful of them, virile enough to satisfy the most demanding of them, and it reinforced his conviction that all women were tramps, anyway. Always with the exception of Virginia, whom he now respected more than ever — he was proud of her as a wife and mother and liked to show her and his family off in public, and he tried to shield her from gossip about his extramarital liaisons.

It all cost money, and he now had expensive tastes. He had bought some expensive polo ponies from Argentina and was thinking of expanding his stable to twenty. He planned to buy a ranch near Encino and was thinking of a house in the desert near Palm Springs. And he was spending money on enlarging the Santa Monica beach house, installing a private cinema and a new and bigger dining room, and beefing up the staff with a butler, another chauffeur, and a couple more maids.

Joe Schenck agreed they had to work out some way they could rearrange their financial affairs to meet their increasing obligations, and meanwhile suggested Zanuck should take Virginia on a vacation trip to Europe (he called it a "post natal operation"). Leaving the three young children in charge of a nanny, the Zanucks took off for France, and they spent the next three months driving around Europe and sunning themselves on the Riviera.

It was a happy trip for both of them, and, in the circumstances, particularly pleasing for Zanuck because, as it turned out, Jack Warner paid their expenses. The Zanucks ran into Jack one night in the casino at Monte Carlo and his old boss invited him to a game at the chemin-de-fer tables. Even though he didn't have the money to gamble with the big ones, Zanuck could never resist a challenge, and while an apprehensive Virginia looked over his shoulder, convinced they were about to lose their all, he dealt himself in. Jack lost heavily and Zanuck won, and it doubled the value of the money just to see the expression on Warner's face.

While he was away in Europe, Zanuck had had to find someone reliable to look after Twentieth's filmmaking activities (Joe Schenck, of course, was ably in charge of administration), and he had picked one of his most reliable producers, a veteran movie man named Harry Joe Brown. Louis B. Mayer was extremely angry when he heard about that. Why had Zanuck overlooked his son-in-law, Bill Goetz? Was he not a director of the company and a film producer in addition? He called up Zanuck when he got back to Hollywood to ask him why he had so "grossly insulted" Goetz by passing him over.

"Because the whole operation would have gone to pieces if I had left him in charge," Zanuck replied. "Bill is a born thumbtack. He doesn't function when the thumb is missing."

During his absence, Joe Schenck had been busy sizing up the studio situation in Hollywood. He had discovered that the head of one of the oldest companies in the film colony, Fox Films, was looking around for help. Its operating chief, Sidney R. Kent, feared that a series of bad years had brought the company to the edge of bankruptcy. Under its original founder, William Fox, the company had once been a Hollywood giant, but mishandling, bad films, and financial double-dealing had put its future in jeopardy.

To Joe Schenck, it seemed like a golden opportunity for Twentieth Century Films to get out from under the money-grabbers at United Artists.

"Fox still has the best distribution system in the movie business," said Joe, "and it makes the worst films. The reverse is true of us. I've talked to Sidney Kent and he is enthusiastic and would like to take us over." Seeing Zanuck wince, he hurriedly added: "Don't worry. If he swallows the deal I propose to offer him, it will be a case of the gnat eating the elephant. We'll be taking over Fox."

The arrangement that Schenck eventually persuaded Kent to accept was a neat and persuasive one. In return for a merger with Fox Films, Twentieth would transfer to the ninety-six-acre Fox lot all its operations and assets, including its contract stars, its scripts, its directing, producing, and organizing talents, and would receive in return half of the common stock and one-third of the preferred stock of the combined companies.

But very quickly the newcomers demonstrated who would be the real bosses in the new organization, by persuading Kent to swallow two vital conditions for the merger. The first concerned the new company's name. Kent wanted it to be called Fox–Twentieth Century Films. Joe didn't care much about that, but Zanuck said no way. It must be named 20th Century–Fox or he would not be a party to the agreement. Kent took a deep breath and agreed.

Next came the question of who would be in charge of the new studio. The man who was running Fox at the time of the merger was a former partner of William Fox named Winfield Sheehan. Sheehan was an old-time newsman who had once been one of the brightest operators in Hollywood, full of enterprise and panache. In his heyday, at the height of his powers, he had directed a powerful and successful operation, thrown great parties, and publicly wooed, pursued, and finally married the most beautiful, expensive and tempestuous grand opera soprano of the day, Maria Jeritza. Before William Fox's shady deals had run the studio into the ground, Sheehan had made many exciting and spectacular films, but now he was an old man and had lost his touch. Zanuck bridled when Kent suggested he should split control of the studio and the film program with Sheehan, but before he could verbally object, he hastily added:

"But you, Darryl, will always be in charge and have the last word on major decisions."

When Sheehan heard this and realized how things would be in future, he let it be known that he was prepared to resign — at a price. The price was steep for those days, but it was decided to pay it, and Sheehan departed with a golden handshake of half a million dollars.

So it was done. Sole charge and sole responsibility for the film program of Hollywood's biggest studio was thus passed over to Darryl Francis Zanuck. As part of the contract which he was given, both Schenck and Kent agreed not to interfere with him in any way, providing he kept the Fox distribution system and its nationwide chain of cinemas fed with a minimum of thirty-five new films a year.

The first time Zanuck and Schenck drove through Fox, it was a secret and unofficial visit. Schenck looked over the ninety-six-acre lot, with its five miles of streets, its twelve stages, its complex of one-story administration buildings, and said scornfully: "It looks like a bunch of stables, and we've got a lot of shit to sweep out of them."

The analogy was far from matching Zanuck's mood. He had done his homework about the Fox Film Company and he was impressed with its record and its past. He would no more have thought of comparing Fox to a stable than the United States to a banana republic. Instead, he was measuring it up against the only other big studio complex he had known, which was Warner Brothers, and it stood up well to the comparison. In fact, he told himself, this was bigger, richer, better equipped territory than Warners ever had been.

And he was now its boss.

Did the fact that it covered more acres, could make more pictures, owned more stars, make him bigger than the boss of Warners, Jack himself?

That remained to be seen. But certainly, there could be no doubt who would be in charge here, and who would wield the power, and no member of the Warner family would ever be able to deny it to him. It was all his, to run to the best of his powers and ability. It was an exciting prospect to savor at the age of thirty-three.

When Darryl Zanuck had quit Warners to form Twentieth Century Films, he had asked his young assistant, Milton Sperling, to go with him. But by that time, Sperling, already acting as Jack Warner's "beard" in his adulterous deception of his first wife, had become deeply involved in other ploys Warner adopted to hold on to his clandestine services. When, for instance, Warner realized Zanuck was leaving him and feared Sperling would go with him, he sent for the young man and said:

"Now don't you quit on me, for Christ's sake. I'll give you a raise. How much are you getting?"

Sperling told him he was being paid twenty-five dollars a week.

"I'll give you fifty," said Jack.

Sperling was tempted and fell. Fifty dollars a week was a lot of money in Hollywood in those days, and a young man of nineteen or twenty could live very well on it.

"As a matter of fact," Sperling said later, "I've never felt richer in my life. I actually saved money and was astonished and heartened one day when I found I had three hundred dollars in the bank. Three hundred dollars was a fortune."

He stayed on at Warners for another six months, and because he was a bright kid and some of Zanuck's boldness and enterprise had rubbed off on him, he soon found that more and more responsibility was being loaded on his shoulders. They were willing shoulders, but he felt that, in view of his extracurricular activities protecting his boss's secret love-life, he ought to get more pay for what he was doing, even danger money.

So he went to see Jack Warner and pointed out that he was working sixteen hours a day and thought he was worth more than the fifty dollars a week he was getting. Warner said:

"How much do you want?"

Sperling swallowed and said: "Seventy-five."

"Impossible," said Warner.

"In that case," Sperling said, "I'm quitting."

Warner laughed. "You're gonna quit? Don't make me laugh. Didn't you tell me last week you're bringing your mother out here from New York? You can't quit. You can't afford it!"

Sperling drew himself up and said defiantly:

"I'll have you know I have three hundred dollars in the bank, and I don't need you."

And he quit. He soon got another job working for Eddie Small, an independent producer, and that lasted a year. Then he got an offer from Winfield Sheehan at Fox Films to go over there as his executive assistant.

"And shortly after that," Sperling said, "the studio was sold from under us, and Zanuck came in."

Sperling has a vivid memory of the arrival of the Twentieth Century people on the Fox lot, and if Zanuck thought of it as an incognito appearance, that was not how it seemed to those who were there. Later on, Sperling compared it to the entry of Adolf Hitler into Prague after the Nazis conquered Czechoslovakia, with the natives watching, weeping, and wondering what was going to happen to them as their new masters swept in.

"The whole studio was shuddering behind drawn blinds and peering out at the main street of the lot," Sperling said later. "A cavalcade of black cars came through the main gate and drove slowly through the studio, examining the premises, and we watched those sinister cars, with Zanuck in the leading vehicle, and we said: 'Boom! Now he's going to fire everybody!' "

He did indeed fire a lot of people. On his first weekend after taking over, he read all the story properties Fox Films owned and went through the production program. He threw a dozen scripts into the wastepaper basket at once, canceled several productions already in the works on the grounds that they were "overpriced crap," and went through the list of contract players and technicians, running a pen through name after name. Then he called in the studio manager, and told him to "pay them off at the best price you can get, and have them out of the studio by the weekend." Players, producers, directors, cameramen, publicity people were all included in the list, and the studio manager did a ruthlessly efficient job of eliminating them. Then, finding that his own name was in the list, he gave himself a week's salary and quit the studio, too.

Actually, Fox had few potent stars under contract, and those with some impact on the box office Zanuck retained. The studio's most popular star was undoubtedly the child actress Shirley Temple, whose appearances in practically any kind of story produced lines at the movie theater, and after her came the cowboy philosopher-comedian, Will Rogers, whose homespun personality was also powerful enough to triumph over poor plots and incompetent direction. There was also a highly popular female star named Janet Gaynor, who specialized in simple, wholesome, romantic roles; Warner Oland, whose Charlie Chan films were popular; and a player named Warner Baxter, whose romantic and heroic roles were a mask for a stubborn and often quarrelsome personality. To add to this roster of players Zanuck brought with him from Twentieth Century some of his loyal stars, including Loretta Young and Fredric March, and he also retained for the future a player who was under a nonexclusive contract to Fox Films. Zanuck was impressed neither by his personality nor his price, but decided to hang on to him just in case. Which was how he came to have Henry Fonda available when he was needed.

To replace the technicians he had fired, he brought over his two best screenwriters, Nunnally Johnson and Bess Meredyth, and his associate producers, Raymond Griffith and Kenneth MacGowan, and, since he was still a shareholder in the company, the Louis B. Mayer son-in-law, William Goetz, came too.

One of the Fox staff who escaped the Zanuck axe was Milton Sperling, who remembered being summoned to Zanuck's office at this time. He feared Zanuck had not forgiven him for staying on at Warners after his departure, and presumed he was going to be given a roasting before being dismissed.

"You son of a bitch, you double-crossed me, you bastard," Zanuck said as he came into the office. "I swore I'd get you for that." He paused and then he went on: "But you've got a contract and I can't fire you." Another pause and Sperling's spirits rose, because he knew Zanuck could fire him if he wanted to, contract or no contract. Then he continued: "What I'm gonna do is punish you — I'm gonna make you one of my writers."

At which he burst into laughter, held out his hand, and Sperling shook it and wished good fortune and good luck to 20th Century–Fox. Zanuck was only too well aware he would need all the luck he could get.

Nineteen thirty-five was a good year for Hollywood. For the first time, screenwriters, directors and producers were beginning to lose their obsession with sound in films, and had begun using dialogue, music, and background noise as handmaidens of their productions rather than as an easy way of jolting moviegoers out of their seats with deafening vocal and sound effects. In consequence, producers and directors turned down the decibels, stopped worrying about how certain stars sounded on the track, and paid more attention to how they could perform in general. Players from the stage in New York, London, Paris, and Chicago began to arrive at the studios, and were taken in not simply because of their mellifluous voices but because the movies had now become a medium for the expertise of the all-round professional player. It was true, of course, that looks were still invaluable. So was a melodious vocal delivery. But the flag-waving eyebrows and the violent body-language of the old silent films were out, and so were the shouts, screams, bangs, and whistles of the early talkies. Instead, control and personality were in.

Everywhere in Hollywood studio chiefs were looking for these new kinds of performers, and were ready to pay fabulous amounts of money to keep them, which was the reason Zanuck found them in such short supply at Fox. There just wasn't enough money in the studio reserves to pay the fees the established stars, or the newcomers from New York and London, were demanding. To compensate, he called his staff together for a morale-building session and assured them they could overcome all their shortages by hard work and enterprise. "Stars don't make movies," he told them. "Movies make stars." All the same, it would have made things easier had he been able to use a Garbo or a Joan Crawford. But until new productions came along, he knew he would have to rely upon the studio's two most reliable moneymakers, Shirley Temple and Will Rogers, to pay the expenses. At which point Will Rogers was killed in an airplane accident, before he could make his first film for the new regime.

That was a misfortune, but there were mistakes and oversights too. Typically, Hollywood was waiting for the thirty-three-year-old wonder-boy to fail, and he certainly did not have a good first year. It was as if Zanuck's arrival at Fox, and the challenge he represented, quickened the blood of his older rivals and prodded them into showing him how it should be done. Over at Warner Brothers, they were soon most effectively compensating for his departure by exploiting the trend in films which he had pioneered just before quitting them. They began a new cycle of money-making gangster films, using the stars he had created for them, in particular James Cagney and Edward G. Robinson. One of the biggest successes was even based on a story Zanuck had been forced to leave behind — because it was written under one of his pseudonyms, Gregory Rogers — and this became a box-office winner entitled *G Men*, with Cagney as its star.

He did not fire Fox's talent scouts, and he regretted that later, because they missed potential talent when it became available. Over at the Goldwyn studios, when he was chief of Twentieth Century, he had produced a turkey named *Born to Be Bad*, and he had blamed the censors rather than the stars for its failure. But he had been particularly pleased with the performance of its young male lead, Cary Grant, whom he had borrowed from Paramount. He cursed himself for not moving in with an offer when he discovered that Grant had since been let out of his contract at Paramount because they saw no future for him as a star. He heard about Grant's departure too late, and Grant had immediately been snapped up by Pandro Berman at RKO. Zanuck groaned that he had been so blind and his talent scouts so slow.

Running through *Born to Be Bad* and trying to work out why it had been such a disaster, he had honestly had to admit that the censors at the Hays Office, who had ordered its emasculation, may not have been entirely to blame for its failure. Maybe if he had let Cary Grant in the male lead lighten up his role and play the situations for laughs rather than emotion, he might have got away with it.

Zanuck watched with envy and irritation as Berman took Grant in hand, gave him a role with the rising star Katharine Hepburn in *Sylvia Scarlett*, and demonstrated what kind of talent was available — and he had missed.

Nor was his amour propre improved when word spread around Hollywood that Warner Brothers had made a new and potentially big star discovery, this time at the expense of Pandro Berman. In casting *Sylvia Scarlett*, Berman had picked for the male lead a handsome and dashing newcomer who he was convinced possessed genuine star quality, but when he mentioned his choice to Katharine Hepburn she had threatened to quit the film if he were chosen. She had a close friend of her own for the leading role, an English actor with whom she had formed an attachment in New York, called Brian Aherne. Faced with losing Hepburn's services (and the consequent cancellation of the film), Berman was forced to fire his chosen actor and assign the role to Aherne instead.

The other actor shopped around for another part, and was finally picked up by Warners, where Jack Warner signed him to a five-year contract.

"Why didn't you bring him to me?" raged Zanuck to his talent scouts when he heard the news. "He has just the kind of pizazz we're looking for."

He had indeed. His name was Errol Flynn.

But perhaps Zanuck's worst mistake in that first year at Fox was his failure to grab the talents of a young dancer named Fred Astaire. Astaire was in Hollywood at that moment facing a crisis in his life and career, and none of his friends, including Zanuck, seemed able to tell him what to do. Until recently, he had been a member of the famous brother and sister dancing act, the Astaires, which had appeared in many successful musicals on the Broadway and London stages, but then Adele Astaire had fallen in love with an Irish peer, married, and given up the stage. Astaire, at loose ends, had come to Hollywood to try to rebuild his career. At RKO he was cast with a newcomer named Ginger Rogers in a musical film called *Flying Down to Rio*, but their roles were meant to be subordinate to those of the stars, Gene Raymond and Dolores del Rio. The singing and dancing sequences that the Astaire–Rogers pair performed proved to be, however, the only highlights of an otherwise mediocre movie. Astaire, who had hated himself in the film, wondered what he was going to do next, and no one seemed able to tell him.

It so happened that he and his sister, Adele, while still dancing together, had met and become close friends of Sam Goldwyn and his wife, Frances, and he spent a good deal of time mooning around the Goldwyn house while he was in Hollywood. A frequent visitor there, too, was Zanuck, in whom he confided his dilemma. Not only had he disliked himself in

*Flying Down to Rio*, he told Zanuck, but he suspected that RKO had done so too. At least that was the way they were behaving towards him. Although he was under option to them for another film, they had kept him in the dark about their plans. The only rumor he had heard was that if they decided to use him in another film, it would be as a partner in a dance act. And he didn't want that.

"Everybody seems to think that I was the minor member of the team when I was dancing with Adele," he said, not without bitterness. "It was always she who got the notices. No one seems to think I can stand on my own, but I can and I need to prove I can. I'm not going to team up again with anyone."

Zanuck, who had seen *Flying Down to Rio*, might have been expected to jump at this obvious appeal for advice and help, but he failed to do so. Astaire went away, deflated and disappointed with his friends the Goldwyns and with Zanuck, the boy wonder, and he did not forget the way in which he considered they had let him down.

It was several weeks later that word began to spread that *Flying Down to Rio* was doing far better at the box office than anyone had a right to expect, and that undoubtedly what was bringing the customers in were the electric dancing sequences performed by Astaire and Rogers. By this time, Goldwyn and Zanuck had begun to realize what they had missed, and Sam made haste to call up Pandro Berman at RKO. A few months earlier, he had lent RKO one of his contract stars, the young Englishman David Niven, for a loan-out fee of $5,000. Now he reminded Berman of the "favor" he had done him over Niven, and went on to tell him that he was now ready to do him another.

"You know that dancer you've got over there, Fred Astaire," Goldwyn said. "I feel sorry for the kid. I'll take him off your hands."

"That's nice of you, Sam," Berman softly replied. "But I'm afraid it's too late. We've got plans for him."

Indeed they had. Berman had finally seen the potential in Fred Astaire, and had rushed off to New York and London to buy up new vehicles for him. He had now come back with two: *Gay Divorce* and *Top Hat*. His problem had been to persuade Astaire to team up once more with Ginger Rogers.

"Not that he had anything against Ginger,"* Berman said later. "He loved working with her. But he just wanted to be an individual. We

---

*In fact, when they had both worked on the New York stage, they had dated each other and become close friends.

overcame that little by little. Gradually he got to where he fought less about it, but it was a struggle."

What really ended the struggle was an offer by RKO, now well aware of the treasure they had snared, to give Astaire ten percent of the profits of all his films, and it was one of the earliest deals of its type in Hollywood. Astaire, Berman, and Irving Berlin, who wrote the songs for the musicals, each got ten percent, and that, felt Berman, "had some effect in keeping him working with Ginger, because the money started rolling in."

Berman did not fail to inform Astaire later that Goldwyn and Zanuck had tried to get him, and Astaire was delighted to hear how they had been turned down.

"He took a perverse pleasure at the fact that they couldn't get him," said Berman, "because, as he once said to me: 'You didn't know me and I didn't know you, and you gave me these marvelous opportunities. These people, who are my friends, whom I've known for years, never even thought I was any good for films.' He was quite delighted."

Zanuck always liked to cite his mistake over Clark Gable as an example of the mistakes even bright tycoons can make, but he rarely mentioned how he had failed to sign up Grant, Flynn, and Astaire.

The first Darryl Zanuck Production for 20th Century–Fox was a film starring the operatic tenor Lawrence Tibbett, called *Metropolitan*. Its setting, as the title indicates, was the Metropolitan Opera in New York, and it was hailed by the critics as a film of great dramatic and musical quality. It died a death at the box office and soured Zanuck on any faith he had ever had about the ability of critics to promote a film.

He needed a hit badly by the time his second film came to the cutting room, but he was confident of its chances. He had written the story himself under his pseudonym Melville Grossman, and Nunnally Johnson had done the final script. *Thanks a Million* was the story of a popular crooner who fortuitously finds himself running for governor of a state, and Bing Crosby was the star they had in mind to play it. Crosby backed away because his would be the only starring role, and he didn't like that.

"He had it in his contract that he had to co-star," said Nunnally Johnson later. "Even when he was at the top of his fame, he would never assume the responsibility of being the sole star of a picture. That was very smart of him, but few actors are that smart."

In consequence, Zanuck had to cast Dick Powell, very much the poor man's Crosby, in the leading role. He backed him up with two good supporting players, Ann Dvorak and Fred Allen, and brought in one of his best directors, Roy del Ruth. Viewing the movie in the studio cinema, knowing his future and that of the company were riding on the success of this film, he waited for his Geiger counter to give him guidance. There was no warning click. He was so confident that he had a good movie that he called up all his friends (and enemies) and arranged for a sneak preview in Santa Monica. It was a terrible evening. The audience collectively squirmed. When the preview cards came in, words like "awful!" and "bilge!" and "crap!" were among the kinder comments.

How could he have been so wrong? Had his nose for smelling out trash — or boredom — failed him? Why hadn't *anybody* liked it? It was supposed to be a light, satirical musical, and there were songs in the film, catchy tunes written by the most popular writers of the day (Gus Kahn, Harry Ruby, Bert Kolmar). And they were not just sung by Dick Powell, who was certainly no Bing Crosby; they were also played by Paul Whiteman's band, the biggest and most popular jazz orchestra of the time. Zanuck stared in puzzlement at the hostile cards, and then abruptly collected the cans of film and drove back with them to Fox.

"I was just sick that night," he said later. "Before I ran [the film] again, I remember going into the toilet and thinking, *How could I make this? How could I do it?* Then I went back to the projection room and worked on it. I ran it reel by reel, stopping after each reel, making notes."

As he studied those notes, the Geiger counter in his head started working at last: *click-click-click.*

"Suddenly I found the weakness. I cut twelve minutes, that's all, and rearranged the rest. I previewed it in Santa Barbara to an absolute ovation. The preview cards were tremendous."

This time he had no complaints about the critics. Not only did they give *Thanks a Million* good notices, but the crowds seemed to agree with them and it was soon "an enormous hit."

"More than anything else," Zanuck said later, "the success of that movie saved my first year at Fox from disaster."

He could have added that it was his work in the cutting room which actually did it for him.

While Darryl Zanuck was looking everywhere for potential stars to add glamour to his films — and missing several of them — he never lost sight of the fact that Shirley Temple was the studio's life insurance. Now that Will Rogers was dead, she was the only star upon whom Fox could rely to bring in the revenue. Every film she made was a copper-bottomed, guaranteed success at the box office. One endearing quality about Zanuck was that he loved children. He would always be grateful to Virginia for giving him a family, and if he preferred his daughters to be pretty, dimpled, and undemanding (whereas he had much more equivocal expectations from his son), he was always delighted to have them around and quite astonished when, in later years, they confessed they were always afraid of disturbing him.

To his credit, he seemed to take as much pleasure in other people's children as in his own, and his affection for Shirley Temple seemed quite genuine. He had begun by being skeptical about her, fearing she would prove too saccharine-sweet, but further acquaintance with her changed his mind and he came to think of her as delightful. "What a shame it is that she has to grow up," he was always saying, as if he thought of her as a cub who would become a tigress rather than a girl child who would develop into a woman.

One day, during a script conference, the telephone rang and it was the director to say that Shirley had had an accident and lost a tooth.

"Oh God," the director moaned, "we'll all be ruined, we'll have to halt the film!"

"Never mind about that," said Zanuck. "Is the kid hurt? Is she in pain?"

He rushed down to the set and took the child in his arms, drying her tears and soothing her. Only after she was quite calm did he allow the doctor to look at her mouth and decide whether a falsie could be inserted in the gap in her front teeth.

"And if it hurts the slightest bit, kid," he said, "just you yell — and we'll stop the film."

He meant it, too.

"I always thought of him as a second father," Shirley Temple said later.

Shirley was a frequent visitor to the Zanuck home, where she played with his daughter, Darrylin, and, though she was now one of the richest children in the world, envied her the dolls and ponies with which her doting father provided her. She had no such luxuries lavished upon her, not because she was stinted by her parents but because they were not that kind of people.

Nunnally Johnson, who "thought she was a darling little girl," also thought she lived a most extraordinary life. Thanks to Zanuck, he got to know her father and mother and often visited them at their home in Santa Monica. It was just a modest suburban frame house, and what amazed

Johnson and amused Zanuck was the fact that they never quite realized how big a star, and how renowned, their daughter had become.* Shirley would go down to the beach with a bucket and spade and be surprised when she found herself surrounded by other children, just staring at her. When she invited them to join her, they giggled, but never did.

It was only after the crowds began visiting their Santa Monica house all day, walking up to the porch and peering through the windows, that Shirley's parents moved to a house, on a back road near Westwood, with a wall around it. One day the director Norman Taurog was driving along this road, which not many people used, and he saw a little stand with two small kids behind it selling lemonade at five cents a glass. He slowed the car, and looked back.

"I'm sure that's Shirley Temple," he said.

It was. At that moment she was the only thing that stood between Fox Films and bankruptcy.

One day, Shirley's father came in to see Zanuck in some embarrassment. He was a teller in a Santa Monica bank and he had been promoted to a better desk because so many people wanted to do deals with Shirley Temple's father. Deals of all kinds.

He was a plump, simple, amiable man with little sophistication. Now he hemmed and hawed and finally told Zanuck:

"I've had some letters." Pause. "They're all from women." Longer pause. "They make propositions. They want me to father a child for them."

Zanuck grinned.

"Can you guarantee you'll give them a girl?" he asked. "Or even another Shirley?"

"Nope," said Mr. Temple.

"Then don't be unfaithful to your wife," Zanuck said.

The father of the world's most famous child looked shocked. "I've certainly no intention of doing any such thing," he said. "I just thought you ought to know that there are women around like that."

"Terrible, isn't it?" agreed Zanuck.

"Don't tell Mrs. Temple," said Shirley's father as he departed. "She'd be ashamed of her sex."

*Mrs. Temple once explained to Harry Brand, chief publicity man at Fox, that she was taking Shirley on a holiday to Hawaii but didn't know anybody there. Could he give her some introductions to people who would show them the sights? Brand told her to leave it to him and sent off a cable. When she and Shirley arrived in Honolulu they were "absolutely amazed" to find 100,000 people were waiting to greet them, and the city's schoolchildren had been given a day's holiday in Shirley's honor.

\*        \*

When General George C. Marshall was Chief of Staff of the U.S. Army during World War II, he used to warn the mothers of America to start worrying about their sons when they wrote home from the wars to say how kind, thoughtful and considerate were their commanding officers. In wartime, Marshall believed, it was the "nice" generals who hesitated, suffered pangs of conscience and doubt, and only too often got their soldiers unnecessarily killed, whereas the more ruthless, selfish, and hard-driving ones went ahead, won battles, and saved lives.

Darryl Zanuck had the same feeling about film directors. He knew that he had several of them around the 20th Century–Fox lot who were loathed as "absolute bastards" by the writers, actors, and crew who had to work with them, but in his experience they got results and came up with better movies than the nice guys. Among the nastier types who could always be relied upon to come up with a successful movie, the most unpleasant was probably John Ford. Ford was a grouch, a grinch, a drinker, and he hated everyone around on a movie set, particularly actors. He never read the book from which a script was taken, and maintained he never paid much attention to the script, either, except as a map to chart his way through the plot. He despised players who blew their lines and actresses who got overemotional, and sometimes he had half the people on the set either weeping tears of humiliation or seething with rage.

But the critics loved his pictures, which were always critical successes, and sometimes even profitable at the box office. And Zanuck was well aware that he kept actors, writers, and technicians on their toes and giving of their best, because "they were so goddamn mad at him all the time, they just had to show the bastard." Which was one of the reasons why Zanuck liked to have him around.

But sometimes Ford was too much even for him. Since running his own show, first at Twentieth Century and now with the bigger operation at Fox, Zanuck had decided that being the head of a studio was rather like being the captain of a ship. You took the blame and responsibility for everything that went wrong, so you had to make sure that nothing did, and that meant you must know about every decision, have the final word on every movie, and constantly remind everyone around — stars, directors, crews, office staff alike — just who was boss, and that his eye was upon you.

Shortly after he took over at Fox, he asked John Ford to come over and direct his first film for the new administration, and handed him what he was convinced was a choice assignment. It has already been mentioned that one of the stories he had almost literally torn from the pages of a newsmagazine was *The Prisoner of Shark Island*, which had been scripted by Nunnally Johnson. It was the story of Doctor Mudd, who was one of the conspirators arrested after the assassination of President Lincoln and imprisoned in the Dry Tortugas.

Zanuck was so enthusiastic about the story that he decided to make it one of his personal productions, and it was he who had chosen John Ford to direct. The part of the Southerner, Doctor Mudd, was filled by a Fox contract star, Warner Baxter, who was a good actor but had a reputation for being wayward, temperamental, and with an ego equaled only by that of Ford himself.

By this time, Zanuck was so busy on half a dozen projects around the studio that he could not afford to be constantly on the *Shark Island* set, but he had come to trust the judgment of Nunnally Johnson and instructed him to keep his eye on how things were going. The writer was soon distressed to notice that whenever Warner Baxter spoke his lines, he used a very phony Southern accent. Ford, who was hitting the bottle quite considerably about this time, didn't seem to notice anything peculiar about Baxter's accent, particularly as he was known to believe that "Southerners talk funny anyway," and was obviously quite satisfied with what he was getting. In any case, Johnson was afraid of approaching the director, who took criticism badly. As for Baxter, Johnson feared he would throw a violent tantrum if he brought up the matter with him, so instead he took Zanuck to the projection room and waited for his reaction when he heard Baxter talking in the rushes.

"I think it's godawful," Zanuck said. "Why did you have him speak like that?"

Johnson explained that the accent was Baxter's own idea, and that Ford didn't seem to notice what was going on.

"Come on," said Zanuck, "let's walk down to the set and see what we can do about it."

Everybody on the *Shark Island* set was tense and watching Ford warily, because he was in a particularly tetchy mood. Johnson remembered the story of the time when the great director had worked at RKO and his two chief assistants used to toss coins to see who would look at the rushes and report to Ford about them. The loser saw the rushes, and then had to give Ford his honest opinion about them. He often came back with a bleeding nose. So now, as Zanuck approached the director and took him to one side, Johnson hung back. But he was near enough to hear Zanuck say: "What about this accent Baxter is using?"

Ford, who was a giant of a man, leaned over his producer. "What about it?" he asked, belligerently.

"I think it's terrible," said Zanuck. "The effect is bad. I've never heard anything like it. Have you talked to him about it?"

"Yes," said Ford, shortly.

"And he's still talking that way? I thought you were a tough guy. I thought you could handle actors. You'd better do something — and do it quick."

Suddenly Ford was towering over Zanuck, who was at least a foot smaller, his broad shoulders squared, his face flushed, his bloodshot eyes blazing.

"Are you threatening me?" he shouted. "If you're threatening me, you'll get off this set! Or I'll — "

While all the actors and crew waited breathlessly for the Ford fists to make mincemeat of Zanuck, he was meanwhile bristling like a bantam cock. He didn't seem cowed in the least.

"It's you who are threatening me," he shouted back. "And no one does that around here. I'm the one who tells you when you can stay or quit. I throw people off the set — they don't quit on me!"

Johnson thought for a moment that it was Zanuck who was going to punch Ford in the nose. But Ford, who could give the producer at least fifty pounds, suddenly backed off. Still glowering, he turned and walked across the set to talk in low, tense tones to Baxter. What he said no one heard, but Baxter began talking naturally from then on.

But Zanuck went on being mad at Ford, particularly when he read the criticisms after the premiere of *The Prisoner of Shark Island*. As usual, since he was a great favorite of the critical fraternity, Ford was lavishly praised for the "typical Ford touches" that he was credited with having inserted into the movie, when, in fact, Zanuck and Johnson had between them written them specifically in the script. He was also lauded for the way he kept the action sequences moving, and this particularly irritated Zanuck.

"He's an arrogant and ingrate bastard," he said. "He screamed like a banshee when I knocked minutes out of his long-winded sequences. And then he has the sauce to take the bows when he's praised for it in the *New Yorker*."

It was almost as good as having his revenge when he called Ford back to the studio some months later and told the director he was picking up his option, and he was being assigned another movie. When Ford asked what it was, Zanuck informed him with a wicked grin that he was teaming him up with Shirley Temple in a film to be called *Wee Willie Winkie*. It was a savory moment when he trapped the expression on Ford's features, for he knew he loathed child actors and hated sentimental stories.

This was, indeed, a soapily sentimental story, an adaptation of the Kipling story with Shirley Temple playing the part of Willie, transformed for movie purposes into a little girl. But if Zanuck expected the great director to turn down the assignment, he was mistaken. He accepted without a word. Not only that. He got along with Shirley splendidly, so much so, in fact, that Zanuck was rumored to be jealous of his success with her, especially when Ford taught Shirley to come into Zanuck's office and call him "Uncle Pipsqueak."

*Wee Willie Winkie* was, of course, a great box-office success. But then, since it starred Shirley Temple, it would have been one no matter who directed it.

# THIRTEEN

# WILD OATS

HREE YEARS after his arrival at 20th Century–Fox, Darryl Zanuck was making $260,000 a year and earning every penny of it. A glance through the list of his movies from 1935 to 1938 does not include any which have since become classics or even many whose titles are likely to be remembered by aging cinemagoers. They were the doldrum years so far as Hollywood was concerned, and the most you can say for the thirty-five movies that Zanuck was turning out every year over this period is that they were usually more stimulating, and better entertainment, than those most rival studios were producing at the time. Where Zanuck excelled over the others was that he never forgot to fill his movies with action and make sure they had a hard-driving narrative line. Looking at some of his product nearly fifty years after it was made is a revelation of the kind of trash movie fans so easily swallowed two generations ago, when twice-a-week visits to the movies were a national habit and hunger for entertainment was more easily appeased.

The films he produced or wrote under one or other of his pseudonyms during those years included eight or nine that cleaned up at the box office and completely restored Fox's financial situation. They included *Shark Island* and *A Message to Garcia* (with John Boles, Wallace Beery, and Barbara Stanwyck), *The Country Doctor* (about the Dionne quintuplets), *Under Two Flags* (with Claudette Colbert and Ronald Colman), *One in a Million* and *Happy Landing* (with Sonja Henie), *Little Miss Broadway* (with Shirley Temple), and *Suez* and *Lloyds of London* (with Tyrone Power, Madeleine Carroll, and Loretta Young). None of them is ever likely to become a favorite with the film societies, but when they make their occasional appearances on late-night TV, one thing is likely to be noticeable about them: none of them has the hacked-about, mutilated appearance of so many other rerun movies, because right at the start, when they were first made ready for the movie houses, Zanuck had already cut them to the bone and left very little else to be excised from them, except by deliberate evisceration.

Furthermore, they may be trashy but they aren't boring, because they always have action.

"They don't call them moving pictures because they stand still — they move!" Zanuck once said, and the message was subsequently hung all over Fox studios.

Seeking as he was in those days for money with which to float the new Fox enterprise to success, he never did succeed in creating the big stars he needed — not of the caliber, anyway, of Gable, Crawford, and Garbo. But he did find some, usually in unexpected places where the more affluent studios like M-G-M would never have thought of looking.

He found Sonja Henie, for example, on the ice-rink at the time when she was the world champion amateur skater. He signed her up without even giving her a screen test and subsequently discovered, as he put it later, "that she was the original dumb Swede.* The moment she took her skates off, she looked and acted like the girl next door's ugly sister. But on the rink, she was a princess, a flying angel, a quick-silver goddess, and she hit everyone who watched her right in the heart and the stomach." He cast her in a junky story called *One in a Million*, and it made a fortune at the box office. He followed this with *Thin Ice* and then with *Happy Landing*, exhorting his writers at every script conference to eschew non-rink encounters and "for Christ's sake keep the dame on ice."

Henie made so much money for 20th Century–Fox in 1938 that the studio had a surplus at the bank for the first time in twenty years, and since the "dumb Swede" had now hired an extremely undumb agent, Zanuck quickly upped her salary to $210,000, making her (in 1937) the highest paid star in Hollywood, and worth every penny of her earnings.

If Sonja Henie was a not very bright skater, Tyrone Power was an extremely dull actor, and practically every studio in Hollywood had tested him and turned him down. He came from a famous American theater family and hated everything about acting, from using makeup and learning lines to pretending to be anybody other than himself.

"All right, I'm dull," he once told one of his wives, "but that's all I ever want to be — dull me."

One of the Fox talent scouts in New York did a test of him after watching

*She was, in fact, a Norwegian.

him play a small part on Broadway, and Zanuck chanced to see the film when it was run in the projection room in Hollywood. He hated it.

"Take it off," he ordered, "he looks like a monkey."

But Virginia, who happened to be with him, saw possibilities. It was true that Power at that time wore his black hair very low over his forehead, and he also possessed thick and bushy brows that drooped right down over his eyes. She agreed that he looked very like an apeman, but on the other hand, there *was* something . . .

She suggested they should sweep his hair back and trim his eyebrows, and the result was startling. Zanuck gave him a couple of walk-on parts, including a small speaking role in the final scene of *The Country Doctor*, where he walks up to one of the grown-up Dionne quintuplets and says "May I have this dance?" At the sneak preview, there were scores of cards mentioning "the guy in the last scene," and, subsequently, gushing fan letters saying "Ty Power can dance with me any time!"

Zanuck decided to cash in on him quickly, and the result was a starring role in *Lloyds of London*, which he had originally intended for Don Ameche, and Tyrone Power's career was launched.

As Zanuck later remarked: "It couldn't have happened to a duller man."

Even after Power became one of the hottest properties in Hollywood, Zanuck, an inveterate practical joker, could never resist getting a rise out of Power. He now had a brand-new steam room on the Fox lot to which certain producers and directors were invited, but actors rarely. One of the few exceptions was Tyrone Power, who liked to come in after a day's shooting and plunge into the pool, which Zanuck always kept at a refreshing sixty degrees. One day, after a particularly strenuous scene on the set, fighting a duel, swinging from the chandeliers, Power stripped off his clothes and plunged with a whoop of joy into the pool. His cry swiftly changed to a howl of pain as he realized that the pool was frigid. Zanuck had had a load of ice poured in just before Power's arrival.

By this time the Zanucks were comfortably settled in their beach house at 546 Ocean Front, Santa Monica, and Virginia was later to describe it as the happiest period of her life. In fact, it must have been a difficult period for her, and one of considerable readjustment. True, their financial situation had never been better and Darryl's manner towards her and her growing family had never been more thoughtful and attentive. He never forgot a birthday, and his gifts were lavish — jewelry from Cartier, a well-trained German shepherd dog for her to walk the beach with; a puppy, a tropical fish tank, bikes, model planes, kites, ponies for the kids.

For one Christmas, he bought her a new open touring car, and she loved it, except that its color was green, like his Cadillac. She did not need to be told that the green was called Zanuck Green at Fox studios, where it was specially blended and sent to Detroit solely for use on the Zanuck cars. Later on, his daughter Susan asked Zanuck where he had found the original blend for the paint, and he told her he had given the painters at the studio a bottle of his mother's green nail varnish and told them to imitate that. Susan guessed her mother had known that all along, that she had one day realized she was riding around in Louise's nail varnish, and didn't really like it.

Louise, who was getting on now, sometimes came down to Santa Monica to see her grandchildren, and she still did herself up for the visit and still wore green varnish on her fingernails, and Virginia thought that for a woman of her age it was kind of outlandish. For a woman of any age, in fact, even a film star.

In 1938, Darryl took Virginia to the premiere in Hollywood of *Alexander's Ragtime Band*, with Tyrone Power, Don Ameche, and a new star named Alice Faye. Virginia had heard rumors about Miss Faye but had never met her. All she knew was what she read in the gossip columns, which told her that Zanuck had recently replaced Jean Harlow, who had been taken ill, with this newcomer with the straw-colored hair. Anxious to find out what her husband saw in her, she watched her intently on the screen and then went to a party to meet her afterwards. If she was impressed, she did not say so.

Virginia was still deeply in love with her husband, but both she and the children were aware that the relationship had changed. When Darryl came home at a reasonable hour, which was not very often, the friends who were present got the distinct feeling that she was being treated like a senior wife in a well-run harem. She was awarded affection, respect, as the honored mother of the master's children. But there were no signs of heat or the tactile contacts that indicate physical passion. And for those who heard the rumors around Hollywood of Zanuck's extraterritorial activities, that was hardly surprising. Sexually speaking, everyone who worked in the studios knew that Zanuck was leading a double life, and the principal speculation among Virginia's friends was how much she knew about it.

Her closest friends suspected she knew quite a lot, and that she well understood what they were talking about when they sometimes slyly referred to him as "the stray lamb." They also suspected she had come to accept the situation, and she and her husband now had an arrangement, though maybe an unspoken one. After the Dolores Costello incident, he had resolved never to embarrass her again by concentrating on one particular woman, especially now that she had established her niche as the mother of his children. On the other hand, she had accepted conditions herself, about her husband and other women. He could never leave them alone because having them, sleeping with them, proved something to him. And her friends believed she had given tacit agreement to that, so long, of course, as Darryl played the field. And, in future, kept his girlfriends from wearing green nail varnish, as one of them had once publicly dared to do.

Except for the skiing holidays which they took every winter at Sun Valley, Virginia and Darryl no longer traveled so frequently together. Not in those first, hectic years of getting Fox established, that is. Zanuck followed the same routine every day. He was up between nine and ten in the morning, though he sometimes tried to be around in time to see Virginia take his daughters off to school. He never came home until the early hours of the morning, having been up most of the night seeing rushes and movies at the studio. Some weekends, he and Virginia would bundle the kids into the car and take them to the ranch at Encino, and that was fine because they would ride across the sagebrush together, compete with their father in races, wrestle, swim, crowd around a barbecue, and he would give test papers on their lessons in the ranch house later before packing them off to bed.

But even on these sunny and memorable occasions, he had usually left before they were up next morning to go visit his stable of polo ponies, and they did not see him again until they crowded the rails and cheered him on at the Sunday-afternoon game. He liked to cuddle his two pretty daughters, who were eminently cuddlable, but somehow they never dared to confide in him as other girls did with their fathers, and they envied Shirley Temple when she came down to stay with them at the ranch and would gravely say, on frequent occasions:

"Uncle Pipsqueak, can I ask you something?"

And they would go off to discuss Shirley's childhood problems, while his two daughters stared after them, wishing they had that kind of courage.

As for Richard, his son, even from the earliest age he was in awe of his father, and was always aware of him as an electric charge quivering and vibrating through the household whenever he was on the scene.

"He was a very scary person to me," Richard said later. "I wasn't a shy little kid hovering in a corner or anything, but I did find his presence overwhelming. I was always aware of my father's need to compete and dominate everyone with whom he came in contact." He used to watch the directors, the stars, the writers who came out to the house to talk to him, and was always conscious of his father's haughty, abrasive manner.

"Sometimes he didn't even look at them when he was talking to them, but just rasped out words at them while he busied himself with something else. And they took it. They were big stars, big names, and they let him push them around. And I sensed that everyone feared him, were afraid to stand up to him, and capitulated to his domination."

He was still a health fanatic, worried about his lung power, his weight, his muscles, and after a session on the trapeze or a half-hour boxing with his trainer, Fidel la Barba, he would spend some time in front of the full-length mirror in the gym, scrutinizing his body. Tyrone Power was once a witness of one of these muscle-flexing sessions and mentioned it afterwards to his girlfriend, wondering why a man in Zanuck's position took so much care of himself.

"You'd think he was an actor," he said. "Actors have to keep track of themselves because of their audiences. But not a guy like Mr. Zanuck."

"Ah," said his girlfriend, "but don't forget he has an audience to worry about too — girls."

Over breakfast each day, he took French and Spanish lessons as he swallowed his yogurt and fruit, and then he was off in his Zanuck Green Cadillac to the studio, driving at breakneck speed over the hills to Westwood, where he arrived promptly at 11 A.M. Everybody else had to be in the studio by eight o'clock and work was already in progress, but somehow the atmosphere of the place subtly changed as the Cadillac swerved through the gate and sped up to Zanuck's office complex, where Milton Sperling and his secretaries were waiting for him and took him right in to the first script and casting conferences of the day.

Milton Sperling was going through a complex period of his life at this time and reexamining his relationship with his boss and benefactor. It was through Zanuck that he had now found what he believed was his niche in the movie business, as a scriptwriter, and, thanks to the opportunities his boss had given him, he had enjoyed some success at it. It was Sperling who had been assigned the screenwriting jobs for Sonja Henie's films, with the result that he was basking in the glorious financial success that those productions had enjoyed. Admittedly, Henie's graceful wizardry with her skates had done most to make her films into box-office bonanzas, but all who had contributed to her success, especially her scriptwriter, inevitably shared some of the credit. Sperling, though still in his very early twenties, had become one of the better-known writers in Hollywood and respected by his peers.

As a result, he had been invited by a number of them to become a member of a newly formed professional organization known as the Screenwriters Guild, which planned to affiliate with the Authors Guild in New York. He was flattered, but shortly after he had accepted the invitation and joined, he was informed he had strayed into enemy territory and volunteered to fight with the rebels. For once more the old war had broken out anew in Hollywood, with the technicians (the screenwriters, this time) organizing an independent union to look after their interests and the studios determined to prevent them. They used the same ploy as they always did in these circumstances, by creating a rival, studio-approved association called the Screen Playwrights, which, they maintained, would do a far better job for the writers than any "outside" union, and they began bringing pressure upon their contract writers to turn their back on the Screenwriters Guild and join the Screen Playwrights instead.

Sperling was in something of a quandary. He knew that 20th Century–Fox was standing squarely with the other studios in opposing the drive for membership in the Guild, and he felt guilty about having joined it, especially when Morrie Ryskind, who represented the Screen Playwrights at Fox, tracked him down one day and said: "How can you betray Darryl after all he has done for you?"

Sperling went to talk to Zanuck about it and got no comfort from their conversation. His boss made no threats of reprisals, but used a much more effective form of blackmail.

"We've gone through too much together," Zanuck said to him. "You've got to resign from that union. Look at all I've done for you. You gave me stories and I turned them into pictures." Which was true, of course. He would have been much farther back down the road to success had it not been for Zanuck.

So he resigned from the Screenwriters Guild but did not join the Screen Playwrights. He did have the feeling he had been subtly pressured, and for a time his feelings towards Zanuck were ambivalent. Before, although Zanuck was not much older than he was, he had always thought of the relationship between the two as that of father and son. Now he felt it was boss and favored employee, and it made a difference.

That did not stop him from continuing to admire his boss and he was constantly astonished at his grasp, flair, and energy. "He was aware of everything, took care of everything," Sperling said later. "From midday onwards he would answer mail, dictate notes, go for a hasty lunch at the

Cafe de Paris, in the studio commissary, and then come back for a series of conferences which lasted all day. There were casting conferences, in which actors and actresses were paraded before him and expected to show off their abilities. He was good with players. He had always read the scripts and the parts for which they were auditioning, and knew what to ask of them. He was always polite and respectful to them, especially to mature actors. It was hard to believe he had once stamped on an old ham's foot out of petulant rage, because he always said 'please' and 'thank you' with such humility. And then, after that was over, he would go down to the makeup salons to make sure a star's hair was all right or a feature player's jacket fitted."

Sperling once saw him take a hank of Betty Grable's hair and slice it off with a pair of scissors he grabbed from the makeup table, and she burst into tears and screamed he had scalped her and ruined her looks. He just laughed at her, told the hairdresser to "tidy it up," and walked out. Later on, she came up and kissed him and apologized, because, with shorter hair, she looked much more attractive.

Back in his office, directors and their assistants came and went. "He had absolutely no respect for directors until they got on the set," Sperling said, "and they must have dreaded the script conferences to which he subjected them. He sat them all around the wall of his office, and there was one chair in the middle of the room, right in front of his desk, and this of course was known around the studio as the Hot Seat. It was usually where 'the Present Writer,' as he called him, or the director, sat and it was a lonely spot, because all the criticisms and awkward questions were flung, like bullets, in that direction. Everyone else had to sit absolutely still and listen while Zanuck walked up and down the office, tearing ideas out of his head, suggesting scenes and special shots, and then swinging on the Hot Seat and rasping: 'Waddya think of that? Does it grab ya?' Whether the poor guy agreed or not, he still had to say why he liked or disliked it. For a time it was part of my job to send a copy of Zanuck's remarks to everybody present after the conference was over. Later Molly Mandeville took over as script coordinator. But the writer was in deep trouble if he tried to use in his amended script Zanuck's own words and dialogue he had conjured out of his brains during the conference. Zanuck's remarks were not to be considered the Word of God, and the writer was expected to use them solely as a base for new script ideas."

Nor did Zanuck mince his words when the new treatments arrived and he thought they failed to measure up.

In a typical memorandum, he would write:

The new treatment of *The Great American Broadcast* is, in my opinion, an almost deliberate attempt to sabotage an excellent story idea. All character, punch and vitality have been eliminated.

He could be even rougher than that:

I know audiences today want popular crap, but I cannot believe we are so lacking that we cannot dish it up to them with some traces of originality. This treatment made me vomit.

"He respected writers, and only the worst screenplays got the really rough treatment," Sperling said. "Despising directors as mere mechanics, he delivered approved scripts to them — approved by him, of course — rather as if he were delivering the morning newspapers. 'Go and shoot this,' he would say, and implicit in his instructions was the added message: 'And don't change a word.' "

There was one period in Zanuck's daily routine that never failed to amaze Sperling. Every day at four o'clock on the Fox lot, everything would come to a halt.

"You know that Darryl was mad about women," Sperling said. "Everybody talked about it in Hollywood and the rumor was that his prowess as a cocksman was just unbelievable. I don't know whether it was true or not. I was a shy young man, a bit backward in that regard, I guess, but even I knew that every day at four o'clock in the afternoon some girl on the lot would visit Zanuck in his office. The doors would be locked after she went in, no calls were taken, and for the next half hour nothing happened — headquarters shut down. Around the office work came to a halt for the sex siesta. It was an understood thing. While the girl was with Zanuck, everything stopped, and anyone who had the same proclivities as Zanuck, and had the girl to do it with, would go off somewhere and do what he was doing. I honestly think that from four to four-thirty every day at Fox, if you could have harnessed the power from all the fucking that was going on, you could have turned the tides at Malibu. It was an incredible thing, but a girl went in through that door every day."

It was usually a starlet who was chosen for this daily assignation, and it was rarely the same one twice. The only one who ever seems to have been called in more than once was a Fox contract feature player named Carole Landis, who was casually referred to by personnel as "the studio hooker." (She subsequently committed suicide after her name had been linked with a Fox star, Rex Harrison.) Otherwise, any pretty and willing extra was picked for the daily session, and after her erotic chore was completed, she departed by a side door with or without a little present or promise from her temporary lover. Only then would Zanuck's door be unlocked again, the telephones would begin to ring, work would be resumed, and conferences would be called.

At 6:30 Zanuck would leave his office for the Fox gym, steam room, barbershop, and pool (decorated in Zanuck Green) where he would first be shaved by Sam Silver, his barber, and then retire to the steam room. If he was feeling good, he would ring up a friend like Joe Schenck or Sid Grauman or one of his polo-playing friends to join him. Sometimes his boxing instructor, the ex-champ Fidel la Barba, would come down to spar for a few rounds in the ring of the studio gym, and an instructor would be around to give him a ten-minute lesson in conjugating French verbs. After this he would plunge in the pool and then come out to be briskly massaged by Sam Nikios, otherwise known as Sam the Barber (who was also the house bookmaker for the gambling element on the lot). And then, but only then, would Zanuck stretch out and take a delayed postcoital sleep.

Watching Zanuck being massaged, Sperling said later, reminded him of Jack Warner, because Jack too had often liked to have him on hand while his Turkish masseur went to work on him.

"I must say, watching Zanuck's and Warner's bodies, having seen them nude so many times," said Sperling later, "inevitably forced me into comparing them. They were both self-confident men and indulgent men. Both were proud of their physical equipment and their sexual prowess, and, I suspect, secretly pleased they could get it up with so many attractive women. Jack had a fleshy, soft, puddingy body, but a very healthy color, and he was strong, physically strong. Zanuck had a body like a bantam cock, very stringy but also very strong. Jack had a body like an elephant. Zanuck had a body like a whippet, a jaguar, and a kind of restless strength, whereas Jack was a kind of steam roller. In their different ways they were both very conscious of themselves. They made a very interesting contrast."

After Zanuck's snooze, he would go back to his office, where dinner would be served. Then he would take out a cigar and light it up and have what he said was the most rewarding smoke of the day. The cigars were always the same. They came from a plantation in Cuba that was later bought by Douglas Fairbanks, Sir Alexander Korda, and Zanuck, and for the rest of the evening Zanuck would chain-smoke them.

"And then about nine o'clock," said Sperling, "he would go into the projection room and he would begin to see the rushes. There would always be at least six or seven films shooting at a time, so he would see the dailies on these, and I would take notes. At Warners, and, later, at Fox, Barbara McLean, a cutter, or Molly Mandeville would be there. He was very sharp and alert and he would continuously be suggesting cuts or alterations in the films that were ready for showing. After that he would see movies which had been made by other studios, and often be just as scathing about them as he was about our own."

Sperling noted that when Zanuck was bored he could drop off to sleep like a baby and never make a sound — a sharp contrast to his sleeping habits at home — or he would get restless and look around for something to distract his attention. He even brought his propensity for practical jokes into the projection room, and once enlivened a dull movie by switching a set of false teeth that a regular at the screenings always took out while watching the rushes. He had had another set made by the man's dentist, slightly different; so far as Zanuck was concerned, the man's discomfiture when he put his dentures back in his mouth more than made up for a boring evening.

"It was often three or four in the morning before he finished viewing, writing memos, conferring with writers, cutters, and directors," said Sperling. "Only then did he get back in his car and drive home to the beach house. I don't know whether Virginia waited up for him or not. I doubt it. Then he was up again next morning, to run, box, exercise, drive back to the studio. That was his life. With that all-important interlude at four o'clock. That's how he worked every day. Those who had to be with him through these grueling daily sessions, as I did, felt the strain of it. It was a good thing I was young. I'd get out of the studio around three or four in the morning and have to be back to clock in at nine, and then have to go through that exhausting process after he arrived at the studio and started work. He must have found it more tiring than I did. True, he didn't turn up until eleven, and so had two hours extra on me. But then, I didn't have the physical effort of that daily four-o'clock interval."

Yet even a superman like Zanuck had to have some help to be able to keep up such a strenuous routine. 20th Century–Fox was now sometimes exceeding its quota and producing between thirty-six and forty movies a year, and Zanuck was always looking around for producers onto whom he could unload the burden of responsibility for individual films. Good, bright, reliable producers were thin on the ground in Hollywood. He finally told Sperling he was taking him out of the writers' pen at Fox and turning him into one. It was the nearest Sperling came to disaster in his movie career.

Betty Grable was one of Fox's contract stars, and everyone around the studio liked her. She was bright, blond, sassy, and pretty. She had graduated first into stage musicals and then into films by way of the big bands that played around the country in those days, and she had been vocalist for both the Dorsey Brothers and Artie Shaw (she later married the trumpeter Harry James). Zanuck signed her up when Alice Faye suddenly announced she was sick; skeptical studio doctors examined her and found that her illness was quite genuine. Zanuck never had any doubt that nothing made female stars get well quicker than the knowledge that a female rival was waiting in the wings, and Betty Grable was eagerly waiting. He replaced Faye with Grable as the female lead in a musical called *Down Argentine Way*, in which Don Ameche played opposite her. She was a great success. Alice Faye hastened back to the studios when she realized her rival was a hit, and, with effective but mischievous inspiration, he cast both stars in the same film, as a sister act in *Tin Pan Alley*. Later Grable did another sister act, this time with Zanuck's erstwhile four-o'clock special, Carole Landis, in *Moon over Miami*.

Now Sperling was told he could have her as his star in his first production for 20th Century–Fox. He had always been a fan of Grable's and he had studied every film she had made. He had become convinced that the bright, leggy blonde was not just an amiable and attractive singer and dancer but a potentially serious actress. When Zanuck gave him the assignment, he decided to make it Betty Grable's first dramatic and non-musical role. Instead of being filmed in spangly tights in Technicolor, he would make her wear all her clothes and show her in stark black-and-white.

Sperling had urged Zanuck to buy a book and was partly responsible for the screenplay, and it was given two working titles, "Hot Spot" and the other, the title of the novel, *I Wake Up Screaming*. He teamed Grable with a newcomer to the studios, Victor Mature, in his first film role, and Zanuck at the last minute ordered him to find a role for Carole Landis.

"The film was directed by Bruce Humberstone," said Sperling later. "He was known as Lucky Humberstone, for the very good reason he somehow continued to find work in Hollywood despite the fact that he had so small a talent. Well, we made the film, and it was a dark film, with low-key lighting, very ususual for those days. I was very proud of it. I liked the script, by Dwight Taylor, who was a very good writer. I had convinced Zanuck to go for the whole thing because I talked fast and convinced him it would be a strange, new type of film, and reveal an entirely new Betty Grable."

They showed the film, under the title of "Hot Spot," at a sneak preview in Pasadena, and it is not a night Sperling likes to remember. It so happened that Joe Schenck and Sidney Kent had come in for a visit from the New York office and they went along to the preview, together with William Goetz, Betty Grable, and, of course, Zanuck.

"Seeing Betty Grable's name up there and a title like 'Hot Spot,' " said Sperling, "the audience thought they were going to see a musical. Instead they saw this grim murder story, and they began drifting out after the first two reels, and I knew it was a disaster, a total disaster. Well, I was aware that Schenck and Kent and the others were all there, and I decided I couldn't face them and I sneaked out by a side door. But I ran right into them because they had sneaked out too. And as I came on to the sidewalk, Schenck pointed a finger at me and cried: 'There he is!' It was a stop-thief kind of thing. They were all glowering at me."

It was at this moment that Darryl Zanuck stepped forward and put his arm around Sperling's puny shoulders. Turning to the others, he said:

"Whatever he did, I told him to do. It's my responsibility, not his. I okayed the script. I okayed the cast and the budget."

Then he bent forward and whispered into Sperling's ear: "Let's leave these cocksuckers and go back to the studio and fix it up."

They drove back to Fox, spent the night in the cutting room, and they fixed it up. Zanuck decided that the title should be *I Wake Up Screaming* and the publicity department added a strapline to the posters saying: "Betty Grable as you've never seen her before!" The critics quite liked it and it made money at the box office.

But for Sperling it had been a close thing.

"Zanuck saved me," he said. "He stood with me. He won my love and admiration for that."

Not surprisingly, Zanuck calculated that if he could turn a youngster like Sperling into a producer of sorts, he could make a really successful one out of a real professional like Nunnally Johnson. He appointed him a producer too, but the result was not quite what he had anticipated.

He called Johnson into his office one day and asked him: "Have you ever heard of a director called Doctor Otto Ludwig Preminger?"

Johnson said he knew the name as belonging to a Mittel-European who had directed a successful play on Broadway. Zanuck nodded and said he had signed Preminger up as a director for Fox, and would Johnson object if he made his debut directing one of Johnson's stories, Johnson to be in charge as producer. Easygoing as ever, Johnson said he was quite willing to work with "Doctor" Preminger on his first Hollywood venture.

About a week later, Johnson received another summons from Zanuck, and when he saw him in his office he seemed to be worried. He asked the writer-producer carefully how the picture was going but did not seem to be reassured when Johnson assured him it was going along all right.

"Don't you think it's a little slow?" asked Zanuck, and when Johnson shook his head, he went on: "Well, I certainly do. Goddamn slow. And I think it not only looks slow in the rushes, but he's taking too long with all the stuff he's shooting. Wasting money. I can't have it. The budget won't stand it. Now you go down there and replace Doctor Preminger at once."

At this Johnson bridled. "Now look, Darryl," he said, "I don't fire people. I only hire them. Firing's not in my contract."

Zanuck laughed. "Okay," he said, "I'll do it. I'll go down and bounce him."

Preminger was off the picture an hour later, and a new director assigned. Johnson felt badly about it and guilty that Preminger should have received such rough treatment on his first film, for he did not think he had deserved it. In fact, he went on brooding about it for months, and some years later, when Zanuck wasn't around, he brought Preminger back to make another film with him, *The Pied Piper*. By that time, however, he had decided that Zanuck had been right and Preminger was no director. So he used him as an actor.

On the other hand, Johnson thought Zanuck had been quite wrong in thinking he would make a producer. He hated all the chores and all the worries involved, especially on scripts other people had written. Finally he went to see Zanuck and said, "Look, I think I'd better quit. I have a script on my desk right now and I cannot open the thing. I know it's no good, and don't know what to do about it. I just cannot tell this fella [who wrote it] what to do about it, and I can't do it all myself. It's unfair to the writer. I can't do it. I can't tell him."

Zanuck sighed. Producers with consciences were new to him. "Why can't you be like Ray Griffith?" he asked Johnson, naming one of his long-time executive producers. "He doesn't know a goddamn thing about scripts but he just flips through it and says, 'Not right.' The writer doesn't know Griffith wouldn't even know what time it is, so when Ray says, 'Try again,' the writer goes on trying." Zanuck grinned. "I bet Ray outlives the both of us. He certainly isn't going to worry himself to death about scripts."

But Johnson, who hated hurting people, insisted on quitting as a producer, and Zanuck, who greatly admired him, sent him off on a vacation to Miami Beach to straighten himself out. While Johnson was there, he was called to the telephone, and it was Zanuck.

"Look," said Zanuck, "would it be all right if you just produced pictures you write yourself?"

Johnson agreed he might be able to manage that, so long, he added, as he was given charge of the casting too. Zanuck said he would have carte blanche, and Johnson was back on the lot a week later. By that time he realized why he had been called back. Zanuck was planning the program for 1939, and since 20th Century–Fox had made so much money over the past three years, he felt he could start introducing some quality into the company's movies. He had come up with a new idea for a film, snatched, as usual, from an article he had read in a magazine. It was a life of the cowboy bandit hero Jesse James.

"It's a natural for Tyrone Power," said Zanuck, and added, when he saw Johnson's grimace: "I know he's a great big sissy, but the audiences out there don't think so. He's almost as big as Gable and the women just love him." And then he went on: "In addition to which, there's a good part in the script for Jesse James's brother, Frank. A very strong role."

"How about Henry Fonda?" said Johnson.

"Jesus, I hate that arrogant bastard," said Zanuck. "He's not even under contract to us, and he'll cost us a fortune."

"Listen, Darryl," said Johnson, "you promised me casting rights if I produced. If you insist on Power, I insist on Fonda. And Henry as director."

He meant Henry Hathaway, who was one of the toughest and meanest directors in the business. Secretly, Johnson agreed with Zanuck that Henry Fonda, with a few snorts in him, could become extremely cantankerous and uncooperative on the set, and he figured only soneone as ornery as Hathaway could keep him in line. But Zanuck deliberately chose to misunderstand Johnson.

"Okay, you can have Fonda and you can have Henry," he said.

But shortly afterwards, Johnson discovered he had been assigned one of the contract studio directors, Henry King, and not Henry Hathaway, but it was too late to do anything about it by then. In any case, Fonda liked his role and behaved impeccably throughout, and *Jesse James* proved to be a critical and box-office success and a good augury for the more distinguished movies Zanuck had decided to make.

*        *

Actually, Zanuck took production credit on the Jesse James film, and Johnson acknowledged later he had earned it. He spent a good deal of time both on the Fox backlot and in Arizona when the riding scenes were being filmed, and was responsible for some of the most spectacular sequences involving riding and horses. It was Johnson who wrote the famous scene in which Jesse James rides his mount right through a plate-glass window, but it was Zanuck who thought up an even more dramatic moment when the James brothers and their gang ride their horses straight over a cliff.

Henry King couldn't believe it could be done, since not even the best-trained horse was willing to commit suicide by doing such a stunt.

"Besides, it's cruel," he said. "Even the horses that come out of the stunt alive will have their limbs broken and will have to be destroyed."

"Not if you leave it to me," Zanuck said, and went to work with the unit horse coper.

On the day appointed to shoot the scene, the horses and their riders were assembled on top of the cliff, and Fonda, Power, Johnson, and Zanuck (doubles were being used for the stars) stood by, watching them. King and his camera crew were nowhere to be seen, but were understood to be below. Zanuck pointed out that the stunt riders and their mounts, as they approached the edge of the cliff, would come onto a concealed wooden trough which had been mounted on rollers. It would tip like a seesaw when it felt the horses' weight and spill them down to the plain below. Johnson and the others winced as the team of horses and riders cantered up at the assistant director's signal, moved onto the concealed platform, and then plunged wildly over the cliff's edge.

"My God, it's murder!" said Tyrone Power. "Those poor horses!" Zanuck laughed, ran quickly towards the cliff himself, and plunged over with a cry that might have been a yell or a cheer.

"The bastard has a conscience after all!" muttered Henry Fonda. "He's killed himself!"

But he hadn't, of course. Nor had any of the horses been injured. Under Zanuck's direction, a short distance down the cliff, on a conveniently broad platform, the unit coper had arranged a soft landing for the horses — and, as it turned out, for Zanuck too. Henry King and his crew had captured the scene as the animals came tumbling past him and it proved to be one of the most vivid highlights of *Jesse James*.

"What were you worried about?" asked Zanuck, triumphantly, when he came back up to the top of the cliff. "I'd never ask an animal to do something I'm not prepared to do myself."

"Animals ain't gonna get much comfort out of that, Mr. Zanuck," drawled Henry Fonda, "considering what *you're* ready to do."

In fact, Zanuck loved animals, probably more than he did people. He was especially good with dogs, and Virginia was always complaining that her German shepherd dropped everything, including her handbag, which he had been taught to carry, the moment he smelled her husband anywhere in the neighborhood. In Africa once, after he gave up hunting, he was tempted to bring home a baby leopard and keep it around the house as a pet, but was dissuaded after it was pointed out it might prove dangerous for the children. Clyde Beatty, the animal trainer and lion-tamer, was around in Hollywood at the time, and on one occasion Zanuck did stints in the ring with Beatty at shows in Fresno and San Francisco. But then he watched Beatty at a training session with some young animals, and decided it was not so much too cruel as too humiliating for such handsome animals, and lost interest.

On the other hand, he couldn't abide cruelty to any animals. He lectured his son, Richard, when he found him blowing up a frog with a straw. He once fired a whole second unit on a Western when their use of illegal tripwires in a gallop sequence resulted in a couple of ponies breaking their legs. He hated anyone who mistreated horses, as he believed Big Boy Williams did at polo, and even though he rode his own ponies hard, he always brought them in well short of exhaustion.

"I'll never ask more from a horse than I will from a man," he once said. "I'll get more, because horses seem to try harder for me, but I'll never demand more."

He hero-worshipped anyone who could ride better than he could, and he once brought a horseman to work at 20th Century–Fox and gave him a good job there not, one suspects, because he had any flair for the cinema but because he was one of the three or four greatest riders in the world. His name was Aidan Roark and he was a charming Englishman and a ten-goal player of polo. Aside from his skill with a mount and a polo mallet, Roark really didn't have a brain in his head. Zanuck installed him in an office at Fox and set him to reading scripts, and told Sperling:

"If Aidan understands a script, it should be crystal clear to a ten-year-old kid in the front seat at a movie. Anyway, think what it means to our prestige, having a ten-goal man on our payroll."

This was a period when Fox was doing so well and making so much profit that Zanuck was handing out several well-paid posts to many of his nonprofessional friends. He put the restaurateur, Prince Mike Romanoff, into the Fox fan-mail office and pinned his royal crest on the office door. He had Nick the Greek, Sam the Barber, and his English butler pass judgment on the studio's product, on the grounds that they were "dumb, ordinary people." Romanoff stayed on until one night, in the Brown Derby, Zanuck heard him complaining that "all the fan-mail letters I see are from people who want to know the anatomical dimensions of our players. I tend to ignore most of these ignorant missives." Zanuck fired him for pomposity, but not before remarking: "Mike, what those people want to know is how big are Betty Grable's tits, and the moment they stop asking and we stop telling them, we're out of business."

Aidan Roark stayed on longer, but finally was kicked out when he started learning the studio lingo but not really understanding what it meant. He once sent a memo to Zanuck about a script, in which he said: "This is a machinegun-paced comedy that seems to drag a little."

"Jesus," said Zanuck, "that's the first time I've ever seen anyone do a U-turn in the middle of a sentence."

The polo-playing wizard was let go shortly afterwards, on the grounds that he had become too sophisticated.

Zanuck would have liked to retain Henry Fonda on contract at Fox after *Jesse James*, but Fonda, who was a freelance at the time, didn't want to be tied down. The bait Zanuck held out to him was a sequel to the Jesse James story in which he would play the starring role in a film about Jesse's brother, Frank James. Since Jesse had been killed in the previous film, there would be no Tyrone Power around. To sweeten the bribe, he even offered to have a part written into the film for Fonda's favorite actress, Barbara Stanwyck. In those days, Stanwyck was not only a great star and a good actress but also one of Hollywood's special people, seductive, beautiful, and nice. One of Hollywood's legendary characters, Herman Mankiewicz, once said of her: "Barbara Stanwyck is the nicest woman I ever met. I could just dream of being married to her, having a little cottage out in the hills, roses round the door. I'd come home from the office, tired and weary, and I'd spy Barbara there through the door, walking in with an apple pie she'd just cooked herself. And no drawers."

Zanuck knew the propinquity of Stanwyck on a film set was a temptation Fonda would find irresistible. But resist it he did. He and Zanuck were antipathetic, and the thought of having "Darryl F-for-Fuck-It-All Zanuck" (as he called him) as his producer blighted the promise of Stanwyck's presence. He turned the offer down. He went on to do another picture at another studio. But Zanuck, who shared the antipathy but knew Fonda's qualities as a star, vowed that one day he would come back to Fox. And this time, he would pin him down to a contract.

The opportunity came sooner than either of them anticipated, in the shape of a movie called *The Grapes of Wrath*.

# GRAPESHOTS

ARRYL ZANUCK was a registered Republican and voted the party ticket in state and national elections, and did so because he believed the Republicans would best protect his interests and those of the movie industry. But most of the people he admired were Democrats or liberals. He was on good terms with Franklin D. Roosevelt and the Democratic administration in Washington. He had visited the President in the White House both as a member of a film industry delegation and as an individual movie mogul, and he had got on famously with him, later remarking to Virginia: "There's a man who speaks my language." It did not, however, prevent him from voting for the Republican candidate at the next presidential election.

He certainly got no pleasure from having the same party allegiance as Louis B. Mayer of M-G-M, Jack and Harry Warner, Harry Cohn of Columbia, and Adolph Zukor of Paramount; with none of them did he have anything in common except the pursuit of box-office bonanzas. During the campaigns against studio unionization in the mid-1930s he had stood solid with the other bosses out of sheer self-interest, but it did not prevent him from despising the pressures used by the others to force their technicians to toe the line. He had one passage at arms with Mayer during which he loudly called him "a malevolent and vindictive bastard." When Jack Warner rose to defend the M-G-M chief, Zanuck rounded on him in a sudden spurt of anger and resentment and shouted: "And don't you talk, Jack. You're such a Scrooge you think you can starve your people into submission. Well, you can't. They're not serfs. They're artists, professionals — and you need them, you idiot, to make your films for you. Without them, you're dead. So pay them what they're worth and stop whining."

Those sentiments still didn't prevent him from fighting unionization, though. He simply believed, as a good Republican, that if you paid people enough they wouldn't want, or need, unions.

By 1939 the political climate in Hollywood was bad. The seeds were being sown, both by right-wing bigots and disingenuous Communists, for the antiliberal persecutions of the postwar years. Already it was getting hard for an honest writer to sell an idealistic or progressive-minded script to the studios, most of whose bosses (especially Louis B. Mayer) would have termed a rewritten version of the New Testament to be Communist propaganda and classified the author as a dangerous Red.

They were turbulent times and the world was teeming with good, filmable stories about what was happening out there. But Hollywood filmmakers were shying away from them, some out of fear, some out of sheer political prejudice and bias. And yet Zanuck knew that if he was to improve the quality of his product, and get away from Sonja Henie and Betty Grable musicals and Tyrone Power swinging from a masthead, he had to tackle controversial subjects and themes, and take the risks or the consequences.

"Every time I got together with Louie Mayer or Jack Cohn," he said later, "they used to try to fill me with pious crap about giving the public what they wanted in those troublous times, which was entertainment pure and simple — by which they meant Garbo's grunts and Lana Turner's tits, and nothing to worry about except was Janet Gaynor going to get to the state fair and Andy Hardy get to kiss the girl next door. And meanwhile, out there, the Nazis were on the rampage in Europe and our own country was going through a crisis of hunger and unemployment and upheaval."

He added: "I guess I was just apolitical, because whereas Louie and Jack threw up their hands and said 'Red propaganda' whenever I mentioned them, I kept on thinking that every single happening I was reading about in the newspapers and newsmagazines was the stuff of moving pictures. But they kept warning me to stay away from such things. 'Give 'em cowboys, tits and gangsters,' said Jack Cohn. 'That's the way to keep 'em happy.' Louie Mayer put it more pompously. 'Give them glamour,' he said. Glamour! In 1939, when the world was going to pieces!"

One day about this time the telephone rang in Zanuck's office and it was someone from the Hays Office, the voluntary censorship bureau set up by the motion picture industry. The Hays Office was supposed to read Hollywood scripts in advance and advise on whether they were likely to contain scenes offending good taste or public morals. It was the Hays

Office that had recently ordained that no man or woman could be shown in bed together unless one of them had a foot outside the bed and on the floor. Zanuck hated the organization because it had once mangled and ruined one of his films, *Born to Be Bad*, and he was apt to call the bureau's officials "a bunch of goddamned bluenoses." Now he was to discover that the Hays Office was venturing into politics. A voice informed him the bureau understood 20th Century–Fox was interested in making a film from John Steinbeck's latest novel, and did he know that several Hollywood studios had already turned it down?

"I've never heard of the goddamn book," said Zanuck. "Why would they do that?"

"Because it is much too political and controversial," said the voice. "Mr. Mayer at M-G-M says it is nothing but downright Red propaganda, and very dangerous."

"If Louie says that," replied Zanuck, "I guess I ought to read it right away. What did you say its name was?"

Its name was *The Grapes of Wrath*, and it was Nunnally Johnson who was causing all the fuss at the Hays Office because he had sent for the galley proofs (the book was not yet out) and was telling all his friends it was the most moving tale he had read for ages. Set in Oklahoma, it was a saga of how a family of homesteaders, having at last achieved a small farm of their own, find their dreams shattered by the drought which turns their land into a dustbowl. There are no jobs around and they have no one to turn to, so they just pick up sticks and head west for California, which they hope will prove to be their land of Canaan.

Zanuck sent for Johnson and rebuked him for not talking to him first before spreading stories about the book all over Hollywood. Johnson explained he hadn't called Zanuck because he hadn't wanted to embarrass him. He liked *The Grapes of Wrath* and thought it would make a wonderful movie, but in the political climate of the time it didn't read like the sort of theme the studios were looking for.

"Everybody in Hollywood says it can't be made like it's written," Johnson said. "It's downbeat, I suppose, certainly not optimistic or hopeful. Your friend Jack Warner would call it pure Communist propaganda."

Zanuck held out his hand for the galley proofs, and called Johnson in next day to say he had bought the film rights of *The Grapes of Wrath* for $100,000 and wanted it put into the program at Fox right away. He told Johnson to go away and write the screenplay. "It's a great story," Zanuck said. "Don't pull any punches."

From that moment on, he became involved in seeing Johnson produce a good and faithful version of Steinbeck's memorable saga, and sat in with him throughout the writing of the first draft. It was he who insisted on cutting extraneous characters out of Steinbeck's sweeping story and concentrating the action upon the Joad family, Ma, Pa, Grandpa, Rosasharn, and Tom Joad, struggling through hunger, suffering, and despair to reach what they hope will be the Promised Land. At all costs he was determined it should be seen not as a political tract but as a very human, personal story.

He was still not satisfied they had done justice to the story when he looked around for a director, and finally picked John Ford. Time had not improved relations between these two arrogant and self-confident moviemen, and after their personal differences in the past they had mutually resolved never to work together again.

But Zanuck knew of no other director in Hollywood who could handle such a story, and Ford, once he read the script, was aware that he was being presented with the cinematic opportunity of a lifetime. He too, like Zanuck, was a Republican. Politically, the Joads were beyond his ken. But like Zanuck, he recognized the compulsive quality of the story and knew he had to make it.

When news spread around Hollywood that Fox had done a screenplay and hired a director to make *The Grapes of Wrath*, Henry Fonda was immediately interested. He was already an enthusiastic admirer of John Steinbeck and had every book he had ever written on his shelves. He was therefore quite excited when his agent, Leland Hayward, telephoned to say Darryl Zanuck had been on to him and wanted Fonda for the part of Tom Joad in *The Grapes of Wrath*. Hayward rushed over a copy of the screenplay and told him John Ford would be directing, and soon afterwards Fonda was prepared to kill to get the part, for Joad was the kind of character a good actor dreams of playing.

Hayward explained that before signing up Fonda for the role, however, Zanuck wanted to see him. This was unusual, since he did not normally spend time dealing with outside players. But Fonda did not suspect any ulterior motives when he was shown into Zanuck's office at Fox.

"I hear from Leland you like *Grapes of Wrath*," Zanuck said.

"You betcha," Fonda replied.

"Like it well enough to sign a seven-year contract with me?"

"Hell, no!" Fonda jumped to his feet, determined, as he said later, not to allow Zanuck "to tie me up like a calf ready for branding." Facing the great man, he burst out: "I'm a freelance actor and I intend to stay one."

"Well," said Zanuck, calmly, "I'm not going to give you Tom Joad and then let you go off and do some picture with M-G-M and Joan Crawford."

He waited and there was a long silence; Fonda sat down again. Zanuck got out of his seat, walked up and down, swinging his polo mallet. Then he turned to Fonda and his tones had softened.

"I've got big plans for you, Fonda," Zanuck said, "and I want to be able to control you and keep you, and I've got to have a contract with you to do it."

All Fonda could think about was the script and the part of Tom Joad, and he knew Zanuck had trapped him. He would have to sign up if he wanted the role — and he desperately wanted the role. His agent got Fonda as good a deal as he could, but, in the circumstances, Zanuck held the cards and Fonda had not much choice. He signed a seven-year contract with 20th Century–Fox, albeit reluctantly. And he was given the part of Tom Joad in *The Grapes of Wrath*, and played himself into movie history. He inveighed against the contract later, because he maintained no other role Zanuck gave him stood up to Tom Joad. But he never regretted his decision, and the contract was worth signing just to get the part. As Fonda's biographer wrote:

> [The film] stands as Fonda's masterpiece. The elements were all there. John Steinbeck's shattering novel of the social injustice to the "Okies" during the Great Depression, the talent and craftmanship with which Nunnally Johnson adapted the novel for the screen, Gregg Toland's revolutionary camera work, Alfred Newman's moving use of "The Red River Valley" as the musical theme, and, ultimately, John Ford's direction.*

Since this is quoted from the authorized biography of Fonda, and Fonda cordially disliked Zanuck, it is not perhaps surprising that the one who gets no credit for the quality and impact of *The Grapes of Wrath* is the one without whom it could never have been made.

Even John Ford, for once, was grateful for the contributions which Zanuck made to the final film, although, typically, he only mentioned the superficial ones.

"One of his greatest assets," Ford said later, "was to supply the proper music — and sound effects. He held music down to a minimum. And with sound effects he was absolutely uncanny. He'd put things in I'd never dream of. In *Grapes of Wrath* there was a scene with an itinerant preacher [played by John Carradine] and a swamp under a bridge, and Darryl put in the sound of crickets, and you *knew* you were in a swamp.

*\**Fonda: A Life*. As told to Howard Teichmann (New York: New American Library, 1981), p. 129.

Later there was that English picture, *The Third Man*, in which they had
a zither playing alone on the sound track, but it was not the first time
that was done. In *Grapes of Wrath* Darryl used a single lightly played
accordion — not a big orchestra — and it was very American, and very
right for the picture."

What Ford does not add is that, as was quite usual in those days, he
left the studio immediately after the shooting of *Grapes* was over and
went on a new assignment abroad. Zanuck took over the rolls of film, and
got to work on them. He did not just cut, speed up, insert snatches of
music and sound. He fussed over the film and pondered the nature of its
impact, and then he made a big decision. He altered the ending. As
Johnson had written *Grapes of Wrath* and Ford had shot it, the movie
ends in California on what was almost a political note. In keeping with
the militant feelings of the time, Tom Joad leaves his family in a government camp and sets off for one of the big cities. There he intends to enroll
in the labor movement as an activist, resolved to fight in the future not
only for the Joads but for all downtrodden members of the proletariat.

For Zanuck, this climax grated on all that had gone before. It took the
human sufferings through which the Joad family had passed and turned
them into a struggle for which there could be only a political solution.
And, as far as Zanuck was concerned, that diminished the movie by
diminishing the Joads as people, as characters, and turned them into
symbols. And who cares what happens to symbols?

He wanted the film to end on an upbeat note, with the Joads seeing
hope ahead, at least, if no immediate answer to their problems. And since
they were Americans, he wanted them to act like Americans, with spunk,
guts, courage, and optimism. So, without consulting anyone else, he wrote
a new ending. He inserted a scene in which the linchpin of the family,
Ma Joad, is leaving the government camp when her husband turns to her
and asks, in despair:

"What's to become of us, Ma?"

And she says:

"Can't nobody wipe us out. We'll go on forever, 'cause we're the people."

*The Grapes of Wrath* had its world premiere at the Coronet Theatre
in New York in 1940, and long before it opened there was controversy
about it, since, in spite of all Zanuck's efforts, rumors had got around that
this was a "political" film. To rebut this impression, he deliberately set
out to turn it into a big social occasion, and the premiere had an invited
audience of some of the most distinguished leaders of New York's fash-

ionable, business, and artistic life. Both Johnson and Ford were appalled when they realized that *le tout New York* had been invited, for they took their work seriously and hardly cared whether the film was a smash hit or not so long as it was recognized as a prestige motion picture.

Zanuck, on the other hand, viewed any movie as a failure if it did not win popular applause, and if that was not exactly what he was going after on this first night, what he wanted was the glamour, press attention and fancy names, to which he could attach the movie in all future publicity.

Johnson could not see this point of view and never really forgave Zanuck or the Fox publicity office.

"The whole thing had been turned into a fashionable event," he said later. "Everybody came from dinner (because it started at 9:30) with, you know, caviar dribbling from their chins and champagne, the goddamnedest collection of people you ever saw. Upstairs was where the press was, and when the picture finally ended the audience downstairs was fast asleep. I was just in despair. I thought this premiere was one of the worst calamities I have ever seen."

At the party following the premiere, he tackled Zanuck about it but his complaints got nowhere because, he maintained later, his boss was already "so crocked" he couldn't understand why Johnson was angry. Meanwhile, John Ford, who had come back from abroad for the premiere, was furious at Johnson, accusing him of walking out of the film and audibly expressing his disgust at it. Johnson wrote back to Ford to say he had indeed walked out of the cinema, but the reason he had done so was his disgust at the nature of the audience and not with the movie. So Ford wrote back to apologize and blamed "that son of a bitch Zanuck" for messing up the first showing, and denouncing him for presenting a movie "which couldn't do anything but bore and depress a bunch of rich people who don't give a fuck about what is going on in the world."

In fact, that first-night audience gave a warm round of applause to *The Grapes of Wrath* and many were in tears after the final fadeout. Next day there were not just rave notices from the critics but lavish displays of pictures of the premiere audience. And it all helped to make *The Grapes of Wrath* into one of the biggest box-office smashes of the year.

Zanuck was so galvanized by the praise and financial rewards garnered by this, his first prestige film, that he was encouraged to embark on yet another "serious" film, and he almost immediately bought the movie rights of a current best-selling novel, Richard Llewellyn's *How Green Was My Valley*, about life in the coal-mining valleys of Wales, for which he paid the record-breaking sum of $300,000.

Since he and Johnson were not on speaking terms following their quarrel over the presentation of *Grapes* (they made it up later, when the box-office returns came in), Zanuck called in the American writer, Ernest Pascal, to do him a treatment of *How Green Was My Valley* and was displeased with the result. The Welsh coal-mining book certainly had a good deal in it about miners' strikes, union troubles, brutal mine-owners, and the like, but what Zanuck was once more looking for was a moving and romantic story about people — in trouble, maybe, and in danger, from disasters in the mine and threats from the mine-owners. But as in *The Grapes of Wrath*, he was convinced he would lose a popular audience if he stuck with all the ingredients of the novel and made it too "political."

He left a memo behind in the archives of 20th Century–Fox after Pascal delivered his first draft, and it well expresses his feelings about "serious films on working-class problems":

> I am disappointed in the script, mainly because it has turned into a labor story and a sociological problem story instead of a great human, warm story about real living people. I think we should take a revolutionary viewpoint of the screenplay of this story and we should tell it as the book does — through the eyes of Huw, the little boy. We should do much of the picture with him as an off-stage commentator, with many of the scenes running silent and nothing but his voice over them. And then, of course, from time to time we will let the voice dissolve into scenes. If we can use this technique we can capture much of the wonderful descriptive dialogue of the book, particularly when the boy talks about the valley and about his father and mother.

He had concluded that Pascal had approached the book from entirely the wrong angle:

> I get the impression that we are trying to do an English "Grapes of Wrath" and prove that the mineowners were very mean and that the laborers finally won out over them. All this might be fine if it were happening today, like "Grapes of Wrath," but this is years ago and who gives a damn? The smart thing to do is to try to keep all of the rest in the background and focus mainly on the human story as seen through Huw's eyes.

Philip Dunne was brought in to replace Pascal and he agreed, making Huw the constant presence behind the action on the screen. Zanuck picked William Wellman as his director, but by the time he had a script with which he was satisfied, which was not until the middle of 1941, Wellman had gone on to other things and John Ford was once more called in to direct.

Again, Zanuck took possession of the completed film and went to work on it, cutting, eliminating characters, rejigging. The film, with Walter

Pidgeon, Maureen O'Hara and Roddy McDowall, was premiered late in 1941, and won the Oscar as the best picture of that year.

"When I think of what I got away with," Zanuck wrote later, "and won the Academy Award with the picture, it is really astonishing. Not only did we drop five or six characters but we eliminated the most controversial element in the book which was the labor and capital battle in connection with the strike."

But that was always the trouble with turning big novels into films. "We were very successful," he wrote later, "with the critics and the public, yet we never attempted to do anything but dramatize a certain portion of each book . . . yet the films carried the true spirit of the books, and we were enabled to expand and dramatize the incidents and characters we retained."

It was a satisfying peak to have reached in his career, and he savored it. Not since he had made *I Was a Fugitive from a Chain Gang* back at Warner Brothers had he felt that he was a real film creator, not just making movies that were successes at the box office — anyone with a Crawford, a Grable, a Henie, a Turner, or a Gable could do that — but ones that made the public talk, think, argue, discuss, and ask for more of the same.

The only trouble was, time was temporarily running out so far as "serious" movies were concerned, and soon a very different kind of picture would be all the rage.

While *The Grapes of Wrath* was still showing across the United States and Zanuck was wrestling with the script problems of *How Green Was My Valley*, World War II was marching on in Europe, and it was not only Pa Joad who was asking the question "What will become of us, Ma?" Everyone was aware that at any moment now the United States might be involved in the conflict, and every American home speculated about how it would affect them. Darryl Zanuck was one of those who looked forward to the conflict. He had sympathized with the French and British against the Nazis from the start, and he and Virginia had long since been contributing money and food parcels to the Allies. With the schizophrenic zeal of a smart showman, he had quickly realized that war in Europe would stimulate interest in martial movies, and that the American people would probably pay and enjoy the experience of sharing in the overseas conflict — vicariously, in the movie houses of the nation.

So side by side with his "serious" movies he had begun making films with a martial theme. The first one, put into production just before the great air battles began over the English Channel in 1940, was originally called *The Eagle Squadron,* about an American test pilot who volunteers for the Royal Air Force, and is killed in one of the big air battles.

Zanuck cast Tyrone Power in the role of the U.S. volunteer, but had not yet decided on his female lead when he was approached by the British embassy in Washington. They had read the script of the film, which, with Zanuck's permission, the War Department had sent to them, and they had a request to make. Could Zanuck please arrange for the American pilot *not* to be killed, because Tyrone Power was a very popular star in Britain and when it was shown over there his death would be a severe blow to national morale.

Zanuck temporarily halted his labors on the script of *How Green Was My Valley* to take a more personal interest in *Eagle Squadron,* the story of which he had written himself under his old pseudonym of Melville Crossman. Not only did he arrange for Tyrone Power to emerge from the air battles alive, but he also fixed it for him to get the girl as well — casting no less than Betty Grable in the role and telling her to "act your pretty ass off for Britain."

He had the title changed, too, and it became *A Yank in the RAF* and was a great success everywhere, including Britain. When Tyrone Power eventually arrived there as a member of the U.S. Army Air Force, he was summoned to Buckingham Palace to be received by the King, taken to drinks with Winston Churchill, and mobbed by cheering crowds whenever he appeared in the streets.

Zanuck turned his efforts to a war films cycle, using pretty much the same strategy as he had for his gangster films, tearing ideas out of the newspaper dispatches from war correspondents in Europe and the Far East. In quick succession he made *Secret Agent of Japan, To the Shores of Tripoli, Tonight We Raid Calais, They Came to Blow Up America,* and, when he read about the guerrillas in Yugoslavia, *Chetniks!* Most of these films he wrote himself or under his Melville Crossman pseudonym, and he told his directors to shoot more for thrills and fast action than for thoughtful viewpoints on the war.

There was probably only one film in the war cycle that tried for the poignancies and terrors of war rather than gung-ho thrills, and it turned out to be the last movie Zanuck produced before he went off to war himself. It was the movie version of Nevil Shute's novel *The Pied Piper,* about a group of French refugee children stranded by the Nazi invasion of France who are led to eventual safety by a mysterious stranger (played by Monty Woolley). The script was assigned to Nunnally Johnson by

Zanuck as a gesture of reconciliation following their differences over *Grapes*, and Johnson did a touching and effective job with the screenplay.

He was all the more dismayed, therefore, when Zanuck nominated a mediocre director to helm the movie, and spent a lot of time on the set watching over his script like a worried eagle with her chick. The more he saw the director at work, the more he feared for the film. One day he was appalled when the director came up to him and said he had just had a brilliant idea.

"We'll make Monty Woolley a pipe-smoker," the director said, "and he and the refugee kids will spend the night in a barn. When he wakes up next morning, he will fill up his pipe, and when he tries to light it he'll find he has filled it up with horse manure."

Johnson stalked off to complain to Zanuck.

"This is the first idea this man has offered on my script," he said. "Can you believe it?" Then, leaning over Zanuck's desk: "Darryl, I want this to be quite clear — if there is to be any shit in this picture, I will be the one to put it in."

Zanuck laughed fondly at his old friend, and reached for the telephone. The director was fired the same day, and replaced by Irving Pichel.

Shortly after the attack on Pearl Harbor and the outbreak of war, Milton Sperling remembers that Zanuck called a meeting of all young men of military age on the Fox lot "and delivered a fire-breathing speech about the necessity for this country to take up arms."

Zanuck had just come back from a visit to Washington, where he had been seen both by President Roosevelt and General George C. Marshall, the U.S. Army Chief of Staff. It was generally understood around the studios that Zanuck had arranged with Marshall to have Hollywood's players and technicians brought together and incorporated in the U.S. Army Signal Corps, there to be assigned various tasks in connection with the war effort. "He proudly announced he was commissioned a lieutenant colonel in the Signal Corps," Sperling recalled about that meeting, "and he called every man jack of us to join up under his command. Since he was looking directly at me, I promptly did so and was sent to the wardrobe to be suited up as a second lieutenant in the army. I was thrilled. We were all thrilled. It was exhilarating." Then disaster came down on Zanuck like a thunderclap. He was informed from the War Department in Washington that he was not, after all, to be commander of the Hollywood unit of the Signal Corps but *second*-in-command. He would have a superior officer, and it seemed he would be a Hollywood unknown called Nathan

Levinson, who happened to be a veteran colonel of the line from World
War I. True, Colonel Levinson had a film background. Zanuck even knew
about him, for he had been one of the sound experts Warners had taken
over after buying Vitagraph films, and he had since been functioning in
the sound department at Warners. Zanuck was enraged. If the command
had been handed to Louie Mayer or Jesse Lasky or Sam Goldwyn, it
would have been bad enough. But a lowly sound engineer! He suspected
plots against him, even, perhaps, sabotage from Jack Warner himself.

"Darryl vowed to unseat Levinson and gain command of the Hollywood
war machine for himself," said Sperling. "He launched an intrigue to
match the Borgias. Strings were pulled, threats issued, bribes offered.
To no avail. Levinson was invulnerable. Zanuck was hysterical."

Then one day, Zanuck asked Sperling to come to his office, warning
him on the telephone to tell no one where he was going. When he got
there, Zanuck was in a triumphant mood.

"He'd got the goods on Levinson," Sperling said. "An informant in the
War Department had uncovered his medical records revealing that in
1918 Levinson had contracted V.D. I never found out whether this for-
tuitous piece of information did the trick for Zanuck, or whether all the
previous pressure he had employed at last became unbearable for the
poor guy. Anyway, he resigned his command and Zanuck was in."

Sperling decided he had better resign too. Watching the hard-driving
ferocity and ruthlessness with which Zanuck had pursued his campaign
to get Levinson out had alarmed him. "If I ever get to go into combat
with this man," he thought, "the son of a bitch is going to get me killed."

So he moved out and immediately volunteered for "a less warlike outfit,"
signing up in the Marine Corps for the duration. He was posted to the
Far East.

Shortly afterwards, Lieutenant Colonel Darryl Zanuck got his orders
to ship out, too.

# FIFTEEN

# LEAKED OUT

I F MILTON SPERLING had stayed with his boss in the army and accompanied him on his first posting, some nostalgic memories might have been aroused in him, for the unit to which Zanuck was ordered to report was based at the old Astoria studios on Long Island, where Sperling had served his cinematic apprenticeship. It stimulated no pleasant feelings in Zanuck, however, who was eager to reach combat territory and get into action. In fact, the Astoria studios seemed even more remote from the battlefields than Hollywood, where, at least, you could hear the sounds of shot and shell, phony though they might be. Here nothing stirred except the wind from rustling paperwork.

To add to Zanuck's irritation, he found the senior officer around the base was one of the few Hollywood studio bosses he really despised, Carl Laemmle, Jr., the spoiled son of the old chief of Universal Pictures. A typical *fils de papa*, Junior had found himself a cozy niche in the wartime establishment and was enjoying himself. Although the studio was several miles away, he lived in the Nevada Hotel in Manhattan and was driven out to Long Island each morning in a chauffeured limousine. He signed in, immediately signed out, and went back to the Nevada, free of military duties for the rest of the day.

His second-in-command, who was in charge of the paperwork, was a peppery ex-publicity man named Manny Cohen. He was so very short in stature that most people, including Zanuck, looked down at him, and the story around the studio was that when he got angry, which was often, he paced up and down his desk.

After a week of frustration and nothing to do, Zanuck went to Washington and stormed into the War Department. In the Chief of Staff's office his reputation was already known, his eagerness to get on with the war was appreciated, and General Marshall, who liked bright and belligerent characters, sympathized with his longing for action.

Since there was no available battlefield where American troops were fighting at the moment (at least, not in Europe), Marshall eventually had him posted to London as chief U.S. liaison officer with British Army film units, with the additional duty of looking after the production of army training films. There, at least, he would hear the sounds of war and even have to take a risk or two, since the Nazi blitz against London was still on.

He had a suite on the top floor of Claridge's Hotel, in Mayfair (later to be occupied by another film tycoon, Sir Alexander Korda), and because it had a balcony looking towards Hatfield, where many of the RAF's fighter planes were made, and west towards Hyde Park, where batteries of anti-aircraft guns were sited, he used to give "blitz parties," replete with plenty of PX booze and food, while London was under attack by the bombers of Hitler's Luftwaffe.

Visitors, who included Generals Eisenhower and Mark Clark, Noël Coward, Laurence Olivier, and many British stage and screen luminaries, will not soon forget those occasions. The noise of cocktail party chatter mingled with the thud of crashing bombs, and yellow, green, and red lights flashed across the faces of the guests as bomb bursts, starshells and fires painted the London landscape. "It was quite saturninely exciting," said Coward later.

Oblivious of danger, Zanuck would never go down to the hotel bomb shelters, even when the Luftwaffe attacked the West End of London and bombs were dropping and buildings were afire nearby. His upbeat, excited mood was infectious, and there was always some equally feverish female guest prepared to stay with him while the others departed for shelter. One of them, who came to know him well at this time, said later:

"For some people, the blitz was like an aphrodisiac, and it certainly affected Darryl that way."

Zanuck put it more succinctly when he said: "I don't think there was a single night during the war in London when I didn't get well and truly laid."

At one of the parties for Allied senior officers in London, Zanuck was introduced to Lord Louis Mountbatten, who had recently been given command of the so-called Combined Forces and, as it turned out, was planning a *coup de main* operation against St. Valery, across the English Channel in Nazi-held France. He would be using a special unit of the new Royal Marine commandos. Zanuck, who was beginning to grow bored with being bombed and wanted to see some military action, persuaded Mountbatten to let him go along as a U.S. observer.

The raid was a success (unlike some others in which Mountbatten was involved) and achieved all it set out to do. The landing was made without enemy opposition and an important German radar station on the cliffs above the Channel port was blown up and destroyed. There was some enemy response as the force retreated to their boats and some casualties were suffered when Nazi troops brought heavy fire down on them.

Zanuck, his face blacked, a Sten-gun over his shoulder, was adjudged "a good Yank" by his British comrades as he helped to carry the wounded aboard the boats. When he got back he sent a small package back to Virginia in Santa Monica. She opened it to find a handful of sand inside and the words: "I have just been swimming on an enemy beach and stole this souvenir. It comes from Nazi territory."

It was all the censors allowed him to tell her about his adventure.

He was promised much tougher conditions when he decided to accompany a U.S. Army film unit to the Aleutian Islands, where American troops were guarding the northern sea-route to Russia. But he hated the whole episode, chiefly because there was no sign of the enemy, not even an intruding enemy reconnaissance plane, the weather was foul, and the resident troops were bored out of their minds. He came back with the film the unit had shot and swore absolutely no one would go to see it "unless they goddamn have to. It could have been taken on Jones's Beach in a snowstorm." Where was the war, and why couldn't he get into it?

Finally, he flew back to Washington and pleaded with General Marshall's aide, Frank McCarthy, to give him an assignment "with some sex in it — lights, color, action, bullets, blood." He had wangled his trip back to the States at just the right moment. Virginia, whom he had telephoned as soon as he landed in Washington, had planned to join him in Washington and bring the children with her, but he phoned her to cancel her trip, because he was departing again right away. He could not tell her where. In fact, McCarthy, who was a theater man himself, thought a little drama would not come amiss in this case, and, with Marshall's approval, had handed Zanuck sealed orders for his next assignment. He was to take off immediately for London and not open them until he got there.

When he did so he found he had been posted to Gibraltar, where new instructions were waiting for him. They ordered him to make a movie of the American side of the Allied invasion of North Africa, which had begun while he was recrossing the Atlantic. In vain he sought out the British high command and asked them to airlift him to the other side of the Mediterranean — Algiers, Casablanca, anywhere. He was only a lowly colonel to them and they neither knew nor cared about his Hollywood reputation. Politely explaining it was all a matter of priorities, they complacently told him to hang around the airfield and see what turned up.

What turned up was General Mark Clark's USAAF plane, taking him back to Algiers with instructions to report to General Eisenhower. He agreed to give Zanuck a lift, and it proved to be a bumpy trip. Their destination was Algiers, and they arrived in the middle of a Nazi air raid on Allied supply ships in the harbor, and came down to a hairy landing at Maison Blanche airfield through a barrage of shot and shell. Zanuck loved every moment of it.

"The sky is alive with colored tracer bullets like a Fourth of July fireworks display," he subsequently wrote. "A Nazi plane crashes nearby. Another explodes in the air and floats down, a mass of brilliant yellow and scarlet flames. . . . [T]his is really a battle and I am in it. The excitement of it was like the thrill that possesses one who looks at a dangerous polo spill or a thrilling bullfight."*

He was in North Africa for the next three months, and took his unit wherever there was fighting in Algeria and Tunis. Sperling's instinct about him had been right, and the troops operating under him found he was a dangerous man to be with on a battlefield, because he sensed danger and moved towards it with the swiftness of a shark smelling blood. Many an ex-Hollywood crew member who had signed up with Zanuck must have subsequently regretted he had not volunteered for the infantry, for it would probably have seen much less dangerous action.

As a man, however, his unit liked him, but it was as a unit commander he made their hair stand on end.

"We were confident he would be rank-happy and obnoxious," recalled his staff sergeant, Robert Gordon Edwards, later. "He turned out to be neither. He was dynamic, aloof, full of nervous energy and anxious to get into battle. One got the impression that these were the most exciting days of his life until then, and he was determined to live them at the utmost pitch."†

He flung his sleeping bag on the floor beside his men, and it was a gesture to indicate they were all in it together, except, as Sergeant Ed-

*Tunis Expedition: A Diary (New York: Random House, 1943).
†Quoted by Mel Gussow in Don't Say Yes Until I Finish Talking (New York: Doubleday, 1971), p. 107.

wards recalls, they were just lying on blankets on the bare floor and his sleeping bag was the biggest and most elaborate one you ever saw.

"[It had] the sort of tubular comfort Abercrombie and Fitch would undertake to supply," Edwards said, "to only the right White Hunters on safari, and in a peacetime world would inevitably have found its way to the noggin of a native bearer slogging through the Congo."*

Edwards noticed that Zanuck slept with his boxes of special Havana cigars beside him, wore a .45 automatic in a holster on his belt, and later began carrying around a tommy gun. The staff sergeant was impressed when they attended a ceremony of promotion for General Mark Clark and Zanuck was brought over to talk to Eisenhower. To his surprise, he insisted Edwards be introduced to the Supreme Commander too.

"Zanuck demonstrated a certain deference to Ike," Edwards said later, "which I later decided had nothing to do with rank, but was based on admiration. This was a man from whom he even enjoyed taking orders. There couldn't have been many like that in his life."†

Not even Zanuck's acquaintance with the Supreme Commander could get him a staff car, however, so he "liberated" a late-thirties Chevrolet which had once belonged to an Italian diplomat and was, unfortunately, colored a garish and eye-catching blue.

"The Chevy served us well," said Edwards, "and damn near got us killed any number of times. How, after all, could a Kraut fighter pilot miss seeing a bright blue Chevy coupe on a dusty road, and once having seen it not be determined to twenty-millimeter the hell out of it? I have sometimes wondered if it ever entered Zanuck's mind to paint the damn thing olive drab, or had he promised to return it to its owner in its pristine condition . . . or did he just get a charge out of driving a Chevy coupe into war?"‡

It was while he was at Bône, in Algeria, that Zanuck ran into a British commando unit of which the British prime minister's son, Randolph Churchill, was one of the officers. The author was also along, having come in with the commandos from the Western Desert. Zanuck, Churchill and the author retired to one of the local hotels for a drink, and Zanuck stared enviously at the parachute wings the Britons were wearing, since both had recently completed parachute courses in the Canal Zone and Palestine.

*Ibid., p. 108.
†Ibid., p. 108.
‡Ibid., p. 108.

"That's one thing I've always wanted to do," he said, "bail out of a plane and come down by parachute. I'm told it's better than having a woman."

"We can soon let you find that out for yourself," said Randolph Churchill, and asked the author to fix him up for a course at Ramat David, the Middle East parachute school in Palestine. But Zanuck had left Africa before it could be arranged.

One of Zanuck's old adversaries, John Ford, also happened to be in North Africa at the time. He was now a commander in the U.S. Navy and was furious when he found himself drafted into Zanuck's unit and told to combine filming operations. He took one look at the producer and said, sourly:

"Can't I ever get away from you? I'll bet a dollar to a doughnut that if I ever go to heaven, you'll be waiting for me under a sign reading: 'Produced by Darryl F. Zanuck.' "

They spent some time together moving across Tunisia with the Allied armies, and their aides found them a toothsome sight as they went looking for action, Ford pulling compulsively at a flask filled with hard liquor, Zanuck chewing on one of his inevitable cigars.

"He and I were in an advance outfit," said Ford later. "All the jeeps and camions and tanks were bunched together and we agreed it was a pretty good place for the Germans to strike, so we went down the hill by a beautiful old church and were going to take pictures of it. We were about twenty yards from this church and I asked Darryl if he had any cigars left, and he said: 'I gave you one this morning and I only have one left.' And I said: 'Cut it in half.' And he said: 'Okay, but first why don't you go up in the steeple of that church and take pictures? I'm not Catholic but you are, and what greater place for a Catholic to get killed than in a Catholic church?' And just then a bomb came and blew us over a cliff and into some rocks. And I said: 'Did it hurt the cigar?' And he reached in his pocket, and it was there. The cameras were blown to bits. The blast didn't hurt us much — it didn't help us, either — we felt each other and there were no broken bones. Our clothes were torn and we were bruised up pretty good."*

This particular engagement separated them and it was not until later in the day that Ford saw Zanuck again.

"He was covered with blood," Ford said. "He'd been helping the

*Ibid., p. 110.

wounded, and he was smoking a full cigar. And I said: 'You lied to me,' and that was the only argument we had for years."*

Ford was being charitable, because very soon afterwards they had locked horns again. Zanuck liked action, excitement, danger, but he didn't like it for long periods, so at the end of three months he gathered together all the material his cameramen had obtained, including the film shot by Ford, and, without telling Ford, decided the time had come to edit it for public showing. He hitched a ride back to Gibraltar, with the intention of taking it back to London for cutting. But once more he ran into the priority business, and failed to get a passage on the shuttle back to England.

Finally, he talked his way onto a plane flying to Dakar, in West Africa, and then across the Atlantic to Brazil and on to Washington. The edited footage was sent out to the nation's movie houses under the title of *At the Front*, and Zanuck was given credit as producer in the titles. John Ford did not get any director or producer credit at all, though he had been responsible for a good deal of the footage. When he heard about it, he was furious. Wangling a passage back to the States for himself, he slapped the gun on his belt and declared, with a wealth of profanity, that he was going to get "that thieving bastard, Zanuck," and when he got close enough to him he was "gonna shoot him where it'll hurt him most — and I don't mean in the head."

Zanuck had kept a diary during his sojourn overseas, and he now showed extracts of it to Clare Boothe Luce in Washington and Nunnally Johnson in Beverly Hills. The snippets from his experiences at the front had movement and color, and they urged him to publish it. He thereupon submitted the diary to military censorship, and after he agreed to some substantial excisions, it was published under the title of *Tunis Expedition*. It got better notices than the movie had done, and the *New York Times* praised it for its lively narrative and colorful characters, and drew attention to the cinematic fashion in which its incidents were told, so much more professionally presented, in the opinion of the reviewer, than the slow and often unconvincing sequences in Zanuck's frontline movie, *At the Front*. Flattered though he was at the praise of his book, Zanuck was offended at this attack on his competence as a movie-maker, and he wrote back to the *Times* in rebuttal. He was particularly incensed at the charge that *At the Front* was amateurish and dull, and lacked realism. He wrote:

*Ibid., p. 110.

If the process would not have violated strict War Department regulations concerning authenticity, I flatter myself in saying that I might easily have transposed "At the Front" from a straightforward piece of visual reporting to a bang-up documentary with propaganda overtones.

Give us a couple of broken-down tanks, a platoon of Beverly Hills infantry-men, a few smoke pots, turn us loose on the studio back lot and then permit us to inject this material into our authentic battle episodes, and the result would undoubtedly amaze the uninitiated as well as pep up the entire con-gregation.

It was a temptation to fake that automatically occurred to a professional movie-maker in such circumstances, and he was proud, he maintained, that he had resisted it.

It so happened that Darryl Zanuck had presented his movie at an awkward time, when there was a hiatus in the momentum of the war situation and a scarcity of dramatic frontline news. As a result, the press was looking for juicy stories about "favoritism" in the War Department and felt it had found one in the case of what came to be known as "The Hollywood Colonels."

Practically everyone with a star name or executive rank in the movie industry had by now got himself a good commission in the armed forces. In fact, most of the male movie stars had got their service jobs the hard way, and such big names as Clark Gable, Jimmy Stewart, Robert Mont-gomery, Victor Mature, Tyrone Power, Sterling Hayden, Louis Hayward, Henry Fonda, Jackie Coogan, and Douglas Fairbanks, Jr. had all either come up through the ranks or seen active service in the armed forces (as had David Niven) or the battle zones before being given their commis-sions.

But most of the directors and producers had never even been inside a boot camp, and all of them had won their colonelcies with suspicious ease and speed. Jack Warner was made a colonel in the Army Air Force without leaving the studio, but then he was horrified to get a letter telling him he must in future wear uniform and also report to a base for training. He was even more alarmed when someone suggested he might even be posted overseas, and have to live in a camp.

"My God," he cried, "I've lost my rights!"

Finally he flew to Washington for an interview with General "Hap" Arnold, the USAAF chief, who assured him he would not need to wear uniform if it irked him, would never be called up for duty, but could continue to call himself Colonel Warner. This put him one up on his older brother, Albert, who had only reached the rank of corporal in World

War I but had wangled himself a peacetime commission later and insisted on always being called "Major."

A Senate committee under the chairmanship of Senator Harry Truman announced it was going to investigate some of these "instant" colonels, and, as usually happens in these cases, picked those whose names were newsworthy rather than those who were just plain unworthy. Among those on whom they concentrated their attention (and the press their headlines) were Colonel Darryl Zanuck, Colonel Frank Capra, Colonel Anatole Litvak, and Colonel Hal Roach, all of whom, as it happened, were doing effective wartime jobs, thanks to their cinematic skills. Because his film *At the Front* was in the news and had garnered bad reviews, Zanuck became the particular butt of many of these attacks. President Roosevelt was so distressed about this that he sent an invitation to Zanuck to have dinner at the White House, and he found himself a fellow guest with Robert E. Sherwood, Mr. Justice Frankfurter, and most of the Cabinet.

At one point the President called out: "Hi, Darryl! I want to say one thing. Pay no attention to the press. I know it's annoying but don't dignify them by answering."

All the same, Zanuck went back to Hollywood, brooded for some time, and then flew back to Washington for a personal interview with General George C. Marshall. On May 31, 1943, it was announced that he had asked and received permission to go on inactive duty.

Most people who knew him were surprised. He had shown great courage in the field and shirked no risks, and his friends had fully expected him to be called up before the Truman Committee and give a good account of himself. In fact, it was known around Washington and Hollywood that there was already a recommendation in the works from Eisenhower that he be given a medal for "exceptional bravery under fire" in North Africa. It seemed out of keeping with his feisty character that he should resign under such spurious senatorial and newspaper fire.*

It was, however, not because of the Truman Committee nor any unfavorable publicity that Zanuck retired from active service but for a much more discomfiting reason. After his return to Washington from North Africa he had, for several heady weeks, moved in quite rarefied military and political circles, and had become privy to much information that does not normally come the way of an ordinary army colonel.

Shortly afterwards, on a trip back to the West Coast, he went to the

*He was awarded the Legion of Merit in 1944.

20th Century–Fox lot. As luck would have it, he espied his erstwhile but favorite assistant, Milton Sperling. Sperling had spent some eventful moments in the South Pacific as a member of a Marine Corps photographic unit, but had now been posted for a spell of duty in Washington. He was on furlough in California visiting his wife and daughter.*

Both men were in uniform and Zanuck greeted Sperling like a long-lost son. Then, with a conspiratorial look, he drew the younger man into a telephone booth on the lot and said: "You're a serving officer so I can tell you this. It's a great big secret and it's come to me from the top. Do you know our country has a momentous new bomb? It's only the size of a golf ball, but it can blow up the whole fucking world!"

Sperling was used to Zanuck's extravagant way of talking, and since his tall stories usually turned out to be exaggerations, he had no hesitation in repeating his old boss's story around Hollywood dinner parties about the fabulous "golf ball bomb." Then his leave came to an end and he took the train back to Washington. Stepping onto the platform at Union Station, he noticed two men "in raincoats and trilby hats" waiting for him. They stepped forward as soon as they saw him, put him in a car, and drove him down to the Pentagon. There one of them said:

"Are you the guy who's been going around Hollywood telling everyone we have a bomb the size of a golf ball that can blow up the whole fucking world?"

When Sperling swallowed and hesitated, the man said: "Don't try and deny it. We've got plenty of evidence you said it. What we want to know is where you got your information from."

*Good God*, Sperling thought, *Darryl must have been telling me the truth. There really must be a bomb like this.*

Swallowing again, he said: "How in the hell can I say where I got it from? Everyone in Hollywood was telling the story. It was just one of those things going around."

The two men seemed satisfied with this. Finally they let him go, but not before warning him to keep his mouth shut from now on. "If we ever hear you've told that story again," they said, "we'll have you down here and you won't get out of jail for the next twenty years!"

Sperling was proud he had thought fast and had not implicated Darryl Zanuck. But somebody else must have done so because Sperling heard Zanuck had been urgently summoned to Washington and taken for a private interview with General Marshall. It was immediately after this

---

*He had married the daughter of Harry Warner in 1939.

that the official announcement was issued that he had been placed on inactive duty, "at his own request."

Whether the revelation about the "golf ball bomb" was the reason for his departure is not something that can be pinned down, because that file is missing from his record. But it is the only plausible explanation of why such a proud and belligerent character, who always relished a public controversy, should have dodged an appearance before a Senate committee and quit under fire.

He came back to Hollywood a changed man, and Virginia Zanuck wondered about him. Had his war experiences matured him, or was it the circumstances surrounding his retirement that had left him disillusioned and subdued? Certainly, a lot of the bounce seemed to have gone out of him for the moment. He was forty-three years old, and his two daughters and son were growing up. Darrylin was fourteen and showing an interest in boys. Susan was a darker and much quieter type, and, at twelve, professed to scoff at boys as "a bunch of phonies," made friends only with girls of her own age, and spent hours in her room listening to the phonograph and practicing dance steps. His son, Richard, was eleven years old and had already started his own newspaper route, sold magazines on commission at Fox studios, and spent many hours wandering round the studio stages, talking to grips, watching cameramen, soaking up the action of the movies.

This was a period when, in fact, Richard was spending more time in the studio than his father was. Zanuck seemed to be avoiding Fox, and, instead, spent much time exercising on the beach, swinging on the parallel bars, reading books and scripts, and catching up in his private cinema with the movies Hollywood had been making while he had been away.

This was the time when, Virginia confessed later, she wondered whether she should give her husband another child, another son, if possible, but finally decided against it, wisely concluding that pregnancy was rarely a solution to marital problems, and that theirs — their new physical and emotional remoteness from each other — were probably only temporary.

It gradually dawned on Virginia that the reason Darryl was staying away from Fox was because of the way it was being run at the moment. During his wartime absence, he had put William Goetz, Louie Mayer's son-in-law, in charge of production at Fox. Since the moviegoing public was paying to see any old trash at this time, even an incompetent like Goetz could hardly fail to make a success of the job, so long as he left to the professionals the writing of scripts and the directing of films. Like most other Hollywood studios, Fox was doing well and making large profits.

Unfortunately, success seemed to have gone to Goetz's head. Word had already reached Zanuck while he was still away at the war that his temporary successor, far from regarding himself as a caretaker chief keeping the seat warm for the boss, was behaving like a potential usurper. When Zanuck had come back for a flying visit, he didn't recognize his offices, so many changes had been made. The whole place had been redecorated, and the famous boudoir at the back, where so many starlets had been bedded, had been turned into a filing room. Even the discreet back door through which his four o'clock companions had let themselves out had been bricked up.

Even worse, Goetz had done over the swimming pool, barbershop, and steam room. The famous Zanuck Green had been painted over in blue, and photographs of baseball stars were hung on the walls.

Obviously Goetz resented Zanuck's "premature" return, and there had already been an embarrassing incident the first time Zanuck came into the Fox board room and broadly hinted he wanted to take back the reins of office. Indicating he did not approve of some of the "crap" that was being made in the studio at the moment, he explained that he was drawing up a new production program and throwing out certain projects "which make me vomit — and will make the public vomit too if we make the mistake of showing them."

To everyone's distress, Goetz shouted in a blaze of hysterical anger that Zanuck was back at his old tricks, that he mustn't think he could behave like a bully and a dictator any longer, and that he, for one, refused to be "a doormat." Then he rushed out of the room, on the brink of tears.

In the circumstances, Zanuck thought it best to leave the studio to Goetz until his departure could be quietly arranged. To everyone's relief, when Goetz carried his woes to his father-in-law, Louis B. Mayer advised him to resign and dug into his treasure chest to finance him in a new project. It was announced towards the end of 1943 that William Goetz was joining Universal Pictures as head of a new, independent production unit to be known as International Films.

On his first day back on the 20th Century–Fox lot, Zanuck called a meeting of his principal directors and producers and announced that a new era was opening for the studio.

"The war is not yet over," he said, "but it soon will be. And when the boys come home from the battlefields overseas, you will find they have changed. They have learned things in Europe and the Far East. How other people live, for instance. How politics can change lives and start wars. How something happening in Yugoslavia or China or Singapore can affect the lives of a farmer and his family in Iowa or Nebraska. The war has made Americans think, and they aren't going to be so interested in trivial, trashy movies anymore. Oh yes, I recognize that there'll always be a market for Betty Grable and Lana Turner and all that tit stuff. But they're coming back with new thoughts, new ideas, new hungers. It's up to us to satisfy them with our movies. They'll want to know more about our world, and this is where I think we at Fox have got to plan to measure up to their new maturity. We've got to start making movies that entertain but at the same time match the new climate of the times. Vital, thinking men's blockbusters. Big-theme films."

"Jesus," whispered Nunnally Johnson, who was sitting in at the meeting. "Darryl's gonna make the Hundred Years War!"

Not quite. But it was almost as ambitious.

# SIXTEEN

# DON JUAN — IDEALIST

Z ANUCK'S wartime maneuverings in Washington had brought him in frequent contact with the White House, and he had formed a close attachment and admiration for President Franklin D. Roosevelt. He had often lunched, dined, or gone for drinks with the President and his entourage, and had observed him closely enough to do a pretty good imitation of him expatiating on world problems, with that resonant voice bouncing off the ceiling and arms outstretched to the world. When he had had a few drinks, he could even do a hilarious caricature of Mrs. Roosevelt, talking ten to the dozen about starvation in China, smallpox in India, the rights of the Baha'is in Persia, votes for women in Egypt, and meanwhile fuss-potting around the room and muttering, in between the high-flown rhetoric: "Now *where* did I put that dratted handbag?"

He liked Roosevelt, thought he was an extremely shrewd and able politician, but never voted for him in a presidential election. And the man he preferred, and voted for when he became the Republican nominee against Roosevelt, was a man he really respected as well as admired, Wendell Willkie. He liked him and supported him not because he belonged to the same party as himself, but because, in his opinion, he was the only genuine apolitical idealist in U.S. public life, much more interested in other people's problems than his own political career. "Besides," Zanuck said, "he's such a nice, decent man. He's the only pol I know who doesn't fill the basin with muck every time he washes his hands."

Willkie and Zanuck shared a mutual enthusiasm for a U.S. politician who had, ironically enough, been a Democrat, and it was through their conversations about his achievements on behalf of America and the world that Zanuck eventually took the plunge. In his new conviction that the moviegoing public was ready for "bigger and better and more serious themes," he announced his first big blockbuster since coming home from the war. It would be a screen biography of Woodrow Wilson, America's World War I President and the founder of the League of Nations.

He spent a lot of time, thought, and sweat on getting a good script for *Wilson,* as the movie was called. He hired Lamar Trotti, one of the ablest scenarists in the business, to do the screenplay and they worked and argued for long hours in the house at Santa Monica, surrounded by history books, in their determination to immortalize but at the same time humanize the most idealistic of U.S. presidents.

Zanuck had meanwhile been surveying the field to search for an actor who could portray Wilson and give him depth, humanity, and fire. He must have considered every player in the business from Henry Fonda to Gary Cooper, but finally chose an unknown named Alexander Knox. Then he picked as his director his old friend Henry King, not because he considered him the greatest helmsman in Hollywood but because he was solid, reliable, and did not mind it when Zanuck hovered over him and superintended his direction.

Finally, when *Wilson* was in the cans, Zanuck retired to the projection room and went to work, with even greater zeal and enthusiasm than usual, doing what he was best at, cutting out the deadwood, speeding up the action, heightening the drama, making the audience sit up and gasp at a new and startling development every five or ten minutes throughout the film.

When he had finished he showed it to Virginia, and she was thrilled, wept at the poignant moments, and was radiant at the final fadeout.

"It's the greatest film you have ever made," she said. "I'm proud of you."

"I'm kind of proud of myself," he said. "I think it will win the Oscar."

He was so sure *Wilson* would be a triumph, the benchmark of his movie career, that he told the publicity department at Fox to spare no effort in launching it, and one of the flacks came up with an idea. Why not hold the premiere of the movie in Zanuck's hometown of Wahoo, Nebraska? He had not been back there since his youth. It could be a great celebration, even worth national press coverage, a classic American story of small-town boy making good and coming home to be saluted by his former neighbors.

A special train containing such stars as Betty Grable, Bette Davis, Dana Andrews, Gene Tierney, Joan Fontaine, Tyrone Power, and Jennifer

Jones, with all the Hollywood columnists and critics, arrived in Nebraska on October 10, 1944, with Zanuck and his family at their head, and the whole town feted the returning hero.

There was a civic luncheon at which the mayor saluted the "Wahoo lad who went out into the world and made good." Zanuck responded with a gung-ho speech that ended with he words:

"If my movies have reflected the spirit of America, the inspiration came from my boyhood days in Nebraska. I am proud to be a Nebraskan."

But was he? In the odd hours before the world premiere, he took Virginia and his son and daughters for a tour of Wahoo, and though little had actually changed since his boyhood, to his grown-up eyes it seemed to have diminished, become meaner. The sight of Le Grande Hotel (its name now even more incongruously changed to La Grand Hotel) depressed him, because it brought back a flood of melancholy memories of his father and mother, of a small boy creeping along the corridors in the dead of night, watching his father drinking and gambling, spying on his mother slobbering over a salesman in their bedroom. And the place where it had all happened wasn't a "grand" hotel at all, but a drab little dump, just a small brick building. Everything now seemed so small, though it had loomed so large in his memories.

"I drove out to the place where I had hunted," he said later. "I remembered it as a monumental bluff, but it was only a one-hundred-fifty-foot slope. Early memories can murder you."

At least the critics did not do that to his film. If anything, they overpraised it, and several of them forecast, as he himself had done, that it would be that year's winner of the Oscar. At the Wahoo premiere the local cinema was jammed and everyone loved the movie, cheered it, praised it, lauded Darryl Zanuck for making it. Virginia and the children were ecstatic. It was one of the high points of their lives.

But next day the theater, which had been packed for the premiere, was almost empty of paying customers. Zanuck couldn't understand why and was irritated when a local told him: "The people of Wahoo wouldn't have come to see Woodrow Wilson if he'd rode down Main Street in person, so why in hell should they pay to see him in a movie?"

Those sentiments were shared by the rest of the American moviegoing public. *Wilson* left them cold. Those who went to see it liked it and thought it did nobly, even movingly, by its subject. But the subject bored them. They just didn't want to see or to know about President Wilson. They stayed away in their millions, and *Wilson* was one of the box-office disasters of the year.

True, it did get an Oscar nomination, but it didn't win an award. Zanuck was crushed by the failure of what he was convinced was his greatest film.

It was not, in fact. Seeing it again, in the 1980s, it has its moments, a good performance from Alexander Knox, a splendid re-creation of World War I and the turbulent postwar world. But worthy is the word for it.

Not that Zanuck ever stopped believing in it. He still remembered it three years later, when he did win an Oscar (for *Gentleman's Agreement*). "I should have got this for *Wilson*," he said, in his thank-you speech.

He never went back to Wahoo again.

It was not the end of his "idealistic" phase. He resolved to make one more try to give the American public the "serious" blockbuster that, he still believed, the returning GIs would soon be demanding as their movie entertainment.

When he heard that his hero, Wendell Willkie, had toured the war-torn planet and written a book about it called *One World*, a plea for a united effort to solve the festering problems left behind by the conflict, he went out and bought the screen rights for $100,000.

What Willkie was actually pleading for was a Marshall Plan, and, shortly afterwards, Secretary of State George C. Marshall came up with one. But Zanuck persisted in thinking that here was a dramatic movie, and he envisioned a semifictional film in which Willkie would be one of the principals. If he had been self-critical enough at this time he might have suspected there was something wrong with his judgment when he considered casting Spencer Tracy in the Willkie role. Zanuck had a blind spot about Tracy, and thought he had "no juice." What, then, could he have contributed to a book that needed "juice" above everything to turn it into a box-office film?

In any case, when Tracy was approached, he turned down the role. Zanuck labored over the script of *One World* for nearly a year (with Lamar Trotti once more writing the actual screenplay). When he had a draft with which he was half-satisfied, he approached his old adversary, John Ford, and asked him if he would direct it. Ford glanced over the draft and turned it down, being too canny to tackle such an esoteric subject as the future of the postwar world.

Finally, and reluctantly, Zanuck decided to shelve the project, because, as he said later, "By the time we got the first scenario, situations had changed."

Actually, he had changed himself. Some said he had come back to his senses. Others were relieved that he had regained his flair. Certainly, he

was back in show business again. At one time he had been so sure that
*Wilson* and the *One World* project would succeed that he had taken a
vow: "If they aren't successful," he said, "I'll never make another film
without Betty Grable."

Now he began looking around for the Betty Grable of 1945.

Many people suspected that if Nunnally Johnson and Milton Sperling
had been around when Zanuck was dreaming about *Wilson* and *One
World*, they would never have let him get beyond the planning stage. It
was not that they knew more about movies than he did, but they were
experienced cinema buffs, with instinctive knowledge of moviegoing habits, cynical about public taste. They would certainly have cautioned Zanuck about being too optimistic about the box-office prospects for *Wilson*
and they would probably have sown enough doubts in his mind to question
his own judgment, though whether they would have persuaded him to
abandon his plans is another matter. He had come back from the war
filled with idealistic feelings and was determined to put them on film,
and it would be doing Zanuck's memory an injustice to say he regretted
this period of "postwar folly," as Jack Warner later called it, expensive
though it proved to be.

Unfortunately, neither Johnson nor Sperling was available at the time,
and Zanuck missed being able to bounce his ideas off them. Johnson was
his biggest disappointment. After Zanuck, returned from the war, had
succeeded in ridding Fox of William Goetz, he had been astonished to
see Nunnally Johnson coming through his door with his resignation in his
hand.

Johnson announced that he was leaving Fox in order to go across to
International Films, Goetz's new outfit at Universal, as one of his producers. Zanuck was both angry and hurt, and immediately suspected a
conspiracy, thinking "Goetz and I had been plotting together while he
had been away defending his country on far-off battlefields," as Johnson
put it later. Johnson insisted that this was not the truth. He was really
leaving Fox, he said, for the same reason Zanuck had left Warner Brothers:
because he had gone as far as he could in the organization, would never
be boss, and needed new goals, new challenges. He had chosen to go
with Goetz because he thought Goetz was a no-man, a neuter, who would
never have the brains, the initiative nor the knowledge to interfere with
what he was planning, and allow him to strike out on his own.

He was quite right about that. Goetz subsequently interfered with him
hardly at all. But to Johnson's dismay, far from challenging him, it took

all the zest out of things. He began to long for the badgering and argument to which Zanuck had subjected him — and finally went back to work for him.

At the same time he lost the services of Nunnally Johnson, Zanuck also got word that Milton Sperling did not intend to come back to work for him either. Hearing he had been discharged from the Marines and was back in town, Zanuck sent Sperling a welcome-home note and asked when he planned to report back to the studio (he was still under contract to 20th Century–Fox). It was then Sperling informed him he didn't plan to return and would like to be let out of his contract. It seemed he had fallen for the same kind of blandishments that had once put Zanuck himself under the spell of the brothers Warner.

Sperling was now married to Harry Warner's daughter, and both his wife and his in-laws continually reminded him that this made him a member of the Warner family. He had "prospects," his wife pointed out. Jack Warner, having ditched his first wife, had also married the mistress on whose behalf Sperling had once acted as Jack's "beard." Jack had also repudiated his only son by his first wife, which left him without an heir. At the same time, Jack was beginning to spread his wings outside the family film business. Using his rank as a USAAF colonel, he had taken to making trips abroad in air force transport, and from one such journey, to the South of France, he had returned the proud owner of a Riviera villa on Cap d'Antibes, which he had picked up at a bargain price.* He talked grandly of retiring to the sybaritic delights (and the gambling casinos) of the South of France and leaving the movie business to "younger members of the family." Harry Warner now used Jack's promise of retirement as an inducement to his son-in-law to hang on and join the Warner studio.

"We need you," he said. "With Jack's son it's hopeless. His father will never speak to him again. My own son is dead. We want to keep the studio and the business in the family. So come on and work for us, and for yourself."

When Sperling went to Zanuck and told him this, he was greeted by a snort of angry derision.

"I thought you were a smart guy," he said. "Those cocksuckers! They're terrible people, they really are! Jack and Harry, they're a couple of thieves,

---

*It was the Villa Aujourd'hui, which had been the residence during World War II of the Nazi army commander in Southern France. Warner used his air force connections, and the Enemy Properties Department, to pick it up cheap.

they're no goddamned good, they're liars, they'll never make good on anything they promise you. If you go there, you'll be making the greatest mistake of your life."

Sperling shrugged helplessly. "What else can I do, Darryl? I have to live with these people. They're in my house all the time. I have to listen to my wife, to Harry, to all of them."

Finally, Zanuck agreed to let him go and tore up his contract. But he was still fond of Sperling and he made him a generous offer. The moment Sperling found the situation intolerable, Zanuck told him, he was to come back to Fox and Zanuck would put him to work in the studio where he really belonged.

"He was quite right, of course," Sperling said later. "My father-in-law turned out to be a straight shooter. But Jack! He was very jealous of his two brothers, Harry and Albert, particularly Harry, and the moment I came to work at Warners he regarded me as a threat and an enemy. And it became so political! The brothers were fighting. I spent most of my time on the Warners lot carrying truce flags from one to the other, to stop the brothers from destroying the studio. I said: 'Listen, you're killing each other, you're killing the studio, why go on like this?' I tried to persuade Harry to go into quasi-retirement and not come to the studio — because they were like gamecocks; they'd walk into the same room and they'd bristle and jump at each other's throats. It was just chaotic. Darryl was quite right. It was a mistake. But so long as I was married to Harry's daughter, I had to stick it out."

With *Wilson* a two-million-dollar disaster and *One World* written off at a cost of half a million dollars, Zanuck needed a box-office hit to recoup Fox's postwar losses. He hoped to find it in the studio production of *The Song of Bernadette*, which had been put into production while he was away at the war, and had been moldering away in the vaults ever since. William Goetz, who had been studio chief during his absence, had refused to have anything to do with it, for complicated personal reasons. The film starred Jennifer Jones, who was now married to David Selznick, and David Selznick had once been married to one of Louis B. Mayer's daughters. Since Goetz was married to the other Mayer daughter, he hesitated to get himself into family trouble by meddling with it.

One of the problems with the film, which Zanuck had discussed at long distance, was how to show the visions of the Virgin Mary that Bernadette sees during her miraculous experiences at Lourdes. George Seaton, who wrote the screenplay, wanted no screen appearance of the Virgin at all, but Henry King, the director, thought she ought to be shown. Finally they consulted Zanuck while he was at the front in Tunis and he cabled back the suggestion that Linda Darnell play the part of the Virgin, draped in suitable robes and bathed in an unearthly blue light. He was kidding, but so far as Henry King was concerned, this was the word of God and he proceeded to translate it into celluloid. When Seaton saw Darnell posing like a Ziegfeld Girl in the role of the Virgin, he felt like dying of shame, and Franz Werfel, author of the original book, threatened to make a public scandal. Zanuck cleared up the mess by having a muzzy figure of no particular identity or shape shown whenever Bernadette sees her visions.

When Zanuck came back and took over control of the studio, he had *The Song of Bernadette* brought out, and he was appalled by the dullness of the movie and its interminable length. "Jesus," he said later, "I had terrible fights with Henry [King] and [William] Perlberg [the producer]. You cannot hope to put an entire novel on the screen. You have to select and eliminate. These two had crammed in everything, and the problem was length. They had literally taken the book. There were hours of [Jennifer Jones] scrubbing the floor. She had blisters on her knees — and if you know Jennifer Jones, they were real blisters and they showed. Ugly."

Zanuck once more took the rolls of film, shut himself away with his editor, and went to work. The result was a film that touched a nerve with the moviegoing public — who turned out to be much more interested in religion than in politics — and was not just a big box-office success but also won an Oscar for Jennifer Jones for the best screen performance of the year.

At one of the parties held after the ceremonies, Jennifer Jones lifted her skirts and showed Zanuck some scars on her knees. "Those are my scrubbing blisters," she said, proudly.

Once more Darryl Zanuck was bestriding the studios of 20th Century–Fox like a collossus, an entourage brought up a few paces in his rear, following him around from office to stage set to commissary to the gym, where he waved them away at the door. He looked like a movie tycoon and expected to be treated like one, exemplifying by his attitude and in every gesture that he was the boss "and the only boss I believe in is me."

But those who knew him well noted that though he had had his steam room and pool redecorated in Zanuck Green and still drove back and forth in his Zanuck Green limousine, he had not had the bricked-up exit door in the boudoir behind his office reopened, nor did the shooting in the studio come to a halt at four o'clock every afternoon so that a starlet could go minister to the boss's sexual needs. It was not that he had given up sex, but he was much less casual about it, and much more secretive, as if he no longer felt it necessary to demonstrate to the world that he could perform with any woman, and that when it came to sex, all women were the same. There were strong rumors around that he was regularly sleeping with Linda Darnell, which was one of the reasons why her potential appearance in *The Song of Bernadette* as the Virgin Mary had caused much hilarity in Hollywood, and his name was linked in the gossip columns at one time or another with Gene Tierney, Myrna Loy, and other Hollywood stars.

But for the time being he had become much less flamboyant. No longer, for instance, did he walk around the studio with a goosing stick, nor did he swing a mallet in the office during script conferences. In fact, his polo days were over. In one of the last games he had played before going off to war, he had ridden like an avenging angel, particularly against his archantagonist on the field, Big Boy Williams.

It had become something of a needle match between the two players, and as the spectators tensely watched the duel between them on the field, they got the feeling Zanuck was rehearsing for battle and Big Boy Williams was the enemy he was planning to kill. Time and again he charged madly at the other player, then wheeled at the last moment, putting Williams's pony off his stride and his rider off his mark.

Williams had become increasingly nervous, especially as Zanuck rode harder and more dangerously close, until it seemed that no way could even the most skillful rider avoid a dreadful, bone-breaking crash. In the end, Zanuck had achieved what he had obviously set out to do. Williams's nerve crumbled, he began to panic, and on one final charge he had swung wildly with his mallet at this maniacal nemesis.

The result was disaster — for Zanuck. One of Williams's wild swings connected with the ball, which sped like a cannon shell straight at Zanuck, caught him in the shoulder, deflecting onto his face and breaking his nose and his cheekbone. Fortunately, none of his family was there to see it. He made light of the accident, was patched up by the club doctor, and went on to a Hollywood party that night with Myrna Loy as his companion, his face swathed in bandages and a cigar sticking out through the slit where his mouth was supposed to be.

But it was much more serious than he made it out to be, and much more painful. In the weeks before Pearl Harbor, Zanuck was undergoing plastic surgery to restore the shape to his face. And somehow he had never got back to polo again. Before he went off to war, he donated his splendid stable of ponies to West Point for use by the cadets. He put away his polo mallet. And what was that he was seen to be carrying, when he needed to have something in his hand? Why, it was a mallet, yes, but a croquet mallet!

One of the legacies left behind from the regime of William Goetz at Fox was a character named Dr. Otto Wilhelm Preminger, whose name has already figured in this narrative. Some years earlier Zanuck had seen a play on Broadway that Preminger had directed, had brought him to California and given him a chance in the movies by teaming him up to direct one of Nunnally Johnson's films. It had not worked out and Zanuck had sacked him, and, he thought, got rid of him for good.

Johnson, however, had had pangs of guilt about Preminger's abrupt departure, feeling he had been given a raw deal by Fox and Zanuck. So he had arranged for Preminger to get another chance. He had given him an acting role in his film *The Pied Piper,* as a Nazi officer, and Preminger had done well.

After Goetz took over the studio, he heard rumors Preminger had been a victim of Zanuck's "spite," and immediately took him under his wing. He arranged for Fox to buy the screen rights of the play which the Mittel-European actor had directed on Broadway, *Margin for Error,* and offered Preminger an acting part in it. Moreover, Preminger discovered Goetz was prepared to pay $75,000 for his services, which was an enormous sum for a player in those days.

But Preminger didn't want to be an actor. He saw himself as a director, and he was prepared to make sacrifices and take risks in order to fulfill his ambition. He therefore went to see Goetz and said that if only the studio chief would allow him to direct *Margin for Error,* he would do it for free, as well as performing the acting role. It was too good an offer for the cost-conscious Goetz to turn down, and Preminger was given the double assignment. He brought it off, too, and Goetz, pleased to be able to put one over on his departed chief, decided he would make Preminger a permanency around the Fox lot. He therefore signed him up to a long-term contract as both producer and director.

Preminger made another film, *In the Meantime, Darling,* with Jeanne Craine, which performed quite successfully in the cinemas. And by the time Zanuck got back and took over his old job, Preminger was a fixture around the place and working on several scripts, including two called *Laura* and *Army Wives.* Then Zanuck, becoming aware of Preminger's presence for the first time, called him in. He was not pleased to see him.

"What's that bum doing around here?" Zanuck was heard to remark when he first noticed Preminger.

"He and Bill Goetz had had a tremendous falling out," Preminger said later, "and anyone who was thought to be a Goetz man was anathema to him. So one day, after he had taken over again, I got a call from Zanuck to go to his house on the beach, and he still remembered we had had that damn fight over *Kidnapped* [the movie from which he had been fired by Zanuck]. Zanuck owned this beautiful house on the beach at Santa Monica, and on entering you walked into the living room. The butler took me outside to the pool and Zanuck sat at the pool with his back to me. The butler said: 'Mr. Preminger is here,' but Zanuck didn't rise or offer me a seat or anything. Speaking tersely, he said: 'You're working on several properties. I think two of them, *Army Wives* and *Laura*, are not bad. You can produce them. As long as I am at the studio, you *will never direct*. Goodbye.' I was dismissed like some errand boy."*

When the script of *Laura* was sent to various directors in Hollywood to ask whether they would be interested, several of them, including well-known ones like Walter Lang and Lewis Milestone, turned it down mainly because they were friends of Preminger and knew he wanted to direct it. But finally it was accepted by Rouben Mamoulian.

"From the moment he got the script," Preminger said later, "[Mamoulian] treated it like dirt, and me too. Whatever I said about the story, he didn't listen."†

Zanuck had already cast Gene Tierney as the female lead in the film, and Preminger, as producer, told Mamoulian he should cast Clifton Webb in the important role of the "menace" in the film. "You can't have Clifton Webb play this part," the casting director said. "Darryl would blow a gasket."

When Preminger asked why, the casting director explained: "Because he flies."

"I'm just a poor foreigner and I don't understand the American language," said Preminger, "so tell me what you are talking about. Clifton Webb, he flies. What do you mean?"

It was explained to him that Webb was a well-known homosexual, and Zanuck was known to be opposed to them and would never stand for a homosexual in this particular role. Refusing to believe such a thing, Prem-

---

*Quoted from *The Cinema of Otto Preminger* by Gerald Pratley (New York: Castle Books, 1971), p. 9.
†Ibid., p. 456.

inger secretly shot a test between Webb and Gene Tierney and then screened it for Zanuck, who was delighted with it. But Mamoulian disliked working with Clifton Webb and the rushes were terrible. Zanuck was so appalled at what Mamoulian had done to a taut, tense, exciting story that he fired him on the spot. Then he turned to Preminger and said: "All right, you son of a bitch, you can start directing this picture Monday."

Preminger was both delighted and appalled, sensing that it was too late to catch up with Mamoulian's errors and save the film. When he had finished shooting and he assembled the rough cut for Zanuck, he was already conscious he had a failure on his hands, and he wold certainly never get another chance in Hollywood. He was right about the film. Zanuck hated it. As the final scene faded he got up and walked out of the projection room, only pausing to say at the door: "We certainly missed the bus on this one."

But Zanuck did not give up that easily. Next day he took over the rough cut of *Laura* and began to work on it. The main contribution Preminger as director had made to the movie was the ending, which he had shot with loving care and, he thought, reasonable success. But Zanuck didn't think it worked. He called in a new scriptwriter to write new scenes and a new ending, and these were shot and inserted into the film, which Zanuck meantime had tightened up, rejigged, and cut.

Preminger mourned the loss of the ending he had directed, but could not prevail upon Zanuck to save it.

Again the rough cut of the new version was ready to be shown. Zanuck instructed Preminger to be in the projection room promptly at 9 P.M. that evening. He dreaded the thought of it. Zanuck had done a pretty good job and he had certainly saved the film from the mauling it had received at the hands of Mamoulian, but Preminger thought Zanuck had made a big mistake with that new ending. "Mine was better. I just knew it. But how could I convince him now, when it was so late in the day?"

And then the kind of luck which Preminger always believed has worked for him in films came to his aid on this occasion. "At lunch that day in the directors' dining room," he said, "there was a guest. This is remarkable and why you have to believe in fate or something. The guest was Walter Winchell [then a famous Broadway columnist], a friend of Zanuck. And Zanuck leaned over and said to him: 'Walter, I have to work late tonight, and then I'll be seeing a film at nine. Come and see the film. After the film we can go out and have supper together.' "*

*Ibid., p. 60.

That night, in the Fox projection room, Winchell turned up with a girl. The movie started to unroll and both Winchell and his friend started to laugh, as they were meant to, and had a merry time right to the end. And at the end, Winchell got up and said to Zanuck: "Darryl, that was big time, big time! A great film, great, great, great!" And then he added: "But are you going to change the ending? What's happening at the end? I didn't understand."*

Zanuck looked at Preminger, who was trying not to smile, and then suddenly Zanuck was smiling too and then laughing.

He said, "Do you want to have your old ending back?"

"Yes, sure," said Preminger, his heart thumping.

"Okay," said Zanuck, reached out for the girl's hand, and he and Winchell went off with her, laughing and talking, to have supper.

"This was Zanuck," said Preminger in a conversation with the author later. "He was a flexible and a professional man. Instead of being mad, like many studio people would have been, he just looked at me — and gave me back my film."

Preminger threw out the new ending, put the old one back, "and we had a preview and it was brilliant. That is how *Laura* became a success, and how I became a director again."

*Ibid.

# SEVENTEEN

# ROVING EYE

ESPITE HIS antipathy towards directors, Zanuck was only too well aware of how necessary they were to the making of a good movie. He would always believe that the two most important elements in the composition of a motion picture were an excellent script and a clear-minded and, if necessary, ruthless editor, which usually meant himself working away in the cutting room after the shooting was over. The trouble with directors was, he believed, their tendency to get above themselves and to think of a picture they had just made as their masterpiece and theirs only, sacrosanct, not to be messed around with by anybody else, including the producer. Whereas, in his experience, a director often didn't know whether his picture was any good or not, and it was he, in the cutting room, who only too often succeeded in editing out the faults and turning a boring flop into an exciting success.

That was one reason why he was always falling back upon John Ford to direct his pictures. Despite his drinking, his hatred of actors, his general orneriness, Ford didn't give a damn what happened to a film once he had finished shooting it. He just took off and left the editing to someone else. And it was Zanuck who took the wrinkles out, livened it up, made it into what all the critics subsequently called "a John Ford picture."

"He knew I hated to go into the projection room," Ford once said, "so I had this tacit agreement that he would cut the picture. If it was up to me, I'd cut everything out. He'd say, 'What do you think of it?' and I'd say, 'It's just another picture.' He was a great cutter, a great editor."

He added: "I never look at rushes. You see, I'm not very proud of my own work."

But most directors were, and so many of them threw temperaments or wailed and moaned when Zanuck hacked at their beloved masterpieces. They all blamed Zanuck if it didn't come out right in spite of his efforts, but they never handed on the bouquets when their rejigged movies were hailed by the critics.

Still, he knew the movies could not do without them, that a good director could make all the difference to a performance, a sequence, a conception. In consequence, he was always looking for new ones, and hoping against hope that when he found one, he would not be like all the others, ready to scream, "Don't touch! Over my dead body!" at the sight of the editor's scissors. That was the reason why Elia Kazan was such a success when Zanuck brought him out from Broadway to direct his first movie. After a successful career in the Manhattan theater, he was given a contract to direct the screen version of a popular novel titled *A Tree Grows in Brooklyn*. Kazan ingratiated himself from the start by saying:

"Now look, I'm a fine stage director. There's no doubt about that in my mind. But I don't know a goddamn thing about films. I know how to direct people but I don't know what to do with the camera. Even if I knew what to do with the camera, I wouldn't know what to do with the film. I know how a set should be built on a stage but I'm not sure that the same knowledge will be useful in making a motion picture. I need help. I don't need help in telling me how a line of dialogue should read, but I don't know one camera lens from another, why you should move the camera, how it should be used. I need someone to help me do it."

They were honeyed words to Zanuck, who had never heard a director be so humble before. So he called in his most sympathetic and amenable unit producer, Raymond Klune, and told him to baby Kazan through his first film and give him all the help he needed. If Kazan's approach to his new medium had all been a carefully thought-out ploy, as Zanuck subsequently came to believe, it certainly worked like a dream.

"So I assigned him Arthur Miller, a cameraman who in those days was just tops," said Klune later. "I gave him Arthur McClaine, a great editor and art director, Joe Bettin as assistant director, and right on down the line — the best property men, the best key grips, and they were the best of the crop. And I took them aside and told them this man had come and asked for help, and that that was so rare that it was a great opportunity — to have a man who will not only ask for your help but listen when you give it."

No expert could have divined from seeing it that *A Tree Grows in*

*Brooklyn* was Kazan's first film, because it contained no technical errors and flowed along its narrative line like silk. Zanuck took it in hand and worked with Kazan alongside him, looking for parts where he could trim, speed up, improve. But the technicians had lent the director a willing, almost eager, hand, and there wasn't much to edit. *Tree* was a smash. Zanuck was impressed, and decided Kazan was a director who could be used for the big, thought-provoking movies he still longed to make and to which, he went on believing, the public would flock once he had found the formula for (a) getting them into the cinema, and (b) sending them out again, excited, arguing, impressed.

First he gave Kazan Louis de Rochement, a bright young documentary producer, and sent them out on location to shoot *Boomerang*, in which they would marry the realistic techniques of documentary movies with a fast-moving, fictional story. And when Kazan once more brought in a good, exciting film, Zanuck decided he had at last found a director with whom he could collaborate on a new cycle of newsworthy, controversial movies, ideas for which were germinating in his mind. He was still a little wary of Kazan, because he had brought with him from New York a reputation as an intellectual, and "I am naturally suspicious of deep thinkers in relation to motion pictures. They sometimes think so deep they miss the point."

But that was where Zanuck came in. Having fallen into a hole over *Wilson* and *One World* he was determined never to make the mistake of digging too deeply again. Big themes, yes — but torn from the headlines in the newspapers, from controversial novels everyone was talking about, and not from footnotes in the history books. Films about which the critics would write not that they were "laudable" or "worthy" but that they were (as one indeed wrote later) "shocking films — they take you by the throat and shake you."

It was just a question of keeping Kazan in order. And Zanuck was confident he could.

He called Kazan in, handed him a best-selling novel that was being talked about a lot at the moment, and told him to go away and read it.

"Is it too tricky to make into a movie?" he asked.

It was a novel by Laura Z. Hobson titled *Gentleman's Agreement*.

As Zanuck had forecast, the inevitable postwar slump in moviegoing had hit the industry, and people were growing increasingly reluctant to line up to see trash. On the other hand, it was a time when the political skies over the United States were darkening and any attempt by Hollywood to tackle "liberal" themes was being watched suspiciously by the McCarthyites in Washington, and nervously by the head offices of the movie companies in New York. The witch-hunt was on and soon the so-called Unfriendly Ten (writers and directors, most of them) would be called up to have their politics and their motives questioned by inquisitors in the capital. Even a registered Republican of Zanuck's standing had to watch what he was doing. It would not have occurred to him to make a movie lauding the Red Army or a Communist takeover in South America, but even he had become conscious that much less political themes had now come under scrutiny from the right-wing watchdogs in the Senate, and "liberal" themes, which might have been calculated to arouse new interest at the box office, were now taboo in New York, where Fox's purse strings were held. The board of directors at 20th Century–Fox were a nervous lot, and they were desperately afraid of crossing the taboo-line the witch-hunters were now drawing. Even Zanuck, who normally ignored his board as "a bunch of dividend-eaters," was paying attention to them at this period. He wrote to one of his scriptwriters, Preston Sturges: "I realize you have no desire to put me or the studio personally on the spot, but unless it is possible for you to do your screenplay on 'The Symphony Story' in eight weeks after you finish the writing of 'Bashful Bend,' then I will really be over a barrel. I am not in the habit of urging authors to write fast, but in these precarious days when every dollar really counts, I have to give a monthly accounting of my activities to the executive committee of the Board of Directors."

In normal times he could be sure of as much money as he liked to finance his films, because he always returned what he was given three-, four-, and fivefold. But now, with box-office receipts diminishing, every script was being scrutinized, and every budget questioned, and anything "tricky" could mean a hold-up of money that would grind the studio's operations to a halt. Not, of course, that the board of directors was likely to call a halt to such Fox projects as *The Beautiful Blonde from Bashful Bend*, which had nothing more sensational in it than Betty Grable's golden legs. It was the others he had to worry about. Zanuck had no intention of allowing prevailing political conditions to inhibit his movie-making program, nor was he going to let any malevolent witch-hunters in Washington or nervous nellies in New York stop him from making the controversial movies he was now planning. But he had to make damn sure they were not just big movies but financially successful ones too, or he would be in trouble.

Kazan breezed into his office waving some sheets of paper, and announced he had already done a draft screen treatment on *Gentleman's Agreement*.

"When do we start?" he asked.

Seen again in the light of all that has happened since, the film of *Gentleman's Agreement* seems a mild assault on the snobbishness and prejudice against Jews of certain Eastern white-collar clubs. But when it first appeared in 1947, it was hailed as a brave and fascinating attack on anti-Semitism in the exurbic enclaves of Establishment America. What happens when a successful member of the middle-class community of a fashionable suburb applies to join a local club that has an unwritten ban against blacks and Jews? Everyone thinks he is a Wasp like themselves, but he turns out to be Jewish.

Had the principal character in the film been played by someone less clean-cut and Caucasian than Gregory Peck, the problem presented by the movie might have been more honestly and frankly confronted. But nearly forty years ago, when the lines of ethnic segregation were more rigidly drawn, the fact that Zanuck dared to tackle the subject at all gave everyone in Hollywood the twitches, especially the Jewish bosses of other studios. "Lots of rich Jews in Hollywood didn't want *Gentleman's Agreement*," said Kazan later. "Don't stir it up! He didn't pay any attention to them. To the Catholics who got after him — they told him the leading lady [Dorothy McGuire] couldn't be a divorced woman — he said in effect go fuck yourself. Those were the days of censorship — fantastic and prurient censorship. *Gentleman's Agreement* was not very daring, but at the time it marked a step. It made a clear commitment about anti-Semitism."

And if Zanuck was to get away with it, the movie just had to be a box-office success, because he knew that if he failed with this one, his board of directors would refuse to give him a second chance with another. For this reason, he argued fiercely with Kazan about certain scenes.

"He was energetic and vociferous," said Kazan. "I was strong-willed. We'd argue a lot."

But both of them shared the same urgent desire to make this a break-through movie and a successful one. When the scriptwriter, Moss Hart, wrote to Zanuck to complain Kazan was reshooting and cutting his scenes without consulting him first, Zanuck sent back a letter that indicates some of the anxieties he was feeling at the time. Since this was *his* film, and *his* reputation was on the line, he was desperately keen to get it right the first time, and not to have to meddle with it in the cutting room, as he did with other men's films.

"I would rather get it good *now*," he wrote to Hart, "than to have to chop it up and try to trim after the picture is finished. These things are to be expected, particularly in a film where you have eighty percent talk and twenty percent action. Rest assured that to the best of our joint ability we will eliminate nothing that is essential or significant to either the story or the theme, but I am sure you agree that by all means we must not make a dull picture even though it be significant and important."

He pointed out that *Gentleman's Agreement* represented a double challenge to him: "The subject on one side and the utter necessity for an exciting lively drama on the other side."

No one subsequently complained he had failed to meet the double challenge. When *Gentleman's Agreement* was eventually shown it became not only one of the big box-office hits of the year but proved to be a prestige success as well, and the Academy of Motion Picture Arts and Sciences' members recognized that fact by awarding it several Oscars (including one for best actor and one for best picture of the year) at its ceremonies in 1947.

It always seems to be the children who suffer when a head of the family becomes a public figure, and Darryl Zanuck's son and daughters were not exactly happy with their father during those busy postwar years at 20th Century–Fox. For Darrylin and Susan, who had their mother to confide in about their adolescent problems, it was not too much of a deprivation that they did not see so much of him. They basked in his reflected glory, could claim to their girlfriends casual acquaintance with the famous film stars their father employed, and seemed only slightly miffed at the stories they read in the columns about his extramarital love-life. He just didn't seem to be around much, though, and they would have liked to see more of him.

His son, Richard, on the other hand, missed him badly.

"So far as I was concerned, he was an invisible father, and a distant figure during my childhood years," he said later. "He was never there when I needed him. It was hard for me to go to him and have a father-son conversation on the most basic levels because his working habits were so strange. Weeks would go by where I would never see him, even though we lived in the same house. I would go to school in the mornings and come back and he would still be sleeping because he had been out late the night before. On the weekends he'd leave on Friday night right from the studio and go down to the house at Palm Springs, and we would be left on our own for the weekend."

In truth, it was not quite as bad as Richard inferred, because his father had always made it clear to him he was available, whether he was up in bed sleeping or out on the terrace in conference, and that his son was always welcome to barge in on him without necessarily having an excuse. But it was a period when relationships were changing between father and son. Middle age was looming for one and puberty was on the horizon for the other, and dramas were shaping up for both of them.

The house to which Darryl and Virginia disappeared each weekend was called, it may be remembered, Ric-Su-Dar, after the children. Zanuck had bought it from his partner, Joe Schenck, after Schenck had got into trouble with the IRS, been heavily fined, and served a three-month jail sentence for tax evasion. It was one of Palm Springs' showplaces, with tennis courts, a pool, and a large guest house with a banquet hall and several bedrooms.

Every weekend, while the children found their own amusements at Santa Monica, the Zanucks filled Ric-Su-Dar with celebrated guests — politicians from Washington, writers like Steinbeck, Gunther, and Faulkner, five-star generals, and film stars like Ava Gardner, Bette Davis, Clark Gable, Lana Turner, Betty Grable, Myrna Loy, Henry Fonda, and Joan Crawford.

Virginia Zanuck was highly skilled at handling Hollywood's sometimes complex sexual arrangements, and kept a close tab on who was sleeping with whom — and, more importantly, who was no longer doing so. She took it in her stride when Tyrone Power turned up one weekend with his French wife, Annabel, and returned the next with his new mistress (and subsequent second wife) Linda Christian. She had heard that Lilli Palmer and her equally temperamental husband, Rex Harrison, had separated but were thinking of a reconciliation, so she deftly put them in separate but contiguous rooms, and philosophically noted later they had reconciled for one night only in her room but were back in their own quarters, and not speaking to each other, when the weekend was over.

She did not bear grudges against women whom she suspected of having slept with her husband, so long as they had done so discreetly; and a past sexual episode, provided it *was* past, did not necessarily debar one of them from a weekend at the house. "After all," she once remarked dryly, "that could cut down the available guest list considerably."

It was noted in Hollywood, for instance, that after Gene Tierney had had a sexual fling with Zanuck she went on to have a much more serious affair with Prince Aly Khan. When that came to an end, Tierney took the break much more seriously, and Zanuck complained she was greatly jeopardizing her career (and one of his movies) by continually breaking into tears on the set, usually in the middle of a scene. Tierney was sure it was all a great big misunderstanding and that the fickle prince would shortly come back to her. Virginia knew better, and tactfully took it upon herself to inform Tierney of the actual situation. Aly Khan had been down to Ric-Su-Dar the previous weekend, when Rita Hayworth was a guest, and they had eye-locked and sped for the nearest bed without even waiting for nightfall.

To Virginia's experienced eye, it was no casual sexual encounter, and she warned Tierney she had better shape up and stop weeping for lost lovers.

So far as Zanuck was concerned, the main reason for having all these distinguished guests at Ric-Su-Dar was not sexual at all, but to involve them in a game of croquet. He had never taken up polo again after coming back from the war, but had been bitten by the croquet bug after playing a game at, of all places, Blenheim House with Noël Coward and Ralph Richardson during his sojourn in England. Coward had remarked that though Waterloo may have been won on the playing fields of Eton, many more wars had been lost on the croquet lawns of Blenheim. Zanuck had taken croquet seriously ever since, playing long, hard, ruthlessly, and for very high stakes. His principal opponents were Sam Goldwyn, Harpo Marx, Tyrone Power, and George Sanders, and he was so determined to win that Moss Hart, an erstwhile player, once remarked: "Zanuck has the true croquet spirit. He trusts no one but himself. Never concedes, no matter how far behind he may be, and hates his opponents with an all-enduring hate."

What fascinated Zanuck about the game was not so much the skill involved in winning it, but the opportunity it gave a player to "kill" his opponent just when he (or sometimes she) was poised for victory. It appealed to his sense of malice, rancor, vindictiveness. He did not bother about the little things in the game that ordinary players considered important, like getting your ball through the wicket, but schemed for every foot of the game to sabotage his opponent in the most wounding way. He was delighted when quarrels broke out among his guests over positions, scoring, cheating, paying off bets.

"I saw more than one friendship broken on the croquet lawn at Ric-Su-Dar," he said later. "People would get so mad they would pick up in the middle of a weekend and leave. I remember Jean Negulesco [the film director]. Jesus, he was cunning. He could also get so violent! He was always complaining that someone had committed a foul on his ball. He howled and raged. Sam Goldwyn and Mike Romanoff practically broke with each other over croquet. Others broke their mallets over their knees, and wished it had been their opponent's head. Great fun!"

One of the guests who liked watching these games but always politely refused to take part was Rex Harrison. "I learned a lot just from being a spectator," he said. "This was where Zanuck got rid of his bile. Think of how much there must have been churning around in there, considering how nastily he could behave during his working week!"

Another silent and observant spectator was that hard-headed star Olivia de Havilland. "I watched Zanuck play croquet," she said later, "and I learned all about him. He was the strategist. He was not only superb in terms of strategy, he was awfully good as an individual player. He ran the game like a military operation. He took the initiative, the responsibility. As he saw it, he had an absolute right to his position. He knew where every ball was. He would outwit his opponents in advance. As I watched him I saw the whole shape of the man."

To de Havilland, who was one of the few film stars around who had turned Zanuck down, deftly fending off his sexual approaches, it seemed he treated his defeated opponents in exactly the same way he treated women, as if, once he had had them, they were no longer worth considering, challengers who had been overcome and could now be thrown away.

"He had no magnanimity towards anyone he had beaten," she said later. "In Hollywood it was often a done thing to lose to your boss and let him feel superior. But anyone who did that with Zanuck — in bed or on the croquet lawn — won nothing but his patronizing contempt."

On the other hand, it didn't pay to beat him fair and square, either — not at certain things, anyway, as his son Richard discovered about this time. It was a turning point in their relationship for both father and son.

Richard Zanuck not only loved but strongly admired his father, having no doubt whatsoever he was the most talented, most powerful and most wonderful guy in the world. He was quite unabashed in his fan worship. He liked his father's masterful ways, the self-confident manner in which he pushed people around, the enormous success he had with women, even with Virginia, who worshipped the ground he walked on and forgave him everything. From the age of fourteen, Richard's greatest ambition was to be just like his father, a genius at making films, an all-round athlete, a whiz with girls, and he couldn't wait to get out there an emulate him.

"Even when I was quite young, my father wanted me to work, to do something after school," Richard said later. "He used to ask me why I didn't go sweep the school playgrounds or sell newspapers or things like that. So I decided to scheme up something. I realized that if I sold the *Saturday Evening Post* around the studios, I'd have a kind of captive audience. So one day a week I would set up a stand in front of the studio commissary, and I'd sell *Posts* as they went in and came out. My father made only one condition, that I would absolutely take no tips from anybody, because of course people knew who I was and I suppose they thought it might help them if they paid me extra for the magazine."

Later he had a stand in front of the Fox Administration Building, and he would go around the offices, selling the *Post*. And of course everybody bought one, probably because they didn't want to turn down the boss's son. It became so successful he hired his schoolmates to help him, and gave them a percentage of the take.

"Every Wednesday after school," he said, "a car and driver would collect the kids and deposit us on our various street corners between Sepulveda and Pico boulevards. Then afterwards the chauffeur would pick us up and take these poor little urchin newspaper kids home. It was kind of funny. But this was during the war and it was so successful that every month there was a War Bond given for the person who sold the most *Posts*, and every month I won it. My father was pleased because I was learning how to manage a little business, because I had to keep a ledger and mail the money in to the *Post*. It was also a good introduction to the studio, and I got to know everyone from carpenters to executives, and I knew every aspect of the lot. I soon knew more about the Fox studios and its distant nooks and crannies, in fact, than most people who worked there, including my father, did."

So he saw a lot more of his father, one way or another, than he remembered later. But though he admired him so tremendously, he did not get over this business of being a little scared of him. The fact that practically everybody else was scared didn't help, either. His father was such a self-confident, dominating character, everywhere, to everyone. Everyone deferred to him, not just the stars but even the other moguls. He noticed that Jack Warner and Louis B. Mayer would lick their lips or look the slightest bit apprehensive whenever his father breezed across a room to talk to them.

Someone once said of the acting profession that it makes an actress a little more of a woman and an actor a little less of a man, and Richard thought that was true of most of the stars in his father's presence. No matter how big a male star was, whether it was Gary Cooper, Jimmy Stewart, Henry Fonda, Paul Muni, or Gregory Peck, Richard always got the feeling that if his father had suddenly barked out "Crawl!" they would have gone down on their hands and knees and groveled to him. On the other hand, the female stars behaved as if his father was a camera, and they performed for him, Ava Gardner pushing out her tits, Olivia de Havilland acting positively lecherous, Jeanne Crain looking like a little girl about to be ravished. Gee, what magnetism he exuded, to get reactions like that! Richard thought he was wonderful, insuperable, invulnerable.

Richard remembered that every Sunday night, when his parents came back from Palm Springs, his father would put on a film show in the small projection room he had built in the house at Santa Monica. Neither Richard nor his sisters were impressed by the fact that there were always a lot of movie people there. They had long since grown used to them, regarded them as their father's employees, and, for Richard, at least, it was his father who was the star around the place.

When the time for the movie showing began, Zanuck would always pick the same place, on a couch at the back, in front of the controls. And invariably he would indicate to his son that he should sit beside him.

"Well, quite often," Richard said, "it turned out that he had either seen the movie or was bored by it, and when he got bored he got restless. He had come back from a good day at the Springs and was feeling his oats from having wiped out so many people at croquet. So as the movie wound on, he would start fooling around, and we would inevitably end up wrestling on the couch."

He had been only about eight years old when this kind of horseplay first began, and, of course, Zanuck was much bigger and stronger than his son. Nevertheless, Dick sensed even then that, in spite of the fact that they were father and son, his father still regarded him as a competitor, an adversary, and when his father locked his arms around his neck and began to squeeze, squeeze, squeeze, he was doing it "for real." He would get Dick in this tight headlock and keep pressing until his son gasped out *"Give!"* which was their code word for "I give in." Only then would he relax his grip, clip his son affectionately across the chin, and turn away, bored again.

"He just loved to win," said Dick, "and, of course, he always beat me."

This Sunday-night horseplay went on for years, and Dick never gave a thought to the fact that he might one day win it himself. That was just unthinkable. Beat his father, the superman? It never even occurred to him. Admittedly, when he was about thirteen years old, he did find that quite often he was able to resist his father's iron necklocks, and sometimes he even managed to get a grip on his father's own neck and start to squeeze, but Zanuck always managed to wriggle free, and, as usual, he wore his son down and made him say *"Give!"*

"Then came this fateful night I'll never forget," Dick said. "I guess I was now fourteen and partly because of my father's inspiration, and because I was so eager to emulate him, I'd become a pretty good athlete. I'd also started playing around with girls, and I guess my father must have seen me doing — well, you know what randy kids get up to when they have a pretty chick around. Anyway, this night the movie was a clunker and as usual we started fooling around on the couch. And as we wrestled, I could just feel, for the first time, that perhaps I was as strong as he was. Well, suddenly, I got him in a perfect headlock. And I began to squeeze. I played it just as he did, and I showed him no mercy. His face became all red, and his eyes were almost bulging out of their sockets, and I thought: 'Hey, this guy is going to die if he doesn't give up!' But I just kept squeezing, and I could hear a voice saying over and over what he had asked me to do over all these years. And it wasn't until he finally blurted out *'Give!'* that I realized it had been my voice which had been giving him the ultimatum — and my God, I had beaten him! It gave me no pleasure at all, the moment I saw his face. This was my father, for Christ's sake, the invulnerable man! I just wished it had never happened."

Richard Zanuck sensed it was a moment in their lives that neither of them would ever forget, and it changed things for both of them. But neither of them said a word.

"It was just the way he looked at me," Richard said. "It wasn't nice at all. I still loved my father, but suddenly, everything was different — and maybe I didn't admire him so much anymore."

He added: "Incidentally, from that time on, he never wanted to wrestle on the couch anymore. I mean he didn't specifically say: 'Let's not do it anymore.' It just never happened again."

## EIGHTEEN

# IN THE PINK

O TTO PREMINGER was a disappointed man. Since his success with *Laura* there was nothing he wanted more than to direct another film for Fox, but for some reason Zanuck would not take him seriously and assign him another picture. Preminger had divined the way the studio boss's mind was working, and he had been reading omnivorously, searching for subjects he thought would appeal to Zanuck's hunger for controversial movie themes. But what happened when he found one? It was taken out of his hands and passed on to another director.

He had, for instance, managed to get into Zanuck's office after reading a sensational novel called *Quality* (by Cid Ricketts Sumner) and he knew it was the kind of blockbuster Zanuck was seeking.

"Dayrell," he said, in his thick Mittel-European accent, "do you know what means pessing?"

"What are you talking about?" asked Zanuck. "Pissing? Yes, I know what pissing means. It's when you've had fourteen beers and all you can think of is where's the nearest urinal."

It seemed, however, that what Preminger was referring to was "passing," and it was something that rarely got talked about in the newspapers of the day. In 1948, there was still a color bar in the United States, and the way to success for talented blacks was blocked unless they went in for show business or religion. They had found one way, however, by which certain of them could leap the class and financial barriers that kept them imprisoned in the black ghettos of the nation, and that was (providing they were light-complexioned enough) to "pass for white," and pose as Caucasians, Hispanics or Southern Europeans.

*Quality* dealt with the phenomenon in a sensitive story about the daughter of a black mother and a white father who decides to use her good looks and light complexion as a passport to the white world — and what happens when she does so.

Zanuck was intrigued and sent Preminger away to do him a four-page synopsis of the novel; soon after he delivered it, Preminger delighted to learn that Fox had bought the movie rights of the book. But the next thing he heard was that another director had been picked to make the movie, and when he complained was told that Zanuck had shrugged his shoulders and said: "What would a Kraut know about such things, anyway?"

In fact, Preminger, who is an Austrian Jew and an extremely knowledgeable liberal, would have been a far better choice than the director Zanuck assigned to the film. Zanuck had got a good script out of Philip Dunne and Dudley Nichols, a couple of first-class screenwriters, renamed it *Pinky* (after the heroine of the story), and had passed it over to John Ford to direct. With Ford they were immediately in trouble. Zanuck said later: "Some directors are great in one field and totally helpless in another."

However, Ford's trouble was not helplessness but willful blindness. So far as blacks in the movies were concerned, he was still living in the days of Stepin Fetchit, and when he started directing the black members of the cast, he quickly came into confrontation with a famous actress-singer named Ethel Waters. She was playing the role of Pinky's mother, and she didn't like the way Ford saw her part. There were blazing rows, which finally became so intense that Ford came to Zanuck and asked to be taken off the film. And when Zanuck saw the rushes, he agreed.

"Ford's Negroes were like Aunt Jemima," Zanuck said later. "Caricatures."

He still did not summon Preminger, who was waiting hopefully in the wings, but, after some thought, picked up the telephone and called New York. Elia Kazan, after his success with *Gentleman's Agreement*, had gone back to Broadway and had won new fame as the director of the Tennessee Williams play *A Streetcar Named Desire*. Zanuck offered him the earth to return to Hollywood for another movie, but, fearing he might balk at taking on something John Ford had botched, did not mention why he was wanted. He got the script to Kazan in time for him to read it on the plane, and once he landed in Los Angeles he was primed and ready to go.

Zanuck showed him what Ford had already shot and hoped he would be able to salvage something out of it. Kazan junked everything. But he was fired by the subject, aware that this was likely to be much more controversial than *Gentleman's Agreement*, and was determined to avoid the mistakes he and Zanuck had made in that film. For instance, he felt they had copped out in *Gentleman's Agreement* by casting a quintessential Wasp (Gregory Peck) in the role of the Jew.

In *Pinky* he did not intend to make any such mistake and recommended that a beautiful black actress, Dorothy Dandridge, should play the part of the black girl who "passes for white." But this was 1949. It was quickly made clear to both Zanuck and Kazan by the New York office and cinema distributors all over the country that the casting of Dandridge would be likely to "kill" the film.

One of the plot motivations of the film was that Pinky becomes a nurse and falls in love with a white doctor. He asks her to marry him. And Zanuck had had some worry about this. Originally he had let his scriptwriters give *Pinky* a happy ending, with the girl going off to marry her lover. But Raymond Klune, his unit producer, thought that was just too pat for a film of this caliber. He wrote a memorandum to Zanuck in which he said:

> [This] turns the film into a rather sweet love story with a little twist ending. And we need something stronger than that, something that will jolt and outrage the racists, even if we aren't going to be able to show it in the South. So I suggest we end the film with the white man asking the girl to marry him — and she turns him down! How about that?

Zanuck liked it, as drama, as controversy, as a slambang climax calculated to make every racist in the country mad as hell that a black girl could get so uppity.

"He changed the whole third act around," said Klune later, "so that the Negro girl turns down the white boy who wants to marry her. She goes on being a nurse. He walks out of her life. A black girl turning down a white boy who wants to make her established and respectable! That was a pretty violent thing to do in those days. But he adopted it — didn't hesitate at all."

The trouble was that even without these scenes, Zanuck had been told the movie would probably never be shown in the South, and he had braced and decided to accept that financial sacrifice. But now he was informed that even in the North white audiences would never stand for love scenes between a black actress and a white man, and that he must choose between one or the other. Showman that he was, he chose the love scenes and the passionate renunciation scenes, on the grounds that the film would lose its extra punch without them.

So Dorothy Dandridge was passed over, and the part of Pinky was handed to the whitest girl on the lot, Jeanne Crain. She did a good job. And, in a way, the fact that she had to be white-pretending-to-be-black in order to be able to make love to a white man and then turn down his offer of marriage emphasized the point about prejudice that the movie was trying to make.

Zanuck always maintained that *Pinky* was just another version of the boy-meets-girl theme, a romantic story with a twist. But he knew better. Much more than *Gentleman's Agreement*, it was a benchmark film, and it took courage to make it, especially at the time. Even when it is revived today, which isn't often enough, it packs a startling wallop.

Kazan did other films for 20th Century–Fox and they were all personal productions of Darryl Zanuck. They included some distinguished movies, among them *Panic in the Streets*, *Viva Zapata!*, and *Man on a Tightrope*. They made a good combination, because both men could hone their ideas on each other and make the cinematic sparks fly. When Kazan eventually moved across to Warner Brothers and became his own producer as well as director, his movies became, in the words of Raymond Klune, "a big dull bore." He was sometimes patronizing towards Zanuck, characterizing him as the antithesis of a real artist like himself, because Zanuck always insisted the box-office potential of a movie was the most important thing to remember. *"Will he fuck her or won't he? Will he catch her or won't he?* That's what he said we should always keep uppermost in mind when we were making any film."

But when Zanuck was no longer behind him, Kazan missed his presence.

"I sort of liked him personally," he said later. "He was always straightforward when I was working with him. He didn't go behind my back. He's a dominant, aggressive man but not a dishonest one. He was essentially a fair guy when he was not challenged in a competitive way. He often explained it to me that you have to make popular or program pictures in order to afford the others, the pictures he had to nurse, shepherd and look after. He was a tough little guy with a narrow, intense vision. I was completely consulted, but I didn't have the final cut. Either you do or you don't. Zanuck prided himself on being a great cutter."

He added what were big words indeed, coming from a director: "He worked very hard on a script, very hard. He didn't duck a problem. I'd want to sleep on it and he went for an immediate direct attack. He would never double-deal. There was no production chicanery. He'd work days and nights, night after night. He saw every foot of film shot on the lot. He is an excellent executive . . . a one-man organization."

And, considering the tricky political climate of the time, he got away with murder. His films from 1948 to 1952 included some good but non-controversially successful program movies like *Call Northside 777* with James Stewart, *Unfaithfully Yours* with Rex Harrison, *The Gunfighter* with Gregory Peck, *All About Eve* with Bette Davis and Anne Baxter, *David and Bathsheba* with Gregory Peck and Susan Hayward, *Mister 880* with Edmund Gwenn, *Five Fingers* with James Mason, *The Snows of Kilimanjaro* with Ava Gardner, Susan Hayward and Peck, and *People Will Talk* with Cary Grant.

But in that same period came such joltingly challenging movies as *The Snake Pit* with Olivia de Havilland (which subsequently changed U.S. medical practices for treating the mentally unbalanced), *Twelve O'clock High* (which dared to criticize the orthodox viewpoint on war and hero-ism), *Pinky*, *Viva Zapata!* with Marlon Brando (which did what Zanuck as a good Republican said he would never do, and that was take the viewpoint of the rebel leader against the government), and an even more uncompromising view of American attitudes towards its black and white subjects in *No Way Out*, with Sidney Poitier and Richard Widmark.

They were big, they were bold and, on a falling market, they made money. So it was not surprising that in 1950 *Time* magazine put Zanuck on its cover and hailed him as one of the great movie-makers of his time.

In the same year that *Time* magazine saluted him, Darryl Zanuck went to London for the premiere of *Twelve O'clock High*. The star, Gregory Peck, the director, Henry King, and the scriptwriter, Sy Bartlett, went with him, and they were all considerably heartened by the reception the English critics gave to the film. The setting was a U.S. bomber base in England during World War II, and the movie took a frank look at the agonies and painful doubts experienced by the base commander (Peck) as his pilots fly out, day after day, to kill or get killed. It was not the usual hooray-for-our-side movie, but its thoughtful quality seemed to strike a deep chord in the British audience.

After the supper party that followed the premiere, the group of movie people went back to the Dorchester Hotel, where they were staying, and

Zanuck, who was in high good humor, suggested a last drink in the bar. Presently a ravishingly beautiful girl in a low-cut evening gown came into the bar and sat at a table across from them.

John Ware, the local Fox publicity man, whispered she had been at the premiere and was an up-and-coming foreign actress who had made several films in Rome and was now trying London. Zanuck, whose eyes had widened at the sight of her, suggested she be brought over, and Ware went across and returned to introduce her to the Americans. As soon as she realized who Zanuck was, the girl turned her shapely back on all the others and concentrated her charms on him, telling him how eagerly she wished to make a movie in Hollywood and become a "beeg beeg star." High on alcohol and euphoria, Zanuck took his cigar out of his mouth long enough to invite her to come upstairs and examine her ambitions further. She needed hardly any urging at all.

Once they were inside Zanuck's hotel suite, it became quite evident that there was nothing the foreign beauty would not do to please Zanuck, and he had some difficulty disentangling himself from her and going into the adjacent bedroom "to get into something more comfortable."

He was gone a long time. As the minutes ticked by and he did not return, the impatient girl decided to creep along the corridor and find out what had happened to him. Peeping into the bedroom, she saw that a mirrored door of the wardrobe was open at such an angle that it directly reflected the bed, of which she had a very clear view. To her great stupefaction and disgust, she saw that Zanuck was lying on the bed, clad in his dressing gown, and that he had what looked like a script in his hand and he seemed to be reading it out loud. Poof! If this was all the interest this vaunted movie macho man could drum up for her, then he was obviously going to be no good for her future career. She had never known her charms to fail her so humiliatingly before. So she angrily stormed out of Zanuck's suite, slamming the door behind her.

A few days later, at a Mayfair nightclub, Zanuck ran into a British film columnist named Roderick Mann, who had already heard rumors about the fiasco of the big tycoon and the luscious little foreign star. She had obviously made haste to spread the story around town about the inadequacy of Hollywood's most famous Don Juan, and Zanuck was appalled.

"That wasn't the way it was at all," he protested, indignant that his notorious sexual prowess was in danger of being mocked. He proceeded to tell the columnist what he claimed had actually happened. He had gone to his bedroom and had hurriedly donned a dressing gown over his naked body. But then, eager to get back to the beautiful star, he had suddenly cautioned himself not to be *too* enthusiastic since he might have to pay dearly for it in the form of a Hollywood contract.

He resolved to keep the girl waiting for a little time. Seeing a script on his night table, he reached for it, lay down on the bed, and began to read. Suddenly a particular paragraph caught his eye and he sat up, looking for a pencil. His usual cigar was clenched between his teeth, and as he leaned over, he accidentally knocked the ash off the tip.

"My dressing gown had come open," he said, simply, "and the hot ash fell straight down onto my cock. Ouch!"

So, Zanuck explained, at the very moment when the girl had looked into the bedroom mirror and sighted him on the bed, he was doing something very different from what she imagined.

"I wasn't reading the script," he said. "I was in pain. I was looking down at my cock, which was where the pain was, and I was talking to it. 'Aw, come on,' I was saying, 'Don't let a little hot ash put you off. There's a beautiful pussy waiting for you out there.' And all my cock was saying back to me was: 'Ouch!' "

Zanuck never forgave the actress for daring to gossip about his alleged sexual inadequacies. And though she later became a box-office star in Hollywood movies, the studio where she made her reputation was certainly not 20th Century–Fox.

Richard Zanuck realized after a time that he and his father were never going to wrestle again on the couch at those Sunday-night movies, and the fact that he had made superman beg for mercy was not a subject that was ever likely to be mentioned between them. Outwardly, relations between father and son seemed just as they had been before. They greeted each other warmly when they encountered each other. Zanuck still pushed notes under Dick's bedroom door in the morning with messages like:

> Your Mother tells me they're bugging you at school about your French. Chin up, kid. There's only one way to learn Frog lingo, and that's horizontally with a chick. Next time they start hounding you, talk back. The Frog for "Frig you!" is "Merde!"

But somehow, Dick sensed, some of the warmth between father and son seemed to have gone out of the relationship, and whereas before he'd trapped an expression on his father's face that was proud, fond, protective, now there seemed to be something more calculating and speculative about the way he looked at him. If there was any expression at all, that is.

In addition to the Sunday-night shows at home, Zanuck spent every night of the week seeing rushes and rough cuts in the projection room at the studio, and quite frequently he would ask his son to join him. Richard was later to squirm at the memory of some of these occasions, for quite often the producer, the director, and the stars of these unfinished movies would be present at the run-throughs, and when they were over Zanuck would immediately turn to his son and say:

"Well, kid, what did you think?"

"It stinks!" or "It's lousy" or "I thought it was a load of junk!" he would reply, without a thought for the creators of the movie, who were sitting all around him.

"Looking back, I cringe at the whole thing," Dick says today. "I would get very angry if I were sitting in on the rough cut of one of my films here at the studio and the head of the show turned and, out loud, asked the opinion of his teenage daughter. I'd walk out in a rage. But somehow my father got away with it. He was a very tuned man. Somehow, he wasn't trying to be nasty. He was really very interested in what young people of my age thought about films. At home he was always pushing scripts and books under my door at night, and interested in my reactions to them. It wasn't just make-busy time, either. He really believed in getting young reactions."

It was after one of these film shows at the studio that Sam the Barber, his father's masseur, deliberately kept Dick back to talk to him and held on to his arm as he watched his father, through the tail of his eye, beetling away through the door. On the excuse that he wanted his advice on a confidential matter, Sam then kept him back until all the others were gone, after which he led Richard into his father's office, to which he had a key, and suggested he should go through "to the playroom in back." He swung open a part of the bookcase behind his father's desk and gestured him on, and Dick, who had never even realized there was a door there and a room behind, went through and realized why he had been kept in ignorance.

The room was done up like a boudoir, with one of those lounge-beds covered in silk drapes, with soft music laid on, and soft lights and incense burning. And waiting for him was a pretty girl (no, a grown-up woman, in her twenties), in a peignoir. She poured him a glass of champagne, undid his tie, and presently went on from there. It was very different from the petting, which, so far, was all he had indulged in with high school girls in the back of a car.

Later, as the girl was driving him home, he said to her, with a sudden sense of guilt: "You won't tell anyone, will you? There'll be a heck of a row if my father ever finds out about this."

The girl laughed.

"Did you think he doesn't know?" she said, squeezing his thigh as she let him out of the car.

# BELLA DONNA

T HE CANNES FILM FESTIVAL had been closed down for the duration of World War II, but it was too good a stimulus for tourism and publicity for that gilded Mediterranean playground, the Riviera, for the French not to revive it. By 1948, with money pumped in from Paris, it had been resuscitated under the direction of a shrewd former official of the Quai d'Orsay named Favre le Bret, and quickly reestablished itself as the most prestigious and most attractive of the annual film festivals around the world. It was Favre le Bret who traveled to the movie-making centers, from Hollywood to Pinewood, Cinecittà to Hamburg and Munich, Stockholm to Buenos Aires, Delhi to Tel Aviv, inviting any studio with a likely movie to bring it to Cannes to compete for the Palme d'Or, which was awarded annually by the prestigious international jury at the film festival. With deft diplomatic guile, le Bret let it be known that the jury's decision might well be influenced by the number and glamour of the stars each competing country sent to Cannes — which they could do, he added slyly, at not too great an expense, for they would be regarded as honored guests of the French government. Since the festival took place during the first two weeks of May, when the weather in the South of France is cool and uncertain and the hotels are practically empty, this did not cost the French too much, either.

In fact, Favre le Bret invited anybody and everybody likely to boost the festival — filmmakers, film stars, starlets (so long as they were young, busty, and female), film critics and gossip-writers — and offered them free accommodation, food, lots of parties, lots of glamorous photo-opportunities and stories, in return for the generous amounts of publicity in the media. Those were the days when the world was still ravaged by the consequences of the war and was poor, rationed, racked by social upheaval and the financial problems of rebuilding bomb-shattered cities. People were longing for some light relief from their day-to-day worries. Cannes seemed to offer a pink-scented surcease, a taste of caviar and champagne interlude in a bread-and-margarine existence.

Not only did filmmaking nations from all over enter their films in the annual competition, but they also gladly accepted Favre le Bret's invitation to free hospitality and sent large delegations to Cannes, including some of their top stars. At one time or another, Elizabeth Taylor, Joan Crawford, Marlene Dietrich, Olivia de Havilland, Clark Gable, James Stewart, Fred Astaire, and Gregory Peck could be seen posing for their pictures in front of the Carlton Hotel in Cannes. French stars Simone Signoret and Yves Montand came down from their home in St. Paul de Vence and could be seen strolling hand in hand along the Croisette. Gina Lollobrigida and Sophia Loren flew in from Rome and expatiated solemnly on the art of Italian cinematography. Claudia Cardinale and Monica Vitti posed on their balconies and pretended to dip delicate toes in the Mediterranean. On the beach itself a long, lithe fifteen-year-old posed in one of the startlingly flimsy new swimming outfits (called a bikini) for a free-lance American photographer named Robert Hawkins,* and while spectators goggled at the blossoming curves of her remarkable young body, she talked enthusiastically about her budding movie career. Asked her name, she laughed at the photographer and said:

"It won't mean anything to you. Let me spell it for you. It's Brigitte Bardot."

Darryl Zanuck liked the Cannes Film Festival and never failed to visit it every year once Favre le Bret had got it reorganized. On several occasions, he used the festival as a showcase for one of 20th Century–Fox's films, and found the consequent publicity went round the world and helped the international box office. After he had finished cutting one of his favorite films, *The Snake Pit*, which was a sometimes grim look at conditions in U.S. mental hospitals, he sent to Cannes, figuring that a world premiere before all the critics at such a glamorous occasion would take the gloomy edge off it, and that the tinsel atmosphere of the festival would rub off on the movie. With the film he not only sent its director, Anatole Litvak, but also its star, Olivia de Havilland, instructing her to be seen around Cannes always at her most glamorous, in sharp contrast

*Later an editor of *Variety*.

to the drably dressed, unkempt appearance she had made in the movie. De Havilland, who was a beautiful young woman anyway, needed no encouragement to deck herself out in the most attractive productions of the newly revived French fashion industry, and pictures of her went around the world, always mentioning her as the star of *The Snake Pit.*

It was a ploy that not only helped to sell the movie, but changed the course of de Havilland's life. A well-known French magazine editor attending the festival fell in love with her, proposed, married her, and turned her, for a time, into the toast of postwar Paris.

While the Cannes Festival was in progress, Zanuck always stayed in a suite at the Hôtel du Cap at Cap d'Antibes, some twenty miles away, and spent much of his time talking movies with French, Italian, and British directors, most of whom had film propositions to put to him. Luis Buñuel, Alberto Cavalcanti, David Lean, Alexander Korda, Roger Vadim, Marcel Pagnol, and Roberto Rossellini all came to see him at the hotel. He was usually clad only in swim-shorts, but never failed to be smoking his inevitable cigar. Lackeys of various kinds hovered nearby, ready to run messages, make telephone calls, usher in visitors, and while he was there the Hôtel du Cap became an annex of his office in Hollywood. Virginia stayed discreetly in the background, soaking up what sun was going, her swimsuit a modest one-piece outfit, because she felt the new bikinis were only suitable "for kids and tarts."

The Zanucks always ended their day in the same way. Darryl would walk out onto the diving board perched on the cliff overlooking the Mediterranean, perform a spectacular swallow-dive into the sea, and swim for half a mile or so across the bay. One year the waters around the Cap had an epidemic of Portuguese man-of-wars and most swimmers except Zanuck got badly stung. He was untouched. "They were afraid he'd sting them back," said one of his assistants.

After a few more telephone calls to Paris, New York, and Hollywood, conversations with Lord Beaverbrook, Prince Rainier, David Niven, Enid Kenmare, and other acquaintances with villas along the coast, he and Virginia would shower and change for the evening's visit to Cannes.

Zanuck liked to go early into the festival city, and a Fox employee held a table for him each evening on the terrace outside the Carlton Hotel, from which he could watch the spectacle along the Croisette, the equivalent of the boardwalk, at Cannes. It was the time of day when movie fans from neighboring towns and cities, released from their shops and factories and offices, swarmed down to the Croisette in the hope of seeing visiting stars in the flesh. Since most stars were housed in the Carlton or the Majestic, just up the road, the fans hoped they would all be out either posing for the cameramen or sipping cocktails on the terrace.

In fact, as Zanuck well knew, the stars rarely appeared at this hour. They were in their rooms getting themselves ready for their grand entrees into the Palais du Festival for the presentation of the film performance of the evening. The terraces were crowded all right, but by unknowns, so far as the movie fans were concerned — directors, producers, newsmen, mostly male, but surrounded by lots of pretty, young, scantily clad and vaguely familiar-looking girls.

They were a phenomenon of the festival, and pricked the half-contemptuous interest of festival aficionados like Zanuck. They were the desperately ambitious beauty-contest winners, would-be actresses, walk-on players, queens of the wolf whistle on the factory lines and in the offices where they worked, all of whom fervently believed the myth that Lana Turner had been discovered at a drugstore counter, all hoping to be singled out here in Cannes by some producer or director and magically turned into a star. Many of them were so young that they had their mothers with them, a chaperonage that did not, however, put any brake on the often brazen nature of their behavior. These were kids who knew what they wanted and were prepared to give their all to get it. Some were dressed and made up to look like Lana Turner's younger sister; others exaggerated the size of their lips and showed their teeth like Crawford or Taylor; still others slit tight skirts to the thigh and pouted as Silvana Mangano had done in *Bitter Rice,* one of the successful Italian films of the time. And almost all of them wore see-through blouses. This was 1951, and France had not yet gone topless, and one of these avid young would-be stars, eager for any kind of publicity, had been banned from the festival and expelled from her free hotel room for opening her blouse and posing bare-breasted for the press photographers. The talk of the festival in 1951 was a pretty American kid, rumored to be only fourteen years old, who had been brought to Cannes by her mother in the hope of snaring a movie contract. The mother, a faded blonde, would parade her daughter around the tables on the Carlton terrace, accosting any directors, producers, or newsmen she recognized.

"Meet my daughter Cindy," she would say. "Isn't she beautiful? And just look at those breasts! Genuine, too — see, no padding." At which she would take the hand of the director or producer and guide it to her daughter's breast, fitting it firmly over the half-hidden globe. The girl would bare her teeth and smile vacantly while the fondling took place.

One day, seated at a table with Mack Sennett, Sydney Box, Alfred Hitchcock, and a critic, Zanuck had a sudden impulse to surprise this outrageous mother. When she reached over and took his hand, he firmly swerved it away from her daughter's breast and instead directed it almost brutally over her breast instead. He was disconcerted, however, when, instead of a cry of hurt surprise or anger, the woman let him hang in there, while she gave him a lubricious smirk and said: "Naughty, naughty!"

Zanuck regarded all the sleaze surrounding the festival with a genial but worldly eye, fascinated by the spectacle of how far women were willing to go to sell themselves into his world of movies, cynically confident he was impervious to all the sexual come-ons of these greedy and shameless females.

And then one of them hooked him.

There was another festival groupie (as the type later came to be known) at the Cannes Festival in 1951, and she was, it must be admitted, slightly different from the lost nymphets who hovered around the Carlton terrace. She was older, for one thing, and more sophisticated, moving in cinematic circles in Cannes with names and influence. She seemed to get invited to all the parties, aboard Sam Spiegel's yacht riding at anchor off the Croisette, at Jack Warner's villa, the Aujourd'hui at Cap d'Antibes, and at some raffish but no less luxurious suppers in the lush hill houses behind Cannes. She was always being photographed on the arm of a second- or third-rank French, Italian, or English film actor, and she went to the gala nights at the Palais du Festival usually with a critic from one of the avant-garde magazines. In a glittering low-cut evening gown, her hair and brown bare shoulders gleaming in the camera flashlights, she had an attraction with a tigerish touch to it.

Most producers looked at her, and some did more than that. She was rumored to have received quite a few film offers, although whether they were serious is something else again. In any case, she maintained she had turned them all down because they came from Continental or Israeli filmmakers, and she was gambling for more than that.

She was known among the festival regulars as Bella Wegier, but one might have guessed from the Slav shape of her features that she was not French. Wegier, in fact, was the gallicized version of their name, which her parents had long ago adopted. She had also been married to a Frenchman, but there had been a divorce after eighteen stormy months, and she had long since forgotten both him and his name.

Bella's background was Polish-Jewish. Her parents had come to France as immigrants in the 1930s, bringing their only child with them. Like many a refugee in France at the time, her father had been forced to take any job he could get, and Bella's childhood memories were of grinding poverty and a dull, dingy life in one of those dark industrial towns along the Belgian frontier in Northern France. As soon as she was old enough, she had left the family home and run away to Paris. How Bella had existed in Paris once she reached the French capital is something she never talked about. All that is known is that when the Germans conquered France and moved into Paris, she was rounded up and shipped to a concentration camp. She was sent first to Osnabrück and then to Auschwitz. She never talked about that either, and the fact that she came out of the shattering experience alive and showing few physical signs of her ordeal was another of the mysteries surrounding her strange, turbulent young life.

Bella Wegier was well known and popular among regulars at the Cannes Festival, especially the newsmen covering it. Most days she was to be seen at the Blue Bar next door to the Palais du Festival, where the critics and their wives and girlfriends would gather. She was usually dressed in tight white slacks, sandals, and a red sun-top, and she always looked marvelous. She slept with quite a number of the better-known critics, and though she never failed to give them a good time, the more sensitive among them got the feeling there was more expertise than ardor behind her performance and she enjoyed it less than they did. They also sensed she did not really like or trust men, which, in view of her experiences in the past, was hardly surprising. She spoke impeccable French, German, Italian, and Polish, and she pumped the newsmen for all the gossip they could give her about the important movie people around.

She was also always borrowing money from them and never paying it back. She was greedy for money.

"It's the only thing that matters in the world," she once said.

It was almost certainly at a party at Jack Warner's villa, the Aujourd'hui, that Bella first decided she was going to get Darryl Zanuck. She had seen him before in the Monte Carlo casino, but never quite realized who he was. Both Jack and Zanuck liked to go on to Monaco after one of the film galas and play cards in the winter casino, particularly in the early 1950s, when a tough Greek syndicate and the profligate ex-King Farouk of Egypt were nearly always playing, and the stakes were high. Casinos were always favorite hangouts for Bella Wegier even though, in those days, she could never afford to play at the big tables. She seemed to blossom in the heady atmosphere of the *salles privées*, and she stalked the salons like a wild animal, nostrils twitching as she watched the men at the high-stake tables, risking fortunes on the turn of a card. The expression on her face was one of pure envy, as if she longed above everything else to be able one day to do the same. Once, when she heard Virginia Zanuck remark that casinos and gambling bored her, Bella looked at her with both astonishment and incomprehension, for to her there was nothing like it in the world.

Jack Warner knew Bella slightly from seeing her at Riviera parties, and it was he who invited her to drinks at the Villa Aujourd'hui. There was the usual crowd of show-business types there — David Niven, Ava Gardner, Jean-Pierre Aumont, Eddie Barclay (the French record entrepreneur and producer), Edward G. Robinson, Linda Christian — and the guests were drinking cocktails in the little summerhouse that was planted on a tiny rock in the sea, connected to the main villa by a narrow causeway. As they sipped their champagne, the guests gazed out at a luxurious white yacht floating at anchor in the blue waters, only a hundred yards or so away. Jack Warner stared at it glumly. "See that boat?" he said. "I could have bought it with what I lost at the casino last night."

The look on Bella Wegier's face as she listened to those words mirrored . . . what? — contempt? envy? disgust? It was hard to tell. Warner was not one of the producers at the festival Bella was chasing, for she was only too well aware that his ever-vigilant second wife never let another woman get near him. For the same reason she hardly gave a second glance at Darryl Zanuck when he stopped by the villa, because Virginia was with him, and she had the complacent look of a solidly married woman.

But then they were introduced and Bella realized just who he was. Her attitude changed. Her critic friends had all expatiated on Darryl Zanuck's life-style, and she was well primed about his attitudes to women. If it was true that he despised the whole of the female sex and believed they were good for nothing but quick sex, as some of her more cynical critic friends maintained, then what had she to gain by sleeping with him? She had been warned it was no way to win Zanuck's admiration or esteem, that Hollywood was littered with the corpses of the eager girls he had used and thrown away. And what did she have to offer him that was different?

As it turned out, she had quite a lot. And she knew how to deliver it.

The week after the 1951 Cannes Festival, Darryl and Virginia Zanuck motored back to Paris by way of the three-star restaurants in Vienne, Lyons, and Chalons. It was a leisurely journey and should have been a glorious relief after the limelight and gaudy razzmatazz of Cannes. But actually it had not gone well at all. Darryl had been irritable and touchy, and they had bickered and snapped at each other. For some time Virginia had sensed Darryl was going through some sort of emotional crisis, although she could only try to divine by instinct what was the reason for his malaise. There was really no excuse why he should not be feeling on top of the world, because, despite a slump in the American movie market, his films were doing marvelously, every movie-maker was beating a path to his door, and there was now no studio boss in Hollywood with anything like his financial success and his artistic prestige.

Yet he seemed nervy and dissatisfied. At home he had become a grouch. He had grumbled when Darrylin had suddenly decided to get married, maintaining she was too young, and he had quarreled with Susan because she never had any boyfriends and showed no signs of getting married at all. And then there was his relationship with Richard. Something had happened there that had, she felt, somehow separated, even estranged, Darryl from his son. She had noticed before they left for this European trip that there was no longer the instinctive warmth and easy, father-son relationship between them. It had once been such a mutual admiration society between the two of them she had sometimes felt alienated, left out, and she had been jealous and resentful that a father and his son could be so close that the wife and mother who belonged to them both was kept to one side. But then the relationship had seemed to change, and change so suddenly and so radically that when Darryl and Dick met, they did not even act towards each other as they had done before. They no longer seemed to feel the need to hug and pat and slap each other, as men so often did with their male intimates in their boyish, bear-hugging way. Instead, they almost shied away from each other, like two horses asked to share the same paddock and pawing out their territory.

Was Dick to blame, since he was growing up and feeling his oats? Or was it Darryl, who was nearing his fiftieth birthday, and hating having to face up to the fact that even a wonder-boy has one day to grow old? Virginia later confessed that in Cannes she had confided in Anatole Litvak, who was often the receptacle of her confidences, and had chided herself for keeping her husband on too tight a tether while he was at the festival.

"With all these pretty girls around, and all the casinos," she said, "I feel so mean, forcing him to dance attendance on little old me. He hasn't the temperament to be the respectable husband. He's a Tarzan of the Apes, you know, really, and I feel guilty for not letting him go out more into that jungle to thump his chest and swing from trees."

"Providing he comes home in good order afterwards?" asked Litvak, smiling.

Virginia dimpled. "Oh yes," she said. "I'd hate it if he found another Jane."

On their first evening in Paris, the Zanucks took a stroll through the streets and finally went for a drink in the back bar of the Paris Ritz, where they could usually be sure of seeing someone they knew. The only person they saw on this occasion was a feature actor Darryl recognized named Alex D'Arcy, who was sitting in a corner with a beautiful girl who seemed vaguely familiar. Presently, Zanuck waved and beckoned the actor over, and he brought the girl with him. It was Bella Wegier, and all four got on famously. So much so that her animation and charm soon lifted Zanuck out of his gloomy mood, and he suggested they go on to dinner at the Tour d'Argent and afterwards to a nightclub, where they danced until the early hours.

That night Zanuck slept well for the first time for weeks, and Virginia gave most of the credit to the personality, worldliness, and amusingly bitchy conversation of the beautiful Bella Wegier, and her good opinion of her by no means diminished when flowers and a note of thanks, addressed personally to her, arrived later in the day.

The two women met several times after that, and they often went out shopping or for quiet lunches together, and Bella was attentive, knowledgeable, and had marvelous taste. Towards the end of their stay in Paris, Virginia had become so fond of the young Polish girl she gave her a large flacon of Joy perfume as a farewell present. Having heard Bella had ambitions to make it in films one day, she urged Darryl to give her a chance to try out her talents, and Darryl solemnly promised to do so.

"If you ever come to California," he said, "I'll arrange for you to make a test."

And Virginia added: "And if you do come, you must stay with us. We would love to have you as a guest in our house."

Bella thanked her profusely and promised to think about it.

What Virginia did not know was that her husband had already begun meeting Bella clandestinely, and they had slept together. Moreover, he had found it one of the more exciting encounters of a not uneventful sexual career, and Bella one of the most stimulating characters he had ever met. She made him feel young again.

He would have stayed on, and Virginia might have found out what was happening, had not a cable arrived from Hollywood asking him to return on urgent business. There was a crisis at the studios and it concerned the future presentation of films. When he told Bella he was leaving, she was silent for a moment, and then, as if she had taken a decision, asked Zanuck to lend her $3,000. While she had been in Cannes, she aid, she had begun gambling and had lost most of her savings. If she didn't pay her debts immediately, she was liable to be thrown out of her apartment. Slowly, Zanuck reached out of bed for his wallet, and peeled off a thousand dollars from a sheaf of bills. He told her he would deliver the rest to her on the morrow.

"You think I am asking for a payoff, don't you?" she asked, adding, "Because you are leaving."

He shook his head.

"No," he said, "I regard it as an advance on what you'll be earning when you come to California."

"Ah," she said, "I thought you had forgotten about that."

"I may have done," said Zanuck, "I am sure Virginia hasn't. If she has her way, you'll be a movie star. I only hope to God it won't make any difference to us." He added, taking hold of her: "You make me feel my youth again."

It was that murmured remark, Bella said later, that convinced her she had got him — and she could make her plans accordingly. She was not, after all, going to be another of those short-time fucks he would presently contemptuously throw away.

While Zanuck had been watching movies and talking deals in Cannes (and revolutionizing his sex-life in Paris), one of Fox's officials had also been in France on a very different kind of mission.

As Zanuck was only too well aware, the principal problem facing the movies in general at the moment was the growing competition from television, which was just beginning to make its impact felt in the United States.

The network programs were becoming all pervasive in the American home and had begun taking a bite out of receipts in the movie houses, and some urgent meetings to discuss a remedy had taken place all over Hollywood long before the Cannes Film Festival of 1951. The men who ran the major studios in Hollywood realized they had to do something to diminish the impact of TV, and it was generally accepted that could probably be managed only by making TV's small screen seem even smaller than it really was. But how? Obviously, by making the cinema screen seem bigger and better. The head of Fox's research and engineering

division was a man named Earl Sponible, and he was already searching
for a way of circumventing the menace of TV with a more spectacular
kind of movie entertainment. From his point of view, this was not a
question of making better films — although that certainly wouldn't do
any harm — but in finding a new way of presenting them.

While he was discussing the problem with his colleagues (Zanuck among
them), a new system for showing films appeared in selected American
cinemas and created great interest in the press. It was called Cinerama,
and it presented to the public a vast wraparound screen (in fact, three
screens) upon which a main scene was shown with palpitating vividness
on the central screen, while, at the same time, the locale and movement
was extended on either side on two other screens. It was all done in such
size and with such blunderbuss effect that it involved the spectator as TV
could never hope to do.

To most technical experts, Cinerama was really a stunt, a circus trick,
and was hardly suitable for the showing of ordinary narrative films.* For
normal studio purposes, it was too expensive, needing too many special
cameras both to shoot the film and show it, and it would obviously never
be a viable rival to run-of-the-mill theatrical movies. Nevertheless, it had
jolted Zanuck when he saw an exhibition of its capabilities, and he sent
a memo to his fellow directors and all the studio technicians suggesting
that maybe an adaptation of its ideas, with perhaps some whittling down
of its vast screen, might be possible.

Sponible had indicated he thought such an adaptation was feasible, and
he had, for some time, been experimenting in the laboratories at 20th
Century–Fox in New York, looking for some way to increase the size of
ordinary cinema screens so as to "spectacularize" their impact on the
audience. In his regular reports to Zanuck, he called it: "How to bring
about 1.85 to 1," which represented the proportions of what, he hoped,
would be the size of the future cinema screen.

But all his efforts to achieve it had failed, and he and his band of experts
had reported disappointing results of their experiments all through 1948–
1950. Then, in 1951, he heard about a breakthrough in France. A cinematic specialist named Dr. Chretien was reported to have invented an
effective and viable method of large-screen cinema presentation.

Normally at 20th Century–Fox all action on technical developments
was left in the hands of the New York office, whose chairman of the board

---

*Though some successful films were made using the Cinerama system, notably Kubrick's
*2001: A Space Odyssey.*

was an exuberant Greek named Spyros Skouras.* Skouras was inclined to fizz and effervesce like a cross between a firecracker and a glass of Alka-Seltzer, but in fact he knew very little about the film business and was a complete ignoramus about technical cinematic developments.

Skouras had, in any case, gone off on a trip to Greece and left no contact address, so that, when the question of locating Dr. Chretien and his new invention came up, it was Zanuck, through his assistant, who gave permission for Sponible to go to France. Moreover, Sponible was told that if he found the invention to be a viable one, he was to buy the rights to the invention. Sponible went to Paris. He saw a demonstration of the projection camera and the lenses, and he bought them up.

Raymond Klune, who handled the Hollywood end while Zanuck was away, ordered Sponible to rush back with the equipment without delay so that everybody could see a demonstration, and as soon as the experts at Fox had possession of the lenses they began doing experiments with them.

"Actually, we had some of the Bausch and Lomb people working with us," said Klune later. "We proved the lens. The option [Sponible had taken on the rights] was exercised, and 20th Century–Fox thus acquired the full rights of what came to be called Doctor Chretien's Anamorphic Lens. It was still a deep dark secret, but we were in the business of wide-screen movies."

Fox had paid out a lot of money for the rights to the new lens, and there was something of a panic when patent lawyers shortly afterwards discovered that the anamorphic principle was in the public domain and was therefore not really patentable at all. This revelation was made while Fox was in the process of showing off its experiments with the lens to other members of the film industry in Hollywood, and any one of them could have stolen it.

"There were mixed reactions to these tests," said Klune, "ranging from great enthusiasm to little enthusiasm, but there was enough around to encourage us to go forward. On the other hand, in order to keep the patent secure, we had to find a name for it — and then patent the name! That was what the lawyers kept telling us. The system wasn't patentable — so patent the name! That was when we came up with the name Cinemascope, but when we came to patent it we found that someone else had already done so. And we had to go around to these other people and buy the name Cinemascope from them, and they stuck us for $35,000."

*He had taken over from Joe Schenck when Schenck went to jail for tax evasion.

Cinemascope did not revolutionize the nature of Hollywood films, but it certainly made them more pleasant to watch, especially spectacular and scenic films.

But to begin with, the studio did not know how to handle it, which was the reason Zanuck was urgently recalled to Hollywood from Paris. He was later to confess he was confused himself, and for a time thought the new system would kill ordinary narrative films. Just about this time, Elia Kazan came to him with a film script that he was eager to direct and wanted Zanuck to oversee at Fox. Zanuck read it through, thought it was exciting, but turned it down, on the ground that it wouldn't "look well" in Cinemascope. So Kazan took it elsewhere and Sam Spiegel eventually made it with Marlon Brando. It was *On the Waterfront,* and Zanuck regretted letting it get away from him for the rest of his career.

"My only excuse is that I was up to my ears in Cinemascope," he said later, "and I didn't think *On the Waterfront* was a Cinemascope type of film. How wrong can you get? It would have been wonderful and it would have won me another Oscar. But it was like the early days of sound films. We didn't know quite what we were getting into, and all I could think of was that Fox had put itself in hock to buy the new system, and we had to get our money back. So we couldn't afford to experiment."

As it turned out, 20th Century–Fox made a lot of money out of Cinemascope, in spite of the fact that all across the country there were grumbles from cinema owners who had to install new screens and new lenses for their projectors. Bausch and Lomb also charged $25,000 apiece for the lenses for both studio cameras and theater projectors.

When the first films in the new system were shown, there was a lot of skepticism around too. Critics wrote learned disquisitions on the reason why it was dramatically wrong for the cinema screen to change its shape. To which Zanuck replied, truculently: "But who ordained that a movie screen has got to be *square?*" Nunnally Johnson, the screenwriter, took it much more calmly than his old boss. He came back to work for Fox just about this time, and when he was asked how he was going to cope with the new demands of Cinemascope, he said:

"Easy. What I'm going to do from now on is put the paper in my typewriter sideways!"

Bella Wegier arrived in Hollywood at the end of 1952, just when the Cinemascope revolution was beginning. One of the first things she did was telephone Virginia Zanuck, who was delighted to hear from her. True to her promise, she told Bella to come right out to Santa Monica and be a guest at the beach house until she got herself settled in a place of her own. So for the next few weeks Bella was a guest in the Zanuck home, and was given a bedroom next to Susan in the guest house, and they shared a bathroom.

She looked thin and pale when she first arrived, but she quickly blossomed and bronzed in the Pacific sun, and she used to meet Zanuck every morning on the beach, wearing shorts and a halter and joining in his calisthenics. She also accompanied her host and hostess to Palm Springs on the weekends, learned to play croquet quite well, and, to the approval of both her host and hostess, dealt firmly and effectively with the lechers who tried to swarm all over her at parties.

All the cynics wondered how Zanuck managed to keep his hands off her, but she seemed to be quite firm in handling him too, and never gave Virginia a moment's anxiety.

"She behaved like a most circumspect young lady," said Henry Fine, one of the regular guests, "but whenever you came near her, you could feel the heat coming out of her. She was one of the sexiest females I have ever encountered, a great lovely ball of shimmering fire — but wrapped up in an iron control. But you did have to wonder about her, and who was going to get burned when she eventually did burst into flames."

Susan was, by this time, the only member of the Zanuck family still at home. Darrylin had married and gone to live in Santa Barbara. Richard was away at college. Since Susan and Bella were roughly about the same age, Virginia calculated they would become friends. And that gave her a sense of satisfaction. She was quite aware of how potently attractive her young guest was, and she was also no fool about Darryl. Confident his sense of the proprieties was strong enough to keep him from fouling the family nest, she still feared he would eventually find it hard to resist making a pass at such a lovely glowing girl, even if he did it elsewhere. On the other hand, he might well be constrained from trying at all if Bella and Susan became chums, since he had always been a most circumspect father and she calculated he would think twice before sleeping with his daughter's best friend. Actually, it didn't work out like that. Susan was a strange girl. Pretty, with strong ambitions to succeed as a singer and a dancer, she liked to live her own life and did not make friends easily. On the other hand, she did not find herself drawn to Bella, this restless, nervous girl from Europe. Or at least so she said.

"I don't like her," she told her mother. "She's sloppy in the bathroom, uses too much perfume, is always borrowing money from me, and is a great big sexpot — you should hear her when she gets into bed!"

She complained that sometimes when Bella came home late and she was already asleep, she would wake up and find Bella standing in the bathroom doorway, no clothes on, staring down at her.

"Then she goes back to her room," Susan said, "and paces up and down, holding her tummy and looking like she's suffering from period pains. Only she isn't," she added, "because she's still not wearing a stitch."

One day Zanuck asked Virginia to come to the studio to see some rushes, but told her to leave Bella at home. When she went into the projection room, Darryl was sitting with one of the regular studio direc- tors, Michael Curtiz, and when the rushes came on she realized she was watching a screen test of Bella. Her lines were simple and her voice was a bit abrasive, but the accent was attractive, and what the girl had was a beautiful body and carriage. The way she walked was slinky and seductive, and if she could only learn to ring some changes on her single facial expression, which just looked sulky and bad-tempered, they might well make something out of her.

Virginia said as much and emphasized again that Bella would have to learn how to use her features and get some animation into her face. "Why does she have to look as if she's got a pain?" she asked.

Curtiz, who prided himself on being outspoken, said: "Do you know what that girl is suffering from? Deprivation. What she needs is a lover. Any volunteers?" In the silence that followed, he laughed and added: "Line up behind *me* in the queue!"

The question then came up about Bella's name. If they did put her in a film, what were they going to call her? Wegier was no name for a young and attractive artist, and Curtiz said they needed something foreign, exotic, mysterious. Virginia, who was one of those people who loved to scramble names, eventually came up with one that had just the right number of letters for a cinema marquee and sounded intriguing. She suggested they should call her Darvi — Bella Darvi — this being a com- bination of Darryl's first name and her own.

"After all," she said, "she does rightly belong to both of us. She was our joint discovery, wasn't she? And we both feel responsible for the poor child."

So Bella Darvi she became from then on, and was given a contract under that name by 20th Century–Fox. Zanuck, in fact, became so used to the name he soon began denying its phony provenance and maintained its linkage to his own name and Virginia's was just coincidence. Once, at a party, when being teased about it by the guests, he insisted the name belonged to an old Polish family and maintained "there are lots of Darvis in the Warsaw telephone book."

There were others at Fox who saw the screen test of Bella Darvi and wondered what Zanuck and his wife could possibly see in her — as a screen actress, that is. To them, the girl seemed to be wooden and have no cinematic potential, and when the boss ordered the Fox publicity department to turn on the heat and get her name into the papers, there were many Rabelaisian jokes about why he was making such a fuss. To them, she was one of those characters, familiar to every studio talent scout, who seems vibrant and vivid off the screen but becomes deadly dull and lifeless under the eye of the camera.

But remarkably enough, Zanuck, who could be tough and shrewd and percipient about new screen talent, had a blind spot about his girls. The more attracted he was to them personally, and sexually, the more he believed in their potential screen talents. And the fact that Bella Darvi was so wonderful in bed seemed to convince him that she would dispense the same magic vicariously from the screen.

"That was one of the surprising things about my father," said his son, Richard, later. "He had this tremendous enthusiasm for the women he would pick up. He was normally so level-headed, such a shrewd judge of what would sell in the movie houses. But when he fell for one of these girls, this great ability he had to get people enthused about a film or someone in it would betray him. He always insisted that every film he produced was the greatest picture he ever made. Now he convinced his women of the same thing. He actually believed, and made *them* believe, they were the greatest discoveries of all time. He would take people right off the street and convince himself — and convince others. To a lot of these poor girls, he would say: 'You're gonna be a great star. I'm gonna make you a great star.' And they would believe it. And so would he."

Whether Bella Darvi believed what Zanuck told her about her movie talents is one of the big questions one finds oneself asking about this beautiful but bizarre woman. To some of those who knew her well, there was a hardheaded, cynical female behind the seductive exterior, and they calculated her experiences in life had been too harsh for her to take seriously the flattering things that were told her, promised her, especially by men. Her old friends from France cynically presumed she was savoring the luxury and security the Zanucks were providing, taking every day as it came, and not worrying about her movie career because she had a better role in real life — being a middle-aged man's darling determined to squeeze out of him every bit of money he could be induced to part with.

On the other hand, some of her friends remembered that Bella was a gambler, and that gamblers are dreamers. Could she be dreaming about her new life in Hollywood? That what Zanuck promised would come true? That he would make her a star — and she would never have to worry about money or security again?

He ought to have recognized the unhappy truth about Bella Darvi as an actress when he cast her in her first two pictures at Fox, for she made absolutely no impact on the public or the critics. Admittedly, he tried her out in small parts in minor feature films. One was called *Hell and High Water* and the other *The Racers*, and his idea was simply to give her a sense of movie sets and how to take direction. But looking at her, how could he miss the fact that here was a personality that simply did not transfer to the screen?

The unfortunate thing is that Zanuck was no longer in a position to think or feel impartially about Bella. Now that she was working in the studio, he had resumed sexual relations with her and began bedding her in the boudoir behind his office. Most of these assignations took place late at night, after his evenings in the projection theater with the rushes and the rough cuts. If she was tired after a day's work on the lot, she gave no sign of it when she was with him. He was later to say that he was "absolutely besotted with her." Bella was good with men. She may not have known how to act convincingly on the set, but she was a Duse, a Bernhardt, a Garbo in bed. Zanuck was more than fifty years old and beginning to worry about his virility, but Bella rejuvenated him, filled him with the vigor of a seventeen-year-old boy.

Afterwards, they would drive back to Santa Monica together and part with a chaste goodnight kiss beside the pool that divided the beach house from the annex. If Virginia chanced to be watching through the window, she could not possibly have guessed from appearances just how things really were.

Despite the minor impact Bella Darvi's film debut made on the movie world, Zanuck continued to enthuse over her capabilities and her promise. Towards the middle of 1953, he let it be known he was looking for someone to fill "an important cameo role" in a forthcoming Cinemascope production called *The Egyptian*. Marlon Brando would be the star, and Jean Simmons and Gene Tierney would fill the principal female roles.

The well-known Hollywood agent Charles K. Feldman telephoned Zanuck to ask what kind of character he had in mind for the cameo. The studio boss replied that he had been thinking of trying to tempt Greta Garbo to come out of retirement in order to fill the part, but he had now abandoned the idea as being unnecessary. He had found just the actress he was looking for, and henceforward, though stories about the talent search would still go on, Feldman should ignore them, because they would just be part of a publicity stunt. The search was over and he had the actress for the role.

"My God," said Feldman, "You really must have some formidable discovery up your sleeve. If you can afford to shrug off Garbo, just who the hell have you got instead?"

"Bella Darvi," Zanuck said.

From the start, the production of *The Egyptian* was a disaster. The film was an adaptation of an opulent best-selling novel by Mika Waltari, set in ancient Egypt, with a script written by Philip Dunne. It was not one of his proudest efforts. Michael Curtiz, who liked to swagger around the set like a latter-day pirate, rough talk and all, had been assigned to direct. Bella Darvi's part was that of a slinky, bare-hipped courtesan, named Nefer, at the Egyptian court.

By the time the cast had concluded the first read-through of the script, Marlon Brando decided this was no movie for him. He walked off the set and took the first plane out for New York. Gene Tierney had a fit of nerves and fled the studio in tears. Jean Simmons, whose pretty English face concealed a sharp tongue, quickly became disenchanted with Bella Darvi's lack of professional know-how. She was heard to remark that here was "an actress who Nefer was."

When news reached Zanuck of Brando's abrupt departure, he grabbed the telephone and told the star's agent the studio would sue if Brando did not report back for work at once. The agent replied that there was absolutely no possibility of Brando's doing so, and when Zanuck finally asked why the star had walked out, the agent said: "Because he loathes

Mike Curtiz, he hates his part in the film, and he just can't stand Bella Darvi."

Even more outraged, Zanuck called his lawyers and told them to file suit.* Meanwhile, he looked around for a replacement and finally, if somewhat reluctantly, signed up a mild-mannered English actor named Edmund Purdom. Linda Christian, who once had a torrid affair with Purdom, said of him that "he is positively marvelous when he's horizontal, but an absolute dud when vertical," and he certainly did nothing to help invigorate *The Egyptian*. The film was shot in Cinemascope, and if it had been the only example of the genre around at the time, it could have dealt a mortal blow to the new system. It was thumbed down by both public and critics. Bella Darvi's performance was singled out for some harsh comments, and she was variously described as "a slinky-hipped no-no," "the weak spot in the talent lineup," and "a high-priced harlot who comes off like a five cent piece."

Virginia Zanuck was no mean critic when it came to films, and she could recognize a stinker when she saw one. She knew from the first sneak preview that *The Egyptian* was going to be a disaster, and did her best, like the old pro she was, to prepare Bella Darvi for the worst. Nevertheless, the notices were even harsher than she or anyone had expected, and Bella was crushed by them. Virginia tried to be both consoling and sympathetic, but secretly she hoped that this would be the end of the girl's movie career and one day soon she would go back to France.

She knew her husband's habits pretty well and she did not shut her ears to all the gossip from well-meaning friends, so she realized by this time that Darryl had found a way of bedding her pretty houseguest. She was ready to put up with it so long as her husband carried on the affair away from home and left no dirty linen staring her in the face.

But even he, she calculated, must now have realized that as a potential film star Bella was a dud. She hoped the disillusionment would help get Darryl out of Bella's embraces and induce the would-be actress to go back to the boulevards of Paris, where she belonged. It had all been a great mistake.

To her surprise, however, her husband did not seem to be facing up to the obvious. He took the failure of *The Egyptian* badly, inveighing against

---

*Brando subsequently settled out of court by agreeing to make another film for 20th Century–Fox. He did *Sayonara* and *Teahouse of the August Moon* for them thereafter.

the critics, assuring Bella that bad notices didn't mean a thing, and telling her to ignore them. When the girl burst into tears and said she had had enough and was going back to France, Virginia was both amazed and disappointed to hear Darryl say he wouldn't hear of it.

He was "going to show them," he said. Putting his arm around the girl, he swore he was going to make a great star of her yet.

# TWENTY

# THE FLYING TRAPEZE

W HEN MILTON SPERLING heard that Nunnally Johnson had made it up with Darryl Zanuck and returned to 20th Century–Fox, he was envious and wished he had the courage to do the same. He was now an executive of Warner Brothers and earning more money than at any other time of his life. Yet he missed the ruthless but talented warrior with whom he had spent his formative years in Hollywood, and he longed to hear the swish of his mallet again. Sperling was still the husband of Harry Warner's daughter and marrying into the family had brought him distressing involvement in fraternal vendettas and bizarre and Byzantine plots.

"It was a period," he said later, "when my relationship with Jack Warner was a kind of pogo-stick thing, one moment high in his esteem, the next right down in the mud. He was a very volatile man. I had discovered that strange things offended his amour propre. I remember that with my new and impressive salary I bought myself a Rolls-Royce about this time. I had always dreamed of having a Rolls and now I had got one, and I was very proud of it, and I drove onto the Warner lot with it. Of course Jack was informed of this instantly, because he had his spies everywhere. That day when I came into the executive dining room for lunch, he didn't speak to me. He ignored me, he didn't greet me, he stalked past me. I didn't realize then that it had anything to do with the Rolls-Royce."

This silent treatment went on for weeks. From being practically a favorite son, Sperling was suddenly out in the cold without an anorak. Jack suddenly seemed to have taken a total dislike to him. He didn't reply to Sperling's memos or return his telephone calls. One day, when Sperling was leaving the lot in his Rolls, it happened that Jack Warner was driving out at the same time. When he saw who was behind him, Jack wrenched on the wheel of his car and then squealed to a stop, almost causing Sperling to ram his rear. Jack was driving his usual Cadillac, and as Sperling came abreast, Jack leaned out of the window, his face distorted with rage, and shouted: "Listen, you little son of a bitch, how come you can afford a Rolls-Royce and I'm driving a Cadillac?"

Suddenly it dawned on Sperling what was the nature of his fault in Jack's eyes. Trying to make a joke of it he said, "You should have told me you don't like Rolls-Royces."

Jack's expression abruptly changed to one of lofty contempt. "Aw, what the hell does it matter to me?" he said. "You just go on blowing your money. I'm gonna wind up with millions and die a rich man — and you'll die a fucking pauper."

Sperling watched Jack back up his Cadillac and drive away, smirking, and next week Warner was back to recognizing him again.

"I didn't know about corporate privilege in those days," he said. "I suppose it's true of most American corporations. You drive a car according to your status in the company. Second-class executives like me don't drive Cadillacs, and certainly not Rolls-Royces. I had been given a reminder of exactly where I stood at Warner Brothers, and I knew I'd never make it to the top."

Nunnally Johnson was welcomed back to 20th Century–Fox like the prodigal son, and Zanuck made it so plain that all was forgiven that Johnson felt guilty at ever having left him at all. He knew by this time that he had made an error, from every point of view, in going off to work with William Goetz and International Pictures. It had been at the urging of his agent, Johnny Hyde, who had planned the move as a way for Johnson to "make some money for your old age." But Zanuck had been right all along the line. Goetz was a dolt as far as movies were concerned, and Johnson had missed Zanuck's abrasive interference with his scripts, the rows they had had over scenes and players and directors, the impudent way in which he took your film and ripped it to pieces in the cutting room. But at least he had taken an interest. During his stay with International Pictures, Johnson had sometimes wondered whether Goetz knew if he was alive or dead, he intervened so little.

He missed Zanuck's maddening but galvanizing interest so much, in fact, that at the first opportunity he had sold out his interest in International and let it be known around Hollywood that he was available. As soon as the word spread, Louis B. Mayer of M-G-M invited him over to lunch and made him an offer. He asked him to join Metro as a writer-producer, and, listing the illustrious star names in the M-G-M stable, said Johnson could have the pick of them, plus more money than he had ever earned in his life, if he would join the organization.

Johnson turned him down. When Mayer asked him why, he said: "Because Fox has asked me to go back to them."

"What are they giving you in money?" Mayer asked.

"Exactly the same money I got when I left," Johnson said.

Mayer looked astonished that anyone could be so foolish. "How can you do it?" he asked. "What has Fox got that M-G-M hasn't?"

"They've got Zanuck," said Johnson.

He added later: "You know, everyone was right about Louie Mayer. He was a real villain. But he was also a very good movie-man, and I remember that I thanked him very much for his offer and told him I was immensely flattered by it, as indeed I was. But I knew I would be more at home if I went back to Zanuck and Fox. I knew where the water cooler was and where to sharpen my pencil. So I went back to work with Zanuck — on exactly the same terms as before. And it was Zanuck who was the magnet that drew me. There was never a filmmaker like him. Not at the head of a studio, anyway."

In fact, Johnson's return was a godsend for Zanuck, too, for he was swimming in a sea of indecision, both in his personal and professional life, bored with the Hollywood grind, worried about middle age and his virility, about falling receipts at the box office, about what kind of movies the public wanted, and desperately in need of someone with whom he could discuss trends, ideas, stories.

Ironically, Johnson's second cycle with Zanuck at Fox began in almost the same manner as their first professional encounter. Zanuck asked him to script a new version of an old film. "He hadn't changed a bit while I'd been away," Johnson said. "He was still nuts about rewrites."

The movie he asked him to do was called *Everybody Does It*, which had originally been made under the title of *Wife, Husband and Friend*. Johnson thought it was "a lousy story" and was not surprised to learn that it had been a box-office flop in its original version. But Zanuck thought a lot about it, even seemed to have an obsession about it.

"We all get obsessed with something in the film business at one time or another," Johnson said later. "For instance, I was obsessed with a gag which I've put into several films, and I even inserted it again in this clunker, *Everybody Does It*. I have this party scene, see, and there is a young man who is attracted to a very pretty girl on the other side of the room, and finally he goes up to her and says: 'May I take you home?' And she says: 'Yes, where do you live?' I think this is funny. But every time I put it in a film, nobody in the audience laughs. *Everybody Does It* was the fourth time I tried it, and when the audience didn't laugh at it again, I had to admit it had become an obsession. And I gave up."

Zanuck didn't seem to worry at all that the film turned out to be a flop. The moment it was finished, he handed Johnson a book called *The Mudlark* and told him it would make a first-rate film. It was the story of an orphan waif and Queen Victoria, and Zanuck declared that since it had been meticulously researched by the author in London, he had decided to film it there, and Johnson would be writer-producer. Only later, after all the arrangements had been made, was it discovered the author of *The Mudlark* was a Frenchman named Bonnet who lived in the South Seas and had never been in London in his life.

Secretly, one of Zanuck's reasons for picking *The Mudlark* was because it gave him the opportunity of doing a bit of offbeat casting. One of his contract stars was a beautiful actress named Irene Dunne, and it was his considered opinion that she was the most stately and regal woman he had ever met. One day she had happened to say to him over lunch: "You know, one of my favorite women has always been Queen Victoria of England. I'd give a lot to play her in a film." He went around from that moment thinking of Dunne padding herself to look like the queen, dressing in black, putting on a crown and frigidly remarking: "We are not amused," and the prospect teased him. Thus, when he read the synopsis of *The Mudlark* he just knew Fox had to make it, so Irene Dunne could play the queen, and she was the first member of the cast to be announced. Immediately the choice caused a storm of controversy in the British press, and there were protests and expressions of outrage in Parliament that such a quintessential Hollywood star as Irene Dunne should have the insolence to try to play such a revered British queen. Zanuck played up the controversy for all it was worth, and then sneaked a copy of the film over to England for a private showing at Windsor Castle. Queen Elizabeth (now the Queen Mother) said she thought Miss Dunne had given a delicious performance, and King George remarked that "it's a pity Great-Grandmamma wasn't really as pretty as the actress who played her. Much smaller and tubbier she was, and quite pasty."

At the height of the newspaper storm, Zanuck made the announcement that *The Mudlark* had been chosen for a Royal Command performance at a West End cinema in London.

As if to compensate for Irene Dunne's American background, Zanuck cast an indubitable Englishman, Alec Guinness, to play the role of Disraeli, the British prime minister, in the film. Later Guinness was nominated for an Oscar for his performance. One of its highlights was the moment when, as Disraeli, he makes a moving speech in Parliament, and the scene subsequently became a favorite with film buffs for the long and highly dramatic pause in the middle of the speech. It was not something that had been written into the script, and both Zanuck and Johnson considered it one of the most brilliant moments of silence in the history of the movies. So when Guinness came over to Hollywood for the Academy Awards they asked him how he had thought it up.

"I didn't," Guinness said. "In the middle of my speech, I forgot my lines — dried up."

It was while Johnson was still shooting in England that Lauren Bacall and Humphrey Bogart, who were over there on vacation, came down from Stratford-on-Avon and raved about a new young actor who was playing in Shakespeare there. They thought Hollywood should snap him up at once. Johnson went to see the young player himself and immediately cabled Zanuck.

It so happened that Fox had just begun preparations for a movie version of Daphne du Maurier's novel *My Cousin Rachel* and George Cukor, who had been given the directorial assignment, was looking around for the male and female leads. For the female he had his eyes on Greta Garbo — everybody was after her in those days — and was having absolutely no luck in persuading her to make her comeback. So Zanuck dispatched him to England to look at the young actor everyone was raving about and see whether he wouldn't do for the male role.

"YES YES YES!" Cukor cabled back. "AS THE ENGLISH SAY, HE'S SUPER!"

Since it was obviously unanimous, Zanuck cabled his London office to grab the actor, put him under contract, and ship him out right away. That was the reason why, a month later, Richard Burton arrived for the first time in Hollywood. He stopped in New York on the way out and had a short interview with Darryl Zanuck, but Zanuck was in the middle of the annual meeting of the company and had no time to spare for him, except to look him over, approve him, and send him on. He telephoned Nunnally Johnson, now back in Hollywood, to take care of Burton pending Zanuck's return. Johnson, who was wrestling with rewrites on the script of *My Cousin Rachel*, recalled later that Burton came to his office on the Fox lot and he found him "an amiable but rather scruffy fellow."

Henry Fonda in a scene from *The Grapes of Wrath*. (*20th Century–Fox*)

Colonel Darryl Zanuck, Colonel Jack Warner, and Field Marshal Bernard L. Montgomery in Paris during World War II. (*Zanuck Family Collection*)

Richard Zanuck with his father in 1948. Richard is fourteen. (*Zanuck Family Collection*)

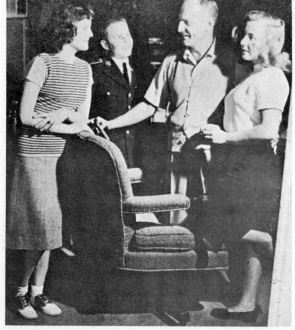

Susan, Richard, and Darrylin Zanuck, with their father in 1948. (*Zanuck Family Collection*)

Dorothy McGuire and Gregory Peck in a scene from *Gentleman's Agreement*. (*20th Century–Fox*)

Ethel Waters and Jeanne Crain in a scene from Zanuck's controversial film *Pinky*. (*20th Century–Fox*)

Anne Baxter, Bette Davis, Marilyn Monroe, and George Sanders in *All About Eve*. (*20th Century–Fox*)

Bella Darvi was a Polish-French woman Zanuck met at the Cannes Film Festival and groomed for Hollywood stardom. Earlier known as Bella Wegier, she was named Darvi after Zanuck and his wife Virginia.
(*20th Century–Fox*)

Bella Darvi in a scene from her first and only big film, *The Egyptian*, also starring Edmund Purdom, Jean Simmons, and Gene Tierney.
(*20th Century–Fox*)

Zanuck showing off at Ciro's Club in Hollywood in 1954.
(*Loomis Dean,* Life *Magazine,* © *1954 by Time Inc.*)

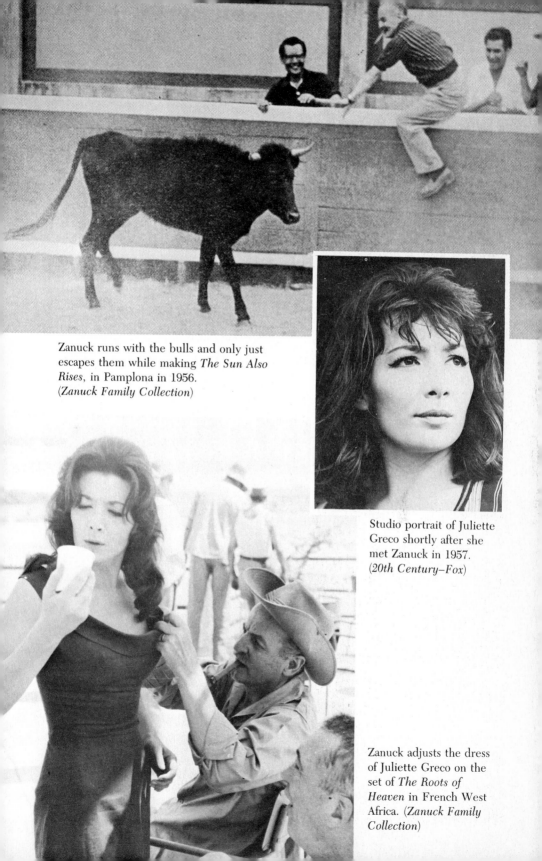

Zanuck runs with the bulls and only just escapes them while making *The Sun Also Rises*, in Pamplona in 1956. (*Zanuck Family Collection*)

Studio portrait of Juliette Greco shortly after she met Zanuck in 1957. (*20th Century–Fox*)

Zanuck adjusts the dress of Juliette Greco on the set of *The Roots of Heaven* in French West Africa. (*Zanuck Family Collection*)

Zanuck and director Ken Annakin
on location in Normandy for *The
Longest Day*. (*Ken Annakin
Collection*)

Elmo Williams and Zanuck, 1962.
(*Elmo Williams Collection*)

Robert Mitchum and Zanuck during
filming of *The Longest Day*.
(*Elmo Williams Collection*)

Director Ken Annakin and Irina Demick in Normandy during filming of the French sequences of *The Longest Day*. (*Ken Annakin Collection*)

Elizabeth Taylor and Zanuck at the premiere of *Cleopatra*. (*20th Century–Fox*)

Richard and Darryl Zanuck together in 1968. Richard is thirty-four. (*Zanuck Family Collection*)

Genevieve Gilles and Curt Jurgens in scene from *Hello and Goodbye*. Gilles was Zanuck's last protégée. (*20th Century–Fox*)

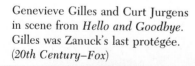

Richard Zanuck addressing the meeting where his father engineered his removal as president of 20th Century–Fox. (*Zanuck Family Collection*)

Genevieve Gilles and Zanuck.
(*Zanuck Family Collection*)

Zanuck at Hôtel du Cap, Cap d'Antibes, 1968. (*Mel Gussow*)

He was shocked when the first question the Welshman asked him was: "How do you get a dame in New York?"

Johnson, who was probably the most respectable character in films in the 1950s, and was an extremely celibate fellow when away from his wife, confessed at once he had never had occasion to need a "dame" when he was visiting Manhattan, and did Burton mean what he thought he meant. Burton did. In that case, said Johnson, he was sure that there were always call girls available in New York, but that, honestly, if someone asked him how to get hold of one he wouldn't have the faintest idea. He might have added that if Burton had needed that sort of information while he was in Manhattan, he ought to have asked Zanuck, but he thought it might be indiscreet to mention this.

"Ah, well," said Burton, "I badly wanted a fuck when I was there and I hadn't any idea of how to go about getting a hooker. I nearly went crazy."

Johnson asked him how long he had been in New York.

"Three days," Burton said.

Johnson wondered what sort of a person this young actor was that three days of sexual abstinence could cause him so much disturbance. Evidently, the same needs were either not pressing him so much in Hollywood or they were more easily appeased. At any rate, he made no request to Johnson for sexual guidance in California.

In any case, when Johnson saw the way Burton was handling the script he had written for him, he forgot about him as a person and was simply glad that Fox had found him as an actor. Watching him on the set confirmed the impression from Stratford-on-Avon, that here was a rare phenomenon, a natural star, full of sheer blazing passion, exuding dramatic craftsmanship and acting skill from every pore.

"What a marvelous man he was to watch in action," Johnson said later. "When he turned a knob to open a door, Burton turned it with his whole being."

The female role in *My Cousin Rachel* had finally been given by Zanuck to Olivia de Havilland, and this had resulted in the departure of George Cukor from the film. De Havilland and Cukor didn't get on. She was very much a woman, strong feminine meat, and she didn't have much time for characters like Cukor, who was gay. He wanted the love scenes in *My Cousin Rachel* to be light, delicate, full of soft sighs and delicious innuendos. De Havilland wanted what Zanuck later called "good old honest-to-God, slambang sex," and Cukor washed his hands of the whole thing with a wrinkle of disgust. Henry Koster was brought in to direct

instead, and he let it be known that he didn't care how the two lovers
played their scenes so long as they did it the way they felt and wanted.

The result was maybe a little more than de Havilland expected. When
she came off the set after the first romantic encounter with Richard Burton, it was noticed she was trembling.

"God!" she said, her hand to her mouth, "what gives with that man?
The first time he grabbed me on the staircase, that was no stage kiss! He
had his tongue right down my throat, right in front of the camera! It
startled the hell out of me."

And then she added: "But he is so good, good, good!"

Their embraces had that same startling, breathless quality when they
were seen on the screen, too, and they helped to launch Richard Burton's
Hollywood career.

Nunnally Johnson thought Zanuck was making a fool of himself over
Bella Darvi's career and had made the mistake of saying so. Asked to
make a comment about her first Hollywood movie, he wrote a memo in
which he said: "Who was that girl who pulled the plug on *Hell and High
Water*?" and only afterwards realized Zanuck was serious about her.

He therefore thought it wise to make himself scarce before Darvi's next
production, *The Egyptian*, came out, and took off with a cast and camera
crew to make his debut as a director, shooting his own script, *Night
People*, in Berlin. His male star was Gregory Peck and his female star a
Swedish actress he had personally chosen, named Anita Björk. Miss Björk
was a lithe, beautiful blonde who had gained a lot of critical attention for
the frenzied, raw performance she had given in a notable Swedish film
version of Strindberg's *Miss Julie*.

Peck was known to be a difficult person to deal with when he didn't
like his director, and he might have been expected to be nervous in
view of the fact that this was Johnson's debut, but instead he went out
of his way to lend all his experience and cinematic know-how whenever the director needed it. As for Anita Björk, she was a sensitive,
responsive actress of the kind directors dream of having. Everybody
thought the rushes looked wonderful. Johnson was therefore somewhat
disconcerted when he received a cable from Zanuck, who had seen the
rushes too, saying: "DO SOMETHING ABOUT THAT GIRL. SHE HAS
NO TITS."

A few days later, he got another cable, a longer one this time. It
concluded with the words: "SHAKESPEARE SAID THOU CANST NOT BE

FALSE TO ANY MAN. HE WASN'T TALKING ABOUT FALSIES. DO SOMETHING
ABOUT THOSE TITS."

As Johnson said later: "As my female star, Anita was very good indeed,
except she had no tits. This was almost unheard of in the movies, where
everybody grows them the size of watermelons."

But what was he to do? When he called in the wardrobe woman, she
shook her head.

"I don't know what to do, Mr. Johnson," she said. "She's got no chest.
She looks like a boy."

Johnson told the wardrobe woman to stuff every dress Anita wore with
loads of cotton wool. At all costs, when the love scenes between her and
the hero came to be shot, he didn't want it to look as if Gregory Peck
was embracing a boy.

Susan Zanuck had long legs, good looks, and a sulky disposition. To
the disappointment of Virginia, her main interest in life was not boys or
getting married and having babies, but making it as a singer and a dancer.
She could deliver a song and do a tap dance with charm and reasonable
efficiency, and if becoming a nightclub entertainer was what she most
wanted to do, her father was ready to give every bit of help she might
ask for. Already, at considerable expense, he had subsidized a week's
engagement for her at a casino in Reno.

Then, in 1953, at the tail-end of the Korean War, she and a shapely
starlet named Terry Moore were engaged by the USO to go out with a
company to Seoul and entertain the troops. They arrived just in time to
celebrate the armistice, and gave concerts all along the demarcation line,
and finally performed some shows for army and navy units in Japan. When
it was learned that they were on their way home, the Zanucks decided
Susan and Terry should be given a welcome-back party. It took place at
Ciro's nightclub in Hollywood on the night of January 18, 1954, and not
only were Susan and Terry there as guests of honor but so were members
of the Zanuck family — and Bella Darvi.

Darvi was still staying with the Zanucks at the Santa Monica beach
house, and if her movie career was marking time, her affair with Zanuck
was certainly not. If anything, he was more obsessed with the girl than
ever, and he was doing something with her that Virginia would have
found unforgivable if she had known — he was now sleeping with Bella
in the house.

He was later to confess that he just couldn't help it. Fouling the family nest though he might be, he just had to have her. And since she was no longer going to the studio — for even Zanuck had not been able to set her up in another film — it had to be at home, in the bedroom next to Susan's in the guest house. And the only good thing about it was that Susan was away, and she could not, therefore, hear them.

But it was a furtive business in the circumstances. Whenever Virginia was away, at a Hollywood lunch, a meeting in Santa Barbara, a trip to Palm Springs, he made an excuse to come home and there was Bella waiting for him, and they went at it together, desperately coupling and proving to Zanuck he was still young, virile, a man, and could satisfy a female again and again and again.

Did he feel guilty about it? It would seem so, to judge by his later remarks. His own desperate need may have reminded him of his mother's behavior, her own sexual abandon. If so, his postcoital moments cannot have been very pleasant ones, and they were not made easier by the growing realization that he was obsessed.

This was the period when Zanuck began to drink. Not all the time. In all things except Bella, he was far too balanced to become an addict. But a lot of people noticed that when he came back to the studio in the evening to work on the rushes (having, almost certainly, sneaked an afternoon with Bella at Santa Monica) he often smelled of drink and kept a glass of strong liquor at his elbow. Virginia noticed it and suggested he should cut down. It was giving him, she said, "a middle-age paunch." She also noticed he was often desperately short of breath when he came back from his workout on the beach in the mornings.

And then, on the night of Susan's welcome-home party, he got drunk.

In view of the fact that the girls were just back from the Far East, it was decided it should be an Oriental party. Virginia wore a kimono, and so did Darryl, over his dinner jacket. Bella came in a tight-fitting, slinky, bespangled cheongsam slit to the thigh. There were three hundred guests, and it was soon noticeable to many of them that not only did Bella seem to be more nervy, restless, and enticing than usual, but that her host was acting towards her with less than his usual discretion. He kept putting his arm around her and kissing her. He became nettled when some young actors came over and began openly flirting with her, telling them to "fuck off and leave the young lady alone."

At one moment the Caribbean playboy, Porfirio Rubirosa, who was present with Zsa Zsa Gabor, came across to remind Bella they had met before in Monte Carlo, and Zanuck angrily waved him away. Virginia had to tell him to stop bothering the poor girl and that she was old enough to look after herself, and finally she remarked that her husband seemed to be a bit under the weather.

"He's drunk," said Susan, fiercely.

There was a cabaret show after the dinner at which Al Jolson, who was still around, did a number of songs, including one from *The Jazz Singer*. Then a trapeze was lowered from the ceiling and some Oriental acrobats came on to give a spectacular exhibition of tumbling, handstands, and spinning with the ropes and rings.

As soon as they had taken their bows and disappeared, Zanuck rose to his feet and made a short speech in salute of his daughter. The spotlight swung onto her and Terry Moore, and they took bows amid storms of applause. Immediately afterwards, Zanuck rose to his feet again and was seen to be stripping off his kimono and the jacket, shirt, and black tie beneath it.

Suddenly alarmed, Virginia leaned forward and tried to pull him back into his seat, but he waved her off and went on stripping. As Nunnally Johnson said later: "The latent Tarzan in him came out." Hands reached out at him, trying to pull him down, but he shouted to the audience through clenched teeth, still gripping his cigar: "Now I hope nobody's going to stop me from doing this." At which he sped towards the trapeze, still swinging over the dance floor, and, taking hold of the rings, drew himself up and did some preliminary swings and pull-ups.

"Among other things," wrote Johnson later, "he made three gallant efforts to chin himself up with one hand, a feat which he told the audience only five men in the world could do. A few minutes later, as every newspaperman in town announced [next day], it turned out there were only four who could do it. . . . As a result of all this jocular publicity, Mr. Zanuck is being treated with particular respect and solemnity these days."


The party drove back in heavy silence to Santa Monica, and it was not until they were alone that a row burst out between Virginia and Darryl. Normally, Virginia was the most long-suffering of wives, and the only thing she asked of her husband was that he not embarrass her. Tonight he had embarrassed her, shamed her, humiliated her, she said.

"Oh, God, I was really in the doghouse," he said later.

It went on for a long time, and it got so bad that Zanuck had a drink, and then another and another. And then, when Virginia had at last gone to bed and cried herself to sleep, he crept out of the house and across to the annex to seek surcease and succor from the ever-open Bella.

He was so drunk he forgot Susan was home again, and was back in her room, next to Bella's in the annex.

And Susan heard them.

It had, as Zanuck later described it, been "a moment of madness," and next day he cursed himself for having been so drunk and indiscreet. All the local papers had snide little stories about his escapade with the trapeze. And then the New York office rang to say they had heard *Life* magazine had obtained a picture of him hanging, stripped to the waist, from the trapeze, and was planning to run it as a whole page in the next week's issue, with an appropriately wry caption. Zanuck got on the telephone to Henry Luce, Time-Life's owner, and asked him to forbid the editor to use the photo. Luce said he could not possibly intervene. Meanwhile, Susan, who had always said she didn't like Bella, had been talking to her mother, and it must have been quite a conversation.

Bella Darvi packed her things and left the Zanuck home the same afternoon. She spent the next few hours in Zanuck's office/boudoir at 20th Century–Fox, and then took the night plane for Paris. She had a first-class ticket and $2,000 in cash he had given her.

Her solemn and subdued lover saw her off at the airport and the last words he said to her were "I'll see you soon."

Bella was satisfied with that. The scene with Virginia had been messy and that was a pity, because she had liked and admired her hostess. But on the whole, it had not worked out too badly.

She was sure of one thing: Darryl was still besotted with her, and he would be back for more.

One day in 1955 Zanuck summoned Nunnally Johnson to his office and handed him a copy of a current best-selling novel, *The Man in the Gray Flannel Suit*. He said he was sure it would make a big movie and wanted Johnson to script it and direct it, with Zanuck producing. He added casually and somewhat mysteriously that it would probably be the last film he would be making in Hollywood.

"So I want it to be good," he said. "My golden swan song. Let's show the cocksuckers."

Johnson went away and came back some weeks later with one of his better scripts, together with the suggestion that Gregory Peck would be the ideal choice for the male lead. Zanuck agreed at once, and then, almost with malice aforethought, suggested that Jennifer Jones be cast as his female co-star. Johnson winced as he saw the wicked grin on Zanuck's face. He remembered Peck had played with Jones before — in a movie called *Duel in the Sun* — and it was rumored in Hollywood that he still bore physical bruises from the experience. On the other hand, he knew Peck was inclined to be a lethargic actor and Jennifer Jones had goaded a blazing performance out of him, and that was what Zanuck was after. This was a drama about New York business executives and it needed fireworks to bring it to life. Jones would provide those, all right. Actually, had Peck not already signed the contract and committed himself to the movie, Johnson wondered whether he would have refused to work with Jennifer Jones. After *Duel in the Sun* he was said to have sworn he would never make a film with her again.

"She carved him up and ate him for breakfast," said Betty Grable, who had also been involved in the making of that movie.

Jones was married at that time to David Selznick, who had once been Zanuck's biggest rival in Hollywood, and he took an inordinate interest in his wife's career. The moment *Flannel Suit* began shooting, he sent long telegrams to Johnson (who was also directing) every day, demanding cameramen be fired, the script be altered, his wife given more closeups. When Johnson tried to talk to Jones about it, he said later, her eyes would cloud over and she would pretend not to hear. Johnson's final defense (he later claimed) was to pass Selznick's complaints over to Zanuck, who would then pick up the telephone and say: "Listen, you son of a bitch, keep your fingers out of my film!"

Jennifer Jones was an actress who burned with intensity and was determined to fulfill every suggestion made about her character in the script. To film the scenes of life at home for the two main characters in the movie, the company had rented a large mansion on Long Island. In one scene there is a fierce domestic quarrel during which Jones runs out of the mansion. He chases her, catches her, kisses her and they fall to the ground in a moiling passion, half fight, half embrace.

Johnson's memory of how this scene was shot differs from that of Jennifer Jones. He remembers it as a tempestuous afternoon of takes, retakes and closeups during which Jones's determination to make the episode as turbulent as the author visualized it severely discomposed her fellow star,

Peck, who was several times mentally and physically ruffled by the intensity of her performance. Jones obviously does not remember it this way, and, in a letter to me in October, 1983, she wrote:

"In my recollection, Nunnally Johnson, Greg Peck and I had very positive relations during the making of *The Man in the Gray Flannel Suit,*" and asks me not to use Nunnally Johnson's version. It can, however, be seen in Johnson's interviews in the Oral Histories of the Motion Picture Industry in America at UCLA.

Gregory Peck remains gallantly silent about the whole affair.

Thanks to Jennifer Jones's burning desire for authenticity, however, Johnson knew his stars had given him two splendidly intensive performances. When he came to screen the first rough cut of *The Man in the Gray Flannel Suit,* he knew he had provided Zanuck with the "golden swan song" for which he had been hoping as his farewell movie production in Hollywood.

Johnson was only too well aware by now how much Zanuck needed to go out in a blaze of glory, for Hollywood was full of rumors about the trouble he was in. All sorts of snide stories were going around the town. Johnson wrote a letter to Lauren Bacall about this time in which he said: "If [Bogey] thinks for one second that I'm going to comment on Mr. Zanuck to a couple of gossipy people like you, he should see a doctor."

And in a note he sent to Richard Burton he wrote: "There is a lot of juicy gossip around here but I'm a son-of-a-bitch if I'm going to put it down on paper and jeopardise my soft berth here."

Now the strongest rumor in Hollywood was that Zanuck was not just preparing to call it quits at the studio but that he and his wife were breaking up for good.

# TWENTY-ONE

# QUEST FOR YOUTH — OR SOMETHING

**E**VERYBODY IN Hollywood had known for a long time that Darryl Zanuck was spending more and more time in Europe, and it was presumed he was flying over at least every couple of weeks to carry on his thing with Bella Darvi. It was a common Hollywood surmise that one of these days he would not come back.

On the other hand, when Johnson heard Zanuck remark that *The Man in the Gray Flannel Suit* would be his "golden swan song," he had suspected that there was more to his boss's plans than a future with Bella Darvi. He had always tried to stay out of Zanuck's private life, but he knew enough about him to have a shrewd sense that it was neither Darvi nor even his relations with Virginia that were upsetting him at the moment, but something much deeper.

Somehow, he seemed to have lost his way.

True, it was ever since the episode in the nightclub at Susan's party that everything in the Zanuck setup had seemed to change, and people realized Bella Darvi had been the catalyst of that. It had been an unfortunate incident, and nothing about Darryl Zanuck (or Virginia, for that matter) had been the same since. Outsiders had a pretty accurate idea of what had taken place when Virginia, Darryl, and Bella got home that night. Virginia liked to gossip and Susan had a habit of confiding in her girlfriends, so most people in the movie world soon learned all about what kind of a showdown had taken place.

Hollywood's sympathies were with Virginia. She had, after all, taken a lot because of Darryl, and the fling with Bella and the foolishness on the nightclub trapeze had obviously been the last straw. But what they saluted Virginia for later was her good sense in extricating herself from an impossible situation. Outraged that Darryl had actually had the ef-

frontery and insensitivity to take his mistress in his own home, with only
a wall separating them from his own daughter, she had succumbed to an
angry impulse and given him an ultimatum — her or me. Then she had
thrown him out of the house.

It was a mistake, and she realized it immediately. How could he possibly
choose anyone but his mistress in the circumstances, given his needs,
given his pride? It was a moment for her to swallow her own and indicate
that so long as he never humiliated her or their children in such a way
again, he did not need to make the choice.

They patched things up and Darryl came back home again. And on a
purely domestic level, things were much better. True, Susan went on
resenting her father, but the fact that he now had to fly six thousand miles
every time he wanted to bed his mistress did not exactly improve the
quality of his sex-life. Virginia, well aware of the nature of the beast,
presumed that very soon now Darryl would find someone perhaps not
quite so exciting as that troubling and restless girl, but nearer home and
consequently more available to him. And no jet lag.

In fact, within months of Bella's return to France, Zanuck's obsession
had begun to lose some of its compulsion and its heat. To begin with,
the reunions were a steamy as ever, and he was tempted on more than
one occasion to tell Bella to pack her things and come back to Hollywood
with him. He would walk out on Virginia, sacrifice his family, and devote
himself to promoting Bella's future career in the movies.

Luckily for him, Bella herself put an end to that idea. So long as she
was in France and he was still in America, he kept her well supplied with
funds, gave her accounts for jewelry at Van Cleef and Arpels, for clothes
at Dior. She suddenly had all the luxuries she had ever dreamed about,
apartments in Paris and Monte Carlo, shops, restaurants, garages, hotels,
flower shops and food emporiums where all she needed to do was sign
the bill.

And she couldn't handle it.

Bella had always been a gambler. But before Zanuck came into her
orbit, she had gambled with her life, her body, her sexual expertise. Now
she began gambling with Zanuck's money, and when the two lovers met,
there was always the same kind of anticlimax to their love-making. Bella
opened a drawer in her dresser and pulled out a list of her bills. She
owed money to every casino on the Riviera, and to lots of other people
too. "She had become a compulsive gambler," Zanuck said later. "Sometimes she won fortunes — a million francs, one time. But winning always

made her feel guilty and she almost literally threw her winnings away, handing out thousands of francs to beggars and hookers on the streets, spending the rest on junk, like gold-plated bongo drums, dancing monkeys with ruby eyes and jingling bracelets, antique chess sets (she didn't play chess), and old music boxes which played 'Please Don't Leave Me Like This' when you sat down on the lavatory seat."

But mostly she lost. And because the casinos knew who her lover was, they let her get away with it. And each time he came over for a visit, Zanuck would go through the bills and pay the most urgent of them. Until even he, with all his money, began to find it hard to meet such enormous debts.

"I remember once we were going out to the Hôtel de Paris for dinner and I asked her to wear the ruby and diamond necklace I had bought her for her birthday," Zanuck said, "and she said she had lost it. So when I said we must call the insurance company at once, she confessed she had put it up as collateral the night before for losses she had sustained in the casino. When I went through her jewel case, she had hardly a trinket left. It had all gone to the casino as guarantees against her debts. That was bad enough, but I soon found out that the jewels weren't enough to cover her. She had even bigger debts and the authorities in Cannes, Nice and Beaulieu, where the government owns the gambling monopoly, were planning to move in on her."

He thought the only way to protect her was to take her back with him to the States and work things out there. But it turned out she couldn't leave. Pending the settlement of her debts, the French had taken away her passport — and she was forbidden to leave the country.

"It was daunting," he said, adding: "And somewhat anaphrodisiac."

At bottom, Zanuck was a simple character, and he almost began to dread his visits. The thought that the moment his passionate reunion with Bella was over there would be all those bills to discuss and settle was not exactly stimulating, nor was the prospect that she was rapidly becoming the most expensive mistress on the French Riviera. There was one occasion when Bella urgently telephoned him to come over with money to save her from the bailiffs who were moving into her apartment, and he borrowed cash from Howard Hughes and flew across with it hidden in a suitcase.

"One hundred thousand dollars for a fuck!" said Hughes, when they met for Zanuck to pay off his debt. "She must be quite something, your Bella."

And indeed she was. Even the financial problems in which she involved him did not prevent him from feeling enlivened, made over, rejuvenated, each time Bella turned her seductive forces on him. She succeeded in convincing him that only he and she together could make such amatory music, and that it was a unique combination. It was wonderful that she could so excitingly turn him on, but even more satisfying that he could respond in kind. She told him there had never been another man like him, and from the way she reacted, he knew it was true. It made him feel a hundred feet tall, and all the money in the world was worth the satisfaction it gave him. She was young, she was beautiful, and she would do anything for him. She was his creature.

And then came disillusion.

It was ironic that what finally broke the magic spell that bound Darryl Zanuck to Bella Darvi was neither gambling debts nor distance, neither boredom nor another man. It was sheer prudery on Zanuck's part.

"It was always being forgotten," said Anatole Litvak, later, "that Darryl, *au fond,* was a provincial American, from Nebraska. Certain basic moral principles were ingrained in him. He never got over the fact that his mother was a tramp and used to cheat on his father, nor the divorce and remarriage which so disturbed his childhood. But that he found a way to live with. It simply confirmed him in the belief that women were weak and fallible creatures, very much the lesser sex, and that so long as a man was big, dominating and strong and vigilant, he need have no worry about them. They would always defer to him and regard him as the master."

He was well aware that women cheated, but only if you were weak enough to let them get away with it, as his father, Frank Zanuck, had been. It never occurred to him, however, that a woman might "cheat" a man with another woman. He did not really approve of homosexuality, but he considered himself broad-minded about gay actors in films and had become particularly fond of some of them, especially Clifton Webb, on whose sage opinions on literature and the theater he laid great store.

But lesbianism he abhorred. The idea that women could make love to each other and possibly prefer it to a relationship with a man filled him with horror. There was no lesbian in the world who couldn't be cured, he believed, by a good fuck. Except that he was not the man who would be willing to bring about the cure. Females who succumbed to lesbianism were, for him, damned as women, and he literally found it difficult to be in the same room with them. They could be the most beautiful and attractive-looking females in the world, and they would leave him cold, flaccid, unturned-on. "Even a nympho's better than a dyke," he used to say.

At the Cannes Film Festival of 1955, Darryl Zanuck heard some gossip about Bella Darvi, and learned she had not been without amorous consolation while he had been away in California. When he demanded to know the name of the man who had been borrowing his mistress, it was slyly explained to him that it wasn't a man at all. Did he not know the truth about Bella? Had he never divined that she really preferred women — and who could blame her, after all, considering what men had done to her?

At one of the gala premieres that year, a woman was pointed out to him, climbing the stairs of the Palais du Festival. She was Bella's special friend, he was told. And what revolted him was the fact that she was not particularly young, not particularly beautiful, and American.

He had to get it confirmed, of course, and it took the private detective he hired in Villefranche-sur-Mer ten days to collect all the gaudy details. In the meantime, he blessed the festival for giving him the excuse not to be alone with Bella. He just could not have behaved towards her in the same way.

And after the report came in, he never slept with her again. "I was cured," he said later. "[Bella] was a sordid, forgotten memory."

And it was therefore not because of her that he told Nunnally Johnson *The Man in the Gray Flannel Suit* would be his last Hollywood film. It was because he was suddenly fed up — with women, with sex, with Hollywood, with making movies, with everything. Here he was, fifty-three years old, and the zest had gone out of his life.

He told Virginia he was leaving her in a long, painful but surprisingly calm session between the two of them — with only one passionate outburst. It wasn't another woman, he told her. It wasn't Bella. He wasn't even asking her for a divorce, although he added that one day he might feel it necessary to ask her for one. For the moment, all he had arranged was a legal deed of separation.

"I'm going to Europe," he said. "I have to get away." And then he added, quickly: "Don't worry, I will not be going to Bella."

He added: "But don't think because it is simply a legal separation that it isn't permanent. I would not like you to think I will ever be coming back. I have to begin my life over again, if I can, when I can. And when I get my act back together again, I am pretty sure it is not going to include you."

Virginia said: "You will have to make up your own mind about that. When the time comes. But for now, you mustn't let yourself feel bitter or guilty about anything. Not about your mother, not about those girls, not about what happened here with Bella. You have no reason to feel ashamed."

It was at this point that he suddenly yelled at her:

"You still don't understand anything, do you? I don't feel ashamed! I don't feel anything, not a goddamn thing. Can't you understand? I just don't care a goddamn about anything!"

"You'll get over it," she said, calmly, as he quietly walked out of the room.

Next day he was gone and forty-eight hours later he was in Paris.

He told his two daughters, whom he saw separately before he left, that he was going away on a long trip and had arranged to work for Fox in Europe. He said he was taking an apartment in Paris and they were to fly over and see him whenever they felt like it. To Susan he added: "You won't have to worry. No one else will be there."

He did not say goodbye to Richard Zanuck, his son, because doing that would have caused him the greatest pain, and he had, in any case, no intention of losing touch with him. So when Richard heard the news from his mother, it was a great shock.

"I wasn't surprised he was leaving Hollywood," Richard said later. "I had heard the talk around the studios that he had lost his zest, that he hadn't made a big film for nearly two years, and that boredom was driving him out of his mind. I sensed from his manner he was planning to quit."

But the news that his father and his mother were splitting up stunned and distressed him.

"It never occurred to me that a thing like that could happen. Naturally, I jumped to the conclusion that the reason was a girl, and I was upset. Even though I'd been on trips with my father where I'd discovered what kind of a talent he had for playing around, I never thought he would completely move out of the house as he did. That was a surprise. And even though I thought he had treated my mother shabbily, I still didn't think it necessary. I thought he was leaving her because of Bella, and that was the revelation — not the fact that he was quitting Hollywood."

He was quite surprised at the way his mother took it. To his astonishment, she said: "I have had thirty-two years of blissfully happy married life, and it isn't over yet. You'll see. He'll be back."

"But, Mother," he said, "if he is walking out like this, that means he doesn't intend to come back."

"You'll see," she said. "I'll wait."

Next day it was announced that Darryl Francis Zanuck had resigned from his post as head of production at 20th Century–Fox after twenty-three years, and that he would be succeeded by Buddy Adler. In future, the announcement continued, Mr. Zanuck would operate from Paris as head of a newly formed company to be known as DFZ Productions. Films made by this new company would be partly financed and released through 20th Century–Fox.

There, it was done. He had thrown off the Hollywood shackles and he was free.

But free for what?

# TWENTY-TWO

# STAR CROSS'D LOVERS

*D*ESPITE THEIR closeness to him, it could never be said that Milton Sperling or Nunnally Johnson ever became intimates of Darryl Zanuck. Sperling would have liked to know more of Zanuck's innermost secrets but was always treated like a son or a younger brother, and fended off. Johnson was one of those who did not believe professional and personal relationships should mix, and shied away from confidences.

If Zanuck could be said to have a real friend and confidant, in fact, it would have to be a most unlikely character named Gregory Ratoff, a Russian-born actor who had become known as a screen comedian but, like many another in Hollywood, fancied himself as a director. He was a big, amiable bear of a man who mangled the English language both on and off the screen, and Zanuck indulged him as he did few other people in the movie business. Not only did he see that Ratoff always had roles in his films, especially when he needed money, but he let him hang around his houses both at Santa Monica and Palm Springs, invited him to all his parties, and also handed out directorial assignments to him which could have been done with more flair, not to say expertise, by more competent studio technicians. When a Ratoff picture was finished and previewed, Ratoff waited in fear and trembling for Zanuck's verdict, which was always the same:

"God, it stinks. How could you make such a goddamn turkey, you bastard? If this gets out to the movie houses, we're ruined!"

Ratoff would promptly burst into tears and sob his heart out, and so heartrending would be his moans and groans that Zanuck would eventually slap him across his shoulders and tell him to quit worrying, that he would take it into the cutting room and make it fit for public showing. At which

Ratoff would smile again. While Zanuck got to work, he would be off to some smoke-filled room to play his favorite game of poker, meanwhile murmuring: "I have left it to my friend Dayril. He can feex *anything!*"

Ratoff, of course, was by no means as naïve as he made out, and there was a shrewd and understanding mind behind that slapstick-comic exterior. But he did truly love and admire Darryl Zanuck and thought there was no one like him in Hollywood, on earth, or in heaven. Once at one of the Palm Springs croquet parties he mishit a ball and caught Zanuck on the head with his mallet. Appalled at the sight of blood streaming down his friend's cheek, he flung his hands up to the skies and cried: "Strike me dead! Punish me!"

It was as if he had done harm to the Son of God himself rather than the chief of 20th Century–Fox, and when a bolt of thunder and lightning failed to descend upon him from the clear blue desert skies, he seized his mallet and battered his own head until it was bleeding too.

It occurred to some of Zanuck's shrewder observers that he was fond of Gregory Ratoff because he saw in him his alter ego, the kind of character he might have become had he not been so consumed by driving ambition and determined machismo. Ratoff was not only everything Zanuck was not, he was also the kind of man he had always feared to become. His body was flabby because he never exercised it. He did not ride or shoot or box. He was scared of animals. He was humble in the presence of women, overindulged them, never showed them who was boss. He had no ambition to be strong and rich, only to get by from day to day. He once remarked he would rather be liked than feared, and looked momentarily appalled when Zanuck replied with an old Armenian saying:

"Only the weak are loved, because they are not strong enough to be feared."

The only vice (except timidity) from which Ratoff suffered was a passion for gambling, and even there, in Zanuck's opinion, he showed the weakness of his character. When he was asked once what kind of a gambler Ratoff was, he replied: "What can you expect? He's a coward — and a loser."

He recalled an occasion at Monte Carlo when he, Joe Schenck, and Ratoff had gone to the casino for an evening's gambling. Schenck was a spectacularly bold player and had remarkable luck; he almost invariably won. Just before they sat down at the chemin-de-fer table, Zanuck counseled Ratoff to "follow Joe. Do what Joe does." Ratoff swore he would.

"And this is the difference between gamblers," said Zanuck later. "At the end of the evening, Joe had won a tremendous amount of money. I had won a nice little sum. And Greg had lost. He just hadn't had the guts to go along with Joe on every round, or he would have won too."

Ratoff was appalled when he heard Zanuck was quitting Hollywood, and with tears streaming down his face told his friend he would not be able to exist without him. Zanuck told him he wouldn't have to, that there would always be a part for him in the films he would be making overseas in the future, and then handed over a voucher to a travel agency. It would ensure Ratoff a free first-class air ticket to Europe every time he got lonely and wanted to see him. Convinced his friend was going through a sexual rather than professional crisis in his life, and that Bella Darvi was the cause of it, Ratoff said he was taking off for France immediately.

"I will go and tell that focking beech to stop focking around with my pal Dayril. I will say to her: 'I am sick of the way you are messing up my friend's life, and I am focked if I am going to stand for it any longer.' "

Zanuck grinned.

"And that's exactly what you will be," he said.

Ratoff looked bewildered. "What — I will be what?"

"Fucked," said Zanuck. Then he added: "And now let me tell you about Darvi. . . ."

It was Ratoff who came up with the idea for what proved to be Zanuck's first independent production overseas, and, on the face of it, the suggestion was a shrewd one. He handed over to his friend a copy of Alec Waugh's novel *Island in the Sun*, about a love affair between a white girl and a black man in Jamaica. Zanuck was enthusiastic at once. He saw the possibilities of stirring up controversy (and publicity) of the same kind as had been engendered by *Pinky*.

He called in a good scriptwriter, Alfred Hayes, and assigned as director Robert Rossen, who had a reputation in Hollywood for being liberal in outlook and an expert, if somewhat stolid, technician. For the role of the young black man he picked a handsome and popular black singer, Harry Belafonte. This time he did not intend to be accused of playing up to the bigots by choosing a white player to fill the black role, as he had been after casting Jeanne Crain in *Pinky*. And what he also did, to emphasize the point of the plot, was pick for the white girl who falls in love with the black man a star who both looked and sounded whiter than white: Joan Fontaine.

As he had anticipated, the moment the announcement of the film and its stars was made, the rows and the controversy began. There were threats of boycotts all over the South. In the South Carolina legislature an irate representative even introduced a bill to fine any cinema owner in the state $5,000 if he dared to show the film. KKK protest meetings were held, and there were parades in Alabama and Mississippi at which effigies of Zanuck, complete with oversized cigar and twirling mustachios, were ceremonially burned. The repercussions of the announcement delighted him, and lifted him out of his depression. When asked how he planned to respond to all the threats and condemnations, he replied: "They've given me the same treatment before. They said I couldn't show *Grapes of Wrath* in Oklahoma and Texas, and I got scared as hell." He mimed someone cringing under a hail of brickbats. "And all I got for all my trouble was an Oscar and a fortune at the box office. Then the censors gave me the same business over *Pinky*, but I fought them and I won, and the opposition never got off first base."

He attacked the South for being behind the times.

"They're threatening us because for the first time we are going to have a film about real people in which real Negroes play Negroes. We didn't have that in *Pinky*. But times are changing, and we're changing with them. And I can tell you this. No matter what they say they'll do to our film, I'm going on with it. I'm not frightened."

Maybe not. But 20th Century–Fox was.

Perhaps subconsciously Zanuck had chosen a man to succeed him who lacked his belligerence, his fondness for getting into a public fight and winning. Buddy Adler had no fire in his belly at all, and when the head of the Fox office in New York, Spyros Skouras, called him and said he and the board of directors were alarmed by the boycott threats, Adler promised to put pressure on Zanuck to water down his film.

Under the contract Zanuck had signed when he quit the studio, Zanuck had the right to choose his own subjects for his movies, his own directors and stars. But it was Fox who would provide him with the bulk of his financing and it was their circuit that would handle the distribution of his films. And this is where he was vulnerable.

After forming DFZ Productions, he had left a small liaison office behind at Fox to handle negotiations with the studio. It consisted of a production manager, Robert Jacks (then married to Zanuck's daughter Darrylin), with his son, Richard Zanuck, acting as his assistant. Dick was newly out of college and this was his first real job in films.

Jacks now reported there were a couple of sequences in the script of *Island in the Sun* that were giving the Fox distributors kittens. One had

Harry Belafonte passionately embracing Joan Fontaine. The other strongly suggested they were having sexual relations. He cabled his father-in-law:

"IF YOU SHOW HARRY CLIMBING INTO BED WITH JOAN, YOU'LL NOT ONLY HAVE TROUBLE IN SOUTH CAROLINA. ACHILLES THE HEEL WILL BE AFTER YOU TOO."

Achilles the Heel was one of the nicknames for Spyros Skouras, the Greek-born chairman of the Fox board. Determined as he was to squeeze every drop of publicity out of the controversy over *Island in the Sun*, Zanuck was also desperately anxious that his maiden movie effort as an independent should succeed, and a threat to deny him a Fox distribution deal would be fatal to his enterprise. So reluctantly he got together with Hayes and did some diplomatic rewriting.

When Belafonte read through the altered screenplay he reacted with the cynicism of someone who has seen it happen before. It was Joan Fontaine who was outraged at the changes, which she thought "emasculated" the movie.

"This might have been a good picture," she wrote later, "but Darryl Zanuck, despite the protestations of the author, Alec Waugh, who was with us on location, felt it was too soon to tackle the race situation with honesty."

All that she and Belafonte were allowed were "an embrace and a kiss toward the end of the film."

Even this, as it turned out, caused trouble when the film was shown in 1957. Fontaine was attacked for being seen in the arms of a black man, and inundated with what she called "reviling missives."

"The hate letters, many containing dimes and quarters," she wrote later, "read: 'If you're so hard up you have to work with a nigger . . .' "

She later got a letter from a more civilized friend who asked her what it had been like sharing stardom with such a handsome and intelligent man as Belafonte, and had she got to know him better "strolling the silver sands in the moonlight with [him]?" She wrote back: "Well, you see, he was black, and I was yellow!"*

20th Century–Fox did not exactly do their damnedest to make Zanuck's first production into a success. The New York opening was badly handled and the places at which Zanuck feared bigoted audiences might hiss or boo aroused, on the contrary, laughter. "At the big preview," wrote Nunnally Johnson, who flew in from Hollywood, "the whole picture was

*No Bed of Roses, by Joan Fontaine (New York: Morrow, 1978).

out of synch. But what dropped everyone into the depths of despair was the fact that every time the story came to a big dramatic climax, the house roared with laughter. . . ."

It did not, however, stop the movie from mopping up.

"Everybody thinks they're going to see Joan Fontaine and Harry Belafonte hop into the hay together," Johnson wrote, "just like the yokel who kept going to see that old picture where a car raced a railroad train across the crossing. Some day, he figured, there was going to be a wreck."

Whatever the reason, *Island in the Sun* quickly became Fox's biggest moneymaker since their box-office smash *The Robe*. By the end of its first six months, it had recouped more than its $2 million cost and was in profit. The film was chosen as a Royal Command film in London and Zanuck went over from Paris for it. He and his six principal players (Fontaine, Belafonte, Dorothy Dandridge, Joan Collins, John Justin, and James Mason) were afterwards presented to Queen Elizabeth, Prince Philip, and Princess Margaret, and photographs taken at the time show him looking cheerful, fit, sunburned, and brimming over with self-confidence. He was obviously fully recovered from his fit of depression, and back in the swing again. Joan Fontaine, who was staying with her children near Cannes that summer, saw him shortly afterwards playing in one of the Riviera casinos. He had a large pile of high-value chips beside him and he was obviously winning. Standing behind him, looking gloomily furtive and frustrated, was Gregory Ratoff.

And at the bar, a glass of champagne in her hand, was a little blond English waif, alone, waiting patiently. Whenever a cruising Lothario approached her and tried to make a pass, she would look across the room at the man with the big cigar, and say crisply: "If you want my telephone number, you will have to ask him. But I don't think he will give it to you."

Darryl Zanuck was back in the movie business, and back on form. In every sense of the term. Even sex was beginning to taste good again. Casual sex, anyway.

Zanuck was in Monte Carlo because he had flown up from Spain to bail out Bella Darvi, who was in the hospital after the first of many suicide attempts. She was, of course, in financial trouble too, and her gambling and other debts were huge. The Hôtel de Paris was holding on to her jewels, furs, and dresses pending payment of their bill. Her passport was still being held by the French authorities. A couple of heavies from a collection agency had accosted her in the street and slapped her around, so when he visited her in her hospital bed she was not only still groggy from the overdose of pills but she had a black eye, a swollen face, and "she looked like hell," as he put it afterwards.

He left her some cash for her immediate needs and got a tentative list of her outstanding obligations, promising to take care of them. Which he subsequently did. But he made it quite clear to Bella that this was the last time he would ride to her rescue. She accepted the inevitable without complaint, as she always had done. She was fatalistic enough about herself to know that whatever terrible things happened to her, they would always get worse, and this was one of those moments. She put a fevered hand on his and tried to smile, and said:

"It's a pity. We made some very good love together."

When he had gone, she cried a little, and then resolved that next time she tried to kill herself she would make a proper job of it. And to give her her due, after several more botched attempts, she eventually did. But this was really the occasion when Zanuck walked out of her life.

If he went to the casino tables to forget about her, a winning streak — and that slim little English blonde — easily enabled him to do so. A couple of days later, after paying off Bella's debts, he flew back to Spain.

Zanuck was making his second independent movie in Spain, and he drove over to rejoin his unit in Pamplona. The film was a version of Ernest Hemingway's bullfighting novel, *The Sun Also Rises*, and he was trying his damnedest to do it faithfully and well, true to the author's intentions.

He admired Ernest Hemingway both as a man and as a writer, and considered himself his friend. They had skied together in Colorado. They had been on safari together in Africa. They had got drunk and wenched together in Paris. But whereas he thought Hemingway could do no wrong ("If I could have been anybody else, I'd like to have been Hemingway," he once said), Hemingway was always a little skeptical of Zanuck. He suspected that inside the film producer's tough and cynical exterior, there was a nice, soft, bourgeois type trying to struggle out (Hemingway's friends could have said the same about him). He once called Zanuck "a Hollywood whore with a heart of gold," and what distressed the film producer was the fact that Hemingway didn't think much of him as a translator of his novels to the screen. When Zanuck showed him his version of *The Snows of Kilimanjaro*, Hemingway stalked out of the theater in a rage and subsequently sent him a telegram suggesting it should be retitled " 'The Snows of Zanuck' by Z. A. Nuck."

To try to prevent his friend from accusing him of once more tampering with one of his masterpieces, Zanuck had, for *The Sun Also Rises*, called in one of Hemingway's favorite companions, Peter Viertel, to write the script. In one of his memos about the movie, he said, in part:

> The trouble with *Island in the Sun* was that we had to "debollick" the story. Nothing and no one will be debollicked in this one, except where Hemingway has done it himself to one of the characters. We want to get every person into the film as they are in the book, cojones and all.

He spent a lot of time picking the cast and one of his first choices was Ava Gardner for the toothsome role of Lady Brett. She was at the height of her career and she was expensive, but Zanuck guessed the choice would win Hemingway's strong approval since she was one of his favorite actresses. He chose Tyrone Power from the Fox contract list for the role of Jake Barnes, and there were other roles for Errol Flynn and Mel Ferrer.

Because it is one of the big scenes in the script, the unit was shooting a sequence at Pamplona during the running of the bulls, and both Power's wife, Linda Christian, and Ferrer's wife, Audrey Hepburn, had come down to see the spectacle. Errol Flynn, who liked to tease Zanuck about his masculinity, casually asked him in front of the women whether he would be running with the bulls himself. Ava Gardner and Linda Christian, both of whom liked to see men flexing their muscles, got so excited that Zanuck was practically forced to accept the challenge.

He trained for the ordeal secretly, finding out at exactly what speed the panicked bulls raced through the streets of Pamplona and pacing himself with a timer to discover whether he could outdistance them. On the great day he surprised even the local Spaniards by joining the stampede at the last possible moment and racing just ahead of the animals through the streets and into the bullring, where he lifted himself onto the rails a wind's breath away from the horns of the leading bull.

When the bull-running sequences were in the can, the film company packed bags and departed for Mexico, where they planned to make the actual bullfighting scenes in Morelia. The small Mexican town resembled Pamplona and had more sunshine and color.

It was here they reached a stage in the shooting where there were two more important roles to fill. One called for a handsome young bullfighter, the other for a striking-looking Spanish girl who has a small but vital role to play. For the bullfighter, Zanuck picked a young executive from New York who had suddenly decided to abandon his career in the rag trade and make it as an actor. His name was Robert Evans, and he subsequently became head of Paramount Films. But though he did a thorough search locally and had some players flown in from Hollywood for auditions, he could not find the actress for whom he was searching to play the Spanish girl.

Audrey Hepburn had read the script and one morning she told her husband, Mel Ferrer, she thought she knew just the girl to fill the role. Once she mentioned her name, Mel Ferrer agreed she would be perfect. He went across to Zanuck, showed him some photographs, and said the girl in them was a personal friend. "Audrey and I think she would be just right in the part," Ferrer said. "She's a cabaret singer and we know her well. She'd love to have a chance to be an actress."

Zanuck asked where she was appearing at the moment, and Ferrer replied she was fulfilling her first engagement in New York, at the Waldorf Astoria. In that case, Zanuck suggested, either Ferrer or Audrey should telephone her and ask her to come down.

She arrived in Mexico City a week later, carrying her small dog under her arm. Her name was Juliette Greco and the dog's name was Crocodile, but it was she who turned out to have the teeth.

Like Bella Darvi, Juliette Greco lived in France and had been one of the victims of the Nazi occupation of that country during World War II. But there was a great difference in the characters of the two women. Juliette wore the scars of her ordeal in very different fashion — as evidences of her triumphant survival rather than as badges of shame — and she showed no sign of the psychological hangups that were helping to wreck Bella's life. Maybe that was because Juliette was not a Jewess and therefore had not had to undergo the same kind of degradations. Everybody knew Greco by her nickname of Jujube. She had been a cheerful Parisian street sparrow of fourteen in 1944 when the Gestapo came along and arrested her sister for working for the Resistance. The sister was presently shipped off to Ravensbrück concentration camp, where her mother was already incarcerated for the same type of Underground activity.

Jujube, angry at her sister's arrest, stormed into the Gestapo headquarters on the Avenue Foch to protest, and was presently carried out screaming and taken to the notorious Fresnes Prison, outside Paris, where petty thieves, prostitutes, and suspected members of the Resistance were inextricably mixed in the cells. After several weeks of incarceration, she was let loose and made her way back to the sidewalks of Montmartre. With no home, no family, no job, no money, and only a thin dress and a short raffia jacket to keep her warm, she learned to live as best she could, on her waifish looks and her hunger-sharpened wits.

Just before the end of the war, she was picked up by one of her old schoolteachers, who now ran a boarding house for young male students, and taken back to become a maid-of-all-work around the house. It was a pretty riotous existence, but it provided her with food and a bed, and it suited her. Moving around among a bunch of strident youths brought out the latent tomboy in Jujube. Since clothes were rationed in postwar France, the students passed their old suits over to her, and the fashion which she was later credited with pioneering began. She wore men's pants from then on, and for the next few years was never again seen in skirts.

Reunited with her mother after the deportees came back from Ravensbrück, she tried living with her for a time. But it didn't work out. They had changed too much, and after a cold embrace, they went their separate ways. Jujube was now sixteen years old, thin, pretty, tough, bouncy, street-wise, worldly-wise and cynical. She had seen and experienced too much to believe in anything — except self-preservation. She took a room in the Latin Quarter of Paris and began to go around with her neighbors, most of them would-be artists, sculptors, actors, and musicians. She still wore pants, though she had by this time learned how to alter them to fit her boyish figure. She was like her companions in that few of them had any money, and in the cold and bitter winter of 1946/7, they might have starved and frozen to death had not one of their number inherited a clothing factory, which the Nazis had stolen from his father. It was a men's clothing factory, and they sold what they could on the black market and wore the rest. Jujube didn't mind; she had now got accustomed to masculine attire and noticed a lot of women around the city were beginning to imitate her.

Since life was not entirely taken up with the hunt for food and a place to sleep, they presently found a meeting place in an old butcher's shop in the rue Jacob, which they turned into a sort of club, called the Bar Vert, where they could buy drinks and dance to the music of a phonograph. But they were driven away by complaints from neighbors about the noise, which went on all through the night. Finally they found an ideal place in the cellar of a nearby café, and this they called Le Tabou. It was soon the talk of Paris, and everybody started coming to see the young men and their girls who frequented it.

They called themselves Existentialists, a name made popular by Jean-

Paul Sartre, the cult philosopher of the time. The young men started a new fashion by wearing their shirts open to the navel, with kerchiefs, keys, and lockets tied round their necks. The girls stuffed white mice down their bosoms and were delighted at the startled expressions of strangers, who stared in astonishment and fascination at the movement beneath the girls' blouses and the occasional glimpse of a tiny pink snout.

Le Tabou was lit only by candles and loud with the music of a student group, and when the Existentialists were not huddled round a table, drinking wine and loftily discussing Kafka or Kierkegaard, they would take the floor and energetically jitterbug.

Jujube first got into the newspapers by smoking a pipe. She did it because cigarettes were scarce and expensive at the time, and she was photographed, pipe in her mouth, holding a candle and leading a customer down the steps to a table. Her gamine good looks, her dark eyes and equivocal smile — and the pipe — started a rush on Le Tabou by *le tout Paris*.

Then she began to sing for the customers, and the numbers were soon being hummed around Paris and symbolized the cynicism of the time. One was "I Spit upon Your Grave" and the other "Live for Today, for Tomorrow There Is Nothing." Jujube was suddenly famous. The newspapers began to refer to her by her full name of Juliette Greco, and found that her amorous adventures — for she boasted about her many lovers — were gaudy, spectacular, and good for the magazine supplements. One lover had killed himself when she threw him over. A husband whom she had left, the father of her child, had involved her in a messy divorce.

"I cannot understand why in French we have just one word for love," she was quoted as saying. "There are so many ways of loving. Love has so many meanings. I love handsome men. I have that in common with Brigitte Bardot and Françoise Sagan. In fact sometimes we have the same lovers one after the other."

Now, according to the newspapers, she was involved with the popular French nightclub singer Sacha Distel, who had once been her guitarist. He was said to be passionately devoted to her and bombarded her with telegrams, telephone calls, letters, and flowers whenever she was away.

Unlike Bella Darvi, whose wartime experiences had taught her to fear, loathe, and despise men, Juliette Greco made no secret of the fact that she adored the male sex, but felt both equal with them and completely liberated and independent.

All this information about her was conveyed to Zanuck in snippets from

Audrey Hepburn and Mel Ferrer long before the arrival in Mexico City
of their friend. He was not impressed.

"My God," he said, "she sounds like the Queen of the Nymphos."

Her first encounter with Darryl Zanuck was not exactly propitious. She
too had been primed beforehand about what he was like, and the gossip
she had picked up in Paris and New York was not exactly flattering.

"I hear he fuck a girl first and ask what her name is afterwards," she
said to Audrey Hepburn. "I am not very fond of anonymous fucks."

Hepburn assured her he had never tried to lay a hand on her, but did
admit that he could be a bossy and dictatorial tycoon. Greco was hardly
reassured when he came to the airport to meet her surrounded by an
entourage of secretaries and yes-men who fawned around him even when
he barked orders rudely at them. When he advanced to greet her she
held out a hand for him to kiss and stared at him with such icy aloofness
that Ferrer whispered in her ear: "Come on, be nice!"

"Why should I be?" she replied, and proceeded to treat Zanuck like a
lowly page, and, when he said he would take her in his car to her hotel,
coolly fobbed him off and said she would rather drive back with "*mes
amis, Audrey et Mel.*" Audrey Hepburn was amused to notice that he
looked quite crushed.

Two days later, Juliette Greco reported to the studio where interior
scenes were being shot and was given a trailer as a dressing room. Shortly
after her arrival, she heard the sound of feet coming up the steps and
there was a tentative rap on the door. When she opened it, there was
Darryl Zanuck. She did not ask him in and there followed what she
afterwards described as a "stilted exchange," during which she noted that
the great man seemed extremely nervous, even shy. He had a large cigar
in his hand and her eyes were riveted on his thumb, with which he was
fiddling with the damp and chewed butt. His other hand was behind his
back.

"A nice day, don't you think?" he said.

"Yes, it is."

"I do hope you are comfortable in your hotel?"

"Yes, very. Thank you."

Pause. Then: "And your dog, Crocodile? Is he liking Mexico?"

"I think so, yes. I hope so."

Pause again. A clearing of the throat, and then he asked her to dinner.

When she appeared to hesitate, he hastened to add that Gregory Ratoff ("my very good friend") would be with them. Greco accepted, wondering if all the stories she had heard about this man could possibly be true. What sort of a person was this who assured her he was bringing a chaperon with him to dinner? To protect her? Or himself?

When she told the others about the encounter at breakfast next morning and laughed about it, she noticed there were no answering expressions of mirth on their faces. Linda Christian and her husband, Tyrone Power, were accompanied by Merle Oberon, who lived in Mexico City at the time, and they obviously thought Greco was treating the subject of Zanuck entirely too lightly.

"Do you know what Darryl told me about you last night?" said Christian. "He said he thought you were a most remarkable young woman and he is most strongly attracted to you."

"And do you know what he told me?" added Tyrone Power. "He said he had heard that you were the most free-spoken woman in France, and that he has read all about your husbands and your lovers, but his impression is that you have never met a real man in your life."

As Greco burst into peals of delighted, and derisive, laughter, Merle Oberon reached out a long, feline hand.

"Don't laugh too quickly, my dear," she said. "You are a self-confident girl, but you must be very careful with Darryl. Where women are concerned, he is the one who likes to win, and mostly he does. If you are not very careful, you will lose your most precious possessions, your freshness, your joy of living. He will devour you!"

Juliette Greco laughed again.

"*Blagueuse!*" she said to Oberon. "You are kidding me!"

In a way, they were right and Jujube was taking the situation a little too casually. For one thing, she did not have a moment of nervousness about her role in the film. She had played in French movies and she was convinced she knew far more about motion-picture techniques than the director of *The Sun Also Rises*, Henry King, whom she quickly decided was slow, doddery, and out-of-date. King was, in fact, one of Hollywood's most experienced professionals and a favorite of Darryl Zanuck, and not only because Zanuck could push him around. He was an amiable veteran who knew just how to handle cocky know-it-alls, and he never lost his temper on the set.

Some of Greco's best friends were among the new wave of directors in the French cinema and she felt she had picked up enough of their revolutionary techniques to be able to criticize King and make suggestions about various shots and camera angles. When he simply smiled but took no notice of her remarks, she began to flare out at him with obscenities and insults in French, of which she had quite a salty vocabulary. She assumed that he did not understand what she was saying, whereas King was quite a good French linguist and understood perfectly well. But he still did not react to her, preferring instead to remark to Zanuck later that this French hoyden was really not worth all the trouble he was taking with her, since she was headstrong, stubborn, and, as an actress, null.

When rumors of these remarks reached her later, Greco became more unmanageable than ever, and failing to get a reaction from King, would start rows with Robert Evans, whom she called "a fop" and "an idiot," and with the amiable and imperturbable Tyrone Power, thus causing a furious Linda Christian to start cursing her in a Spanish that was perhaps even more colorful than Greco's French. Zanuck had to be called onto the set on several occasions when shooting was held up, and he was witness of some of Greco's petulant outbursts. At last he could stand it no longer and intervened.

"I had always heard," he said, "that you were one of the most intelligent women in France. It just shows how misinformed you can be. You are being paid a very good salary. You have been given an excellent role in this film. And you are throwing away the chance of making a hit in it by these ridiculous exhibitions of temper, petulance, and ignorance. That is not how I expect an intelligent woman to behave. You may get away with it in France but in Hollywood, this would be regarded as the tantrums of an ignorant bitch."

Greco rounded on him.

"You call me a bitch?" she screamed. "How dare you insult me like that? And how dare you compare French films with this Hollywood trash? Hollywood!" She spat out the word as if it were an orange pit. "All I hear you talking about all day is Hollywood — which you call The Industry! Not art like we call it in Paris but The Industry! It sounds like Coca-Cola! My God, maybe it *is* Coca-Cola!" she added, laughing hysterically.

By this time there was no stopping her. Her eyes were alight and her cheeks were flaming, and she was fairly dancing with suppressed fury. She stamped over to Zanuck, dragged the cigar out of his mouth, and shouted:

"As for you, Mr. Fuck Machine Zanuck! Is that not what they call you — fuck machine? As for you, with your big fat cigar and your clever manner, why should I take any notice of you and all these —" she searched for the word — "arse-lickers around here! What do they know about making films and how to direct a *vraie* French *artiste?* What do you know, Mr. Fuck Machine Zanuck?"

He waited for the pause that came at the end of her rhetorical question and then he interjected, mildly:

"Well, I have, after all, made nearly six hundred films, and some of them have been quite successful — even in France."

She stood there staring at him. He was smiling at her, not a bit disturbed or angered by her outburst. And suddenly she was so aware of what a fool she was making of herself that the tears began to roll down her cheeks, and after angrily trying to brush them away, she began to laugh. He opened his arms and she began to laugh and cry at the same time on his shoulder, and he was laughing too.

Forty-eight hours later, they slept together for the first time. Thereafter, he came on the set every day, and he told Henry King he was writing new scenes and would be building up her part.

Nevertheless, she was not completely won over by him, and it was obvious he was not entirely sure of himself with her. Linda Christian remembers she often caught Zanuck looking at Juliette with a slightly puzzled expression on his face.

"I guess it must have been the first time he had ever had an affair with a really free and independent woman," she said, "and it was a new experience for him. To feel, I mean, that he had given away as much as he had got. He liked to knock over females like ninepins, and I sensed with this girl he felt a bit like a ninepin himself. Who had knocked over whom? Had he fucked her or had she fucked him?"

They went on sleeping together for the duration of the shooting, but when he called for a wrap-up of the Mexico City sequences, he still didn't seem to be entirely certain of the situation between Greco and himself. He was disconcerted, for instance, when she told him she would not be traveling back with him to Paris, as he wished, nor did she seem to be all that interested when he told her he would be looking after her film career from now on.

She informed him, firmly, she would prefer to travel back to Paris alone, and indicated that when the film was over she would consider that to be the end of their relationship. At first he tried to argue with her, but when she curtly cut him off, he swallowed and seemed to resign himself to the fact that their association would soon be over. Next morning, however, he sent a note around to her trailer on the set informing her his dear friend Gregory Ratoff had suffered a heart attack and had been rushed to the hospital. Would she please go and see him, because he was asking for her — and when she came back, would she report to Zanuck about the condition of his dear friend?

Greco had, in fact, become quite fond of Ratoff, finding him funny, extravagant, and lovable, and when she made inquiries she became in no doubt that the heart attack he had suffered was serious. The doctors at the hospital told her there was even a chance the attack could prove fatal, and all visitors had been banned. She was the sole exception. Señor Ratoff had insisted on having "a last talk" with the beautiful señorita.

Ratoff was a born ham and he insisted on giving a performance even when his life was at stake, and therefore the first thing he did when she came into his darkened hospital room was to croak dramatically that he had sent for her because he was dying. He had one last request to make of her, and only she could see that it was carried out.

"Please look after my friend Dayril," he whispered. "Do not forsake him. He has been looking all his life for the perfect woman, and now he has found her. If you leave him, he will go back to being like he was a few months ago — a ruin, a wreck, a piece of flotsam and jetsam. Please," he croaked, "do not leave him. Only you can save him!"

In spite of herself, she was considerably shaken, and she told her driver to take her straight back to the hotel, where she went up to Zanuck's suite. He listened to what she had to say about Gregory's condition, and gave no sign whatsoever when she told him what the stricken man had said to her about her relationship with Zanuck.

Presently he reached across the divan on which they were sitting and picked up a briefcase.

"I have a little present for you," he said. "I don't know if you will like it. I fear not."

With that, he pulled out what Jujube later described as "a square-cut piece of black suede," with a pocket in it, which he handed to her. In the pocket was a small block of solid gold, with a tortoiseshell comb fitted into a slot at the top, the whole slab encrusted with diamonds. It must have cost a fortune.

"What on earth do you want me to do with this?" she asked. She knew she could never wear a tortoiseshell comb in her unruly mop of hair.

"Put it in your safe," Zanuck said. Then looking at her face: "I'm sorry you hate it. We'll change it for anything else you wish when we get to Paris."

He waited and there was a long silence. She knew what he was waiting for. He was waiting for her to say she was still going to travel back to Paris alone. Only she did not say it. He knew then that — thanks to Ratoff? — she had changed her mind, and would be traveling with him.

Ratoff recovered, of course. Many months later, back on his feet, he cheerfully confessed that his conversation had been prearranged with his old friend.

"It will sound so much more convincing to Jujube if we make it a deathbed conversation," Zanuck had said. "Especially as you are really dying."

It was while they were flying back to Paris from Mexico City that Juliette Greco told Zanuck that Sacha Distel had been her lover for the past three years, and that he would be waiting to meet her at the airport. So she left him when the plane reached Orly. She went off in search of Distel and took him into a bar to tell him the news that their affair was over. He was "very distressed," she said later.

They had some more studio scenes for *The Sun Also Rises* to make in Paris, but when it was over, Zanuck said to her: "Let's get the hell out of here. Let's go to the South of France."

"I'll take my nurse and my child with me," she said, "and put them up at St. Tropez. Then we'll go on to the Hôtel du Cap." On the day they were leaving, they were looking out of the train window when they saw Sacha Distel running up and down the station platform with a bouquet of flowers in his arms.

"Just then, he got a flash of us," Zanuck said. "I seemed to take it stronger than she did. She shrugged it off. I couldn't."

They dropped the child and the nurse off in St. Tropez and then drove up the coast to Cap d'Antibes.

Zanuck had brought a bunch of scripts with him. He was looking for a vehicle for his new star, Juliette Greco.

# TWENTY-THREE

# JUJUBE IN THE JUNGLE

JULIETTE GRECO was twenty-seven and Darryl Zanuck fifty-five when they began their affair in Mexico City during the making of *The Sun Also Rises*, but it was not the difference in their ages that shocked her Parisian friends when they heard about it. He was an American, and that was what really disgusted them.

It was 1957, and the French preferred to forget it had been largely due to the efforts of the United States that their land and people had been liberated from Nazi occupation thirteen years earlier. Gratitude, especially in politics, has a short life. Little remained in France of the enormous fund of goodwill towards the Americans that had been one of the pleasantest Gallic manifestations towards transatlantic visitors of the immediate postwar years. An unsuspecting visitor from Oshkosh could now walk down side streets off the Champs Elysees and see "À bas les Americans!" and "Go home Yanks!" scrawled on the walls, and wonder what he and his fellow countrymen had done to deserve it. The group of artists, poets, critics, actors, and musicians in whose circles Greco had moved before she went to Mexico City was, if anything, even more virulently and contemptuously anti-American than ordinary, chauvinistic Frenchmen. Her friends would have forgiven her if, in search of money and stardom, she had taken up with an Italian, a Swedish, or even an English producer, no matter what his age, but the fact that she had picked someone who was a quintessential Hollywood movie mogul, right down to the rasping voice and the big fat cigar, pained them beyond measure. How could Jujube have done such a thing?

The French, as Greco had once said, may have only one word for love, but they have plenty to describe women who sell out, especially to Yanks, and they let loose the whole vocabulary on her. So right from the start, Greco was made to feel guilty about her relationship with Zanuck.

"What can a young woman see," she wrote later, "in an elderly tycoon with a toothbrush moustache, who smokes like a chimney, speaks through his nose, is perpetually angry, and does not speak a word of her native language."

Admittedly, she repudiated this passage after it had appeared in the newspapers, maintaining it had been written in her name by mischievous friends. But there is not much doubt that it represented one facet of her feelings towards her new lover, even if she was enormously impressed by him, and attracted too. When she was with him, she sometimes seemed to be acting, especially in French surroundings, as if she had betrayed someone or something. And this was unusual for her, for she prided herself on being nobody's creature, independent, free from guilt about everything she said and did. Zanuck, too, seemed to change when ·he was in her presence, almost defensively reacting to her by exaggerating his Yankee bragadoccio, the impressive power of his money and influence. Sometimes it was not a pretty thing to see. Once in the summer casino at Cannes she loudly summoned him to her side by flicking her fingers and saying: "Come over here, my little tycoon." When he did come over he reached out, cupped her breast in his hand, and squeezed, hard.

It was a stormy relationship, with quarrels that reverberated around the garden from their suite at the Hôtel du Cap, and were not always confined to rasping voices and shrieks of rage. Greco could scratch and kick. Zanuck could slap.

But to describe Zanuck at this period of his affair as an "elderly tycoon" was as inaccurate as to call him a non-French-speaker (he spoke fluent French, even if he mangled the grammar and the syntax). Despite his age, he seemed to have recovered all his former vigor, exuberance, and virility. The episode with Bella Darvi and his parting from Virginia had turned him suddenly into a fading middle-aged playboy, but now he seemed to have recovered completely, physically, mentally, emotionally, and from the way he glowed it was obvious life (and the movies) meant something to him once more.

It was certainly a honeymoon period, both professionally and person-ally, and he was relishing every moment of it. For one thing, he was making big money, even more than he had earned as head of 20th Cen-tury–Fox. *Island in the Sun* had made a fortune for him, even if he had been forced to tone it down. *The Sun Also Rises* was also doing well at the box office, thanks to its star cast, and if Greco, despite her fattened part, came over as a zero personality, Ava Gardner's sheer animal magnetism blazed out of the screen and pulled in the audiences. But the reviews were not good, and once more, as with *The Snows of Kilimanjaro*, Hemingway hated it. Zanuck worried about Greco's impact. For a woman of such a heated personality, almost searing when you were subjected to it in real life, why did she come across on the screen so tamely? Why did the camera neuter her? As he always was with his serious girlfriends, he was convinced his vibrant new mistress was potentially a great star, and he was determined that one day soon the whole world would be talking about "Zanuck's latest discovery." But first some new approach to her screen appearance would have to be made.

Meanwhile, he set out to teach Greco a way of life she had only vaguely heard about, and they did the rounds of the three-star restaurants and had midnight suppers of caviar and champagne in the nightclubs of the Côte d'Azur. They dined with Montand and Signoret in the garden of the Colombe d'Or at St. Paul de Vence, played *boules* with César and Alain Delon in the square at St. Tropez, flew to Ischia to loll in the mudbaths with Orson Welles, hobnobbed with Prince Rainier in the palace at Monaco, sailed into the sunset aboard Sam Spiegel's star-packed yacht, and water-skied with the Prince Saddrudhin Khan in Sardinia. And in between, Zanuck gambled, for high stakes, and, as happens when things are going well, he always seemed to win.

Greco, remembering the days when she would do almost anything for a square meal in Paris after the war, never failed to be impressed by the uncaring opulence all around her. Once, in the casino at Monte Carlo, she watched a well-known Hollywood female star with a reputation for acquisitiveness walk over to Zanuck's place at the chemin-de-fer table and casually pick up one of the chips and walk away with it. Zanuck merely smiled indulgently at her, slapping her derriere familiarly as she moved off. When she came to the bar later, Greco noticed she was still clutching the chip. Pointing to it (it was one of those large oval white ones) she asked how much it was worth, and was told ten thousand francs. Her eyes widened. Staring at Zanuck's place at the table, she noted he had now acquired a whole stack of them, at least a foot high. "*Mon Dieu!*" she exclaimed. "There is enough there to feed every starving child in Paris!"

"Or buy a new diamond necklace for you," said the star.

Greco still held on to "my block of gold bullion," as she called it, which

Zanuck had given her in Mexico City, and to this nowadays he added rings, bracelets, earrings, furs, and pictures.

One evening they went out to dinner with the French writer Romain Gary and his young American wife, Jean Seberg. Their marriage was evidently not going too well, and Gary, who looked even more world-weary than usual, remarked in a sad voice that he envied Jujube's luminescent glow and Darryl's general air of well-being and contentment. He congratulated them on their thriving relationship and lifted his glass to toast their "happy partnership."

Seberg gazed sourly at Greco's array of expensive jewelry, lifted her glass and said:

"To the partnership — Van Cleef and Arpels!"

The meeting with Romain Gary was to discuss a movie version of his novel *The Roots of Heaven*, which had much impressed Zanuck after he had read it. It seemed to him to contain all the ingredients he needed for a big Zanuck movie of the kind he had achieved with *The Grapes of Wrath* and *Twelve O'clock High*. It contained an offbeat but appealing hero, an intriguing narrative line, a spectacular African setting, and a moral punch. It even had in it an interesting role for Juliette Greco, as a concentration camp survivor who has suffered too much from her wartime experiences at the hands of the Nazis, believes in nothing, until she meets the hero and is stirred back to life by him and the nature of his mission.

Greco was all fired up about the part too, and believed she could give it more than anybody else. After all, she had actually been through the experience herself. She knew how the character felt.

So galvanized was she by now by Zanuck's belief in her cinema career she had begun to believe she had it in her to become a star of international caliber. She even allowed herself to be talked into changing her appearance for cinematic purposes, and flew with Zanuck to London to see the famous plastic surgeon Sir Archibald McIndoe. He had trimmed the noses of many famous stars, including Kay Kendall, the wife of Rex Harrison, and performed facial jobs on Ava Gardner, among others. He agreed with Zanuck that Greco might benefit from a "nose job," and they spent a week at the hospital at East Grinstead, in Sussex, where McIndoe did many of his operations.

Afterwards, Zanuck and Greco stayed at an obscure resort in Suffolk until her bruises healed, and then went back to London for a screen test. She liked her new nose and thought it gave her a touching pathos, but

Zanuck wasn't satisfied. A little later, he sent her back to McIndoe to have the nose trimmed further.

Greco submitted to these painful surgical interventions despite the fact that, philosophically, she was against such things, considering them as much an indulgence as caviar and diamond bracelets. But Zanuck was persuasive, and, after all, if he didn't know how a star should look, who did? She had now begun to put a lot of faith in his judgment, for the atmosphere of power and persuasion he exuded was highly impressive. And she was completely sold on *The Roots of Heaven* and the opportunity it seemed to be offering her.

For one thing, if it turned her into a world star, what a slap in the face that would be for her friends in Montmartre, who continued to charge her with "selling out to the Yank."

Romain Gary was a good writer with a wry, bittersweet philosophy. Beneath his surface cynicism was a rich vein of humanity, and Zanuck was anxious to tap that quality in the script of *The Roots of Heaven*. To aid the Frenchman with the nuances of the English language, Zanuck brought in an Anglo-Irish writer named Patrick Leigh-Fermor, and together they went to work. Meanwhile, Zanuck started casting the film.

The principal character in *The Roots of Heaven* is an embittered European who has given up his job as a white hunter with safari parties because he begins to fear the elephants of Africa are in danger of becoming extinct. Rich hunters from Europe and America, natives poaching for ivory, have all been slaughtering them to the point when their existence is threatened. He becomes obsessed with the mission of saving them, and decides on highly unorthodox, not to say violent, steps to do so. These are to exact stern revenge against those killers who are killing the elephants off.

It was a part that strongly attracted the Hollywood star William Holden, for both professional and personal reasons. He liked the role, and he also had a deep interest in Africa and its animals. But though he tried hard to do so, he could not extricate himself from prior acting commitments. Reluctantly, he was forced to say no when offered the part.

Zanuck finally turned to Trevor Howard to play the part. He was a better actor but he was not so well known, and he lacked Holden's wry, cynical, worldly manner.

Next, Zanuck picked Errol Flynn, whom he liked both as a man and an actor, for a role that fitted him like a glove, that of a drunken white mercenary. His friend Orson Welles he cast as an extrovert and intrusive

American network radio correspondent, and Eddie Albert and Paul Lukas were picked for other roles. And then there was Juliette Greco in the only big female part in the film.

Zanuck was at first inclined to take his film company to East Africa to make *The Roots of Heaven*. He loved Kenya and Tanzania. He had filmed there before and knew the ropes. There were plenty of game parks available within reasonable distance, the climate was good, and a civilized city, Nairobi, and the beaches of Mombasa were never too far away when cast and crew needed relaxation.

But then Greco reminded him France still had a colonial empire in Africa, and, unlike Kenya, which she seemed to think of as a sort of Miami Beach, most of it was pristine, untouched by the dirty thumbmarks of white civilization. Zanuck was tempted and fell. He knew the French authorities were eager to offer him facilities, and that would save him money on his budget. He finally took the big decision and announced *The Roots of Heaven* would be made in French Equatorial Africa. The company would set up its headquarters at a colonial administrative outpost named Fort Archambault, in Chad.

When Trevor Howard heard the news that the movie would be made in Chad, he groaned and said: "My God, Zanuck must be off his rocker."

He had friends who had served in the Anglo-Egyptian Sudan during World War II and several of them had passed through Chad on their way to and from the United Kingdom. They still shivered at the memory, and from the doses of malaria and other diseases they had contracted during stopovers there. The place was pestilential and the climate almost insufferably hot and humid — as much as 110 degrees during the day and rarely less than 90 degrees at night. It was considered a hardship post even by the French colonial office, and the unfortunate officials posted there kept disease and other things at bay with liberal doses of brandy, and were glassy-eyed drunk by midmorning and moiling in the throes of fearful hangovers for the rest of the day. They solaced the loneliness of their semisober hours by exercizing their droits de seigneurs, and kept flocks of giggling native girls available, most of them no more than children, waiting naked around the house to be called to give service to their masters. Howard presumed things had improved somewhat in the thirteen years since the end of the war, but knowing the French colonial service, he did not hope for too much.

Certainly, it was no place for anyone with a drinking problem, no matter how much local conditions had been cleaned up. And the company would include several drinking problems. John Huston had been chosen as director, and he was known to be fond of alcohol, especially in trying circumstances. Errol Flynn and Howard himself were far from being the most abstemious members of their profession. Huston was later to call Fort Archambault "the asshole of the world." Howard simply called it "Fort Despair." One of the first to succumb to the pestilences of the place was Zanuck's son-in-law, Robert Jacks, who was married at that time to Darrylin. He had been hired to manage the company and flew out first to look over the situation. By the time the rest of them caught up with him, he already had a bad case of malaria. When it did not improve, he was shipped first back to Paris and then rushed back to the States for treatment.

Howard fought off disease (and snakebite, since the camp was full of poisonous reptiles) with whiskey, and this sometimes put this normally amiable character into a hyperactive mood. He would move through the camp doing war dances, with fearful cries and bloodthirsty shrieks. Sometimes he would rouse Darryl Zanuck, who went to bed with bottles of beer and sleeping tablets, to scream in his ear that he was an evil ju-ju man who was bringing down death and destruction upon them. "Ju ju man! Ju ju man!" he would shriek.

Zanuck, thinking he was making insulting references to his beloved Jujube, struggled awake through mists of drugs and drink to assure him that "Juliette is really a gentle, innocent girl who would never do harm to anybody."

Meanwhile, Errol Flynn, who had brought a dozen cases of vodka with him (and was soon sending out signals for more) spent his sleepless nights sitting up in his campbed either writing long, lamenting letters to Beverly Aadland, his teenage Hollywood girlfriend, or plotting practical jokes calculated to infuriate Zanuck. Flynn ate little and took his meals in liquid form — tumblers full of vodka — and could get up enough energy to make the set only by swallowing pills and other stimulants. Patrick Leigh-Fermor, who had come to Africa at Romain Gary's request to "protect" their joint script, was the only one to thrive in the appalling heat. He discovered the climate improved his prowess as a two-fisted Irish drinker. He could out-tipple them all, and after the others had collapsed dead drunk on their beds, he would continue to quaff whiskey alone, spouting dark Irish verse in between drafts, and finally would go crashing into the scrub to defy the flora and fauna, daring the snakes and man-eating lions to come out and attack him.

The crew had already dubbed the movie encampment Zanuckville.

Every morning a tribe of natives moved in, spraying everything with disinfectant. Once every three days a crop-sprayer came over and dispensed clouds of mosquito repellent. Shooting began at dawn and stopped at noon, when players and technicians alike were beginning to drop from heat exhaustion. The bizarre setting was not made less far-fetched by the loudspeakers that hung from tents and huts, blasting out Muzak or rasping exhortations from Darryl Zanuck.

Greco had left her dog Crocodile at home, but she adopted a tame mongoose, which she kept in the quarters Zanuck shared with her. But someone (Flynn was suspect) was always letting the animal out of its cage, and it developed a liking for Zanuck's precious cigars, would consume four or five, and then be sick on Zanuck's bed. It also became extremely protective of its mistress and indulged in frenetic screams of rage whenever Zanuck tried to embrace her, a reaction he found distracting, infuriating, and "anaphrodisiac," to use one of his words.

He had also made the mistake of allowing Greco to bring with her to Africa two of her old Existentialist chums from Paris, a journalist named Anne-Marie Cazalis, who was put on the payroll as publicity-assistant, and Marc Doelnitz, an actor, who was given a small role in the movie. The chief publicity man was, in fact, a tall, handsome young man named Christian Lemaiziere, who was also an old pal of Greco's from Montmartre. To Zanuck's intense irritation, she was soon spending more time with this French trio off the set than with her lover. The climate was affecting everyone badly, exacerbating their moods, and Zanuck began to show distinct signs of jealousy.

Greco, who found she hated the heat, decided to sleep in the open air with a mosquito net over her camp bed. Her lover stayed in the bungalow assigned to them, but fretted about what Greco was up to. Despite the fact that he lulled himself to sleep each night with half a dozen beers and sleeping pills, he would force himself to wake up in the early hours and crawl out of bed, stumbling down the steps to where Greco was sleeping. He would shine his flashlight on the bed to satisfy himself she was there, then stagger back into the bungalow.

Every day he became tetchier and touchier, and conceived the notion that when Greco and her three fellow Parisians were away chattering together, it was because they were mocking or ridiculing him.

The last straw was the sudden arrival at Fort Archambault of members of Greco's old group, who flew in to give a surprise party for her. Zanuck suspected they were really there to try to wean her away from movies and back into cabaret again — which they probably were — and he refused to accept their invitation to the party. Greco went on her own, accompanied by her three Parisian buddies, and she stayed out long and late. Zanuck had sent her and her party in his car and instructed the driver to wait for them, but in the early hours of the morning, when it was evident that no one wanted to go home yet, she came out and dismissed the car and driver, saying she would arrange her own transport home.

It was not until four A.M., blissfully high, that she managed to borrow a gendarme's bicycle and pedaled back to the encampment, whistling to scare the animals away, but out of sheer happiness and joie de vivre too. But suddenly she was silent. Between the wooden gates of the film camp Darryl Zanuck stood, waiting for her.

She had already made the discovery that her love not only took sleeping pills every night, but wore a black mask to keep out the light. Moreover, he wore what was called at the time a "Baby Doll" nightshirt instead of pajamas.

"I can assure you," Greco said later, "it was a most extraordinary apparition, especially in Africa."

He was clad in his nightshirt now, with his mask pushed to the top of his head, and his cigar glowing in the darkness. She applied the brakes and squeaked to a halt in time to hear him rasp:

"Where have you been?"

She said she answered with an outburst of laughter. As if he didn't know where she had been! She immediately regretted making any response at all, however, because it seemed to release all the pent-up fury in him.

"It signaled the start of the most extraordinary behavior I have ever witnessed," she said later. "He insulted me. He raised his hand. Unluckily for him, all the hot quick strength of my youth boiled up inside me."

How dare he treat her like an errant wife — or, rather, like an errant daughter!

"I caught him by the collar of his nightshirt and began to shake him, hammering him with my fist. But I had not counted on those neat strong hands. Zanuck had been a boxer when he was young. He liked to fight, unlike me."

She says he began to attack her so fiercely she had to leave her bicycle in the mud and run for it, for the shelter of the cabin. "He leaped after me, screaming insults," and chased after her into the cabin. "Darryl, perhaps, did not realize my weakness. He loves to win. I remember only his furious cries . . . his swift movements . . . before I fainted on the beaten red earth of the cabin."

When she emerged from the cabin next morning, she discovered both Lamaiziere and Cazalis had disappeared. Zanuck had fired them and sent them back to Paris. Greco, who had been feeling ill for some time, promptly took to her bed and the doctor was called in. After his examination, he told her she was suffering from a severe case of malaria, and that if she didn't get out of West Africa soon she would die.

"The doctor said I had to go home," she said. "It was what I wanted too. Zanuck didn't want it. He wanted me to stay there, with him. But he had to give way. For once, there was nothing Zanuck could do about it."

She came nearest to a breakdown while she was waiting for the plane to take her back to Paris. Opening a box of powder on her makeup table, she was horrified to see "the ugliest piece of fluff " clamber out. "It was a horrible, velvet jet black and it raced up the wall of my room. It was a tarantula."

She screamed so hard Zanuck came rushing in and helped kill the spider with the stiletto heel of her shoe. He took her in his arms and soothed her hysteria, and next day, when she boarded the plane, decided at the last minute to hop aboard and accompany her. She was under sedation and slept all the way back to Paris nestled in his arms.

In the circumstances, it is astonishing that *The Roots of Heaven* was ever finished. When it was eventually shown publicly, it received poor notices from the critics and did only moderately at the box office. Romain Gary complained that Zanuck had "murdered" his book.

"He fucked it up," he said.

Actually, the movie deserved better from everyone than the criticisms it received, and it stands up well to the test of time. Given today's interest in the ecology and public concern with the fate of Africa's dwindling herds of wildlife, it is surprising it has never resurfaced after its appearance in 1958. For all its checkered history in the making, it has some memorable moments and performances (especially from Howard, Flynn, and the elephants) and, reissued today, could easily become a cult film. And that at least would justify some of the pain, sweat, and sickness that went into its making.

"I'm afraid it wasn't a very good picture," said John Huston later. "Or at least it could have been an awful lot better. I take full responsibility for this. Darryl put on a writer I recommended, put all my people in, went all the way with me. But the script wasn't all it could have been. It was a story that called for a sort of profound approach. As it turned out, it became a kind of adventure picture — and it shouldn't have been that at all."

Zanuck blamed himself. For the first time in his movie career, he put the fate of the picture he was making second to personal comfort and personal affairs.

"It was the most difficult location in the entire history of motion pictures," he said later, "and we took the easiest way out. Everybody was so depressed after we had been there a month, we would say, 'Oh, Christ, let's leave that scene out.'"

It was something he had never done before, and he was ashamed of himself. He was ashamed that a mixture of heat, mosquitoes, temperamental actors, drink, and, above all, worry over Greco, had combined to sap his morale and weakened his determination to come back from Africa with a wonderful film.

And it had lost him his girlfriend.

Or had it?

It was not the end of Darryl Zanuck's attempts to turn Juliette Greco into a film star, but by the time he had run the rough cut of *The Roots of Heaven* through a dozen times, he must have begun to suspect it was not going to be easy to achieve. Her role in the film was close enough to her own experience to enable her to mine the seams of her own pain and suffering and then project them at the camera. The trouble was, she did not seem able to project, not cinematically, anyway. This was a young woman who could move her listeners to tears with a cabaret song, who looked ravishingly beautiful in the spotlight of a *boîte de nuit*, but seemed to become denatured on the cinema screen.

"She acted well enough," said Zanuck later, "but she didn't project. The camera is a monster and there is not a damn thing you can do about it."

But he tried, stubbornly, unwilling to admit she did not have what was needed in a star. He resurrected one of his pseudonyms from the past, Mark Canfield, and wrote an original story and screenplay called *Crack in the Mirror*. He cast Orson Welles and Bradford Dillman opposite Greco in the starring role, and flew in Richard Fleischer to direct it. Joseph Mankiewicz later called it "a turkey," but it wasn't really big enough or positive enough to merit such a condemnation. It was simply a forgettable film that whimpered away without most people realizing it had ever been made. Greco didn't even make enough of an impact to be noticed by the critics.

They put down their differences to the evil influences of Africa, and patched up the affair when they got back to Paris. But things were not really going well between Zanuck and Greco, and the lukewarm notices he got from his film, the lack of success she was having with her career, did nothing to help the relationship. Neither was a character who knew how to handle failure, even if it was only temporary, and they began to get on each other's nerves. They were seen more in public than ever before but that was because they were increasingly abrasive with each other in private; and even in public they often openly quarreled. Greco gave him a present of a pet dog, a miniature schnauzer called Iago de Rochefort, and, surprisingly for the admirer of German shepherds and the creator of Rin Tin Tin, he seemed to be fond of it and liked to sit in sidewalk cafés with Iago fast asleep across his knees. In return, he made Greco a present that he later came to regret. As if to solidify their association, he presented her with two blank checks, drawn on his dollar account at the Chase Manhattan Bank (Paris Branch) and told her they were for any amount of money she might care to fill in.

"This is an earnest of my love and trust in you," he said, "and the permanency of our relationship."

She was a little embarrassed and did not do anything with the checks, neither filling in any sums on them nor cashing them. Gregory Ratoff flew in for one last visit with his friend. He was a sick man and it would not be long before he died, but he was worried about Zanuck. He had heard stories from Paris which disturbed him, and he feared the worst. He knew no girl had ever dumped Zanuck, that it was he who had always walked out on them, and he dreaded the consequences if, for the first time, it were to happen to his friend now.

"Dayril," he croaked, "this girl is no good for you. Why do you not tell her to fock off? She cost you money, she does not look clean, she cannot act her way out of paper back. Why waste time on a piece of meshuga when Paris is full of nice clean virgins. Kick her out before she gives you a dose of clep."

In fact, Ratoff was percipient about the situation in which his friend found himself. Zanuck had never had an association with a female like Greco before, and he was finding it difficult to handle. He was not used to young, free, independent women. He was suspicious when she ignored his advice, went her own way, sought out her old friends, as she was now beginning to do. Did he really trust her? No, he did not. He had even been to a private detective agency and hired an operative to keep watch on his mistress whenever she was out of their apartment for any length of time. It was reported to him that she had taken to visiting Montmartre, and the old friend she was seeing was Christian Lemaiziere, the handsome young publicity man he had fired in Chad.

When he taxed her with this, she did not try to deny it, but admitted she was seeing Lemaiziere about making a comeback in the music world, since her film career seemed to be failing. She did not reveal to Zanuck that many of the consultations with Lemaiziere were taking place in bed.

"Unlike Zanuck, who thought singing was a waste of time," she wrote later, "Christian believed in me and encouraged me. In return, I gave him all I had to offer . . . my love."

In a desperate effort both to get her out of Paris and to salvage his star-making efforts, he decided to make one last try. They took off for Davos for a skiing holiday, and there Zanuck met up with Irwin Shaw and asked him to write a vehicle for Greco. It was to be an African story again, but one that could be shot on the more civilized plains of Kenya. Unfortunately for Zanuck, he was a show-off skier and in demonstrating to Greco that there was no one in the Alps more daring or more skillful, he ran straight into a tree and smashed his collarbone.

While he recuperated in the hospital in Davos, Greco went back to Paris to continue her musical discussions with Lemaiziere. But when he eventually limped into Paris, she still seemed willing to listen to Zanuck's siren song about making it in films, and she was still persuaded that the great tycoon might yet make her a star.

So when Shaw came up with the script of a movie to be called *The Big Gamble*, it was one last big gamble she decided to take. It was even more of a disaster than *Crack in the Mirror* and a resounding flop at the box office. Moreover, since it had been made in Africa, it had cost a lot of money. One day a cable arrived from Zanuck's son, Richard, who was temporarily running his Hollywood liaison office.

"BOARD OF DIRECTORS HERE WORRIED ABOUT FINANCES," it began. "ACHILLES THE HEEL SAYS UNWILLING TO MAKE MORE ADVANCES PENDING BETTER SHOWING MOVIES AT BOXOFFICE . . ."

It did not happen overnight, but one day about this time, Greco walked out of his life.

"Everything suddenly became clear to me," she said later. "I was not in love with him anymore."

She moved over to Montparnasse and refused to come to the telephone when he called her. And, as Ratoff had feared, he took it badly. When she looked out of her window, Greco would see "a long, low closed Citroën near my front door. It was full of Zanuck's private detectives."

On the far corner, she could see Zanuck himself, his Tyrolean hat jammed on his head at an angle, pacing restlessly up and down the street, a walking stick in his hand. When she told her friends about it, they asked her whether they should call the police or otherwise do something about him. She shrugged her shoulders. "He did not wish to harm me," she said. "He just wished to speak to me, and he just could not bear the frustration when I refused to see him."

So far as she was concerned, he was out of her life, and all she wanted to do was reach out for the microphone and return to her singing career. And suddenly, all her friends came flocking back to her, to welcome her home, to commiserate with her for the way she had been suborned, tricked, and seduced by that ineffable cigar-smoking Yankee.

The apartment in which Zanuck had been living in Paris was in the Plaza Athenee Hotel, and no guest had been viewed with such favor or treated so royally. Directors, managers, waiters, and maids had all fawned upon him and his slightest whim had been their command. But then news spread around Paris that Juliette Greco had walked out on him. At the same time, there was a story in one of the local papers that Fox was in financial difficulties. And then a ridiculous thing happened.

One morning there was a knock on the door of his suite, and in walked a flunkey with one of the hotel's heavily embossed envelopes. Inside was a bill which, a note informed him, the management would like to have paid at once. The bill contained an itemized list of the damage that, the hotel maintained, had been done to the furnishings of the suite and certain public rooms by Monsieur Zanuck's schnauzer dog, Iago de Rochefort. Iago had scratched the paneled walls, he had micturated on the drapes, he had vomited on the shoes of a chasseur and bitten a tween-maid's ankle. Furthermore, after partaking of a meal in one of the restaurants of the hotel with Monsieur Zanuck, he had barked at the maître d'hôtel, jogged a waiter's elbow while he was serving the soup, growled at neighboring tables, and lubriciously snuffled up the skirts of a distinguished female guest at a dinner party nearby.

For all these regrettable events and the consequent damage entailed, the management of the Plaza Athenee requested payment of $4,000 at once and the imminent departure of Monsieur Zanuck and the afore-mentioned Iago de Rochefort, who would no longer be considered fit guests for the Plaza Athenee Hotel.

As it happened, the note was a godsend. It arrived at one of the worst moments of Darryl Zanuck's life. A woman had walked out on him, which had never happened before, and he found the humiliation of it terrible to bear. This is what had happened to his father, and he had despised him for it. In his opinion, there was no more contemptible person in the world than a man who couldn't hold on to a woman, and it was a sign of age, of weakness, of failing faculties that it had happened now, and it was enough to plunge him into the depths of despair.

And then this. He glanced through the hotel bill, let out a roar of rage, and then reached down and swept up the schnauzer, Iago de Rochefort, who was looking inquisitively up at him, and held the bill up to him.

"Have you seen this, baby?" he shouted, beginning to hoot with laugh-ter. "Have you seen what they saw you've done? Pissed on the drapes, shat on the carpet, poked your nose up a woman's cunt. Baby, baby, are you in trouble! Are we both in trouble!"

Suddenly, he had forgotten about Greco, about his humiliation, about the parlous state of his bank account. He reached for the telephone to call his pal, Art Buchwald, who still wrote a Paris column for the Inter-national *Herald-Tribune*.

"Art," he said, "have I got a story for you!"

A few days later, Buchwald wrote a comic column about Iago de Rochefort's list of complaints against the Plaza Athenee Hotel, and all Paris had a laugh about it — except the hotel management, that is.

By that time, Zanuck had moved out and taken an apartment on the Île de la Cité. He was still a profoundly depressed and shaken man, but, as he said later, that pompous note about Iago had come just at the right time, and momentarily made him forget that a woman had dared to walk out of his life.

There was one other ironic little postscript to the Juliette Greco affair, and that caused him no end of worry. One day, when he was sitting alone in his new apartment on the rue du Bac, his accountant called up and asked him, for tax purposes, what had happened to the two checks which were simply marked "Jujube" in his stubs, with no amounts filled in.

My God. He picked up the telephone and tried to call her, but once more, as always, the baby's nurse answered and swore that Madame was not at home. So then he called his lawyers. They agreed that if Greco desired to do so, she could fill in the checks for any amount she wished, and cause him no end of embarrassment. The checks must be got back from her at once. A letter was drafted in New York and rushed to Paris for Zanuck's approval, and then sent on by special messenger to Greco. It contained a stiff, formal demand that the blank checks be returned immediately.

Greco was afterwards to claim she had, in fact, forgotten all about the checks Zanuck had given her, that she had put them away in some bottom drawer and could not remember where. It took her several days of rummaging through her papers to find them. But she did not send them back. She said the cold, formal, almost threatening tone of the lawyers' note made her see red.

"I do not like being insulted," she wrote later. "The demand for the return of those little bits of paper put me beyond myself with anger. Not for the devil himself would I give them back! In any case, they are mine. He gave them to me and I have no reason to give them back."

She had, of course, no intention of filling in the checks and trying to make money out of them. She had accepted generous presents from Zanuck while they had been together, but she would not try to exploit him now that it was over

But she did not tell Zanuck that. Nor his lawyers.

Soon there were rumors flying around Paris that Greco had in her hands the means of ruining her erstwhile American lover. The news appealed to the anti-American feelings still simmering among her Latin Quarter friends. It amused them to think the hated Yankee tycoon had made a fool of himself over his young French mistress and handed over to her the means to wipe him out.

They urged her never to give back the checks, and she held on to them. They relished the thought that they would hang like a sword of Damocles over Zanuck's head for many years to come.*

---

*They did not, of course. Zanuck simply instructed his bank to cancel the checks.

*TWENTY-FOUR*

# THE LONGEST NIGHT

**A**MONG THOSE who happened to be in Paris during this dark period in Darryl Zanuck's career was a well-known Hollywood executive named Elmo Williams. An amiable and unflappable man in his early forties, Williams had been working in the movies since he was nineteen years old, most of the time spent in studio cutting rooms. He had a reputation almost equaling Zanuck's for being able to salvage a salable film out of the worst kind of cinematic junk, and it was because of his editing expertise that he had been asked to go with Zanuck to make his second African film with Juliette Greco, *The Big Gamble*. He had soon discovered that there was little he could do to turn it into a viable picture.

"Oh, it was a bad movie," he said later. "It was such a bad script, and there was really nothing you could do with it. Darryl and I struggled with it, but we knew from the start that it was hopeless."

Williams had not been impressed by the female star of the picture (not, at least, as she projected herself from the cutting-room screen), and although he did not say so out loud, he wondered how a supremely professional producer of Zanuck's caliber could ever have imagined that in Juliette Greco he had a big international star. Having worked night and day in the Paris studios to try to get something interesting assembled from the hodgepodge of film they had brought back from Africa, Williams finally signed off and left it in Zanuck's hands. Both of them knew without saying so to each other that *The Big Gamble* was never going to be the financial and critical success for which Zanuck was now desperately hoping.

Williams stayed on in Paris for some weeks to await the arrival of Stanley

Kramer, who wanted him for a film called *The Maccabees,* to be made
in Israel. When that fell through he was offered an assignment in Munich
with Walt Disney, and thought, before taking off, that he would say
goodbye to Darryl Zanuck. By that time he had heard that the romance
with Greco was definitely over, and that Zanuck was drinking heavily in
consequence. It worried him. He had always admired Zanuck as the last
of the Hollywood giants, and he had already made up his mind that if he
really was in bad shape and needed help, he would postpone his departure
and do what he could for him.

When Williams rang the bell of the apartment in the rue du Bac, it
was a nurse who opened the door, and inside Zanuck's doctors were
padding around. It seemed that only half an hour before, Zanuck had
been felled by a stroke and they were still working on him. He was
informed that the patient was in no condition to see anyone for the
moment, and he was told to come back in a couple of days.

He returned three days later. Zanuck was in bed and looking "lousy,
and feeling miserable and sorry for himself. But he certainly didn't look
as if he was dying, or anything like that." Williams told him he was about
to depart for Munich, but would postpone it if he could be of any help.
At which point Zanuck seemed so grateful that Williams thought for a
moment that he was going to burst into tears. Williams was terribly
concerned. He had never seen this man looking so woebegone, so downhearted, so miserable. His hand trembled as he reached for and lighted
one of his giant cigars. When Williams raised his eyebrows, Zanuck said,
grinning:

"Those frogs told me to lay off them, too. I told the Doc I'd rather die
with a cigar in my mouth than boots on my feet. The hell with them."

He puffed away contentedly for a few moments, and then suddenly
looked pathetic again. Glancing at Williams, he said:

"You know everybody's gone, don't you? I have nobody here any longer.
Juliette's left me. My whole staff has bailed out. There's nobody around
who gives a damn about DFZ. I still have my seven-picture contract with
Fox, but what the hell does that mean? The last ones I've made have
been flops."

He shook his head, in utter gloom.

"You know movies, and I think you suspect I've lost my touch. So do
I. I've lost my touch, and I don't know why. I've lost my way, and maybe
it's because I've been too preoccupied with other things. And I'll tell you
frankly, Elmo, I don't know what to make next. I own some other screenplays, but I tell you, I don't know which to make next."

He paused again, puffed at his cigar, watching the blue smoke curling across the airless room.

"Look," he said, abruptly, as if making up his mind, "will you do something for me, Elmo? Will you take a look at those screenplays? I'll pay you for a week if you'll take them away with you now and read them — then come back and advise me which I should make. Tell me what you think of them. Advise me. Christ, if ever I needed advice, it's now. And I guess you know it isn't my habit to ask for advice."

Forty-eight hours later, Elmo Williams was back again, with the scripts under his arm. The patient was much better, to judge by the condition of the ashtrays, which were littered with cigar butts. But Zanuck was no more cheerful than before, only more restless, obviously itching to be out of bed.

"Well?" he asked, impatiently, when he saw the scripts.

Williams decided he was recovered enough to be told the truth.

"They're awful," he said. "Every single one of them is a lousy script. I'm sorry to tell you, but I wouldn't put a dime in any of them."

"My God," said Zanuck.

There was a long silence, until he groaned and said:

"I don't know. I don't have anything else."

Silence again.

"The only other thing I've got," he said at last, "is —" Then he shook his head. "Nah."

"What, Darryl?" Williams asked. "What's the other thing you've got?"

"You know the French producer, Raoul Lévy?"* he said at last. "He ran out of money and came running to me, and I lent him seventy-five thousand dollars. It was a personal loan, and he put up a book as collateral. Lévy told me he'd tried to raise the money to turn the book into a movie, but everybody had turned him down. But maybe there is a film in it. Would you take it and read it and see what you think?"

He indicated a fat book lying on the bedside table, and Williams promised to take it back with him to his hotel and read it right away.

It was called *The Longest Day* by Cornelius Ryan.

Back in Hollywood at 20th Century–Fox nobody was worrying much about Darryl Zanuck and his troubles. They had problems of their own. In fact, despite the comparative financial failure of *The Roots of Heaven*

---

*Lévy was a French film producer who made, among others, some of the early films of Roger Vadim and Brigitte Bardot.

as well as the disasters with *Crack in the Mirror* and *The Big Gamble*, DFZ Productions still had money in the bank, and that was more than one could say for the parent company. Zanuck's *Island in the Sun* and *The Sun Also Rises* had made profits hefty enough to tide him over a bad patch,* and his resources had just received a further boost, thanks to the efforts of his son, Richard.

Richard had been operating in Hollywood as assistant to Zanuck's son-in-law, Robert Jacks, running the liaison office between the studio and DFZ Productions in Paris. It so happened that just before he left Hollywood, Zanuck had bought the movie rights to the stage play *Compulsion*, but, under the contract which had been signed, no film version of it could be made until the stage play finished its Broadway run. Now suddenly, the play had begun losing its audiences and been taken off. If DFZ Productions was to cash in on its theatrical reputation, the movie of the play must be put into production immediately. But Zanuck was in Chad, wrestling with the problems of *The Roots of Heaven*. The man to whom the production chores would normally have been handed on, Robert Jacks, was in the hospital with the case of malaria he had contracted in Africa.

So Richard Zanuck took a deep breath, dipped into his DFZ's drawing account at 20th Century–Fox, and, with his father's blessing, launched himself into his career as a producer. It was his first movie venture on his own, and *Compulsion* not only became a box-office hit but also garnered for DFZ quite an amount of critical praise. Subsequently it was presented and acclaimed at the Cannes Film Festival and won awards for its three stars, Orson Welles, Bradford Dillman, and Dean Stockwell. So Zanuck did not really need to worry — not about his financial resources, anyway. Fox, on the contrary, certainly did. The studio hadn't had a hit movie for more than a year — not since Zanuck had left them. The shareholders were beginning to get restless, and were demanding the board of directors do something about it. As a result, Spyros Skouras, the chairman of the board in New York, was harassing the studio and demanding action — and big, prestigious, moneymaking films.

The answer of the studio was to put into production at once a movie that had been planned as "a modest costumer," as *Variety* put it, with Joan Collins as its star. Now Fox paid off Collins, called for a new script,

---

*And helped Fox's finances too, since *Sun* had been made directly for the studio and only incidentally for DFZ.

and dramatically increased the budget. Then they went across to M-G-M and offered one of its contract stars, Elizabeth Taylor, a million dollars to play the lead in what they faithfully promised would be "a real blockbuster." Its title: *Cleopatra.*

Taylor agreed at once. Only after she had done so did she and her agent, Kurt Frings, remember she still had one picture to make under her M-G-M contract. It was to be produced by Pandro Berman (who had recently moved across from RKO) and was a movie version of the John O'Hara novel *Butterfield 8.*

"Liz Taylor didn't want to do *Butterfield 8* at all," said Berman later. "She claimed it was because it was a terrible story and script. The truth of the matter was she had already decided she wasn't going to make this picture, no matter what it was like. This was her last commitment to M-G-M under her long-term contract, and she was committed to do this picture for Metro for $100,000."

Taylor made it plain to Berman that in no way was she going to accept such a paltry sum of money when she could go to Fox and get a million dollars for *Cleopatra.*

"I was not going to let her get away with it," said Berman. "It was very fortunate that this was one time I was able to get front office backing. We simply told her we would never allow her to make *Cleopatra* until she had done this picture. She *hated* making it."

But in order to have a happy star on the set of *Butterfield 8*, Berman was forced to make one concession. At that time Taylor was married — happily married, everyone thought — to the actor-singer Eddie Fisher. She now demanded as a sort of "consolation prize" that Fisher be given a role in the film, and Berman finally, if reluctantly, gave in. He came to regret his decision, because the couple gave him lots of trouble during the production. And Taylor never did let him forget she was doing him a favor in consenting to appear in *Butterfield 8*, which she continued to maintain was unworthy of her as a film.

In fact, as it turned out, *Butterfield 8* scored a fantastic success at the box office and secured rave notices for Taylor. Later the same year her performance in it won her an Academy Award.

As for *Cleopatra* . . .

When Elmo Williams returned to the apartment in the rue du Bac next day, he was enthusiastic about *The Longest Day.* He thought it could make a wonderful film.

"But God, I don't know," he said, "it will take an awful lot of guts to make it. It's a real hazardous project."

Zanuck was improving day by day, and his depression seemed to dissipate with his return to health and vigor.

"Do you really think we can do something with it?" he asked, eagerly.

Williams said he did. Here was a story covering every moment of the first day's invasion of Normandy, the D-Day landings on the coast of Nazi-occupied France, and Ryan had achieved an exciting book about an historic event.

"It's an episodic kind of thing," Williams said. "If anything should go wrong in the course of the production, you could easily substitute another episode, so that takes some of the risk away. But not all of it. It's a risky subject — a great subject but a rocky one. For instance, where in hell are you going to get all the equipment this long after the end of the war? How are you going to show the landing in Normandy — with all those ships and men? And what about the parachute drops — with thousands of American and British paratroopers and gliders? Where are they going to come from?"

Zanuck was going through a transformation. Like Lazarus, he was rising from the dead. Williams could see him regaining his old persona of the quick-thinking, self-confident Hollywood tycoon for whom nothing was impossible.

"Listen," he said, briskly, "how about canceling that trip to Munich and putting your ideas down on paper for me? I'll pay you for them, of course."

"Okay," said Williams.

Next time he came to the apartment, he brought with him a draft of the narrative line he thought the movie should follow. He too was beginning to get excited.

Under his contract with 20th Century–Fox, Zanuck controlled the choice of subject for his movies, and the direction, casting, and location as well. But he still had to go to the studio for the money. Fox had the obligation to finance the projects of DFZ Productions, but they also had the right to approve the budget for each of them, and they could stipulate financial limits beyond which they would not go.

Zanuck sensed that if he did decide to make *The Longest Day* this could create difficulties. He had already had plenty of reports from Bob Jacks and Richard that things were going badly with Fox as far as finances were concerned. The truth was, the successor he had nominated and left behind when he quit Hollywood for Europe, Buddy Adler, had turned out to be a dud. He had eventually been replaced by Robert Goldstein, the head of Fox's London office, who was brought in to pick up the pieces. Among those pieces was the big prestige picture, *Cleopatra,* with which Adler had hoped to lift Fox out of its financial hole. The debris from his expensive tinkering with the project was lying everywhere that Goldstein looked, and so much had already been spent on it the new chief realized they would have to go on and get the film before the cameras somehow. But he was soon convinced it would prove a Sisyphean task. Fox's dwindling resources had been poured out in profligate fashion on paying stars (like Taylor), hiring directors, finding locations, getting a shootable script, but each time *Cleopatra* seemed to have reached the peak and was ready to take off, back it rolled into the hole again.

Zanuck's favorite scriptwriter, Nunnally Johnson, disgusted with Buddy Adler's method of running the studio, had already walked out and gone to make movies in Europe. He was happily at work in England producing a film called *Mr. Hobbs Takes a Vacation* when Goldstein called him. Would he drop everything and go to work on the script of *Cleopatra* and try to whip it into shape?

At that moment Walter Wanger was the official producer of *Cleopatra* and he had already made a monumental and costly error. He had decided the movie could be shot in England. He had spent millions of dollars planting palm trees and building an Egyptian city on the outside lot at Pinewood Studios, only to discover belatedly that English skies stayed stubbornly gray, the buildings were constantly soaked in un-Egyptian rain, and the supposedly nilotic background looked like a Thameside suburb when transferred to the screen. The director, Rouben Mamoulian, was still shooting tests with Peter Finch as the leading male star (he was later replaced with Richard Burton), and Johnson was invited to see them at the Dominion Cinema in London, the only movie house in England at that time equipped with Todd-AO, the system in which the film was being shot.

Johnson was appalled. Mamoulian's work seemed to consist of shot after shot of the drably lit set at Pinewood. He said to Wanger: "I don't think this feller is ever going to shoot this picture. He's testing fabrics. A man's really desperate when he begins testing fabrics. He's afraid to come to bat." And then, he went on: "I'll bet you a pound, just a pound, that Mamoulian never starts this picture."

About a month later, he got an envelope from Wanger with nothing in it except a pound note. Shortly afterwards it was announced that Mamoulian had asked to be taken off the picture, and soon so was Walter Wanger. Peter Finch was replaced by Richard Burton. Johnson was dropped and Joseph L. Mankiewicz came in as writer-director-producer.* The whole company had been told to prepare to move the production to the sunnier skies of Italy.

It all cost a lot of money. Fox had so far spent $6,450,000 and had only eight minutes of film in the can — never used, as it turned out. And the more it cost, the more Fox was likely to jib at a big budget for *The Longest Day*.

Not that any financial jitters at Fox were likely to stop Zanuck from making the film. He had now caught fire and he was determined that neither Spyros Skouras's doubts nor his own state of health was going to prevent him from putting the film into production.

He was out of bed now — for at least part of the day, anyway.

"I wrote a treatment and took it over to Darryl," said Elmo Williams, "and he liked it very much and began to enthuse about it. So he asked me to come to his apartment every day and talk to him about it, and he and I slowly sketched it out. He was well enough to get up every day for lunch, so we would walk from his apartment to Chez Lipp and we would eat and talk, and then we would walk back. He would go back to bed and spend the rest of the day there, while we talked about what should go into the film."

Zanuck was now convinced he could turn *The Longest Day* into the truest film about war that had ever been made. But he also realized neither he nor Elmo Williams — who were visualizers, not writers — could produce a script to live up to the theme of the book. So he offered a lucrative contract to its author, Cornelius Ryan, and asked him to come over to Paris. That was a mistake. The two men did not get on at all. Ryan quickly decided that Zanuck was a cocky little bastard who was trying to take his masterpiece away from him, and he objected vehemently to every suggestion Zanuck made to alter the incidents in his book. Ryan insisted that the book was perfect, and Zanuck, irritated by his attitude, set out to prove him wrong.

"He had all these arguments with Ryan, and he hated to lose to anybody," Williams said later. "Darryl was a pugnacious little guy and he

---

*Before he left, Mankiewicz asked Mamoulian what he would advise him to do about the picture. "Do as I did," Mamoulian replied. "Resign."

now took great delight in finding some place where Ryan had made a mistake. You always can find them when you look."

Such was the antipathy which now developed between producer and author that Zanuck secretly enlisted the help of other writers to help him get the script he wanted. He called in Noël Coward. He flew in James Jones and handed a contract to Romain Gary. Ryan resented the whole thing bitterly and finally went before the Screen Writers to argue about credits.*

But there was one thing Ryan achieved that should have made Zanuck deeply grateful to him. Having been told that the U.S. 6th Fleet in the Mediterranean was about to do landing exercises, Ryan mentioned casually that the fleet commander was a friend of his and might be persuaded to simulate a D-Day invasion, and allow it to be photographed, for the film.

"Well, the upshot was," said Williams later, "that we set up the landings in Corsica in April — though we were not ready to begin the actual picture until the middle of June. I managed to get the art department to simulate all the obstacles and things for the Normandy landings. Zanuck came down and the top brass of the navy came down. And it all worked out spectacularly well. We got what we wanted."

Then they moved to Normandy and set up headquarters in the Malherbe Hotel in Caen. The cast began to arrive from all parts of the globe: John Wayne, Robert Mitchum, Henry Fonda, Robert Ryan, Sal Mineo, Paul Anka from California, Sean Connery from Jamaica (where he was making his first James Bond film), others from Britain, France and Germany. Zanuck and Williams were out all day in a helicopter, surveying the Normandy coastline for suitable places to shoot.

In the middle of all this, Richard Burton arrived. Zanuck had tempted him away from *Cleopatra* (and Elizabeth Taylor, as it turned out) by offering him a juicy fee for a vignette in *The Longest Day* that would take only forty-eight hours to shoot. After it was over, Burton had dinner with Zanuck and told him he was greatly disturbed about what was happening on the set of *Cleopatra*. He doubted that it would ever be finished, that money was just being thrown away, and that it was now such a burden on Fox that there were rumors the studio was going to go bankrupt. Burton strongly urged Zanuck to take a trip to Rome "and scare the hell out of them by just appearing on the set." Burton's news worried Zanuck.

*He received sole credit for the finished film.

He, his son and daughters, and Virginia Zanuck between them were Fox's biggest shareholders, and their future depended on the solvency of the company. So did DFZ Productions. On the other hand, he couldn't get away. *The Longest Day* was by now far too important to him.

It was at this moment that Spyros Skouras called him from New York and told him to report to the board of directors at once.

"Otherwise," he said, flatly, "we're going to stop your picture and take the loss involved."

Zanuck boarded the next plane.

Primed by his son, Richard, who flew to New York to warn him, Zanuck became aware that certain members of the 20th Century–Fox board were out to get him. They were looking for a scapegoat to blame for the disastrous financial condition of the company, and knew he was vulnerable. They hoped to turn shareholders' attention away from the scandalous waste of money that had been involved in the production of *Cleopatra* and persuade them that Zanuck was to blame for the studio's troubles. Had he not made three flops in a row, all because of his mad obsession with some French nightclub singer? Had she not finally thrown him over and made him the laughingstock of France? And hadn't he, in consequence, now become a drunken bum who was bleeding the company white with a monstrously expensive war picture nobody wanted to see?

Richard Zanuck warned his father that the anti-Zanuck forces were convinced they could make their charges stick, and that it was no use relying upon Spyros Skouras, the chairman of the board, to come to his rescue. He was scared to death by what was happening to the company, and would like to load the blame for it on anyone who was available.

"You're it, Dad," Richard said. "They think you're on the skids, and they'll heap all the shit they can on you. They're convinced they can get away with it. They've heard some terrible stories about you from Paris."

In the circumstances, Darryl Zanuck's entry into the board room of Fox's headquarters in New York — it was the spring of 1961 — caused some contemptuous smirks when he first walked in. They slowly changed to expressions of bewilderment and irritation.

"They had expected to see an old bull limping in with his balls cut off," said Zanuck later, and they were surprised to note how fit and well he looked. In fact, at fifty-nine Zanuck acted like a bouncy boxer just itching to begin a bout. No one would have guessed he had suffered a stroke a little more than six months earlier. His mood was belligerent, and as Spyros Skouras sensed how fighting mad he was, he hung his head sheepishly. When he rose to address the board he said he wanted to make it clear that preventing Zanuck from making *The Longest Day* was certainly not his idea.

"I must say that Skouras was against stopping the picture, but he had lost *all* control," Zanuck said later. "Milton Gould was violently opposed to it. He and John Loeb spearheaded the attack. Who wants this kind of picture? Let's take a three million loss and get out before he ruins all of us."

Looking around the table, Zanuck sensed it was a solution that appealed to most members of the board. They had all been hearing from the shareholders, angrily accusing them of gross extravagance, of wasting money on overexpensive pictures. Executing Zanuck was an easy way to appease them. All they had to do was halt production of *The Longest Day* and they could claim they had saved the shareholders millions of dollars.

When he was physically fit and mentally and emotionally well, nothing appealed to Darryl Zanuck more than a challenge of the kind that now confronted him.

"I had to convince these cocksuckers that they were out of their fucking minds," he said later. "Here they were, ready to capsize the ship that was going to bring the goods home for them, just to save a lousy million dollars or so. I knew and they knew that what was to blame was not me or my extravagances but that godforsaken movie they were making in Rome, which was pouring away the company's money like shit down a sewer. But the bastards wanted to make me the reason for the diarrhea. And here I was, with the greatest potential moneymaker the studio had had for years — and I was goddamned if I was going to let them lose it."

He rose to his feet and began to address the meeting, quietly, earnestly, with no trace of passion or bitterness in his voice, even though he was now in a fuming rage. The remarkable thing was that he never mentioned *Cleopatra* once. All he did was talk about *The Longest Day*. He went over the world-shattering events of the day that the Allies landed in Normandy in June 1944, the invasion that led to the defeat of the Nazis and victory in World War II. He painted a graphic picture of Ryan's book, of how it brought home what this momentous event meant to the individuals who were involved in it. He said the world was waiting to hear this story, and would beat a path to the doors of any cinema that showed it. It would be war on the screen as it had never been seen before.

When someone snorted with skepticism, Zanuck became aware that a member of the board had risen to his feet. It was the only general on Fox's board of directors, James Van Fleet. Zanuck knew he had proved himself one of the feistiest soldiers in the war, had taken part in several critical battles, and knew whereof he spoke. Now General Van Fleet lost his temper. His face red, he looked round the room at his fellow directors with angry contempt.

"He practically called them idiots," said Zanuck later. "He had landed in the first wave on D-Day. Usually at board meetings he never said anything, but now he said, 'This picture will make more than any other picture. To stop it now would be suicidal for this company.' "

After several more hours of discussion, Zanuck was asked to wait outside the board room while the directors consulted among themselves. He paced up and down impatiently, puffing furiously on his cigar. Finally, when he was called back, Spyros Skouras announced the decision. By a vote of six to five, it had been decided that *The Longest Day* could go ahead, but only if its budget did not exceed $8,000,000.

"If I spent more," Zanuck said, "they said they would take my cameras away."

By that date, *Cleopatra* had already cost $15,000,000 and was still nowhere near completion.

"The cocksuckers!" exclaimed Zanuck to his son, just before boarding the plane back to Paris. "They know I can never bring it in for that amount. What the hell am I going to do for the money?"

"You know you can count on all of us, Dad," Dick said.

Secretly Richard agreed with those who thought *The Longest Day* was a mistake. Who in hell wanted to see a film about World War II? But on the other hand, if his father's heart was set on completing it, he would do his best to help him.

# TWENTY-FIVE

# COMEBACK

ZANUCK WAS still triumphant that he had saved his film, and the result was reflected not just in his professional activities but in his private life too. It was just about this time that Juliette Greco chose to sell the serial rights of a book she had undertaken to write about her association with Zanuck, and it was not a pretty story as she (and her ghostwriter) recounted it. The series read more like the bitter reminiscences of a woman scorned than of a successful young woman who had walked out on her lover, and *le tout Paris* sniggered rather uncomfortably over her snide references to Zanuck's age, bullying, ill temper, and jealousy. *Innocent French girl meets ruthless Yankee tycoon and falls victim to the Almighty Dollar*. It didn't sound quite right even to those readers who had never seen Juliette except on the TV screen or heard her on discs and the radio, and Zanuck might have been wiser to let the revelations run their course and allow readers to draw their own conclusions from Greco's fevered prose.

Instead, he called his lawyers and forced the withdrawal of the series. The magazine *Paris-Match*, which had used a short extract, found it prudent to run two articles praising the production of *The Longest Day* by way of recompense. The book was never published.* Juliette thenceforward banished the name of Zanuck from her lips. But, in a way, the action he took had proved the correctness of one charge, at least, in her series: that he was ruthless and when he wished to do so he could wield his money and power like a weapon.

As if to underline the fact that there were plenty of other women who found him attractive, and to emphasize he was not only fit again but as

*She has since written her autobiography, published in Paris in 1982 under the title *Jujube*.

*331*

virile as ever, he now began to be seen around Paris with a succession
of girls. In fact, most of them were not much more than high-priced
pickups, one-night stands recruited to service him by members of his
entourage. He was now frequenting many of the fashionable nightclubs,
but rarely seemed to be seen with the same girl twice. Sometimes, as he
fondled a companion in the spotlight glare of a Parisian *boîte,* one could
catch a slightly desperate expression on his features. It was as if he were
defiantly indicating to anybody watching him: "See, I can still get it up!"

Luckily, this sad spectacle ended when the head of Fox's Paris office,
Edward Leggwie, took him down to his private cinema one evening and
ran a series of advertising films for him. Zanuck was looking for someone
to play the small role of a female Resistance fighter in *The Longest Day.*
As he had done in the case of the chief male roles, he had gone after a
star to fill the part — offering a large sum of money for perhaps one or
two days' work. But French female stars were not self-confident enough
to accept vignette roles, even for munificent pay, and both Brigitte Bardot
and Marina Vlady had turned him down. Now Leggwie thought he had
a girl who might fit the role and be glad of the money. Her name was
Irina Demick* and she was a model reasonably well known in advertising
circles in Paris.

Zanuck was taken with her at once, not so much for the acting ability
she showed on the screen — there wasn't much opportunity for that —
but for the air of affection and good feeling she exuded. *"Irina, elle est
vachement sympa"* ["Irina is really simpatico"], one of her friends said
about that time, and it aptly summed her up. Zanuck said he would like
to meet her. Edward Leggwie, who knew his boss well, had already made
the arrangements. He waved to the back of the cinema where a lone
figure was sitting. Irina had slipped into the projection room while Zanuck
was watching her up on the screen. He took her out to supper, and their
association began, professional and personal as well.

He was lucky. Irina Demick, the daughter of Russian émigrés who had
settled in France, was a frank, open, generous girl in the broadest sense
of the term. He was more than thirty years her senior, and if she did not
fall in love with Zanuck, she certainly conceived a profound affection for
him, came to admire his technical skills and judgment, and was constantly
in awe of his prowess as a filmmaker. She was also a beautiful woman,
with the proud, bony face that a sculptor or painter is always seeking as
a model. Best of all, she had no feminist hangups. She liked being bossed

---

*Her name had originally been Demich.

by Zanuck, who, from that moment, took over her life. She let him dress her, change her hair style, show her off at fashionable restaurants and clubs, and was genuinely pleased as he began to grow fond of her as a person, a confidante, and not simply as a woman. Above all, she was modest. Whereas most of the people who surrounded Zanuck when he was making films seemed secretly to resent his power over them, she never did so. She considered herself fortunate that he had found her, and once said about herself and his entourage:

"If Darryl is not there, we are nothing. We are satellites around the sun. If the sun is not there, we die. Before him, I never tried to make movies. If he was not there when it began, I would never be Irina Demick. I cannot be Irina Demick without Darryl Zanuck. I am a cabbage."

She could not have come into Zanuck's life at a more propitious moment, and it did much to restore an ego that was still being buffeted by the mockery and ridicule of Juliette Greco's friends.

The action of *The Longest Day* was filmed from the viewpoints of those who had taken part in it, and Zanuck had therefore hired American, British, and German directors for those segments dealing with their own nations. For the landings in which the British were involved, he had picked a well-known English director named Ken Annakin, who had not only made some highly successful British films but had also directed several live-action films for Walt Disney. But although he had worked for Americans before, this was his first war picture, and Zanuck's reputation as a tough, hard-driving producer had preceded him.

Annakin had been signed for a three-week stint, and his wife, Pauline, accompanied him when he installed himself at the Malherbe Hotel in Caen. On the first night, Zanuck came across to the table of the restaurant where the company usually dined and welcomed him to Normandy, but he didn't sit down or invite Annakin back to his table, where a dark-eyed brunette was quietly watching them. But the next night Annakin and his wife went to the improvised projection room where the rushes were screened, and watched the results from those units that were already shooting. Zanuck and his friend (they had learned by this time that her name was Irina Demick) were there, and the Annakins got a glimpse of what they might be in for.

"Unlike any producer I have ever worked for before," Annakin said later, "Zanuck invited us to see other people's rushes as well as our own. Zanuck and his girlfriend were in the center of the theater, and he would pass very critical and very, very downright remarks while the rushes were on. His girlfriend obviously had her opinions too, because I would notice their heads would go together, and then he would say something out loud. Sometimes they were devastating comments."

About five days later, after Annakin had done his first sequences with his British cast, his rushes came on the screen in the evening.

"And I suppose good fortune must have been smiling upon me that day," said Annakin, "because my rushes were good. Afterwards he came up to me, all smiles, and from that time on I couldn't go wrong."

He took to coming down to Annakin's set-up, on the bridges over the Orne canal and river, but he never tried to tell him how to direct.

"He would pass a remark sometimes," Annakin said, "as to some point in the staging of a shot. It was usually quite a shrewd remark, and we played a sort of game, in which I tried to think of things before he would think of them."

As the days passed, they got on easier and easier terms with each other. Zanuck never used the name of Annakin's wife, always greeting her with the words, "How's the lovely bride?" although, as Pauline pointed out, "we had been married for years by then." By the end of three weeks, Annakin had shot all the British segments of the film and the rushes had all been seen to Zanuck's satisfaction. When the British director came over on his last night to say goodbye, Zanuck said to him:

"I think you know we're not very happy with the Free French sections of this film — the sabotage sequence, for instance, in which Irina stars. It doesn't come off. We want you to reshoot it."

When he told his two cameramen what Zanuck had said, they laughed.

"Aha, that's the sack-getter," they said.

It seemed that four directors already had tried to shoot the sequence with Irina, and all had been fired in consequence. She apparently had approval of the result, and if she didn't like the rushes, out they went. Pauline Annakin, who hated to think of her husband being fired on a woman's whim, was all for persuading him to stick to his original contract and depart forthwith. Annakin had other ideas. He said he planned to treat Irina exactly as he would a child actor, as if she knew nothing about filmmaking at all.

"I'll overshoot and cover in every possible way," he said, "and I'm going to be ultra-patient with her — show her every gesture, every breath."

It worked. She liked her scenes and Zanuck enthused over them. He rewrote Annakin's contract and insisted he try a helicopter shot that he wanted to use to set the scene for the invasion sequences of his film.

Several other directors had tried it, but Zanuck had been satisfied with none of them. Now Annakin went aloft. His masterly sequence, shot close up to the Normandy beachheads, was eventually used in the completed film, and became a collector's item among cinema buffs.

Thereafter, they became sort of buddies.

"Zanuck used to insist Pauline and I have dinner with him and Irina," he said later. "He always spoke French with her, and with us, which was more difficult. His was rather bad American French but perfectly idiomatic. We used to have to tell our stories in French, but worse than that, we had to listen to his funny stories in French. Irina wouldn't say much. She was a great listener, and she always made sure he was at the center of the stage. It became a good association, even a fun association, and it led to my taking over more and more of the film."

The relationship wasn't always as smooth as he makes it sound, however, and sometimes strain developed between producer and director.

"I had a scene where a hundred commandos come in for a landing," said Annakin. "To bring them in Zanuck had succeeded in borrowing thirty American landing craft from the U.S. Army. They made the filming of the sequence part of a tank landing exercise, and I had the right to use them as I wished. They weren't too keen on that, especially when they found we were Brits. The sergeant who commanded the landing craft forces was a sergeant who must at one time or another have had a hard time at the hands of an English girl — maybe she gave him a dose or something — and he made no secret of how he felt about Limeys. Anyway, in this scene, a Stuka divebomber is supposed to come over just as the commandos are going ashore, so we had charges set to go off everywhere, and I had six cameras set up on the shore. I got in the landing craft with the commandos and their commander (played by Peter Lawford). The main thing was to calculate — Zanuck and I had worked it out — at exactly what moment the commandos would jump out of the craft into the water. During an actual operation, they would have gone into deep water. But Zanuck wanted them to drop into water that was only three feet deep, so we could get a shot of a Scotch soldier in full Highland dress playing his bagpipes as he leads the men ashore."

Annakin's split-second timing was to ensure the men jumped into the water just as the Stuka came over and the bombs went off. He asked the U.S. sergeant how long it would take the moving landing craft to lower its ramp and enable the men to go into three feet of water, and when they tried it out during rehearsals the time came to sixteen seconds. So

Annakin boarded the landing craft with Lawford and the commandos, gave the sergeant the order to lower the ramp, and then signaled the Stuka to come over and the charges to go off sixteen seconds later exactly.

"But the fucking ramp comes down in three seconds," he said later, "and the men promptly jump into the water — and disappear. There's nothing I can do. Once the signal is given, I can't stop the plane or the explosions. As for the men, they all vanish into the water.* We can't find Peter Lawford, because, thinking he's only going into three feet of water, he fails to fasten his wet suit, and by the time we get him out he's completely waterlogged. But the other men are magnificent. Somehow they struggle ashore. And out of the surf, holding on to his soaked bagpipes, comes the Scotch piper, blowing strangled sounds as he stumbles up the sand."

It wasn't Annakin's fault. In fact, he discovered later that the anti-British sergeant ("having got pissed as a newt beforehand") had decided it would be a splendid joke if he speeded up the dropping of the ramp and gave the Limeys a soaking.

"On the other hand, I knew what Zanuck's attitude would be," said Annakin. "He wanted exactly what we had planned, and he would be mad as hell that we hadn't got it. So I did what I thought was a tactful thing. I stayed on the landing craft and went back to the landing station, and didn't come back for half an hour, when I imagined the worst of Zanuck's anger would be spent. It wasn't. I was greeted by a shower of profanity."

But what won Annakin's admiration was the fact that though, when they showed the rushes that evening, the sabotaged shot looked like real war, Zanuck wasn't satisfied. He wanted the scene as it had been written.

"So despite the fact that the shot took six hours to set up, and cost a hell of a lot of money," Annakin said, "he insisted that we redo it. We shot it four days later with a new top sergeant who didn't mind the Brits and didn't get pissed, and it was perfect."

It was now the end of the summer and the weather had closed in. Zanuck had moved his vast company down to the Île de Rey, facing the Bay of Biscay, where the beaches were uncluttered and good for shooting over wide distances. He still needed the big shot that would crystallize

---

*Among them was Sean Connery. "If I'd drowned him," said Annakin, "there would have been no James Bond."

the nature of this film and demonstrate the mightiness of the enterprise. It was the scene of the main landing on Sword Beach on D-Day morning, as watched from the shore by Kenneth More playing a British officer who has already landed with a bulldog, mascot of his regiment.

The shot began on the bulldog, then slowly pulled away and lifted to take in the full panoply of the invasion forces — landing craft, tanks, armored vehicles, fighter planes overhead, guns banging away, troops pouring onto the Normandy sands.

To shoot such a massive moving panorama would have been a daunting task for a director under normal circumstances, but there was something special about this one that Annakin was only too conscious of. He knew that this was the make-or-break scene not only for the movie but for Darryl Zanuck as well. He had been informed from Fox's head office that his $8,000,000 limit had been reached and no more money would be forthcoming. He had been ordered to cease shooting. Not only had he disobeyed, but he had dug into his own private resources in order to keep going. Annakin knew Zanuck was personally paying now for every landing craft, every tank, every old plane, every soldier and every member of the camera crews who were about to register this scene, and if he botched this one Zanuck could be wiped out.

Yet Zanuck gave no sign of what this meant to him. He wandered about, quietly watching, during the seven or eight hours Annakin took to set up the scene. Annakin had to move with a certain dispatch, because the French had lent them three thousand troops and they had not reached the island until 11 A.M. and had to catch the ferry back to the mainland by 3 P.M. They carried wooden rifles and were strung out by the assistants along the beach. Then suddenly everything stopped for half an hour while a box lunch was delivered to them.

At only one moment did Zanuck intrude to take a view through the camera lens, and then he said to the director in a casual voice:

"You realize what you've got out there, don't you, Ken? There's three million dollars worth of hardware on that beach."

He did not go on to mention that he had paid for the whole lot of it himself. And the only evidence of his feelings came when Annakin, addressing a group of British troops approaching the camera, cried out:

"Now come on, you're doing this for king and country!"

"Not for king and country," roared Zanuck. "For 20th Century–Fox!"

He could also have added, with ample justification:

"And for Darryl F. Zanuck!"

*        *

They did the interior shots for *The Longest Day* at the Boulogne Studios in Paris, and by that time Annakin had been working for Zanuck for three months. He was now one of Zanuck's greatest admirers.

"He was always there, hovering near the camera," said Annakin, "and I always knew he was racking his brains to think of anything he could suggest to make the scene better. He was a constant spur. But I found him a very human person. All he was interested in was making the most wonderful true war picture ever. He had his guts, his heart and his soul in the movie, and you could feel the pain of the effort he was making."

One day he said to Annakin:

"You know, I've always envied directors." He watched while Annakin set up a scene with Robert Mitchum, and then went on: "I know I'm not a director, but I would really like to feel that this was my picture. Would you help me to take over?"

So for the last three weeks of the interiors, all of them with American stars of the film, Annakin would set everything up and then Zanuck would go behind the camera and make the shot.

"Normally speaking, I would never have allowed it," Annakin said. "But I suppose I had enough experience with him not to be jealous of him in any way, and I thought: why the hell shouldn't I let him do it, if it makes him feel closer to the film? I had got to like Zanuck sufficiently by that time, and it was fun. After all, he had demonstrated at every moment during the production of the film that he was the master of it, and neither writers nor directors had been allowed to interfere with the way he wanted it. And somehow I got the feeling that no matter what might happen to him in the future — and I suspect he was already beginning to worry about what was going on back at Fox in Hollywood — this would be regarded as his swan song, his greatest contribution to the cinema, and that if he never made another movie and departed now, he would be doing it in a blaze of glory."

That was not the way the board of 20th Century–Fox viewed his future. Or his film.

*Cleopatra* was driving 20th Century–Fox inexorably towards ruin, and nobody seemed to be able to do anything to stop it. Spyros Skouras, though still chairman of the board, had lost his grip on the company's affairs and no longer wielded enough authority to plug the drain on the company's resources, which the disastrously expensive and accident-prone film in Rome was now causing. Meanwhile, faced by ever-increasing debts, the finance department was scrambling desperately to pick up money where it could. Fox needed ready cash from any available source to pay its bills, and would sacrifice a million dollars next month to secure a hundred thousand dollars tomorrow.

When news reached the board that Zanuck had made a good film and that it would probably do well at the box office, they could hardly wait to get their hands on it.

Zanuck got an inkling of the troubled waters in which the studio was now floundering when Nunnally Johnson telephoned from London to tell him Marilyn Monroe had been fired and her new film, *Something's Got to Give*, canceled at a cost of $2,000,000. The new head of production at Fox, Peter Levathes, who had succeeded Robert Goldstein, had decided an inflated blonde named Jayne Mansfield possessed much more box-office attraction than Monroe, and had made up his mind to rid the studio of his temperamental star. Zanuck was already convinced of Levathes's poor sense of judgment,* but this decision appalled him for its sheer lack of insight into what makes a big box-office star. He himself didn't think much of Monroe as a woman — she was "just another easy lay" as far as he was concerned — but he shared Johnson's opinion of her public popularity and her potent sex appeal. Her dismissal was a startling indication of the rudderless course Fox was now steering.

Nunnally Johnson blamed her director, George Cukor, for the ruin of Monroe's film, but Darryl Zanuck knew it would never have been allowed to happen had the head of Fox studios been more capable, and had the board of Fox in New York been keeping its eye on its investment in its stars.

If that is what they could do to someone with the box-office potential of Marilyn Monroe, what might they now be cooking up for him and his film, *The Longest Day*? Richard had already informed him from Hollywood that Spyros Skouras was rumored to be on his way out. If so, who would take his place? And whoever was chosen, could he be relied upon to look after Zanuck's financial interest in Fox — and, above all, spend time, money, and effort in the proper presentation of his film?

He was still one of the largest shareholders in 20th Century–Fox, and it might be as well to remind the board of that fact, in case they were proposing to ignore it. To that end, he took time off from the cutting room in Paris — where he was still working on the final version of *The*

---

*He had already canceled one of Richard Zanuck's productions, *The Chapman Report*, on the grounds it lacked box-office potential. Zanuck had intervened on his son's behalf, sent the film over to Warner Brothers for distribution, and seen it become a financial success.

*Longest Day* — and wrote a memorandum for dispatch to New York. In it, he tipped his hand both as to his views of the future of the company and of the role he considered he should now play in its operations. He wrote:

> If and when Spyros decided that he wanted to step out of the presidency, I would present the following concrete recommendations based on the industry as it exists today. Whether or not I become the President is actually immaterial. I own with my family about 280,000 shares of stock, and the voting control of it all. I have a personal interest in the survival of the Corporation as well as a certain amount of pride in what was once described as "the best operating Studio in the industry." I also have selfish interests.

He then dropped his bombshell. He went on:

> I would close down the Studio and only complete the films that are either already in production or committed for. . . . I would sell the Studio to the Fox Realty Company or a third party. . . . I firmly do not believe that our world grosses will suffer radically even if we do not start another picture in the next six or eight months.

He was now so enthusiastic about the chances of *The Longest Day* he was willing to admit his previous failures, and his memorandum, in an unusual spasm of modesty, for him, proceeded to acknowledge his own dismal recent past.

> My record, since my first independent production, *Island in the Sun,* which was a profitable venture, has not been good. I cannot defend my position nor can I blame it on bad luck. The figures speak for themselves, and while most of my films received better than average critical acclaim, they did not live up to expectations and two of them were out-and-out flops. I believe that I have now profited by my error of judgment, and I am no longer confronted with private or personal problems which obsessed me prior to commencing *The Longest Day.* I will continue to make mistakes in this highly speculative business, but the "know-how" I have acquired as a result of my failures and the lessons I have learned have been of enormous value.

It was an obvious appeal to the board to rally around him, elect him the new president, and let him get the studio out of its financial crisis without delay. But whether they recognized this or not, they certainly did not respond to it. Instead, it was his own lawyer, Arnold Grant, who called him to say that Skouras would be retiring at the next board meeting and Judge Samuel Rosenman would be temporarily replacing him while a new president was found. But who? When Zanuck flew to New York and went to talk to Rosenman, he was astounded to be asked not whether he would become president himself, but whom he would recommend from a bunch of names with which he was presented.

"And do you know the names that cocksucker presented to me?" asked Zanuck later. "Well, I can tell you that one of them was Otto Preminger, who was likely to go bankrupt running a kids' softball team. And Mike Frankovich, who couldn't count up to fifteen unless you lent him one of your hands. It made you vomit."

Neither Rosenman nor any other members of the board seemed to be aware that Zanuck might like the presidency for himself, and that he was far and away the best candidate available.

In the circumstances, he was not ready to make a fight for it. Not for the moment, anyway. What he had come to New York principally to find out was what 20th Century–Fox was going to do to help him make *The Longest Day* into a financial blockbuster. The condition of the company was such that they might be tempted to throw it away, just simply to get hold of some ready cash to pay their outstanding loans, and the last thing he was going to do was allow Fox to use his film as a lifebelt. He had quietly been in touch with Jack Warner and discovered Warner Brothers would be delighted to take over the movie and send it out on a road-show basis, which meant it would open in selected spots in selected cities, and be presented and publicized as a prestige film.

In the meantime, he presented his plans to Rosenman for the exploitation of the film. They included a special budget of $100,000 (which Zanuck offered to put up himself) to be handed over to two top industry publicists who would go out and "sell" the film to the media and public. At the same time, the film would open with a bang first in Paris, then in New York and London, and thereafter in selected cinemas throughout the nation — on a specially priced, reserved-seat basis.

Rosenman shook his head at once and said under no circumstances would he allow it. *The Longest Day* must take its chances under a blanket-release simultaneously in cinemas everywhere, to bring in as much financial return as possible in the shortest possible time. He gave the impression he regarded the film as something of an embarrassment, to be shown and forgotten about as soon as possible. It was just another possible moneymaker to him, and the sooner it began bringing in returns, the better he would like it.

Zanuck kept his temper with some effort considering how he now felt about Rosenman, who was kicking his baby to death before his eyes. His impulse was to knock him down. Instead, in a quiet voice, he gave Fox a choice — either send out the film on a roadshow basis, or he would buy it back from them. His lawyer, Arnold Grant, supported this by adding they were ready to pay $8,000,000 — which was what Fox had spent on it — for the rights to the film.

To add insult to injury, Rosenman shrugged his shoulders and said if it were up to him he would accept the offer like a shot. However, he added, it was the company that had put up the money, and therefore the film belonged to them. There was no question of selling it.

That was all he had to say. Abruptly, he rose to his feet, glanced impatiently at his watch, and said he was already late for another appointment.

"What a bastard!" said Zanuck, once they were outside. And later he added: "All my life, I've never been so mistreated. They treated me like a schoolkid."

Now he was determined to fight the board. He was certain of one thing above all else: if *The Longest Day* was to be issued and properly exploited by Fox, he was the only one who would be able to see that they did right by his baby.

And to do that, he *had* to become president of the company.

Darryl Zanuck flew back to Paris on June 16, 1962, to complete his work on the final print of *The Longest Day,* but he had left behind in New York a team of advisers ready to do battle on his behalf for the control of 20th Century–Fox. His lawyer, Arnold Grant, hired the famous attorney Louis Nizer, to help him in the forthcoming battle, not so much because Nizer was an expert on boardroom brawls but because his was a name that was always good for publicity. At the same time, he had heard through the grapevine that anti-Zanuck interests at Fox were planning to hire Nizer themselves, and he thought it would be a neat coup to prevent them from using his services.

Ten days after he got back, Zanuck took time off to write one of his famous long telegrams, addressed to the Fox board, accusing them of being jointly responsible for the company's parlous financial predicament. He insisted it was not the fault of Spyros Skouras alone, pointing out, in case they tried to make him a scapegoat, that they had taken jointly all the decisions that had lost $40,000,000 in 1961 and $25,000,000 so far this year. Far from selling the company short, he was confident he could restore it to its earlier profitability and prestige. He ended by saying that if they wanted him to do so — if they wanted him as their new president —

they would have to offer him "the unqualified and unanimous support of a unified board of directors."

"Over my dead body," replied one member of the board, a corporation lawyer named Milton Gould. Gould, who was known as "Jack the Giant Killer" along Wall Street, loathed Zanuck and all he stood for. It was he who had tried to stop Zanuck from finishing *The Longest Day* by cutting off his money. Then, someone leaked Zanuck's telegram to the press, smearing his name all over town, as a womanizer, a drunk, a profligate gambler, a maker of dismal flops. Zanuck's reply was another telegram, threatening to begin a proxy fight against the board, aware that such a move would panic most of its members. As if to reinforce his threat, he flew once more to New York and was met at the Plaza Hotel, where he kept a suite, by a couple of nervous directors, Ed Weisl and Robert Lehman, who hinted they would be prepared to back his presidential bid if he, in turn, would agree not to hire his son, Richard. Zanuck refused.

"Nepotism only occurs in Hollywood," he said, "when a studio chief hires his incompetent relatives. My son has already won his spurs. He is an asset to 20th Century–Fox. It would be a loss to us to let him go elsewhere."

Finally, he was summoned before a company selection committee to be questioned about his suitability for the presidency, and Gould launched a last-ditch attack, backed by Zanuck's other bitter enemy, John Loeb.

"The bile just poured out of them," Zanuck said later. "It was filthy stuff — mostly about my private life. What the hell had that to do with my competence as a president? But then, they knew they couldn't say much about my ability as a filmmaker. I'd had my flops as an independent, but look at my record while I was running 20th Century–Fox. And look at the mess it had got into since I had left."

He listened to the virulent torrent of abuse in silence until Judge Rosenman turned to him and said: "And now perhaps Mr. Zanuck would tell us what *he* would do for the company if he did become president."

He had brought with him a carefully prepared program of detailed proposals for restoring the fortunes of Fox, but suddenly he was weary and as he rose to present them, he looked around at the indifferent faces and said to himself: *Aw, to hell with them.*

Aloud, he said: "I have nothing to say. If you want me, fine. If not, get somebody else."

On July 25, 1962, at a full meeting of the board, Darryl Zanuck was elected president by a vote of eight to three. The three voting against were Judge Rosenman, Milton Gould, and John Loeb, and twenty-four hours later the latter two had resigned.

The first thing Darryl Zanuck did was to call his son, Richard, in Hollywood and tell him he had been appointed new head of production at the studio in place of Peter Levathes. Two hours later, he called him again from Fox's presidential office and gave him his first order:

"Stop all production and close down the studios."

# TWENTY-SIX

# ANTICLIMAX

UBLICITY MEN have become such expert manipulators of lights, stunts, film stars, and public figures that they can turn any trashy movie — or even a supermarket opening — into a media event, and most people have become blasé about them. On the other hand, few among those who were present are likely to forget the fanfare, the panoply, the gaudy trappings with which the world premiere of *The Longest Day* in Paris in 1962 was surrounded. The spectacle was such that one critic, as he finally reached his seat in the cinema, was heard to remark: "I feel as if I've just gained entry to Valhalla!"

It was an international event, as Darryl Zanuck intended it to be, and nothing was overlooked to help foreign correspondents among the guests find plenty of intriguing items for their newspapers and TV stations.

Almost as if they were making up to him for the mockery by Juliette Greco and her Existentialist friends, the French government set out to salute Zanuck and his film. Not only did they lend him the Palais de Chaillot for the occasion, but they also abandoned austerity measures and lighted up a large section of Paris. General de Gaulle and the whole of his cabinet were the guests of honor, and also present were all the commanders from NATO headquarters, the diplomatic corps, an international bevy of stars and notabilities. From the third level of an illuminated Eiffel Tower, the ageless gamine of the French cabarets, Edith Piaf, sang the "Marseillaise" and the theme song from the film.* Zouave horsemen from North Africa, in their colorful flowing robes, cantered by. And afterwards, while fireworks burst over Paris from the Eiffel Tower and turned Paris for one night back into a City of Light again, Zanuck and a contented

---

*It was written by Paul Anka, who also played the role of a GI in the film.

Irina Demick presided over a banquet that must have cost enough to finance a medium-budget film.

*The Longest Day* was by no means, in the view of most critics, the greatest war film ever made, as Zanuck had hoped, nor was it even a particularly excellent movie. But it had been made long enough after the end of World War II to be able to cover both sides of the conflict with reasonable impartiality, and it pricked both the curiosity of the new generation and stirred the nostalgia of those who had lived through the war. It had been cleverly crafted and cast to give at least a simulation of what D-Day might have been like, and Zanuck's flair for good cinematic effect had paid off in his decision to cast famous stars in the roles of the principal D-Day characters.

"I wanted the audience to have a kick," he said later. "Every time a door opened, in would come a famous star."

It was a trick that seemed to work.

For the New York opening and its subsequent road-showing across the country, Zanuck faced a problem. He had shot the film with each national contingent — American, British, French, German — speaking their own language, and had dubbed it all into English later at the Boulogne Studios. For the big international premiere in Paris, however, the film was shown in all three languages and seemed much more effective as a result. For the press showings in New York, however, the critics were shown the film in English. But it so happened that Bosley Crowther, then film critic of the *New York Times* and one of the most influential reviewers in the country, could not get to the ordinary press showing. The Fox publicists promised that if he would come in from his home in Connecticut the following Sunday, they would give him a special showing. When he heard about this, Zanuck said:

"You know, Crowther is a little bit of a snob, and he speaks French and some German. Why don't we put the three-language version on for him? I think it might appeal to him."

Crowther was so impressed that he commented in his notice very favorably on the original-language version, and it tipped Zanuck's decision in favor of abandoning the English-language version altogether. For the opening night in New York, Cardinal Spellman and General Omar Bradley rode down Broadway (with Irina between them) in a long procession to the cinema, and then a host of celebrities watched *The Longest Day* in the three-language version with enthusiastic approval. Despite some so-so notices, the subsequent publicity was such that the film was a success from the start, and was in profit long before the end of its first six months in the cinemas. By the end of 1962, Darryl Zanuck was able to announce it had made enough to pay off 20th Century–Fox's most pressing bills, and there would soon be cash in hand to finance new movies.

He also confirmed his son, Richard, in the position he had unofficially given him at the beginning of his presidency, and he was now legally head of production at Fox. His salary was $1,000 a week, and when shareholders subsequently criticized the weekly stipend as too high, Zanuck rose to his feet and replied:

"It is very hard for a father to defend his son. I criticize him myself. At twenty-four I was getting $5,000 a week at Warner Brothers. At twenty-nine he isn't doing so well. But then I wasn't saddled with a notoriously successful father."

Although he was now president of a company with its headquarters in New York, Darryl Zanuck had no intention of leaving France. He flew into Manhattan frequently for important meetings at the Fox offices there, and he kept a permanent suite at the Plaza Hotel. But he never went to the studio or Hollywood, and spent most of his time either in Paris or the South of France, with occasional skiing trips to Switzerland. After assuming the presidency, he had flown back with copies of all the scripts owned by the company, including three which the former head of production, Peter Levathes, had planned to put before the cameras just before his contract was terminated. Zanuck read these three with especial care and junked two of them. The one he retained for future consideration was a script adapted from a Broadway play by Nunnally Johnson called *Take Her, She's Mine*.

To begin with, however, his worry was about *Cleopatra* and how he could salvage some of the millions that had been expended in the course of its stormy production in Rome. Joseph L. Mankiewicz, who had become its producer-director-scriptwriter, was now cutting it in Rome in preparation for its presentation, and as soon as he heard Zanuck had replaced Spyros Skouras as Fox's president, he sensed he was going to have trouble.

Mankiewicz was a touchy and temperamental character and he had always suspected Zanuck didn't like him. While that may have been true personally (he could be a hard man to like), it was certainly not accurate professionally speaking. Zanuck, in fact, had several times intervened at Fox to save Mankiewicz from being fired by New York after a succession of his films had failed at the box office. On one occasion, when Spyros

Skouras himself had ordered him fired, Zanuck had offered his own resignation if the order was carried out. And though Mankiewicz did not
know it at the time, that was the only reason why he went on to direct
his most famous and successful film, *All About Eve,* for which he, George
Sanders, and Zanuck all won Oscars.

Zanuck was still catching up with all the details of the *Cleopatra* disaster, so he was ignorant of the fact when he took over Fox's presidency
that Mankiewicz had a special plan for the presentation of the film — or
films, as it seemed.

"My plan was to make two films about Cleopatra," he said later, "the
first, her life with Caesar, the second, her life with Antony. They were
to be released simultaneously and we hoped audiences that saw one would
want to see the other. That was the arrangement I made with Spyros
Skouras, president of Fox. I set out to fulfill that obligation. There were
countless interruptions . . . Elizabeth [Taylor] fell ill, there were casting
changes, and it takes twice as long to make two films. I was proud of my
script and it was one of some daring, as it invaded the land of Shakespeare
and Shaw."*

Then Spyros Skouras was replaced by Zanuck.

"He was impatient to get *Cleopatra* before the public at once," said
Mankiewicz, "and profit by the wide coverage its making had received.
We were not on friendly terms and he was in an irritated state as he had
produced some colossal flops. He wired my cutter to prepare a single
four-hour film from the footage, and would look at nothing else."

From this moment on, the versions of what happened to the film differ
according to whether you are listening to Mankiewicz or Zanuck. According to Zanuck:

"It never occurred to me, after I became president, that I would have
to do anything more than walk in and see the picture. But when Mankiewicz brought me his first cut and I looked at the film I was shocked.
I asked to see the sequences that had been cut and decided some of them
should be restored, but I found to my astonishment that no loops had
been made for certain eliminated episodes. In other words, Mr. Mankiewicz obviously considered the picture finished when he brought it to
me. I was powerless to do anything about it."

Zanuck said Mankiewicz now became angry and demanded the sole
responsibility to finish the editing — "either that, or to be told to get

*In a conversation with Thomas Quinn Curtiss at the Deauville Film Festival, reproduced
in the International *Herald-Tribune,* September 16, 1981.

out." Zanuck told him to get out, and then called a press conference at which he said:

"In exchange for top compensation and a considerable expense account, Mr. Joseph Mankiewicz has for two years spent his time, talent and $35,000,000 of 20th Century–Fox's shareholders' money to direct and complete the first cut of the film *Cleopatra*. He has earned a well-deserved rest."

According to Mankiewicz (speaking in 1981) it was not a direct confrontation between the two men that took place, but an exchange of letters.

"Then he [Zanuck] entered into correspondence with me," he said. "My concept was to show how Cleopatra held Antony as her slave and destroyed him, knowing that he dreaded her comparing him to Caesar as both lover and warrior. Zanuck wrote to me: 'I can't understand your glorifying such a bitch. Why, if Cleopatra had done that to me, I'd have emasculated her!' "

Mankiewicz added:

"I leave that remark for Freudian interpretation."

He went on:

"The finished film you saw was a complete distortion, a parody of what I wanted to do. I disown it. Zanuck hammered it to pieces with that polo mallet he used to carry."*

On the other hand, Zanuck insisted that Mankiewicz collaborated with him on the version of *Cleopatra* the public eventually saw, and that they went to Almería in Spain together to shoot new scenes that Zanuck had drafted and Mankiewicz scripted. They were designed to strengthen Antony's character and allow him to stand up to Cleopatra, because, according to Mankiewicz, Zanuck still went around muttering:

"If any woman treated me that way, I'd kick her in the balls."

*Cleopatra* was finally presented for the first time at a garish premiere in New York, and Times Square was packed with crowds who were not so much interested in the film as in seeing its two stars, Richard Burton and Elizabeth Taylor. That was how it worked out at the box office, too. They paid to see Burton and Taylor, and hardly noticed the film.

It still took a long time, however, for it to earn back its $35,000,000 cost, though it eventually did so.

For the support and encouragement which he had given him during the making of *The Longest Day,* Zanuck appointed Elmo Williams to the

*Conversation with Thomas Quinn Curtiss, op. cit.

post of chief of the London office and head of Fox film production in
Europe. Slowly, Richard Zanuck was bringing the Fox studios in Hollywood back to life, and the old-timers whom he had sacked out of hand
on his father's orders were now being invited back to resume work on
the lot. But in the meantime, the cinemas and the Fox distribution organization which supplied them badly needed movies, and Williams was
urged by Zanuck to do his share in supplying them with product. He
made a couple of minor flops, *The Man in the Middle,* with Robert Mitchum, and *Third Secret,* directed by Charles Crichton, and then had a
stroke of luck. A young Greek actor-director named Michael Cacoyannis
came to see him one day and asked him if he was interested in backing
a film. He had originally promised it to United Artists but felt he had
been insulted by one of its directors, so he had walked out with his script.
Williams read it, agreed to make it, and suggested Anthony Quinn for
the leading role, and subsequently sent *Zorba the Greek* to the Fox
distribution organization.

About the same time, Zanuck telephoned Nunnally Johnson in London
and asked him if he would come to Paris. Johnson looked forward to the
reunion and thought it would be a pleasant social occasion. Instead, he
was dashed to find Zanuck puffing smoke in his face, a script with Johnson's
name on it in front of him, and saying fiercely, over and over:

"This screenplay will have to be rewritten."

Johnson had originally scripted *Take Her, She's Mine* as a film to star
James Stewart, and it had been officially accepted, and paid for, by the
former head of production at Fox, Peter Lavathes. But when he pointed
this out, Zanuck said:

"It's not accepted until I accept it."

"Look, Darryl," Johnson said, "there's nothing about that in my contract. . . . I can't do this without some payment for the extra work. You
point out it may take six to eight weeks, and it's unreasonable to expect
me to do it without payment."

Stubbornly Zanuck shook his head.

"And I can't pay you until you do the work," he said.

Johnson went to see his attorney, who in turn took him to see Fox's
attorney. The Fox attorney agreed Johnson had fulfilled his part of the
contract, and nodded his head when Johnson threatened to sue them and
added: "We'll win."

"I know you will," said the Fox attorney. "But that won't be until next
year, and we'll swap a losing suit next year for not having to pay out any
money right now."

He pointed to a pile of contracts on his desk and added: "See those? They're all suing for money we owe them. We're not paying any of them, not a nickel, because we haven't got it. They've offered to settle, some of them, for fifty cents on the dollar. When they come down to ten cents on the dollar, we might make a deal."

Eventually, Johnson and Zanuck got back together and came to an amicable arrangement. It was then Johnson discovered what kind of alterations Zanuck wanted. *Take Her, She's Mine* was a very American story, about a typical college girl, and Zanuck felt it wouldn't be understood outside the United States, that it needed an international flavor. So he paid Johnson handsomely to rewrite the whole of the last third of the script and move the action to Paris.

"Of course it didn't work," said Johnson later. "I wrote a lousy third act, and the French, when they saw it in the film, didn't understand it any more than the Americans did. But he was very international just then, and he insisted on it."

Johnson got an uneasy feeling during his sessions with Zanuck. He sensed the new president of Fox was already bored with the job, mainly because he felt out of touch with the studios, and that his new post simply didn't give him anything satisfactory to do. The creative side of the business had passed out of his hands. It was his son, Richard, who was in charge of production now, and although they spoke to each other for an hour every day, no matter where they happened to be, and although Richard was meticulous in detailing his activities, decisions, progress reports of movies being shot, it wasn't the same. After so long away, Zanuck plainly missed Hollywood. He missed the Fox studio lot. He missed being able to wander around, go onto any set, argue with a director, criticize a script, a star, a camera angle, bed any starlet who took his fancy.

His son suspected (although he never talked about it) that his father had taken a vow never to return to Hollywood so long as he remained separated from his wife, so long as Virginia was still around and patiently waiting for him. There was guilt lurking around there, somewhere. But in the meantime, in between the board meetings in New York, he just seemed to be marking time. Irina had gone out of his life temporarily, and though he had instigated her departure himself, he realized after she had gone that it was a mistake. He had sent her on a world tour, publicizing the international premieres of *The Longest Day*. Her mothering attitudes had begun to get on his nerves, and there were other ways in which familiarity was beginning to breed apathy and boredom. But her absence, and his own loneliness, his own need to prove that age was not affecting him, spurred him into reverting to his old habits.

"I was running the studio," said Richard later, "and he was in Europe, playing around. He had lots of women, and he became notorious at the gambling casinos all over Europe and on the Riviera as an aging playboy. In some peculiar way during that period of our lives we had reversed roles. I became the father and he was the son. We had some very frank and strange discussions. They were quite unique in that I would be telling him — as he had told me years before — 'For God's sake, can't you go out with the same girl twice? Why do you have to have a different girl every night?' You know, that's just what you tell your high-school son. 'You're staying out too late and not getting enough sleep.' 'Don't make a fool of yourself in public,' and those kind of things."

Richard would endeavor, amid their daily business discussions, to offer his father sensible advice, and although he felt embarrassed in doing so, he believed his father was accepting his words in the spirit in which they were offered.

"I became to him the voice of practicality and realism," he said. "Sometimes he would abide by what I said because I was living a rational life at that time and it made sense to him."

Or so he thought. What Richard Zanuck failed, perhaps, to realize was that his father was not only beginning to be bored out of his mind by executive, noncreative activities, but he was also becoming increasingly envious of his son, who was right there in Hollywood in the thick of things, taking all the risks, making all the creative decisions. A touchy and dangerous period was beginning in their lives.

Richard Zanuck was not at that time a man much given to self-analysis, but he had begun to worry sometimes over the nature of the relationship between his father and himself. He would always remember that curious incident towards the end of his childhood when he had beaten his father in a wrestling match, and he had sensed it had marked a turning point in their feelings one for the other. Why had he so suddenly stopped being willing to play second best to his father and refused to surrender to him any longer when they horsed around together? And why should the fact that he had reversed their roles, forced his father to ask for mercy from *him* rather than vice versa, have filled him with such a sudden surge of triumph, followed by such a pang of guilt? And why had his father looked so stricken when it had happened, refused ever to wrestle with him again, and treated him so differently from then on?

Their relations were different, he had no doubt about that. He not only sensed that his father had changed in his attitude towards him, but Richard knew his attitude towards his father had changed too. In his childhood days, when he had simply worshiped and admired his dad, he had wished for nothing more than to emulate him, be as great as he was, be recognized as a worthy son of a brilliant man. But was that true any longer? Since moving into the studio, since beginning to make his mark as a producer of films, would it not be truer to say that he didn't just want to be like his father any longer? He wanted to be better than his father was. Just as being second best had no longer been good enough when he was a growing boy, now being level with Darryl F. Zanuck was no longer his goal as a grown man. He wanted to pass him, to beat him, to do better than he had ever done. Be Richard Zanuck. Number One. And that made him feel both excited and guilty all over again.

The first sign there was something amiss with their grown-up relation-ship developed during the making of a movie based on the life of a famous World War II general, George Patton. Significantly, it was Richard who caused the upset.

By this time, 20th Century–Fox had made a marvelous financial re-covery, thanks in part to Zanuck's firm hand on the administrative helm in New York, but possibly even more to Richard's skill (and good luck) as head of production at the studio in Hollywood. He had initiated a series of films that more than consolidated the recovery begun by *The Longest Day*.

Richard had shown he possessed an instinctive (or inherited) flair for picking good box-office subjects for movies. It was he who had seen the burgeoning interest among young cinemagoers for outer-space and other-worldly subjects, and he had put into production a film called *Planet of the Apes*, which shrewdly capitalized on growing American skepticism with its own kind by making apes superior beings and humans their often brutish inferiors. Not only was *Planet of the Apes* a large moneymaker for Fox but so were the sequels which followed.*

Then his instinct for anticipating public taste told him to try a musical, and on the recommendation of Fox's story chief, David Brown, who was also his friend and trusted adviser, he bought the rights to a musical about the Trapp family in Austria; and with Julie Andrews as its star, and David

---

*He also made two other smash hits, *The French Connection* and *Butch Cassidy and the Sundance Kid*.

Wise as its director, turned it into one of the most successful film musicals in the history of the movies, *The Sound of Music*. The money from the box office just flowed into Fox's empty coffers. He followed that with a daring, mocking comedy about the Korean war called *M\*A\*S\*H*, which was a box-office success (and also a popular TV series in which Fox retained a financial interest).

"Many of the projects at the studio were completely mine," Richard said later. "*M\*A\*S\*H* was completely mine. To my knowledge, he [Zanuck] never read the book. I don't know whether he ever read the screenplay or not. I would come to the board meetings and give them a description of the subject matter, and he would hear about it for the first time. He was very receptive and encouraging and backed me completely. On other projects, I don't think he ever interfered. Frankly, going back to the very beginning, he literally saw the first frame of *The Sound of Music* at the premiere in New York. He was spending more and more time overseas, and I was having his backing without his interfering at all. Which was wonderful."

But *Patton* was different.

The script for a movie of the life of General George Patton, the brilliant but braggart and bullying hero of the war in Western Europe, had been hanging around Fox studios for some time. It was the enthusiastic baby of a remarkable film man named Frank McCarthy.

Brigadier General McCarthy had served in World War II as chief aide to that brilliant soldier General George C. Marshall, who was Chief of Staff of the U.S. Army during the war. Like Dwight Eisenhower, Patton was one of the men Marshall had picked for advancement, and also one whose career he had several times saved when politicians started screaming for his dismissal.* It was Frank McCarthy who had had the delicate job of getting the rebellious and loudmouthed Patton back in line, and he had grown fascinated with him as a human phenomenon.

After the end of the war, McCarthy had gone to Paris as representative there of the American Motion Picture Producers Association, and then returned to Hollywood, where he became aide to Darryl Zanuck. Zanuck encouraged him to go into the production side of the industry, and from the start he cherished the idea of turning Patton's life into a movie.

"When I mentioned this to Darryl — I guess this was about 1950 —

---

*The nearest he came to being fired was after he slapped a GI suffering from shellshock in a Sicilian hospital and called him a coward.

he said, 'Oh yes, it's a great idea,' " McCarthy recalled later. "But he was busy with a great many other things, and I was still only an apprentice, looking on, and though I talked again about the film to Darryl from time to time, he never let me go ahead, though he did let me employ some inexpensive writers to see what would come out of it."

It was only after the success of *The Longest Day* that the project came up again. Richard Zanuck had now become head of the studio and McCarthy mentioned it to him.

"I think it's a marvelous idea," Dick said. "Let's get going with it."

"Well," replied McCarthy, a little skeptical by this time, "we've tried so many writers on the thing, more than you can think of, that I think the only way to get a treatment is to try something entirely new."

McCarthy called up the Film School at UCLA and asked them who was "the most promising screenwriter who came out of your graduating class last June?"

"A guy named Francis Coppola," they said.

So McCarthy had Coppola over to see him at Fox and asked him whether he would try his hand at doing a screenplay about General Patton. He was so young he knew only vaguely who Patton was, and reluctantly agreed to accept some money to try to turn his life into a film.

"Coppola was an outrageous-looking character," McCarthy recalled. "Did you as a child ever have one of those toys with a round bottom, and you could push it over and no matter how you pushed it would always spring up again? That was Coppola. All bottom and beard. I gave him some stories about Patton and he came and put the material together, and about the second day he arrived in my office with the opening of the film. It was Patton's famous 'blood and guts' speech to his troops, and it was a brilliant attention-getter."

Coppola proved to be expert at re-creating events in Patton's life but he had no sense of narrative line, and he quickly became bored with the subject, anyway. In any case, one of the studios had offered to finance the film script he had written for his film school thesis, and he itched to get away and do it.*

"So I finally let him go," said McCarthy, "and brought in another writer who knitted Coppola's scenes together and gave it a hard-driving narrative line."

So they were ready to go. But at this point Darryl Zanuck "injected himself into *Patton*," as McCarthy put it. A summons arrived for Mc-

*It became Francis Ford Coppola's first film, *You're a Big Boy Now.*

Carthy and the director, Frank Schaffner, to go and confer with him in Europe. "I suppose he wanted to get involved because he was a World War II buff and because of *The Longest Day,*" said Richard. "But it became a problem for me."

It became a problem because Darryl Zanuck did not bother to tell his son he had summoned McCarthy and Schaffner to see him in the South of France, and Richard discovered it only by accident. Moreover, once they arrived at Cap d'Antibes, Zanuck strongly criticized the script that Richard and McCarthy had already approved, and insisted on making drastic changes.

"He was very contentious," McCarthy said. "I think he was still trying to show he could run things by remote control, and I think he also wanted to keep his hand in. I became aware for the first time of the tension between him and his son. However, I think it is fair to say that Dick went along with me on everything, and Dick managed to prevail."

What McCarthy never learned was that Zanuck's objections were not overcome quite as easily as that. There were acrid exchanges between father and son, and several extremely sour and very long telegrams.

"My father had never interfered with any of my other projects," Richard said later. "I did understand that he took a particular interest in *Patton.* But I felt that this was a challenge to my authority, and I told him so in a telegram. It was a challenge to my authority for other directors to think they could go over me to him, and get their way, when I was supposed to be running the show. I had to make him see that."

He added: "In that respect, I suppose I made a little more out of it than I should have done. This isn't known, but I ended up resigning from the company. I walked out over that. McCarthy and Schaffner knew nothing about it. I resigned for a few days. Then my father backed down, sent me a nice telegram, and things were patched up. I came back."

*Patton* went ahead on the script McCarthy and Richard had approved between them. And, of course, it not only proved a highly successful movie but also won an Oscar for McCarthy.* And the scene that grabbed audiences more than any other was its opening, as written by Francis Coppola.

So all seemed to be smoothed over. But neither father nor son forgot their differences over the film. Nor that, in the final confrontation, it was Zanuck who was forced to back down.

---

*The Sound of Music* and *The French Connection* also won Oscars.

*     *

Regularly, once a week, Elmo Williams would fly over from London where he was now head of Fox's British operation, to report or consult with Darryl Zanuck about his projects.

"He rarely came to England himself," Williams said later. "It was as if he had suddenly conceived an antipathy for England. He only visited it two or three times in the whole three years I was there."

Two of those occasions were in connection with the making of the film *Those Magnificent Men in Their Flying Machines,* which had been written by the English screenwriter, Jack Davies, about a 1910 cross-Channel air race. Fox took it over from the Rank Organization, to whom Davies and his collaborator, Ken Annakin, had sold it. Once Zanuck knew that Annakin was connected with it, he gave it the studio's fullest backing, contingent on Annakin directing the film. He now had great faith in him and knew how well he could capture spectacular scenes. He did not fail to have a small and irrelevant role written into the script for Irina, and both Davies and Annakin hated to have to put it in, but in the event it proved an effective contrast to the part played by the main female star, Sarah Miles.

Zanuck flew in a party of eighty journalists from Paris to watch the main flying sequence in the film, when all the pre–World War I planes took to the air, but otherwise kept away from the production. But once a rough cut of the completed movie was ready, Annakin departed to direct *The Battle of the Bulge* in Spain, and Williams and Zanuck took *Flying Machines* to the cutting rooms and polished it.

"I have to admit," said Annakin later, "that when I saw *Flying Machines* next it was on opening night at the Dominion Theatre in London. I flew in from Madrid and I hadn't seen the final dub until that night. I think they did a marvelous job. Zanuck was there — with Irina. He had obviously worked quite closely with Elmo and he was very high on the film. He put on a dinner afterwards and was very complimentary."

Annakin felt let down by Zanuck on only one aspect of the film.

"Both Jack [Davies] and I wanted Dick Van Dyke for the leading male role in *Flying Machines*," he said, "and in fact Jack had written the part especially for him. [This was the period when Van Dyke was enjoying world popularity as a TV star.] We relied upon Richard Zanuck and Fox studios to supply our Hollywood stars, and so we sent a script and a request for Van Dyke through Zanuck *père* to his son. Back came word that Van Dyke had turned us down."

Two years later Annakin and his wife, Pauline, ran into Dick Van Dyke in the South of France, and the actor congratulated them on *Flying Machines* and said he wished he had been in it.

"Well, you *were* sent the script," said Pauline Annakin.

"I swear the script never came to me," said Van Dyke.

"And of course that was Dick's doing," said Annakin. "He allocated Stuart Whitman to us, because he was doing a two-picture deal with him. That was one time when I felt that Zanuck, with all his power and all the good things about him, deliberately accepted the second best. He knew Whitman was not a comedic actor, but he wanted to be nice to Dick — and that was a let-down, a bitter disappointment."

But if he wished to be nice to his son, he did not always show it in his dealings with him. The strain between the two was now beginning to tighten, even if neither of them was aware of it, and Elmo Williams noted Zanuck was increasingly restless. His moods were not improved by his need now to divest himself of Irina. Zanuck always liked to convince himself — and his girlfriends — that he could turn them into great stars, but once again he was beginning to realize that this one, like Darvi and Greco, would never make it. Sometimes he was heard to say that "Irina isn't bitch enough, she's far too nice," and the cynics around him would wonder, "Is he talking about her film career or their sex life?"

"During that period," said Richard, "when he was in Europe playing around, I had many hard decisions to make. He was acting foolishly, and there were times when I had to cover for him. He was concerned with my efforts to try to hide his lack of activity. He became a little paranoid about my help, and he interpreted that as putting him out to pasture. That's an exact quote, 'You're trying to put me out to pasture.' "

Determined that he would not be remembered solely as a playboy who put his girlfriends into flop movies, Zanuck was searching desperately for a subject that would get him back into production in a manner commensurate with his past reputation. Williams would walk around Paris with him while they discussed possible projects, and in the course of their peregrinations Zanuck would take him into all the Left Bank restaurants where Hemingway used to sit and drink, pointing out the places where he had once held court among his circle of admirers.

"He worshipped Hemingway," Williams said. "It was a sort of pilgrimage. He seemed sad that he might not be remembered in the way that Hemingway was, and sometimes speculated whether *The Longest Day* would earn him a place in the pantheon."

He toyed with all kinds of subjects. One of them that took his fancy was a movie about a World War I hero of the battles in East Africa, General Paul von Lettow-Vorbeck, who drew a quarter of a million British Empire troops away from the battlefields in France between 1914 and 1919, when he surrendered on orders from the exiled Kaiser. Since I had written a book about it, *Duel for Kilimanjaro*, he had a long series of discussions at the Cannes Film Festival with me about it and I got to know him very well as a result.

Finally, however, he decided it was still too soon after the end of World War II to make a German the hero of an American war film, and he went on to other things. Going through Fox's list of acquisitions in New York, he came across a book called *The Broken Seal*, by Ladislas Farrago, which had been bought as a possible movie, but a succession of scriptwriters had tried to find a film plot and failed. The book dealt with code-breaking and other intelligence secrets of World War II, and Zanuck was convinced he had discovered a good story-line when he read the section dealing with Pearl Harbor. He contacted Richard Zanuck in California and asked for a treatment to be written. At the same time, Elmo Williams tried his hand at drawing up a plan and an outline. He had been promised that if and when a film came out of it, he would be the producer. It would deal with the events leading up to the Japanese attack on Pearl Harbor, and Zanuck was soon certain it would do for the Pacific war what *The Longest Day* had done for the war in Western Europe. Someone came up with a striking title: *Tora! Tora! Tora!* (Japanese for "Tiger! Tiger! Tiger!")

From the production point of view, Williams realized that it would be very different from *The Longest Day*.

"Because there," he said, "I had managed to find all the equipment and promoted the navy into helping. In the case of *Tora! Tora! Tora!* there was nothing left, because we had destroyed all the Jap planes. The only ones left were wrecks in the jungle somewhere in New Guinea or the Marshall Islands. So I had no aircraft to work with, and I had no physical way of doing the picture."

Nevertheless, Zanuck was now fizzing with enthusiasm, and during a succession of meetings with Richard in New York he managed to pass on some of it to his son. Richard was at that time involved in making a movie of "John Brown's Body," to be directed by the British director Guy Green, and he had financial problems. After the tremendous successes of the past few years, he was moving into a cycle of hard times and badly needed a hit. But he was so pleased to see his father active, eager, and around films again he readily agreed to the *Tora! Tora! Tora!* project, confident he could fit both films into his budget.

Then he heard what his father and Elmo Williams had in mind for the production of *Tora!*

"Not only did I have no Japanese planes to work with," said Williams, "but there were no ships, either. They'd all been sunk. I decided that a lot of the film should be done from the Japanese point of view, which would enable me to buy aircraft miniatures of Jap planes to show the attack. And when I studied the ships, I found out that we had two basic types of battleships, and one of them had a unique superstructure and a spiral observation tower with a ladder that gave it a very unusual look. I decided if I could build part of the two of these ships as set pieces, we could do the whole picture."

He called in an artist and set him to making a series of drawings to illustrate his concept.

"How much is it going to cost?" asked Zanuck.

"How much do you want it to cost?" replied Williams. "Darryl, we can build a whole fleet for millions of dollars and make it very real, or I can have a guy run out of a house and you can put an explosion over him and a big sound track, and indicate that that's the end of the fleet — and it'll cost you nothing."

Zanuck waved a lordly hand.

"It's got to be like *The Longest Day*," he said.

"In that case," said Williams, "I'll have to see what I can do."

"*Tora!* was a picture that we were all involved in — my father, myself, David Brown [head of the story department], Elmo, and a couple of other people," said Richard Zanuck, "and initially we were very enthusiastic about it. There was some concern — and I shared it — that unlike *The Longest Day* this was the story of a defeat, and that the ending, no matter how we tried to twist it to get over that, was too downbeat. Then too somehow this film would be more difficult to personalize than the way my father had personalized the characters in *The Longest Day*. It would be more difficult to cast, because, unlike *The Longest Day*, which had only a brief scene with Eisenhower, *Tora!* constantly dealt with characters whom we recognized, especially in Washington, D.C. They were real people."

When the first provisional budget came out, Richard Zanuck was appalled. It was $20,000,000.

"Everybody was shocked," he said. "We never anticipated that it would cost that much."

Then, as the weeks went by, the budget grew and grew.

"The project became a pet of my father's," said Richard, "because of his love of the whole period. He had studied it, he was quite an expert on it."

At a meeting of the Fox board in New York, doubts were expressed both about the box-office possibilities of the film and its growing cost. Zanuck, seething with anger, determined now not to be thwarted, rose to his feet and poured scorn on the doubters. He had encountered the same stupid opposition when he had started making *The Longest Day*, he reminded them, and had come perilously close to having it halted in mid-production by the board. And what had happened after the film was completed? Its success had saved 20th Century–Fox in its hour of financial need.

"He got very excited and he ramrodded it through," said Richard. "And there were casualties on my production list. 'John Brown's Body' was one of them, and there were several others. We just couldn't afford to make them once *Tora!* was decided upon. And my God, was it a nightmare!"

Elmo Williams was now working full-time on the production preliminaries. He "did not find it a very happy experience for a lot of reasons," he said later.

"First of all," he said, "Dick and Darryl weren't getting along at all well. And Dick being head of production, that meant that I was reporting to him. Darryl, on the other hand, was taking a very personal interest in the film and on several occasions he said: 'Now look, you report direct to me. Don't report to Dick.' This made a very difficult situation for me, and I tried reporting to both and keeping things straight."

He said he had one idea that he found difficult to persuade either of them to accept at first. He proposed that Akira Kurosawa, the famous Japanese director, be given the job of directing the Japanese sections of the film. (Richard Fleischer would be directing the American sections.)

"Oddly enough," Williams said, "neither Dick nor Darryl knew much about Kurosawa. I mentioned his name and they asked me who he was — two or three times, before they understood."

It was Richard who eventually finalized the deal for Kurosawa's participation through his representatives, since he refused to come to America. Williams went to Japan to work with him on the script, and then shooting of the Japanese sections began. To Williams's dismay, Kurosawa immediately "started spending money like crazy." He had ordered built a full-size replica of the battleship *Nagato* out of plywood, with its prow sticking out into the sea.

"The costs escalated quite a bit," Williams said, "and then he started shooting, and he only shot six minutes of film in six weeks. So we were obviously in real trouble, and Darryl came over. He ordered me to fire Kurosawa, and I said I couldn't do that. That caused a real crisis. Darryl and Dick got together in New York, and eventually I got a telegram some time in December [1969] to say: 'FORGET ABOUT JAPAN. FORGET ABOUT MAKING ANYTHING OVER THERE. TAKE THE WHOLE PICTURE OVER TO HAWAII. CANCEL ALL THOSE SETS.' And I felt that if we couldn't make the film with part of it in Japan, using the Japanese and using a Japanese director, then we wouldn't have the right kind of film. So I demanded to talk."

It was now Christmastime. Zanuck, having flown to Switzerland, had gone out skiing with a new girlfriend (who was very young) and had once more taken a tumble, this time breaking his leg. Richard Zanuck had taken his wife down to Acapulco for the holidays. Williams put in a conference call from Tokyo, via the studio in Hollywood, to talk to the other two "and it was a fiasco." Richard Zanuck was all in favor of calling the whole thing off.

"We'll have to take a bath," he said. "It will cost us two or three million dollars to pay all those people off."

Zanuck was adamantly against that, and furious with his son for suggesting it. Williams offered his resignation, and was dissuaded by Zanuck. It was finally decided that the film should go ahead, "and it was all systems go from that point on," Richard said.

Then the footage from Kurosawa started coming in from Japan, and Richard Zanuck found it "quite dreadful." There was something about the style and the acting that made it seem comical to Western eyes.

"They all moved around like they were in speeded-up motion," Richard said. "And this was a picture costing twenty-three million dollars!"

Since Williams was producer of the whole picture, he had to spend a good deal of time in Honolulu, where Richard Fleischer was directing. And while he was away from Japan, high winds partially destroyed the *Nagato* and it had to be rebuilt at great expense.

"Then we began getting certain reports from Japan," said Richard, "that disturbed us. Kurosawa seemed to be having a nervous breakdown. On one particular day, I remember, he drove onto the set in a tank, and he was wearing a steel helmet. Then there was a scene in a room which was painted white, and he decided it wasn't white enough, so he had everybody, including members of the cast, take paint brushes and start painting the white walls whiter. And then he had the habit of rolling up his script and hitting people over the head with it when he was displeased."

Abruptly, Kurosawa was hospitalized, and so the unit had to shut down.

"At this point I got a terrible assignment," Richard said. "I was told by the board of directors to go over and fire Kurosawa. I called up my father and told him what I was doing, and he agreed it had to be done. But he did not take it well. He thought it should have been done sooner."

Richard flew into Tokyo with Stanley Hough, who was then part of the Fox production department, and they went straight to the Imperial Hotel.

"I was actually very scared," Richard said. "[Kurosawa] was a national hero. He was a king over there. I was worried for my personal safety. Some rather threatening telegrams arrived at the Imperial Hotel."

He tried to make an appointment with Kurosawa, but the director refused to see him. Finally, he had to send him a message through the head of Fox's local office that he was through.

"You know, the whole thing was a shambles," Richard said. "I stayed there about a week looking at all kinds of Japanese films, and trying to find a substitute director. Well, none of the top Japanese directors wanted to find themselves in the position of replacing Kurosawa, so I found myself watching karate pictures, we were down to that level. In addition to that, the cast refused to go on. It was really a mess, a terrible mess. I remember how glad I was to be boarding the plane and getting out of there."

But he dreaded the moment when *Tora! Tora! Tora!* had its world premiere. He felt in his bones that this was a disaster film, and there was no chance it would repeat the success of *The Longest Day.*

He was right about that. *Tora! Tora! Tora!* opened to a chorus of nitpicking reviews and never really succeeded at the box office. It had some splendidly spectacular scenes, but it had to be faced that — unlike the British, for example — the American people got no lift out of hymning their military defeats, and their spirits did not soar at the sight of the disaster of Pearl Harbor, to which the movie devoted much of its action. Sage old movie veterans predicted that nevertheless *Tora!* would eventually cover its costs and make a profit, even if it failed to become an immediate hit — and that is what has since happened. But Richard Zanuck knew his father longed — and needed — a hit now, for psychological as well as financial reasons. He had a pang as he watched his face as they came away from the premiere. Darryl was too old a hand not to realize that this was far from being the big blockbuster hit on which he had set his sights. Just the opposite, in fact, for it was almost a flop. What was it going to do to his morale when he began to measure the full extent of his failure?

There were troublesome times ahead for Darryl Zanuck. And also for his son.

# TWENTY-SEVEN

# O ABSALOM!

**D**EEPLY INVOLVED though he might be in the outcome of his *Tora! Tora! Tora!* production, Zanuck did not allow it to interfere with the other activities in France that his post as president of 20th Century–Fox allowed him to indulge. He was still busy collecting new girlfriends and proving to the world that though he was now 67 years old, he was still fighting fit, attractive and virile. He was rarely seen around without a pretty girl on his arm, and he still liked to reward these girlfriends for their devotion to him by trying to turn them into stars. Gossip writers in Paris and London would speculate about which of the girls he escorted to premieres, clubs, and openings would be the next to have her shapely feet set on those golden stairs. Britt Eklund? Claudia Cardinale?

The gossips whispered that the only reason he made films in France these days was to pay off his mistresses for sexual services rendered, and pointed out that most of them had Irina Demick in them, until he tired of her, and then someone equally unknown and even less experienced, Genevieve Gilles. It was not so, he replied. Even if it were true that the films were made "economically" and did not have famous stars, and even if they did feature very young girls who were known to be his mistresses, these films were still being made for a very important purpose. "He kept telling us that from a distribution standpoint, we had to have these locomotives,"* said Richard Zanuck later. "He maintained you couldn't get our American pictures played in French cinemas unless you made a certain number of pictures over there in France. Well, I saw this as just hooey. They were just going down the drain, down the drain. I kept

---

*An industry term for "program" films.

telling him: 'It's better that our American pictures don't play at all than waste all this money on these terrible pictures.' Of course a lot of the girlfriends were in the pictures and it kept them happy."

They were terrible pictures largely because the girls in them were so inexperienced. Just about this time, Milton Sperling was in Paris. It was 1969. He was walking along a street off the Champs Elysees when he suddenly saw Darryl Zanuck sitting at a sidewalk table in the Café Alexandre.

"He was fondling a small poodle, wearing dark glasses, and looking haggard. He was waiting for the mistress of the dog, and I presume she was also his mistress. He looked like an old man. It broke my heart, just broke my heart, to see him like that because I had known him when."

He learned Zanuck was making a film at the Billancourt Studios, and later that day he got a call from his old friend, Jean Negulesco, who told him he was directing the film. It starred Curt Jurgens, Michael Crawford, and the new girl in Zanuck's life, Genevieve Gilles. Negulesco told Sperling that Ronald Neame had originally been hired as director of the film, but after a few days had "arranged to have himself sacked so he could collect the money." Zanuck had searched all over for a replacement but could not persuade anyone to take it on, and so had called on Negulesco out of old friendship.

"Come out and see this monstrosity," Negulesco said, "with this awful girl."

"She couldn't act at all," said Sperling. "Jean, who had been out of work for three years and was desperate, had reluctantly taken five thousand dollars a week to make the film. I came onto the set to watch the following scene: telephone ringing, and Gilles having to come out of the bedroom to the living room and down three steps to answer the phone. Zanuck was at the back smoking his large cigar. Lights — camera — action. Negulesco: 'All right, dear, come on.' She came down the steps and stumbled on the first step. He said, mildly: 'You must look down at the step when you come down the step.' She finally got to the phone, where she was supposed to say: 'Hello.' She said 'Yes' instead. It was 11 A.M. They wrapped for lunch."

That was the only scene they made that morning. So Sperling said to Negulesco: "How long is this going on?"

"Forever, I hope," said Negulesco.

The film was called *Hello and Goodbye*. It was finally completed at a cost of $4,000,000 and died a horrible death at the box office.

For a time, the fact that Zanuck was making these "locomotives" did not unduly worry the Fox board, and Richard was glad that they "kept him busy and kept his girlfriends happy." He did not try to be too censorious about them.

"I didn't try to be a Goody-Two-Shoes but it was an uncomfortable situation from many standpoints, especially when we ceased to be as successful as we had been. No one wants to see his father making a fool of himself in front of other people. But there was another factor. What happened fundamentally was that there was a fear among his closest associates in New York that if something weren't done, there would be severe criticism by the board and the stockholders."

Richard was approached by some of the board members who were closest to Zanuck with the suggestion that he avert criticism by moving in and becoming president of Fox himself, with his father filling the role of chairman of the board. When Zanuck came over to New York he listened to the proposal and agreed at once.

"It was the logical move to make," Richard said. "He was out of touch with Hollywood and the studio. In the whole period of eight or nine years, he couldn't have spent more than two or three days out here [in Hollywood] the whole time. He had his own personal reasons for that. At any rate, he was spending more and more time overseas, and, quite frankly, he seemed to be going through an early stage of senility. They convinced him and they convinced me. He was moved up to chairman of the board and I was made president."

Richard later maintained he really didn't like his promotion at all, especially since it meant he had to spend even more time than ever flying back and forth between the studio and New York. But he would not have been human had he not been proud of his new eminence in the world of cinema. He was now in control of everything, both the creative and the administrative side of Fox, and what he now decided was the law of the studio. No man, not even his father, could now tell him what to do. He was the master of everything.

On the other hand, Darryl Zanuck would not have been Darryl Zanuck had he not begun to regret his acceptance of the decision once it was made. He was only too well aware of its significance. He had been kicked upstairs. While it was not yet a question of *The king is dead, long live the king*, it certainly reflected the board of directors' conviction that the king was moribund and a regent was needed to rule in his place.

His suspicion he had been outmaneuvered was hardly soothed by the reaction of his girlfriend when he got back to Pais and told her of the new development. She was indignant. A Paris newspaper had picked up the rumor from Hollywood that Zanuck was becoming senile, and she was outraged — not so much on his behalf but as an insult to her. What did they think she was? Did they really think she would cast in her lot with a senile old man?

"You have been tricked," she said. "Tricked by your son."

So furious was she, indeed, that she persuaded Zanuck to fly back to New York at once and try to reverse the board's decision. And when the board refused to do so, Zanuck angrily stormed around the board room, complaining loudly that he had been the victim of "the con job of the century."

"He was convinced I had deliberately put him out to pasture," Richard said. "He did not consult me about it. He simply started drinking again, angrily complaining that I had taken everything away from him. Egged on by his girlfriends, he began stalking around New York and Paris and saying there was no longer room for the two of us at 20th Century–Fox. The situation deteriorated rapidly. He became certain I had just weaseled my way in in order to eliminate him. Of course it wasn't so."

It was unfortunate that father and son did not meet at this time. Richard maintains that if he had fully understood how his father was feeling, he would have flown to see him and tried to explain the situation to him.

But it didn't happen. Richard Zanuck, the new president of 20th Century–Fox, was snowed under with problems, and did not communicate with Darryl Zanuck, the new chairman of the board. And the result was disastrous.

"What was happening," said Richard of his father, "was that he was determined to be revenged and draw some blood himself."

Hollywood can be a cruel place when things are going wrong for a producer, a writer, a director, a star — or the head of a studio. Decent motives and honest toil do not count for much in this company town if all they lead to is failure. Failure elicits no pity, no sympathy, only contempt. As Richard Zanuck said:

"This is a town where only success counts. You can get away with anything except murder so long as your pictures are successful. And if they are super-successful, maybe even with murder too."

Unfortunately for him, his honeymoon at Fox was over. After his great successes with *Patton*, *M\*A\*S\*H*, *Planet of the Apes*, and *The Sound of Music*, his flair for picking winners had faltered. Desperate to repeat the box-office bonanza created by the success of *The Sound of Music*, he had brought together the same star (Julie Andrews) and the same director

(Robert Wise) in another musical, hoping that the formula would work again. But with *Star!* it did not. The film died at the box office. Two other musicals that looked good on paper to Richard and his partner, David Brown, turned out to be expensive failures. *Dr. Doolittle* (with Rex Harrison) whimpered away and barely made back its costs. *Hello, Dolly!* (with Barbra Streisand) was a particularly costly disaster, because Fox had paid heavily for the film rights. Not only did the subsequent film wilt in the cinemas but its receipts did not even bear comparison with the profits made by the producer of the Broadway stage and touring company versions. And, of course, *Tora! Tora! Tora!* was a big financial disappointment.

In the volatile way in which these things can happen in Hollywood, Fox's reserves were swirling away like laundry water out of a washing machine, and the only detergent left behind to clean up the scum had been loaned by the banks. Fox was now getting by only thanks to huge overdrafts, and though the whole industry was going through a bad time, this did not prevent Fox's directors from being both uneasy and unhappy with the state of affairs, especially when the value of their shares dropped sharply on the New York Stock Exchange.

It was a moment when Richard Zanuck was particularly vulnerable. Seven fat years of big successes had been followed by two lean years of failure, and though his father and the board had all participated — or at least concurred — with his production ventures, it was he who was going to be saddled with responsibility for their failure. He was doing what he could and following the lead of the rest of Hollywood studios in cutting costs to lessen the impact of his losses. The general situation in the film industry was summed up in a story published by the *Hollywood Reporter* towards the end of 1969:

> The film studios are continuing to trim staffs as they liquidate inventories estimated at $400,000,000. MCA (which owns Universal) and 20th [Century–Fox] hit new lows for the year on the New York Stock Exchange. Universal has pink-slipped a number of senior executives and writers and members of the new Talent Division. . . . MGM has trimmed about 29% of its personnel and is expected to extend pink slips to another 25%. . . . At Warners the process will be extended over the next three or four months with new dismissal notices before the year end. . . . 20th Fox, where about 50 were pink-slipped about a month ago, is expecting another wave of dismissals.

To handle the tough financial measures he now considered necessary, Richard Zanuck had brought in an expert who had formerly acted as chief financial adviser to the *Los Angeles Times*. His name was Dennis C.

Stanfil. Stanfil was doing his best to ameliorate the fraught financial situation, and Richard was convinced they would get by — provided the
program he had set in motion for new productions paid off with some
real successes, and provided he could ride out the present financial crisis
by persuading both the board and the banks that he was going to weather
the storm. For that he needed his father's fullest support. But in the
circumstances, was he likely to get it?

Just about this time, Ken Annakin, who was living at that period in the
South of France, got a call at his home in Vence asking him if he would
come to Paris to talk to Genevieve Gilles. He saw her in her small
apartment not far away from the Hotel George Cinq, where Zanuck kept
a suite of rooms, and she said she wanted to discuss a film project. She
was a young, vital, very lovely young girl, hardly twenty years old, who
had already made a reputation in the fashion world of Paris as a model.
She had about her that air of supreme self-confidence and determination
that all film directors recognize in the young women with whom they so
often have to deal. It usually means that they have already had their eyes
on a goal and know exactly how they are going to get there. Annakin,
who is as susceptible to charm and beauty as the next man ("a director
who gets too cynical about actresses has lost the battle," he once said),
realized how completely she had won Darryl Zanuck's support when she
mentioned she had written a film story and wanted Annakin to direct it,
with herself, of course, as its star. She had called the story *Julia of the
Wolves* and it was all about a small, lonely girl, neglected by her parents,
who runs away into the forest and takes up with a pack of wolves; they
adopt and protect her. Annakin, reading the story with a certain skepticism, ended by being impressed both by Gilles's skill and knowledge
of wolf behavior, but also by her insight into loneliness and neglect. Only
at one moment during their talk did the subject of Darryl Zanuck's relationship with his son come up, and Annakin thereupon saw another side
of her completely. She was obviously deeply distressed by what she
considered the poor treatment her good friend had received at the hands
of his son.

It so happened that in Hollywood the question of Genevieve Gilles
had come up for discussion. Since he was now president of the company,
Richard Zanuck had to approve of all film projects for which 20th Century–
Fox would be paying the bills, and these inevitably included his father's
"locomotives." Most of them, nowadays, had Genevieve Gilles as their
star. She had been given a contract by Zanuck and this now came up for

renewal. It involved a substantial amount of money, and no critics who had seen her performance in *Hello and Goodbye* thought she had the qualities to make a star. Except Darryl Zanuck, of course.

When Dennis C. Stanfil mentioned the question of Gilles's contract and asked Richard what he was going to do about it, the moment of truth had obviously arrived — even if the younger Zanuck did not recognize it as such at the time. In a financial climate where economies were being made in every branch of studio activity, where veteran employees with many years of good and faithful service were being "pink-slipped," had he the right to approve an arrangement whereby the company went on paying for his father's girlfriend? That, at least, was the way he rationalized it. As president of the company, he felt he had no alternative.

"Tell Mlle. Gilles," he said, "that her contract is not being renewed." But who was going to tell his father?

By the fall of 1970, Richard Zanuck was well aware that his father was hurt and angry with him. He had become convinced that he had been victimized by his own son, and was determined to reverse the process and restore the situation. He was certain it had only been by a trick that he had been dethroned as king of 20th Century–Fox, and he wanted his powers back and all the trappings that went with them. His mood was savage and, some would have said, unbalanced, and he was demanding not just his own restoration but the humiliation of a son he now believed to be an upstart and an ingrate.

He could hardly have asked for better conditions in which to plot his revenge against his "usurper." Fox now had loans from the banks of over $110,000,000 and no immediate prospect of paying even the interest owing on them.

At the beginning of November 1970, Richard Zanuck heard his father was getting ready for a showdown. Darryl Zanuck moved across the Atlantic to the Plaza Hotel in New York. Genevieve, who had her own apartment on the East Side, moved into the Plaza when she discovered Zanuck had started drinking heavily, and she spent a good deal of time hiding bottles from him. They made one quick trip to Hollywood where they took two bungalows at the Beverly Hills Hotel. Zanuck did not go near the studio nor did he see Richard, but he received lots of visitors and was making all kinds of dispositions. Genevieve kept her eye on him.

"He was very clever, very subtle," she said later. "When he had an important business conference or something like that, he would never touch a drop, but he carried a flask and would take one drink just before

his conference began and one after . . . the icebox was in my bungalow
[in Hollywood]. He would sneak in at night and empty a full bottle. I
decided to tell his doctor, Lee Siegel. Siegel saw him on several occasions.*

There was a series of messy scenes in which Gilles cooly gave her lover
an ultimatum. Either he would give up drinking or she would walk out
on him. Coming on top of all the other humiliations he considered he
had suffered recently, this was a prospect he found too awful to accept.
There was a maudlin scene in which he wept and pleaded, and it finally
ended when he faithfully promised that he would never touch any alcohol
again. Gilles did not expect him to keep his promise. What old man of
sixty-eight, secretly drinking a bottle of spirits a day, could be expected
to straighten himself out? But he did.

"At first it was terrible for him," said Gilles. "He lost weight and could
not eat. When we left [Hollywood] for New York he could hardly walk.
The TWA man had almost to carry him onto the plane. When we arrived
in New York he had to be almost carried off the plane and Henry, his
chauffeur, helped me get him to his car. He never spoke a word. . . .
Gradually he began to eat and walk normally."†

She said later that she took no pride in his recovery, "but I would
never go through it again for any man, even if he was a combination of
Dustin Hoffman, Prince Philip and the Pope."

At Zanuck's behest, an emergency meeting of the board of directors of
20th Century–Fox was called for December 29, 1970. The day before,
Richard got a telephone call from Ted Ashley, who had taken over as
president of Warner Brothers studios.

"I hear DZ is starting a witch hunt against you," he said, "and terrible
things are being planned at that board meeting. I just want you to know
that if things go wrong, there's a place for you at Warners."

Richard thanked him and went to work himself. He had not watched
his father operate over the years without learning some of the tricks of
corporate life, and his objective now was to try to neutralize whatever it
was that his father was planning. One way to do it was to ensure that a
quorum failed to turn up at the meeting. That shouldn't be too hard to
arrange. After all, it was the holiday period between Christmas and New
Year's. Lots of people were away, in Florida or the Caribbean, or home

*Quoted by Mel Gussow, op. cit., p. 275.
†Ibid., pp. 275–276.

with their children. He knew his financial adviser, Dennis Stanfil, had been summoned to New York to supply information and vote, if and when called upon to do so. He called him in and said:

"For God's sake don't go to that meeting. Invent a diplomatic illness."

Stanfil decided he had to go, and took the plane for New York.

Even so, Richard only just failed to thwart his father's plans.

"There was barely a quorum, in fact," he said later, "because a lot of the members were aware of what was going on and didn't have the stomach to turn up. They just didn't show. They knew what was going to happen, that this was a railroad job. On the other hand, those who did show up didn't have the stomach to speak up against what was done."

Richard became fully aware of what was about to take place when a press release was circulated to members of the board before the discussion began, and when he glanced through it he saw that it contained an announcement of his resignation. When his father rose, the first thing he did was read the report of a committee he had initiated to inquire into Richard's competence as president of the company. It indicted him in severe terms for his lack of vision, lack of control over production programs, wastefulness, and administrative incompetence. Zanuck then proceeded to summarize the criticisms and to recommend that Richard be replaced as president of the company. He also proposed that the direction of Fox's affairs be placed back in the hands of those who handled them so efficiently in the past — in other words, his own.

Someone rose to put a motion. Richard was asked whether he had any comments to make before the motion was put to a vote, and he rose to his feet and tried to defend himself. But, in fact, he was stunned.

"I felt terribly let down that my own father could do this to me," he said. "He was very cold ass at that meeting, very cold ass. Jesus Christ, it was brutal. And my father, talking, just sitting there, he showed absolutely not any ray of compassion for me. And that hurt me. It was an execution — a very tough pill to swallow. It was cold, really cold."

The motion was put and carried. In a kind of painful daze, Richard sat in his chair and heard them discussing the question of his successor.

"Nobody was looking at me," he said. "It was like I had the plague, or something. And the loss of the company, my position. Everyone makes the mistake of assuming that their positions will go on forever, and it only came to me afterward that this was an occupational mistake, that nothing was permanent. Fox studios, which I had been controlling for so long, for nine years, a semi-demi king there, was suddenly no longer mine. It came as such a great loss that I no longer controlled it. And it made it no less agonizing that the man who had taken it away from me, who had replaced me, was my own father."

It might have been easier to bear had Zanuck shown any sympathy at all towards his son at that moment. Those who were present said he made no move, showed no emotion, listened without a glance at Richard as his own succession was voted. His son's numbness lasted all through the procedures that followed until, staring across the room at his father, Richard suddenly had a moment of realization.

"Here was the great tycoon restored," he said, "proving to the world — and particularly to me — that he was still a power to be reckoned with. But in a flash, I knew what had happened at that moment. If I had lost, so had he. He thought he had succeeded in getting everything he wanted. But I had heard a member of the investigating committee my father had set up [a director named William Gossett] insert a significant phrase into the resolution proposing that Darryl Zanuck be restored as president of Twentieth Century–Fox. He added what seemed to me to be fateful words — 'At the pleasure of the board.' I said to my father: 'Do you realize what that means? It means that at any moment they choose, they can dismiss you too.' Without more than a flicker of a glance at me, he shrugged his shoulders and casually said: 'It will never happen,' and went on to other business. I said: 'But it will. Watch out. You will be next.' He took no notice. He had won. I expect that night, when he told his girlfriend, she would be delighted."

Zanuck did not bother to say goodbye to Richard when the meeting was concluded, and few of the members of the board could bear to look at him when they went their separate ways. It was New Year's Eve when he flew back to Los Angeles, and he took the car straight to Fox studios, where his secretaries were waiting for him. Only then did he realize the extent of the humiliation his father had arranged for him.

When he came into his office, it was to find a studio guard waiting outside the door. His chief secretary, Lucy Ballentine, handed him a note. It informed him he was expected to be out of his offices and the studios by six o'clock that evening. As he went through his drawers, the guard kept interrupting him, pointing out that he could not be allowed to remove this file or that.

"It gave me an extraordinary feeling," he said later. "From being a king, or a crown prince, suddenly I was made to feel like a criminal. The guard was watching me as if I was about to steal an ashtray."

As it came near to six o'clock, and the time limit began to expire, Lucy Ballentine, close to tears, whispered to him that perhaps it was the moment for his departure. He went out of the administration building at last and crossed to the parking lot, where there was a place assigned for his car with his name painted on the curbside.

"When I got there, I saw there was a painter there," he said, "and I literally couldn't get into my car because he was on his hands and knees painting out my name. I said: 'I can't get into my car,' and he reluctantly stood up and backed off, so I could get in. I started the car and drove off down the lot and out of the gate. It had happened so fast it was like a death of some kind. I couldn't believe it. It was a nightmare and I kept wondering when I was going to awaken."

For the next few weeks he walked the beach at Santa Monica, going over and over the events as they had happened. On the few occasions when he did drive into Hollywood or Beverly Hills, "I didn't go by my customary route or even go anywhere near the studio, because I couldn't abide the place."

He added:

"All the columnists were writing, day after day, about what had happened to me. And everybody was talking about it, saying how shocked they were. It became a very boring subject eventually."

Not a word came from his father.

One person who was not bored by the subject, however, was Richard's mother. Virginia Zanuck was outraged at what had happened to her beloved son at the hands of her once-beloved husband. And she emerged from self-imposed purdah to make it clear to the world how she felt about it.

# TWENTY-EIGHT

# VIRGINIA REDUX

IN THE EARLY DAYS of Hollywood, when Virginia Zanuck was a dimpled Mack Sennett Bathing Beauty playing in custard-pie two-reelers, her producer once told her why she would one day make it to the top.

"There are two qualities that make a star in this business," Mack Sennett said. "One is acting genius, and not too many have that. Take comedians, for example. Any comic can make an audience laugh when he falls down, but the genius is the one who can make them laugh while he's getting up again."

She waited for him to name the second quality.

"Patience and tenacity," he said. "A strong bladder, a pair of durable feet, and the ability to hang in there and never give up. That's what you've got, Virginia. Patience and tenacity. Looks too," he added, hastily. "But that's your secret, staying power. If you want to, you can outlast them all."

It was true, and she knew it. She had an infinite capacity for hanging on.

When her husband had walked out on her fifteen years earlier, the one thing he had not said to her was: "Hang in there." He had, in fact, given her no hope at all that he would ever come back. And yet as the years went by, and one mistress succeeded another, she had begun to get what she was convinced was a message from her departed husband. For one thing, he had indicated clearly through his lawyers that he never intended to divorce her, and what else could that mean except that he was leaving his options open, and one day might be back?

"If I had gotten a divorce or a legal separation [from Virginia]," he was once quoted as saying, "I would have been married three times since. I would have had three more divorces. I would have had a lot less money and a lot more misery." But he had had his marriage to Virginia, still legal if inactive, to protect him from all that. What did that convey if not the fact that she was always there in the back of his mind, the life-belt he could grab when his follies threatened to engulf him?

Virginia Zanuck knew enough about her husband's proclivities to presume he would stay away from her, once having made the break, so long as the philandering was plentiful elsewhere and the young girls were still available. But how long could that last? He was now nearly sixty-nine years old, and even younger and younger female companions could not be expected to turn him on forever. The latest one was only just twenty. What would happen when she began to seem old at twenty-one, and even teenage tots failed to excite him?

The way Virginia saw it, Darryl must always have it clear in his mind that she was more than a barrier against the marital ambitions of rapacious mistresses. He must realize he was welcome home any time he became weary of the hunt, and the door would always be left unlocked for him.

To that end, to give him that reassurance, their son, Richard, had been a useful liaison between them over the years of separation, quite apart from his movie-making activities. She knew she had Richard's loyalty and love, and she knew he also cherished a strong affection for his errant father. So, as long as Richard maintained his personal and professional relationship with her husband, he was the golden link by which she hoped one day to draw Darryl back home again.

But now, abruptly and brutally, the link had been smashed. By breaking so coldly and ruthlessly with his son, Darryl had severed the escape route by which he might one day make his way back to her. It was a blow. It made the years of waiting seem unendurable in retrospect.

And there were other reasons, not just personal, why the repudiation of Richard aroused her concern. It affected the family fortunes, too. One of the settlements Darryl had made upon her during their marriage was a sizable block of 20th Century–Fox shares, and these had been increased, to make her feel secure, when he went away. She now held at least 100,000 shares in the company, making her one of Fox's most important stockholders.

So it was not just as a wife and a mother but as a shareholder that she was angry over the manner in which Richard had been treated. She was knowledgeable enough about the movie business to surmise that, once conditions improved, Richard would have been more than capable of getting Fox back on its feet again, despite the losses the company had suffered. All the studios had done badly, Metro, Paramount, Warners, RKO, all of them. So she regarded her son's departure from control of Fox as a threat to the future of the company once things turned around. And it put Darryl in peril. She did not think much of the movie-making capabilities of Fox's board of directors, but she knew they were highly skilled in plotting, scheming, and back-stabbing in their search for corporate power. Once she would have matched Darryl Zanuck against the lot of them and never had any doubts about the outcome. But now? At sixty-nine? With no one beside him (as Dick had been) to help plan strategy and tactics — except teenage girls whose expertise belonged in the bedroom and not in the board room? She was living at Ric-Su-Dar, the house in Palm Springs, when news reached her of Richard's brutal dismissal, and she promptly did something she had always avoided in the past, through the years of Darryl's absence. She called up the press and made a statement.

She said she was proud of the way in which her son had refused to use her husband's influence to make his way in the movie business.

"My son has overcome his father's name and is respected by the whole industry," she declared. "But [20th Century–Fox] is now run by a board of wishy-washy old men who take orders from DFZ and are, for the moment, scared to cross him. Mr. Zanuck thinks he is the same old genius he used to be. Next year could be a great year for Fox. If they throw out my son and put someone else at the helm who is inexperienced, they could go down the drain in two months. I intend to fight not only for my own survival but for the protection of other stockholders."*

The writer of the story added:

> It is no secret that some of the father-son problems at Fox are over Genevieve Gilles, who starred in a frightfully forgettable bomb titled "Hello and Goodbye." It seems Dick Zanuck stepped on Papa's toes by not picking up Miss Gilles' option.

He went on to quote Virginia as saying:

> "As a large shareholder, I am not going to see any more pictures made like 'Hello and Goodbye,' which was nothing but a $5,000,000 screen test for Miss Gilles. She can't even act. That's all *our* — the stockholders' — money. As far as I am concerned, there will be no more $5,000,000 or even $1,000,000 screen tests. . . . Darryl Zanuck always bought stories for the girl he was trying to build up. They were all flops."

*Chicago Tribune*, December 30, 1970.

Virginia told the reporters she was waiting to talk things over with her son, and then would fly to New York to begin her fight.

But when Richard arrived at Palm Springs and went over the situation, she changed her mind, on his advice. He was still a deeply distressed young man. He warned his mother his father was in "a terrible mood." He tried to explain his motives at the board meeting by saying:

"He simply felt he was losing control, and that, for him, was unthinkable. In business, he couldn't care less who goes down, even his own son, even his wife."

He told his mother he wouldn't be able to bear watching his father and mother rip each other to pieces in a public battle. His own trauma had been shattering enough. This one would destroy both them and him, and that was too much to contemplate.

So he pleaded with his mother to stay out of it and wait and see what happened. Patience and tenacity were what were needed now — and those qualities, of course, Virginia Zanuck had in abundance, as Mack Sennett had told her.

It was a period in Hollywood's history, in fact, when the age of the movie tycoon was passing, and Darryl Zanuck was one of the last of them clinging desperately to power. It was not just his philandering, his little girls, his profligate habits, that were menacing his position in the industry. It was change. Change in the ways the studios were run. Change in film tastes. Change in mass entertainment.

If Zanuck had not quit Hollywood for Paris, he would have seen the Hollywood revolution at close quarters, and possibly learned to adapt to it. Those who had failed to do so had already gone. The most ruthless, nastiest and most unscrupulous of them all, Louis B. Mayer, had already been unseated in a bloodless coup at M-G-M, but he had gone not because he had been an unfeeling tyrant but because he had failed to accommodate himself to the new ways in which the studios were being run.

The day of the independents had arrived, and it meant death to the tycoon because, for the first time, he was forced to share power. And how can you continue to be a dictator and do that? First Hollywood had accepted the idea that not just Fred Astaire and Katharine Hepburn and other stars be allowed to "participate" in the movies they made, but all players, directors, and writers with any clout. Percentage deals became the norm in Hollywood, and the big agents, representing the big names, moved in to parlay and wheel and deal, withhold, threaten, and blackmail.

In the old days, a studio boss could ruin a star by putting him or her "on suspension" if he or she dared to refuse an assignment. Not anymore. It was now the agents who were doing the arm-twisting: *Buy this story, hire this director, use this cameraman or you don't get my star.* As Pandro Berman said: "In the old days anybody who wanted to work for Metro had to sign an optional seven-year contract, and they could let them go any year or keep them on a fixed salary. And that's when guys like Louis Mayer and Jack Warner and Darryl Zanuck were the bosses. They could use their muscle. They could threaten. They could boycott. But the moment percentage deals came in, the actors became part owners of each picture that was made. Everything was radically changed. No one would sign for more than a one-picture deal, and the studio bosses couldn't threaten any longer. They had nothing to threaten with. No star would sign a deal that didn't ensure them a fabulous amount of money, and everything in the studios from then on was predicated on how much profit a movie was going to make — for the studio, for the star, for all those with participation deals. The day of the accountants arrived and they weren't interested in the whims and temperament of the big tycoons, not even those with the genius to visualize super films. All they worried about was the balance sheet."

So one by one, the tycoons were departing, and the tyrants too. No one in California was allowed to make a decision anymore. At Warners, the situation had changed too, and the brothers had at last decided that the time had come to sell out. But like Zanuck, Jack Warner refused to see the writing on the wall and clung to the temptations of studio power to the last.

"Jack and Harry Warner were still at each other's throats," said Milton Sperling, "and even at the last moment Jack did a final outrage to his brother. They all agreed to sell their stock and get out of this terrible situation. But Jack had made a secret agreement with the buyers whereby, the day after the sale, he would regain his stock at the price he had sold it, and would be given a twenty-year contract as head of production. When Harry, who was still my father-in-law, heard about it, he had a stroke — out of sheer anger."

Harry Warner died. Jack heard about it while he was staying at his Riviera villa, the Aujourd'hui. As a practicing Jew, he should, of course, have taken the first plane back to America to attend the funeral. But he was gambling every night at the casino, he was having his nightly girls, cheating furtively on his new wife, and when the family urged him to come back for his brother's interment he decided not to go. His relatives were horrified at his decision.

"And at the very hour that Harry was buried," said Sperling, "Jack was driving back along the Corniche from the casino and he ran his car into a tree. The first words he said when he regained consciousness were: 'God punished me.' "

So did the new owners of Warners. They made life such hell for him that he sold his shares all over again and walked out on them for good.

Louis B. Mayer had taken up racing. Sam Goldwyn had made his last film. Jack Warner eventually retired to Palm Springs, where he grew very fat and took up with a pretty nurse who looked after him. Even Nunnally Johnson, though no tycoon, decided the new Hollywood was not for him and was retiring from the scene. Only Darryl Zanuck was clinging on.

But how long before he, too, was forced to recognize the new situation?

The man who took over from Jack Warner as the operator of the re-constituted Warner Brothers was a lively newcomer named Ted Ashley. He was young enough to fit easily into the way the new Hollywood worked. He liked to make deals and to have producers, directors, and stars make deals with him, and he neither looked like an old-school tycoon nor acted like one. It was Ted Ashley who had warned Richard Zanuck just before the fateful board meeting that his father was out gunning for him. Now that the worst had happened, he telephoned to repeat his invitation to Richard and his partner, David Brown, to join Warners as executive producers — on a participation deal, of course. Brown accepted at once. Richard, still in a state of trauma, took longer to make up his mind. It was as if he was waiting, as he walked the beach at Santa Monica, for some gesture from his father that might ease the pain he felt over what had happened between them. But Darryl Zanuck did not call his son. Eventually, Richard went across to Warners and began a new career, for the first time completely dissociated from his father's presence and influence. So far as the making of films was concerned, that is.

On the other hand, both Richard and his mother were acutely conscious that the annual general meeting of 20th Century–Fox was scheduled for May 18, 1971, and the subject of Richard's abrupt dismissal and Darryl's part in it might well come up for discussion. Virginia Zanuck became aware that even more serious moves were being considered when an emissary arrived at Santa Monica from New York. He represented two so-called dissident stockholders in Fox named Charles M. Lewis, a movie industrial analyst and stockbroker, and Lewis H. Powell, an attorney, and they proposed to organize a proxy fight to get rid of the directors, led by Zanuck, who, they maintained, had brought down the value of Fox shares from $71.51 a share in 1969 to $14 in 1971. Lewis, a bouncy and self-confident man whose last successful campaign had been on behalf of John F. Kennedy, said he would like to have solicited Richard Zanuck's support in the campaign to sack the board of directors of Fox, but realized the shares he and his two sisters owned in the company were controlled by Darryl Zanuck, who had the power to vote them any way he wished. He was not likely to use them against himself or his fellow directors.

"He has no power over *my* shares," said Virginia Zanuck. "And I have over a hundred thousand of them."

That, said the emissary, was precisely why he had come. Would Virginia Zanuck join in the proxy fight and help clean out Fox's stables? The dissidents were prepared to spend $350,000 on a campaign to rally other stockholders to their cause, and were confident they would collect enough votes to win. Still angry at her husband and still anguished over the traumatized state of her beloved son, Virginia signed a proxy giving her vote to the dissidents.

Soon news of the approaching fight spread to the newspapers, and their pages suddenly sprouted with propaganda from both sides. There were charges and countercharges, and it became evident that the target of the insurgents' anger when the meeting was held would undoubtedly be Darryl Zanuck himself, because there were repeated references in newspaper advertisements to "Fox's tired, old and wayward leaders" and barbed remarks about "the use of films as playthings for playmates."

But if anything was calculated to stimulate Darryl Zanuck and get the red corpuscles coursing through his veins, it was a stock fight of this nature. He roared back that the dissidents were nothing but a bunch of "opportunists," but he did take two deft and expert steps to divert their criticism. To Richard Zanuck's initial stupefaction, he did not assume the position of president of 20th Century–Fox, the job he had wrenched away from his son, but passed it on to Dennis C. Stanfil, and the irony was not lost on Richard that he had been replaced by one of his former subordinates. Zanuck then stepped down from his position of chief executive of the company, and added chief operating officer to Stanfil's title. He himself faded into the background as a modest chairman of the board responsible only for the subject he knew most about, making films.

"I told him this is what would happen," said Richard Zanuck when he learned of the change in his father's status. "I told him at the time that he would be the next to go. They are now plucking his feathers out one by one, picking him to pieces one toenail at a time. They've been stripping him of power ever since I left."

Or was this simply Zanuck's tactic for circumventing the dissidents and deflecting their fire?

On May 8, 1971, ten days before the annual meeting was due to take place, *Business Week* published a long article on the situation, which began:

> The 20th Century–Fox Film Corporation, famed for its spectaculars, is now the objective of a spectacular proxy fight for control. Insurgent shareholders are making a strong bid for Fox at a moment when the management is in a last-ditch struggle to turn the company around.
>
> Fox lost $114.1 million in two years and defaulted on loan agreements last June. The showdown is likely to come at Fox's annual meeting in Wilmington, Delaware, on May 18. Even the troubled Fox is a prize well worth fighting for. One of the two remaining independent movie makers, it is the largest producer and distributor of films. Fox also has a large film inventory valued at about $100 million and considerable California real estate.
>
> Both Fox and the insurgents are blazing away at each other in newspaper advertisements and letters to Fox shareholders. The situation is getting so heated that Fox directors even hired a debugging outfit for the boardroom and then played a transistor during their meetings to foil an eavesdropper.

It was likely to be quite a battle, and Darryl Zanuck looked forward to it. Observers noticed that he now looked fitter and moved around more briskly than at any time since he had suffered his stroke in Paris. He gave a number of confidential interviews to Hollywood columnists to be published after the annual meeting was over, making clear that he intended to take over again after the conflict had been resolved in the board's favor. Whenever Genevieve Gilles came into the room, he would bound to his feet, slap her on her bottom, refer fondly to "her dandy little derriere," give her a bear-hug, sometimes wrestle her onto the couch, and even neck a little. If she was never as embarrassed over these intimacies as some of the others present, she did occasionally look surprised at their nature.

Occasionally Dennis Stanfil would come in to see him when the interviews were taking place, and he would be treated cavalierly by Zanuck almost to the point of being humiliated. Stanfil had already been written up in the newspapers as an Annapolis graduate, Rhodes scholar, and Oxford graduate, and it was almost distasteful to watch him being ordered around by Zanuck, rated for slowness and stupidity, and made the butt of snide references to his capabilities.

"The good thing about Stan is he always does as he is told," Zanuck once remarked to his listeners. "The bad thing is he's so goddamn slow about it."

From the expression trapped on his features when this was said, some of those present suspected that Stanfil was not quite the willing doormat Zanuck made him out to be. There were whispers on Wall Street that he was having secret consultations with a big Fox stockholder, William T. Gossett, but no one read too much into that, since Gossett, an attorney, former Ford Motor Corporation executive, and chairman of Fox's executive committee, was known to be on Zanuck's side. Or, rather, on the side of the present board of 20th Century–Fox.

The annual general meeting of the 20th Century–Fox Film Corporation took place in Wilmington, Delaware, because it was registered as a Delaware company to take advantage of that state's special privileges and concessions to big corporations. Members of the board began arriving, by car, by Metroliner from New York, by private jets, on the evening of May 17, and all of them put up at the palatial Du Pont Hotel in downtown Wilmington, built by the du Pont de Nemours family to accommodate and cater to their powerful and discriminating clan in a manner to which their riches and lineage had accustomed them. That night the board members and some of the wives who had accompanied them dined in style in the hotel restaurant, where the food is French and first class and the clarets and Burgundies in the hotel's cellar are excellent. Later that evening, when Zanuck had gone upstairs to his suite, changed into a dressing gown, and was puffing on a bedtime cigar, there was a knock on his door and when he opened it, William Gossett was there. He asked to be allowed to come in and talk for a few minutes. Zanuck, who thought it was a discussion of last-minute strategy, invited him in and poured him out a brandy.

Gossett then gave him the good news. For the past few weeks, he and Dennis Stanfil had been having continuous discussions with the Broadway stage producer David Merrick, who, it had been discovered, was one of Fox's biggest shareholders. He held 207,000 shares. It so happened that Fox owed Merrick $1,800,000, being the amount they had agreed to pay him for the film rights of his stage hit *Hello, Dolly!* They had now arranged to give Merrick a guaranteed note for $1,800,000 in liquidation of that debt. It was in no sense a quid pro quo, Gossett said, but during one of the meetings Merrick had indicated that he supported the policies of the Fox board completely, and, when it came to voting in the forthcoming proxy fight, he would be swinging his 207,000 shares behind the board.

Zanuck slapped his thigh with glee.

"That'll show the cocksuckers!" he said. "We've got the bastards on the run! Is that enough to get us through?"

Gossett gravely agreed it was enough. They had made an estimate, and with Merrick's shares voted their way, plus all the others they had been able to round up from loyal shareholders, they now felt they had the necessary votes to defeat the dissidents. He waved away another brandy Zanuck was pouring him and paused, finally mentioning, with lots of hesitations, that there was one more thing. In order to get the requisite number of shares together to win the battle, he said it had been necessary to approach some of the big Wall Street holders, who had promised their support. But on one condition.

"And what's that?" Zanuck asked.

Gossett hesitated again. Then, in a rush, he said the condition was that the chairman stepped down. In other words, they wanted Zanuck out. Without his announcement at tomorrow's meeting that he would not be standing for reelection, the Wall Street people would probably swing their votes the other way.

"For God's sake, why?" asked Zanuck.

Again a lot of hesitation.

"Maybe they think you a little too — er — flamboyant," Gossett said, "for these times. Think you've lost your touch, perhaps. All that publicity. Those girls."

He looked pleadingly at Zanuck. If those Wall Street votes were swung the other way, then not just Zanuck but all of them would be out, and God knows what would happen then.

Zanuck had flopped back in his chair and was draining his brandy. He suddenly looked old and gray and tired.

"The bastards!" he said. A long pause. He leaned forward and put his head between his knees, then suddenly straightened. "Okay," he said, "I'll write out a statement for you."

Gossett told him there was no need for him to do that. He fumbled in his pocket and drew out a piece of paper. The committee had already written the statement for him, and all he needed to do was sign.

He waited until Zanuck had scrawled his signature, and then, paper in hand, he went to the door, leaving Zanuck sitting blankly on his chair, hand on his chest as if he had a pain.

Gossett turned as he went out. "Thanks, old man," he said, gratefully, and added: "You'll see. We have a little surprise for you. We'll make it up to you tomorrow."

Next day they did too. Sort of. By a unanimous vote, the board "reluctantly and with regret" accepted Zanuck's decision not to stand for reelection, and then announced that, "in return for his meritorious and imaginative service to this company for so many years," he had been voted president emeritus of 20th Century–Fox.

It was, of course, a position without power or function. He would have no say over any decisions the company would make in the future, including what films would be on their program. If he had not felt so crushed, deflated, defeated, he would have said he had been most neatly, but ruthlessly, "debollicked."

As for the balloting, the board of directors won "handily," as the *New York Times* reported next day, in their fight with the insurgents, who were defeated by a vote of 3,900,000 to 2,400,000.

"We lost," said Virginia Zanuck that night, when the news came through.

"No," said Dick Zanuck. "Dad was the one who lost."

## TWENTY-NINE

# FADE-OUT

**O**NE DAY in the late summer of 1972, some time after the demeaning events in Wilmington, Delaware, Pauline and Ken Annakin went to see Darryl Zanuck in his suite at the Plaza Hotel in New York, and were chastened and concerned at what they found. Never before had they realized how small in stature Darryl Zanuck really was. Somehow, there had always been such an oversized personality pulsating from inside him it had tended to conceal his actual physical dimensions. But now he seemed to have shrunk. It gradually dawned on them that the diminution was probably because the vigor had leaked out of him, and he was unwell, depressed. And, somehow, bereft too. Annakin concluded he missed the atmosphere of the film studios, the lights, cameras, actors, action, and he listened eagerly to the gossip they brought him about Hollywood. His air of authority, his cocky self-confidence, seemed to have vanished. His vibrant young girlfriend, Genevieve Gilles, seemed, on the other hand, to be humming with energy. She was obviously genuinely fond of him and was inclined to fuss, and instead of being irritated by it, he seemed almost grateful, humbly grateful.

They thought it quite pathetic. Strangers probably didn't notice it. But they had known him when.

They had heard he had suffered a physical collapse in the wake of the Delaware meeting, and that Gilles had been a tower of strength. Shortly after this visit, he became ill again and this time was rushed to the hospital.

When news of his hospitalization reached Richard Zanuck in Burbank, where he was working with David Brown at Warner Brothers, he hesitated for a long time about what to do. He missed his father. He had talked to him several times on the telephone and had long since forgiven him for what he had done. His instinct was to rush to his side, but he was reluctant to risk another rebuff. Finally he picked up the telephone and called him.

"Dad," he said, "I hear you've been ill. Would you like me to come and see you?"

"Of course," said his father.

"And shortly after that," said Richard, "every time I would go to New York on Warner business I would go and see him, and we came close again."

Richard had expected the reunion to be painful, and he feared his father might be disturbed by feelings of guilt over the hurt he had inflicted on his son. On the contrary, he gave no sign there had ever been any rift between them, and seemed unaware he had dealt his son a wounding blow.

"Later, when I reconstructed what had happened, from his point of view," Richard said, "I decided he didn't feel he had wronged me at all, and therefore had no guilt about it. He had simply felt he was losing control [at Fox] and that, for him, was unthinkable. In the movie business, he didn't care who got hurt, even his own son, so long as he didn't get hurt himself. It had been simply a case of *sauve qui peut*."

It had been a stroke, and a second one after Delaware, and when Zanuck came out of the hospital it was obvious he would never be his old self again. His swashbuckling days were over. Even young girls were unlikely to turn him on any longer. Yet his relationship with Genevieve Gilles remained close, and if there was no longer any heat to it, they still stayed "cuddly," as one female visitor described it.

To aid in his recuperation, his doctors advised him to get out of New York, and presently it was rumored he was planning to return to Ric-Su-Dar in Palm Springs, and that Genevieve would be going with him. It seemed safe to presume she would be staying on once they got there. Virginia had gone back to the house at Santa Monica ("where my memories are"). She still kept Darryl's humidor filled with his favorite cigars. He had sent her a bronze bust of himself (not a very successful one) from Paris and the original of the *Time* portrait used when he was the week's cover subject, and she proudly displayed them in the den she kept waiting for him. No one thought she would ever leave Santa Monica.

But when Zanuck and Genevieve arrived in Palm Springs, they found Virginia installed in Ric-Su-Dar and waiting to welcome back her husband. And it was made very plain indeed that there was no place anywhere in the house, particularly not in the bedroom, for Genevieve. It was a puzzling and frustrating period for the young Frenchwoman, and she had some difficult moments before she finally gave up on her erstwhile lover.

In 1973 Richard Zanuck and David Brown bought up their contract with Warner Brothers and went across to Universal Pictures to form a new independent production company. Their first film, *Sugarland Express*, was directed by a newcomer to the movies named Steven Spielberg, and it lost them money.* Richard took it down to Palm Springs and showed the film to his father and Virginia, and neither was particularly impressed. Virginia tried to keep her husband as up-to-date as possible and arranged for most of the new films to be shown to him, but she confessed that Darryl often fell asleep during the showings.

When Richard had talked to Gilles in New York, she told him that Darryl seemed to have grown bored with the movies.

"He only wakes up when there are films of naked women," she had complained. "And then only if they have what he calls tits. Why are you Americans so obsessed by tits?"

But when Richard finished his next film, *The Sting*, he took it down to show to his father and mother and was gratified that both of them sat through it without nodding off and also warmly applauded it at the end.

"That movie could win you an Oscar," Darryl said.

And it did.

But Richard worried about his father. His speech was often slurred and he looked as if he had had another stroke. His only interest in life seemed to be sitting around the pool, and it made his day when someone young, bronzed, and shapely turned up whom he could admire as she exposed her body to the sun. Virginia did not seem to notice the deterioration in her husband's condition. It was just, she told her friends, that he was a little weak in body and mind "and needs a little mothering."

And who better could mother him than she? After all, unlike his real mother and all the others, she was the only woman in his life who had never let him down.

"I heard stories about him," said Milton Sperling. "I heard Darryl had lost his mind, so I went down to Palm Springs especially to see him. And when I spoke to Virginia, she said: 'But Milton, you knew him when he was the most brilliant and powerful man in Hollywood. Do you really want to see him now?' And I said: 'I guess not.' And I went back to

---

*He more than made up for it with the next film he did for them. It was *Jaws*, which broke the record for U.S. box-office returns previously held by *Gone With the Wind*.

Beverly Hills without seeing him. I still remembered him with that poodle on his knee in Paris, and that was bad enough. I didn't want to see him like that again."

Gilles would like to have seen Zanuck again before he died, but she never did. Richard would like to have shown him his further film successes (particularly *Jaws*, of which he was very proud) but *The Sting* was the last of his movies his father ever saw. "But it was quite remarkable, a heart-warming thing," said Richard, "to see my mother and father back together again after twenty years of separation."

But how much Zanuck appreciated Virginia's return is something only he could have answered, and he was not really in a condition to do so. When he reached out his hand, he must have missed those glowing curves Gilles had once presented to him so generously, both around the pool and elsewhere. But there were consolations. There were other kinds of precious comforts that Virginia could bring him. They were the qualities she possessed that he had never really found in any other woman, his mother included — solidity, fidelity, loyalty, security. These Virginia now gave him in added measure. They might not be as exciting to touch and cherish as a young brown body, but they were comforting beyond words when you were feeble, failing, and seventy-two years old.

He gave that one last performance in January 1974, for the fiftieth anniversary of his marriage to Virginia. Richard planned the party and surprised him with it at the last moment, so that he had no excuse for opting out of it. He dressed in his old Signal Corps uniform and looked as slick as if he were to be presented to the President instead of to a few friends and selected members of the press. And when he turned up at the Raquet Club, he even seemed to be the original Zanuck, cocky and self-confident as ever. One veteran columnist muttered: "All he needs is a polo mallet in his hands, and it will be just like old times."

But the polo mallet had been put away for good.

Watching that scene, Richard Zanuck felt the tears pricking his eyes, and realized with a pang that the life of the man he had once admired more than anyone else in the world was ebbing away under the desert sunshine.

It was a lovely day, but a desperate moment.

There he stood, doing his stuff for the cameras, the last Hollywood tycoon. And what Richard knew, and he was sure his father knew, was that Darryl Zanuck's life was over — even if he was not yet dead.

# EPILOGUE

*I*N FACT, it took another five years of lingering illness before Darryl Francis Zanuck finally died in 1979, and that, as any good film technician would have pointed out, was far too long to wait for the final fade-out. Zanuck himself, always proud of his skill as a cutter, would have done a lot of rejigging and considerably speeded up the action in the final reels had he been in charge of the production. Unfortunately, like 20th Century–Fox, it had long since passed into other hands.

Still, he did retain some control over his own funeral, and though his son, Richard, and his daughter, Darrylin, wrote the script, and Virginia was around as the director, it was plain to those who attended the last rites — and they included everyone who was or had been anyone in Hollywood — that Zanuck himself was in overall control. For one thing, there were no hymns, no chorales, no Dead Marches nor laments played during the service, but only the theme tune from *The Longest Day* repeated over and over again. Cineastes would remember Darryl Zanuck for what one obituarist described as "the movie gems sparkling in his cinematic crown." The writer went on to enumerate Zanuck's great productions, like *The Grapes of Wrath, How Green Was My Valley, The Snake Pit, All About Eve, Viva Zapata!*, and *Twelve O'clock High*.

But Zanuck himself had preferred *The Longest Day*. It was dearest to his heart because it was the one into which he had put his guts and sunk his own money, and he never had any doubt that it was a monumentally splendid film. So it was to the strains of its rather mediocre theme song that he had chosen to ride out into his last sunset.

Listening in his pew to the organist grinding away at the tune, Elmo Williams was slightly embarrassed. He hardly thought it was quite suitable for a funeral service, but since he had been responsible for getting it written, how could he really object? He thought back as the song jangled on to the day in Normandy, during the shooting of *The Longest Day,* when he had asked Paul Anka to try to work out a theme song for the movie. Some hours later they had gone together to the Malherbe Hotel in Caen and Anka had taken out his mouthorgan and played the tune for Zanuck. Everyone knew Zanuck had a tin ear for anything except brass band marches and advertising jingles, and he obviously did not know whether he liked it or not. But when Williams had nodded his head, he had agreed at once.

"Okay," he had said. "Let's use it."

Now it was the signature tune for his departure to Valhalla, or whatever other-worldly destination for which he was bound.

Williams looked across the heads of the congregation, and wondered idly what they were thinking. Sprinkled here and there were the women whose cinematic destinies Zanuck had so coldly controlled. They seemed to have come to no harm from their experience, and though most of them now were established stars or solidly substantial matrons all of them seemed to feel sentimental over the passing of the man who had once bossed them around. At least, they were all dabbing at the mascara on their eyelashes.

Nunnally Johnson was dead and therefore was present only in spirit. He had despised movie directors and always been offhand about producers, of whom he had once said: "A producer has only one important decision to make, and that is 'Let's make the picture.'" But he had made an exception in the case of Sam Goldwyn, Sam Spiegel, and, particularly, Darryl Zanuck.

"He had a kind of tough, stubborn faith," he had once said, "and if he believed in your project, by God, he would see that it got made. There weren't many men who could read a script and recognize a good one, but he could."

Henry Fonda had loathed Darryl Zanuck because he had tried to push him around and was never his kind of person, but he was present at the funeral too, because he knew that without Zanuck he would never have made *The Grapes of Wrath* and his career would never have flown to the same heights it eventually did. You could say the same for Gregory Peck, Bette Davis, Elizabeth Taylor, Richard Burton, Richard Widmark, Dorothy McGuire, Ava Gardner, Olivia de Havilland and Jennifer Jones. All of them, in large or small ways, owed their cinematic eminence to Zanuck.

All of them realized that, with his death, there was no possible chance that the making of movies would ever be the same again.

"He was the best of the movie moguls," said Milton Sperling, "a single-purpose machine, a filmmaking machine. And he was so good at it! I remember when he would lay out his program at Warners on a big sheet of paper — all marked up with fifty-two pictures, one a week for a year. And then at the top would be the names of the stars, and at the side a column with the names of the stories. And all movable, like a production board. So he would gather his people around him, his producers, his writers, and he would say: 'Okay, we want three Bette Davises, four Cagneys, four Eddie Robinsons, three Bogarts, two Errol Flynns. Who's got a good story for Bogart — anything we can put Bogart in?' That would go on for a couple of days, and at the end of forty-eight hours he would have an entire program for the studio for a year. With stories and directors assigned, the whole thing. It was like a well-run factory and its product was slick, yes, run off a production line, yes, but if it sometimes spewed out a lemon it also sometimes proudly gave birth to a Rolls-Royce."

Richard Schickel, one of the more percipient of the movie critics, once wrote:

> Any movie's largest potential is for disaster. The process by which films are made is akin to those long, skidding, agonizing chase sequences shot along the rim of a cliff. Inside their chosen vehicle the egomaniacs scream at fate and one another, all the while kicking and kneeing, punching and gouging as they struggle for control of the wheel. Most movies, as everyone knows, end up in the ravine, bottoms up among the broken and rusting remnants of last year's improbable dreams. A few — sensibly designed or well-balanced or inherently powerful — seem to steer themselves into the theaters, oblivious to the uproar that attended their journey.
>
> Then, every once in a rare while, one arrives in style, its owner-drivers still glaring angrily at one another, but somehow the better for its terrible travails. These are the miracles of the industry, the stuff of Hollywood legends.

The congregation at his funeral was paying tribute to a man who had been something of a miracle himself and certainly a Hollywood legend. And everyone knew just who and what they were saluting. With Darryl Zanuck dead, they would never see his like again. And the Hollywood they had all known and cherished — which he had done so much to create — was being buried with him.

No one was sadder at his disappearance than his old employee Milton Sperling, and later he put his grief down on paper in a letter. It seems fitting as an epitaph to Darryl Zanuck: "I shared the intimacy that all his co-workers enjoyed (or endured). Even at a distance . . . his presence was always felt. His life style, his pleasures, his prejudices influenced me far past my period of employment. Green, for example, was his favorite color. It was mine. His noon to dawn working hours became my habit. He took up skiing, so did I. He studied French. Me, too. And so on. My single unconformity was in politics. . . . His vulgarity made me laugh, as it was intended to. His cruelty impressed me with its manliness. His insatiable appetites awed me. Don't forget I was very young, very impressionable. He was a role model and in unconsciously emulating him, I caused myself no end of trouble.

"I wish Darryl was around now. He loved film, made instant decisions, encouraged talent. He'd deride today's committee-ridden, computer-oriented, agent-accountant management apparatus.

"He was the Sun King. On reflection, I'm glad he escaped the deluge."

# THE SCREEN CREDITS
# OF DARRYL F. ZANUCK

# THE SCREEN CREDITS OF DARRYL F. ZANUCK

*Note:* The records cover the years 1924–1970 and are, in some cases, incomplete. It should also be noted that Zanuck used several pseudonyms during his screenwriting career. These are marked with an asterisk in the list below.

**Warner Brothers Films**

*Find Your Man* (1924)
Director: Mal St. Clair
Star: Rin Tin Tin
Original story and screenplay: DFZ

*Lighthouse by the Sea* (1924)
Director: Mal St. Clair
Star: Rin Tin Tin
Original story: Owen Davis
Screenplay: DFZ

*On Thin Ice* (1925)
Director: Mal St. Clair
Stars: Tom Moore, William Russell
Adaptation and screenplay: DFZ

*The Limited Mail* (1925)
Director: George Hill
Star: Monte Blue
Adaptation and screenplay: DFZ

*Red Hot Tires* (1925)
Director: Eric Kenton
Stars: Monte Blue, Patsy Ruth Miller
Story: Gregory Rogers*
Screenplay: DFZ

*Hogan's Alley* (1925)
Director: Roy del Ruth
Stars: Monte Blue, Ben Turpin, Louise Fazenda
Original story and screenplay: Gregory Rogers*

*The Little Irish Girl* (1926)
Director: Roy del Ruth
Star: Dolores Costello
Original story: C. D. Lancaster
Screenplay: DFZ

*The Social Highwayman* (1926)
Director: William Beaudine
Star: Montague Love
Original story and screenplay: DFZ

*Footloose Widows* (1926)
Director: Roy del Ruth
Stars: Louise Fazenda, Jacqueline Logan
Screenplay: DFZ

*Across the Pacific* (1926)
Director: Roy del Ruth
Stars: Monte Blue, Myrna Loy
Story and screenplay: DFZ

*The Better 'Ole* (1926)
Director: Charles Reisner
Star: Sydney Chaplin
Original play: Bruce Bairnsfather
Screenplay: DFZ

*Oh! What a Nurse!* (1926)
Director: Charles Reisner
Star: Sydney Chaplin
Story: Robert E. Sherwood,
    Bertram Block
Screenplay: DFZ

*Tracked by the Police* (1927)
Director: Ray Enright
Stars: Rin Tin Tin, Jason Robards
Story: Gregory Rogers*
Screenplay: DFZ

*The Missing Link* (1927)
Director: Charles Reisner
Star: Sydney Chaplin
Story: Charles Reisner
Screenplay: DFZ

*Irish Hearts* (1927)
Director: Byron Haskin
Stars: May McAvoy, Jason Robards
Original story: Melville Crossman*
Screenplay: Bess Meredith,
    Graham Baker

*Old San Francisco* (1927)
Director: Alan Crosland
Stars: Warner Oland,
    Dolores Costello
Story: DFZ
Screenplay: Melville Crossman*

*The Black Diamond Express* (1927)
Director: Howard Bretherton
Star: Monte Blue
Story and screenplay: DFZ

*The First Auto* (1927)
Director: Roy del Ruth
Stars: Barney Oldfield,
    Russell Simpson
Screenplay: DFZ

*State Street Sadie* (1927)
Director Archie Mayor
Stars: Conrad Nagel, Myrna Loy
Story and screenplay: Melville
    Crossman*

*The Desired Woman* (1927)
Director: Michael Curtiz
Stars: Irene Rich, William Russell
Story: Mark Canfield*
Screenplay: DFZ

*The Jazz Singer* (1927)
Director: Alan Crosland
Star: Al Jolson
Original play: Samson Raphaelson
Screenplay: Alfred A. Cohen
Produced by: DFZ

*Tenderloin* (1928)
Director: Michael Curtiz
Stars: Dolores Costello, Conrad Nagel
Story and screenplay: Melville
    Crossman*

*The Midnight Taxi* (1928)
Director: John Adolfi
Stars: Antonio Moreno,
    Helene Costello
Story and screenplay: Gregory
    Rogers*

*My Man* (1928)
Director: Archie Mayo
Star: Fanny Brice
Story and screenplay: Mark Canfield*

*Noah's Ark* (1929)
Director: Michael Curtiz
Stars: Dolores Costello,
    George O'Brien
Screenplay: DFZ

*Say It with Songs* (1929)
Director: Lloyd Bacon
Star: Al Jolson
Story and screenplay: DFZ

*Disraeli* (1929)
Director: Alfred Green

Star: George Arliss
Original play: Louis N. Parker
Screenplay: Julian Josephson
Produced by: DFZ

*Madonna of Avenue A* (1929)
Director: Michael Curtiz
Stars: Dolores Costello, Louise
    Dresser, Grant Withers
Story and screenplay: Mark Canfield*

*The Life of the Party* (1930)
Director: Roy del Ruth
Stars: Charles Butterworth,
    Winnie Lightner
Story: Melville Crossman*
Screenplay: DFZ

*The Office Wife* (1930)
Director: Lloyd Bacon
Star: Lewis Stone
Based on novel by Faith Baldwin
Adapted and produced by: DFZ

*The Doorway to Hell* (1930)
Director: Archie Mayo
Star: Lew Ayres
Story: Roland Brown
Produced by: DFZ

*Little Caesar* (1931)
Director: Mervyn LeRoy
Star: Edward G. Robinson
Novel by: W. R. Burnett
Adapted and produced by: DFZ

*Illicit* (1931)
Director: Archie Mayo
Star: Barbara Stanwyck
Original play and screenplay: Edith
    Fitzgerald, Robert Riskin
Produced by: DFZ

*The Public Enemy* (1931)
Director: William Wellman
Stars: James Cagney, Jean Harlow,
    Mae Clark
Story and screenplay: John Bright,
    Kubec Glassman
Produced by: DFZ

*Smart Money* (1931)
Director: Alfred E. Green
Stars: James Cagney,
    Edward G. Robinson
Story and screenplay: John Bright,
    Kubec Glassman
Produced by: DFZ

*Five Star Final* (1931)
Director: Mervyn LeRoy
Star: Edward G. Robinson
Story: Louis Weitzenkorn
Adapted and produced by: DFZ

*The Crowd Roars* (1932)
Director: Howard Hawks
Stars: James Cagney, Joan Blondell
Story and screenplay: Howard Hawks
Produced by: DFZ

*The Mouthpiece* (1932)
Directors: James Flood, Elliot Nugent
Star: Warren William
Original play: Frank J. Collins
Adapted and produced by: DFZ

*The Dark Horse* (1932)
Director: Alfred E. Green
Stars: Bette Davis, Warren William
Story and produced by: DFZ

*I Am a Fugitive from a Chain Gang*
    (1932)
Director: Mervyn LeRoy
Star: Paul Muni
Original novel: Robert E. Burns
Screenplay: Sheridan Gibney,
    Brown Holmes
Adapted and produced by: DFZ

*42nd Street* (1933)
Director: Lloyd Bacon
Stars: Ruby Keeler, Warner Baxter
Story: Bradford Ropes
Produced by: DFZ

*Baby Face* (1933)
Director: Alfred E. Green
Stars: Barbara Stanwyck,
    George Brent

Story: Mark Canfield*
Screenplay: Gene Markey,
  Kathryn Scola

**Twentieth Century Films (released by United Artists)**

*The Bowery* (1933)
Director: Raoul Walsh
Stars: George Raft, Wallace Beery
Screenplay and produced by: DFZ

*Broadway Thru a Keyhole* (1933)
Director: Lowell Sherman
Stars: Constance Cummings,
  Paul Kelly
Story: Walter Winchell
Adapted and produced by: DFZ

*Blood Money* (1933)
Director: Rowland Brown
Star: George Bancroft
Adapted and produced by: DFZ

*Advice to the Lovelorn* (1933)
Director: Alfred Werker
Star: Lee Tracy
Original novel: Nathanael West
  (*Miss Lonelyhearts*)
Produced by: DFZ

*Gallant Lady* (1934)
Director: Gregory La Cava
Star: Ann Harding
Story: Gilbert Emery
Adapted and produced by: DFZ

*Moulin Rouge* (1934)
Director: Sidney Lanfield
Stars: Franchot Tone,
  Constance Bennett
Story and screenplay: Nunnally
  Johnson
Produced by: DFZ

*The House of Rothschild* (1934)
Director: Alfred Werker
Star: George Arliss

Original play: George Westly
Screenplay: Nunnally Johnson
Produced by: DFZ

*Looking for Trouble* (1934)
Director: William Wellman
Stars: Lee Tracy,
  Constance Cummings
Story: J. R. Bren
Produced by: DFZ

*Born to Be Bad* (1934)
Director: Lowell Sherman
Stars: Cary Grant, Loretta Young
Story: Ralph Graves
Adapted and produced by: DFZ

*Bulldog Drummond Strikes Back*
  (1934)
Director: Roy del Ruth
Star: Ronald Colman
Story: H. C. McNeile
Screenplay: Nunnally Johnson
Produced by: DFZ

*The Affairs of Cellini* (1934)
Director: Gregory La Cava
Original play: Edwin Justus Mayer
Produced by: DFZ

*The Last Gentleman* (1934)
Director: Sidney Lanfield
Star: George Arliss
Story: Katharine Clugston
Adapted and produced by: DFZ

*The Mighty Barnum* (1934)
Director: Walter Lang
Star: Wallace Beery
Story: Gene Fowler, Bess Meredyth
Adapted and produced by: DFZ

*Clive of India* (1935)
Director: Richard Boleslawski
Stars: Ronald Colman, Loretta Young
Original play: R. J. Minney,
  W. P. Lipscomb
Produced by: DFZ

*Folies Bergere* (1934)
Director: Roy del Ruth
Star: Maurice Chevalier
Story and screenplay: Bess Meredyth,
    Hal Long
Produced by: DFZ

*Cardinal Richelieu* (1935)
Director: Rowland V. Lee
Star: George Arliss
Screenplay: Maud Howell,
    W. P. Lipscomb, Cameron Rogers
Produced by: DFZ

*Les Miserables* (1935)
Director: Richard Boleslawski
Stars: Charles Laughton,
    Fredric March
Original novel: Victor Hugo
Screenplay: W. P. Lipscomb
Produced by: DFZ

*Call of the Wild* (1935)
Director: William Wellman
Stars: Clark Gable, Loretta Young
Original novel: Jack London
Screenplay: Gene Fowler
Produced by: DFZ

*Note:* During 1935 Warner Brothers
produced *G Men*, which DFZ had
left behind when he quit to form
Twentieth Century. He wrote the
screenplay under the pseudonym
Gregory Rogers. William Keighley
directed; James Cagney starred.

## 20th Century–Fox Films

*Metropolitan* (1935)
Director: Richard Boleslawski
Star: Lawrence Tibbett
Story: Bess Meredyth
Screenplay: Bess Meredyth,
    George Marion, Jr.
Produced by: DFZ

*Thanks a Million* (1935)
Director: Roy del Ruth

Stars: Dick Powell, Fred Allen,
    Ann Dvorak
Story: Melville Crossman*
Screenplay: Nunnally Johnson
Produced by: DFZ

*The Man Who Broke the Bank at
    Monte Carlo* (1935)
Director: Stephen Roberts
Stars: Ronald Colman, Joan Bennett
Screenplay: Nunnally Johnson,
    Howard Ellis Smith
Produced by: DFZ

*Show Them No Mercy* (1935)
Director: George Marshall
Stars: Cesar Romero, Bruce Cabot
Story and screenplay: Kubec
    Glassman
Produced by: DFZ

*King of Burlesque* (1936)
Director: Sidney Lanfield
Stars: Alice Faye, Warner Baxter,
    Jack Oakie
Story and screenplay: Gene Markey,
    Harry Tugend
Produced by: DFZ

*The Prisoner of Shark Island* (1936)
Director: John Ford
Star: Warner Baxter
Story and screenplay: Nunnally
    Johnson
Produced by: DFZ

*Professional Soldier* (1936)
Director: Tay Garnett
Star: Victor McLaglen
Story: Damon Runyon
Screenplay: Gene Fowler
Produced by: DFZ

*It Had to Happen* (1936)
Director: Roy del Ruth
Star: George Raft
Story and screenplay: Rupert Hughes
Produced by: DFZ

*The Country Doctor* (1936)
Director: Henry King
Stars: The Dionne Quintuplets,
  Jean Hersholt
Screenplay: Sonya Levien
Produced by: DFZ

*A Message to Garcia* (1936)
Director: George Marshall
Stars: Barbara Stanwyck,
  Wallace Beery
Screenplay: W. P. Lipscomb
Produced by: DFZ

*Captain January* (1936)
Director: David Butler
Star: Shirley Temple
Screenplay: Sam Hellman, Gladys
  Lehman, Harry Tugend
Produced by: DFZ

*Under Two Flags* (1936)
Director: Frank Lloyd
Stars: Ronald Colman,
  Claudette Colbert
Screenplay: W. P. Lipscomb
Produced by: DFZ

*Half Angel* (1936)
Director: Sidney Lanfield
Star: Brian Donlevy
Screenplay: Gene Fowler,
  Bess Meredyth
Produced by: DFZ

*White Fang* (1936)
Director: Daniel Butler
Stars: Lightning, Slim Summerville
Screenplay: Gene Fowler, Hal Long
Produced by: DFZ

*Sins of Man* (1936)
Directors: Otto Brower,
  Gregory Ratoff
Stars: Don Ameche, Jean Hersholt
Story and screenplay: Sam Engel
Produced by: DFZ

*The Road to Glory* (1936)
Director: Howard Hawks

Stars: Fredric March, Warner Baxter,
  Lionel Barrymore
Story: William Faulkner, Joel Sayre
Produced by: DFZ

*Sing, Baby, Sing* (1936)
Director: Sidney Canfield
Stars: Gregory Ratoff, The Ritz
  Brothers, Adolphe Menjou
Story and screenplay: Milton Sperling
Produced by: DFZ

*Lloyds of London* (1936)
Director: Henry King
Stars: Tyrone Power,
  Madeleine Carroll
Screenplay: Ernest Pascal,
  Walter Ferris
Produced by: DFZ

*Pigskin Parade* (1936)
Director: David Butler
Stars: Bette Davis, Judy Garland,
  Stuart Erwin, Jack Haley
Screenplay: Harry Tugend, Jack
  Yellen, William Conselman
Produced by: DFZ

*One in a Million* (1937)
Director: Sidney Lanfield
Star: Sonja Henie
Story and screenplay: Leonard
  Praskin
Produced by: DFZ

*On the Avenue* (1937)
Director: Roy del Ruth
Stars: Alice Faye, Dick Powell,
  Madeleine Carroll
Screenplay: Gene Fowler
Music: Irving Berlin
Produced by: DFZ

*Seventh Heaven* (1937)
Director: Henry King
Stars: James Stewart, Simone Simon
Screenplay: Melville Baker
Produced by: DFZ

*Wake Up and Live* (1937)
Director: Sidney Lanfield
Stars: Ben Bernie, Walter Winchell
Screenplay: Harry Tugend,
  Jack Yellen
Produced by: DFZ

*Wee Willie Winkie* (1937)
Director: John Ford
Star: Shirley Temple
Screenplay: Gene Markey
Produced by: DFZ

*Lancer Spy* (1937)
Director: Gregory Ratoff
Stars: Peter Lorre, George Sanders
Story and screenplay: Philip Dunne
Produced by: DFZ

*In Old Chicago* (1938)
Director: Henry King
Stars: Tyrone Power, Don Ameche,
  Alice Faye
Screenplay: Lamarr Trotti,
  Sonya Levien
Produced by: DFZ

*Happy Landing* (1938)
Director: Roy del Ruth
Star: Sonja Henie
Screenplay: Milton Sperling,
  Boris Ingster
Produced by: DFZ

*Kidnapped* (1938)
Director: Alfred Werker
Star: Freddie Bartholomew
Original novel: Robert Louis
  Stevenson
Adapted and produced by: DFZ

*Little Miss Broadway* (1938)
Director: Irving Cummings
Stars: Shirley Temple,
  George Murphy
Adapted and produced by: DFZ

*I'll Give a Million* (1938)
Director: Walter Lang
Stars: John Carradine, Peter Lorre

Story and screenplay: Cesare
  Zavattini, Giaci Mondaini
Produced by: DFZ

*Alexander's Ragtime Band* (1938)
Director: Henry King
Stars: Tyrone Power, Don Ameche,
  Alice Faye
Music: Irving Berlin
Adapted and produced by: DFZ

*Josette* (1938)
Director: Allan Dwan
Stars: Simone Simon, Don Ameche
Screenplay: DFZ, Allan Dwan
Produced by: DFZ

*Three Blind Mice* (1938)
Director: William Seiter
Stars: Loretta Young, Joel McCrea
Screenplay: Raymond Griffith
Produced by: DFZ

*Hold That Co-Ed* (1938)
Director: George Marshall
Stars: John Barrymore,
  George Murphy
Screenplay: George Marshall
Produced by: DFZ

*Suez* (1938)
Director: Allan Dwan
Stars: Tyrone Power, Loretta Young
Screenplay: Allan Dwan
Produced by: DFZ

*Submarine Patrol* (1938)
Director: John Ford
Star: Preston Foster
Screenplay: Nunnally Johnson
Produced by: DFZ

*Straight, Place & Show* (1938)
Director: David Butler
Stars: The Ritz Brothers
Screenplay: David Butler,
  The Ritz Brothers
Produced by: DFZ

*Just Around the Corner* (1938)
Director: Irving Cummings
Star: Shirley Temple
Screenplay: Irving Cummings, DFZ
Produced by: DFZ

*Thanks for Everything* (1938)
Director: William Seiter
Stars: Adolphe Menjou, Jack Haley
Screenplay: William Seiter
Produced by: DFZ

*Kentucky* (1938)
Director: David Butler
Stars: Loretta Young, Walter Brennan
Screenplay: David Butler, DFZ
Produced by: DFZ

*Jesse James* (1939)
Director: Henry King
Stars: Tyrone Power, Henry Fonda
Screenplay: Nunnally Johnson
Produced by: DFZ

*Tail Spin* (1939)
Director: Roy del Ruth
Stars: Alice Faye, Constance Bennett
Produced by: DFZ

*The Little Princess* (1939)
Director: Walter Lang
Star: Shirley Temple
Produced by: DFZ

*The Story of Alexander Graham Bell*
  (1939)
Director: Irving Cummings
Star: Don Ameche
Adapted and produced by: DFZ

*Young Mr. Lincoln* (1939)
Director: John Ford
Star: Henry Fonda
Screenplay: Nunnally Johnson
Produced by: DFZ

*Susannah of the Mounties* (1939)
Director: William Seiter
Star: Shirley Temple
Produced by: DFZ

*The Gorilla* (1939)
Director: Allan Dwan
Stars: The Ritz Brothers
Screenplay: Allan Dwan,
  The Ritz Brothers
Produced by: DFZ

*Second Fiddle* (1939)
Director: Sidney Lanfield
Stars: Sonja Henie, Tyrone Power
Screenplay: Milton Sperling
Produced by: DFZ

*Wife, Husband and Friend* (1939)
Director: Gregory Ratoff
Stars: Loretta Young, Warner Baxter
Screenplay: Nunnally Johnson
Produced by: DFZ

*Stanley and Livingstone* (1939)
Director: Henry King
Star: Spencer Tracy
Produced by: DFZ

*Hotel for Women* (1939)
Director: Gregory Ratoff
Stars: Linda Darnell, Elsa Maxwell
Adapted by: Gregory Ratoff, DFZ
Produced by: DFZ

*Hollywood Cavalcade* (1939)
Director: Irving Cummings
Stars: Don Ameche, Alice Faye
Adapted and produced by: DFZ

*Drums along the Mohawk* (1939)
Director: John Ford
Star: Henry Fonda
Original novel: Walter D. Edmonds
Produced by: DFZ

*Daytime Wife* (1939)
Director: Gregory Ratoff
Stars: Tyrone Power, Linda Darnell
Produced by: DFZ

*The Return of the Cisco Kid* (1939)
Director: Herbert Leeds
Stars: Lynn Bari, Warner Baxter
Produced by: DFZ

*Rose of Washington Square* (1939)
Director: Gregory Ratoff
Stars: Tyrone Power, Al Jolson,
  Alice Faye
Screenplay: Nunnally Johnson
Produced by: DFZ

*The Rains Came* (1939)
Director: Clarence Brown
Stars: Myrna Loy, Tyrone Power
Original novel: Louis Bromfield
Produced by: DFZ

*Swanee River* (1940)
Director: Sidney Lanfield
Star: Don Ameche
Produced by: DFZ

*The Blue Bird* (1940)
Director: Walter Lang
Star: Shirley Temple
Produced by: DFZ

*Little Old New York* (1940)
Director: Henry King
Star: Alice Faye
Produced by: DFZ

*The Grapes of Wrath* (1940)
Director: John Ford
Star: Henry Fonda
Original novel: John Steinbeck
Screenplay: Nunnally Johnson
Produced by: DFZ

*Chad Hanna* (1940)
Director: Henry King
Stars: Henry Fonda, Dorothy Lamour
Screenplay: Nunnally Johnson
Produced by: DFZ

*Johnny Apollo* (1940)
Director: Henry Hathaway
Star: Tyrone Power
Produced by: DFZ

*He Married His Wife* (1940)
Director: Roy del Ruth
Star: Joel McCrea
Produced by: DFZ

*Star Dust* (1940)
Director: Walter Lang
Star: Linda Darnell, John Payne
Produced by: DFZ

*I Was an Adventuress* (1940)
Director: Gregory Ratoff
Star: Vera Zorina
Screenplay: Nunnally Johnson
Produced by: DFZ

*Lillian Russell* (1940)
Director: Irving Cummings
Stars: Alice Faye, Henry Fonda,
  Don Ameche
Produced by: DFZ

*Four Sons* (1940)
Director: Archie Mayo
Stars: Don Ameche, Betty Grable
Produced by: DFZ

*Maryland* (1940)
Director: Henry King
Stars: John Payne, Walter Brennan
Produced by: DFZ

*The Man I Married* (1940)
Director: Irving Pichel
Star: Joan Bennett
Produced by: DFZ

*Public Deb No. 1* (1940)
Director: Gregory Ratoff
Star: Brenda Joyce
Adapted and produced by: DFZ

*The Return of Frank James* (1940)
Director: Fritz Lang
Stars: Henry Fonda, Gene Tierney
Screenplay: Fritz Lang
Produced by: DFZ

*Brigham Young — Frontiersman*
  (1940)
Director: Henry Hathaway
Stars: Tyrone Power, Linda Darnell
Screenplay: Henry Hathaway
Produced by: DFZ

*Down Argentine Way* (1940)
Director: Irving Cummings
Stars: Betty Grable, Don Ameche,
   Carmen Miranda
Adapted and produced by: DFZ

*The Great Profile* (1940)
Director: Walter Lang
Star: John Barrymore
Produced by: DFZ

*Tobacco Road* (1941)
Director: John Ford
Stars: Gene Tierney, Charles
   Grapewin
Original novel: Erskine Caldwell
Screenplay: Nunnally Johnson
Produced by: DFZ

*Blood and Sand* (1941)
Director: Rouben Mamoulian
Stars: Tyrone Power, Linda Darnell,
   Rita Hayworth
Story: Blasco Ibanez
Produced by: DFZ

*A Yank in the RAF* (1941)
Director: Henry King
Stars: Tyrone Power, Betty Grable
Story: Melville Crossman*
Screenplay: Karl Tunberg
Produced by: DFZ

*How Green Was My Valley* (1941)
Director: John Ford
Stars: Roddy McDowall, Maureen
   O'Hara, Walter Pidgeon
Original novel: Richard Llewellyn
Screenplay: Philip Dunne
Produced by: DFZ

*Son of Fury* (1942)
Director: John Cromwell
Stars: Tyrone Power, Gene Tierney
Produced by: DFZ

*To the Shores of Tripoli* (1942)
Director: Bruce Humberstone

Star: John Payne
Screenplay: Melville Crossman*
Produced by: DFZ

*This Above All* (1942)
Director: Anatole Litvak
Stars: Joan Fontaine, Tyrone Power
Adapted by: Anatole Litvak
Produced by: DFZ

*Thunderbirds* (1942)
Director: William Wellman
Stars: Gene Tierney, Preston Foster
Story: Melville Crossman*
Screenplay and production: Lamar
   Trotti

*The Pied Piper* (1942)
Director: Irving Pichel
Stars: Monty Woolley, Roddy
   McDowall, Anne Baxter,
   Otto Preminger
Screenplay: Nunnally Johnson
Produced by: DFZ

*China Girl* (1943)
Director: Henry Hathaway
Stars: Gene Tierney,
   George Montgomery
Story: Melville Crossman*
Screenplay and production: Ben
   Hecht

*At the Front* (1943)
Army Signal Corps Film
In charge of production:
   Lt. Col. D. F. Zanuck

*Lifeboat* (1944)
Director: Alfred Hitchcock
Stars: Tallulah Bankhead, William
   Bendix, Walter Slezak
Screenplay: Jo Swerling
Producers: Kenneth Macgowan, DFZ

*The Song of Bernadette* (1944)
Director: Henry King
Star: Jennifer Jones
Original novel: Franz Werfel

Screenplay: George Seaton
Production: William Perlberg
Produced by: DFZ

*The Purple Heart* (1944)
Director: Lewis Milestone
Star: Dana Andrews
Story: Melville Crossman*
Screenplay: Jerome Cady
Produced by: DFZ

*Wilson* (1944)
Director: Henry King
Star: Alexander Knox
Screenplay: Lamar Trotti
Produced by: DFZ

*Laura* (1944)
Director: Otto Preminger
Stars: Gene Tierney, Clifton Webb
Original novel: Vera Caspary
Screenplay and production: Otto
    Preminger
Produced by: DFZ

*Winged Victory* (1944)
Director: George Cukor
Original play and screenplay:
    Moss Hart
Produced by: DFZ

*A Tree Grows in Brooklyn* (1945)
Director: Elia Kazan
Stars: Dorothy McGuire, James
    Dunne, Joan Blondell
Original novel: Betty Smith
Adaptation: Elia Kazan, Louis
    Lighton
Overall production: DFZ

*The House on 92nd Street* (1945)
Director: Henry Hathaway
Screenplay: Louis de Rochemont
Overall production: DFZ

*Dragonwyck* (1946)
Director: Joseph Mankiewicz
Stars: Gene Tierney, Vincent Price

Screenplay: Joseph Mankiewicz
Produced by: DFZ

*The Razor's Edge* (1946)
Director: Edmund Goulding
Stars: Tyrone Power, Gene Tierney,
    Herbert Marshall
Original novel: W. Somerset
    Maugham
Screenplay: Lamar Trotti
Produced by: DFZ

*My Darling Clementine* (1946)
Director: John Ford
Stars: Henry Fonda, Linda Darnell
Adaptation and production:
    Sam Engel
Produced by: DFZ

*13 Rue Madeleine* (1947)
Director: Henry Hathaway
Star: James Cagney
Screenplay and production:
    Louis de Rochemont
Overall production: DFZ

*Boomerang* (1947)
Director: Elia Kazan
Star: Dana Andrews
Screenplay and production:
    Louis de Rochemont
Overall production: DFZ

*Miracle on 34th Street* (1947)
Director: George Seaton
Stars: Edmund Gwenn, Maureen
    O'Hara, John Payne
Screenplay: George Seaton
Production: William Perlberg
Overall production: DFZ

*Gentleman's Agreement* (1947)
Director: Elia Kazan
Stars: Gregory Peck,
    Dorothy McGuire
Original novel: Laura Z. Hobson
Screenplay: Moss Hart
Produced by: DFZ

*Kiss of Death* (1947)
Director: Henry Hathaway
Stars: Richard Widmark,
Victor Mature
Screenplay: Ben Hecht,
Charles Lederer
Produced by: Fred Kohlmar
Overall production: DFZ

*The Snake Pit* (1948)
Director: Anatole Litvak
Star: Olivia de Havilland
Original novel: Mary Jane Ward
Screenplay: Frank Partos,
Millen Brand
Produced by: Anatole Litvak,
Robert Bassley

*Unfaithfully Yours* (1948)
Director: Preston Sturges
Stars: Rex Harrison, Linda Darnell
Story, screenplay and production:
Preston Sturges
Overall production: DFZ

*Sitting Pretty* (1948)
Director: Walter Lang
Star: Clifton Webb
Screenplay and production: Sam
Engel
Overall production: DFZ

*Call Northside 777* (1948)
Director: Henry Hathaway
Star: James Stewart
Adaptation and production: Otto Lang
Overall production: DFZ

*A Letter to Three Wives* (1949)
Director: Joseph Mankiewicz
Star: Linda Darnell, Jeanne Crain
Story and screenplay: Joseph
Mankiewicz
Produced by: Sol C. Siegel
Overall production: DFZ

*Pinky* (1949)
Director: Elia Kazan
Stars: Jeanne Crain, Ethel Waters

Original novel: Cid Ricketts Sumner
Screenplay: Philip Dunne,
Dudley Nichols
Produced by: DFZ

*Yellow Sky* (1949)
Director: William Wellman
Star: Gregory Peck
Story, screenplay and production:
Lamar Trotti
Overall production: DFZ

*Twelve O'clock High* (1950)
Director: Henry King
Star: Gregory Peck
Story and screenplay: Sy Bartlett,
Bernie Lay, Jr.
Produced by: DFZ

*The Gunfighter* (1950)
Director: Henry King
Star: Gregory Peck
Screenplay and production:
Nunnally Johnson
Overall production: DFZ

*Panic in the Streets* (1950)
Director: Elia Kazan
Stars: Richard Widmark, Jack Palance
Screenplay: Elia Kazan
Produced by: Sol C. Siegel
Overall production: DFZ

*No Way Out* (1950)
Director: Joseph Mankiewicz
Stars: Richard Widmark,
Sidney Poitier
Screenplay: Joseph Mankiewicz,
Lester Samuels
Produced by: DFZ

*All About Eve* (1950)
Director: Joseph Mankiewicz
Stars: Bette Davis, George Sanders,
Anne Baxter
Story and screenplay:
Joseph Mankiewicz
Produced by: DFZ

*Mister 880* (1950)
Director: Edmund Goulding
Star: Edmund Gwenn
Screenplay and production:
Julien Blaustein
Overall production: DFZ

*David and Bathsheba* (1951)
Director: Henry King
Stars: Susan Hayward, Gregory Peck
Screenplay: Philip Dunne
Produced by: DFZ

*People Will Talk* (1951)
Director: Joseph Mankiewicz
Stars: Cary Grant, Jeanne Crain
Story and screenplay:
Joseph Mankiewicz
Produced by: DFZ

*Viva Zapata!* (1952)
Director: Elia Kazan
Stars: Marlon Brando, Anthony Quinn
Story and screenplay: John Steinbeck
Produced by: DFZ

*Five Fingers* (1952)
Director: Joseph Mankiewicz
Star: James Mason
Screenplay: Joseph Mankiewicz
Produced by: Otto Lang
Overall production: DFZ

*The Snows of Kilimanjaro* (1952)
Director: Henry King
Stars: Ava Gardner, Susan Hayward,
Gregory Peck
Original story: Ernest Hemingway
Screenplay: Casey Robinson
Produced by: DFZ

*The Robe* (1953)
Director: Henry Koster
Stars: Richard Burton, Jean Simmons,
Victor Mature
Adapted by: DFZ
Produced by: Frank Ross
Overall production: DFZ

*The Egyptian* (1954)
Director: Michael Curtiz
Stars: Gene Tierney, Jean Simmons,
Edmund Purdom, Bella Darvi
Original novel: Mike Waltari
Screenplay: Philip Dunne,
Casey Robinson
Produced by: DFZ

*The Man in the Gray Flannel Suit*
(1956)
Director: Nunnally Johnson
Stars: Gregory Peck, Jennifer Jones
Original novel: Sloan Wilson
Screenplay: Nunnally Johnson
Produced by: DFZ

*Island in the Sun* (1957)
Director: Robert Rossen
Stars: Joan Fontaine, Harry
Belafonte, James Mason
Original novel: Alec Waugh
Screenplay: Alfred Hayes
Produced by: DFZ

*The Sun Also Rises* (1957)
Director: Henry King
Stars: Ava Gardner, Tyrone Power,
Errol Flynn, Mel Ferrer,
Juliette Greco
Original novel: Ernest Hemingway
Screenplay: Peter Viertel
Produced by: DFZ

*The Roots of Heaven* (1958)
Director: John Huston
Stars: Trevor Howard, Errol Flynn,
Orson Welles, Juliette Greco
Original novel: Romain Gary
Screenplay: Romain Gary, Patrick
Leigh-Fermor
Produced by: DFZ

*Crack in the Mirror* (1960)
Director: Richard Fleischer
Stars: Juliette Greco, Orson Welles,
Bradford Dillman
Story and screenplay: Mark Canfield*
Produced by: DFZ

*The Big Gamble* (1961)
Director: Richard Fleischer
Stars: Juliette Greco, Stephen Boyd
Story and screenplay: Irwin Shaw
Produced by: DFZ

*The Longest Day* (1962)
Directors: Ken Annakin, Andrew
  Marton, Bernhardt Wicki
Original book and screenplay:
  Cornelius Ryan
Produced by: DFZ

*Those Magnificent Men in Their
  Flying Machines* (1965)
Director: Ken Annakin
Stars: Sarah Miles, Stuart Whitman

Screenplay: Jack Davies, Ken
  Annakin
Produced by: DFZ

*Hello and Goodbye* (1970)
Director: Jean Negulesco
Stars: Genevieve Gilles, Curt Jurgens
Screenplay: Mark Canfield*
Produced by: DFZ

*Tora! Tora! Tora!* (1970)
Director: Richard Fleischer
Screenplay: Larry Forrester, Hideo
  Oguni, Ryuzo Kikushima
Produced by: Elmo Williams
Overall production: DFZ

# SOURCE NOTE

In the introduction I have expressed my thanks to those authorities on Hollywood and the cinema who have been so helpful to me in the research and preparation of this book. As anyone who knows the history of Hollywood generally and Darryl Zanuck in particular will have divined from the preceding pages, my debt is particularly large to two important sources. The first is, of course, Mel Gussow, already well known as a critic of both theater and cinema, whose devoted attention to the cinematic achievements as well as the producer's robust — and very special — personality produced a biography of Zanuck, *Don't Say Yes Until I Finish Talking*, which should be required reading for all students of the cinema as well as aficionados of Hollywood life and behavior. For me, as for many, many readers, he has brought Darryl Zanuck back to life in all his pulsating, zestful reality, and his book proved both a splendid guide to sources and an inspiration.

A number of quotations from Darryl Zanuck and others including Virginia Zanuck, Jack Warner, John Ford, Robert Gordon Edwards, Romain Gary, Elia Kazan, Olivia De Havilland, Juliette Greco, John Huston, Irina Demick, Joseph Mankiewicz and Genevieve Gilles first appeared in Mr. Gussow's book. Several of these quotations are footnoted, others appear on pages throughout the book.

The other, of course, was Darryl Zanuck's son, Richard, who not only spoke of his father with such warmth, affection and insight, but also pointed me towards other books, documents, papers, and former associates in his effort to show his father as the great, and fallible, man he was. I shall long be grateful for his help.

There are many other sources to which I have gone for information and enlightenment, and I have mentioned some of them in my introduction. Here I would also like to add that invaluable help was given to me by the indefatigable staff of the British Film Institute in London, who not only helped me from their special cinematic resources in compiling a list of Zanuck's films and a bibliography of important and relevant books on cinematic matters, but also searched out pictures from Zanuck's film dossier which, as I hope this book will show, illuminate many of the producer's activities in a manner that has rarely been seen before.

The filmography reproduces the selected list of Zanuck films that first appeared in Mr. Gussow's book, with the occasional addition and subtraction of individual credits, plus selections from Nunally Johnson's filmography (he made many films with Zanuck) to be found in UCLA's Oral History.

To Gussow, to Zanuck, and to all the other authorities I have consulted — including so many producers, stars, technicians and others too numerous to mention here — I give my warm gratitude and thanks.

*   *   *   *   *   *   *   *   *   *   *   *   *

# INDEX

# INDEX